To Yvonne and the road we're on together

Advanced Visual Basic™

A Developer's Guide

Mark S. Burgess

Addison-Wesley Publishing Company

Reading, Massachusetts   Menlo Park, California   New York
Don Mills, Ontario   Wokingham, England   Amsterdam   Bonn
Syndey   Singapore   Tokyo   Madrid   San Juan
Paris   Seoul   Milan   Mexico City   Taipei

Library of Congress Cataloging-in-Publication Data
Burgess, Mark S.
    Advanced Visual Basic : a developer's guide / Mark S. Burgess.
       p.   cm.
    Includes bibliographical references and index.
    ISBN 0-201-60828-6
    1. Windows (Computer programs) 2. Microsoft Visual BASIC.
  I. Title.
  QA76.76.W56B87 1993
  005.4'3--dc20   92-38339
                                         CIP

Sponsoring Editor: Keith Wollman
Project Editor: Elizabeth Rogalin
Production Coordinator: Gail McDonald Jordan
Cover design: Jean Seal
Set in 10 point Palatino by Benchmark Productions

1 2 3 4 5 6 7 8 9 -MA-9796959493
First Printing, November 1993

Addison-Wesley books are available for bulk purchases by corporations, institutions, and other organizations. For more information please contact the Corporate, Government and Special Sales Department at (617) 944-3700 x2915.

Table of Contents

Acknowledgments

As books do, this one took too much time—from its inception soon after the release of Visual Basic 1.0 until its release several months after the release of Visual Basic 3.0. During that time a host of people helped with the research and the assembly of these materials.

First, I'd like to thank Elizabeth Rogalin of Addison-Wesley for her many polite but insistent phone calls as I assured her that another version of Visual Basic was just around the corner. And thanks to Keith Wollman of Addison-Wesley for permitting her to continue to call and to Barbara Milligan for not losing her train of thought between chapters or figures and to Gail McDonald Jordan for all the art shuffling! Next, I want to thank a good friend, Kenn Nesbitt, for his sometimes playful, often challenging technical critiques of each chapter.

In their leading role, the cast of thousands on the CompuServe MSBASIC forum asked many of the questions that I've tried to address in this book. (Because of my online charges for downloading all those messages, I may only break even with my royalties from the book!) Thanks to Jonathan Zuck, Keith Pleas, Mark Novisoff (Microhelp) and Ethan Winer (Crescent) for their tireless work in responding in that forum. And thanks to Micrografx for the new copy of ABC FlowCharter.

Lastly, thanks to Jeff Heath for answering the phone and taking on the real and paying programming jobs while I wrote. And thanks to Yvonne Burgess for answering the phone, straightening out my accounting and reviewing each chapter in a hurry, even as she drove the chapter to the overnight mail drop. And thanks to Dave Saunders for midnight rescues of my system after I'd done something I shouldn't have.

Preface

Visual Basic passed through two revisions while I worked on this book, which made things go a little slower than everyone would have liked. However, the Visual Basic programming environment got stronger along the way. With the appearance of Visual Basic for Applications, the concepts in this book now spread to an even wider audience. Many of the techniques useable in the Visual Basic programming environment will be transferable to VBA enabled applications.

I set out to write a book to help programmers move past the first gloss of Visual Basic. While the environment makes programmers immediately productive, it doesn't take too long for them to find where to push the tool a little in order to get what they want. The first couple of chapters serve to give you my view of the Visual Basic environment and to provide a quick start for adventurous folks who have not yet worked in Visual Basic.

I tried to target this book to professional programmers who want to produce something useful while they learn. That's why many of the utilities contained on the source code disk and in the examples also serve as programming tools or language extensions I used while writing the book. The rebel module unloader FREEVB is handy when you're coding a new DLL that gets left in memory after the calling program terminated. I use the Reader program when I want to do some targeted research using the Microsoft KnowledgeBase on CompuServe. And we use the Stomper program in Chapter 10 as a means of tracking everything from product ideas to bugs and enhancements in development projects.

I hope your projects go successfully and I'll be pleased if something in this book helps you.

M.S.B.
San Diego, California

Chapter 1

Programming Visually

To explain the difference between an application and an operating system in his 1979 book *Micromillenia*, Christopher Evans uses the example of filling your car's gas tank with fuel. If you drive up to the attendant and say, "Fill it up, please," that's equal to asking your word processor to print a letter. Then Evans takes us to the operating system level. Imagine you have to get out of the car, he says, and without touching anything yourself, tell the attendant exactly what to do to fill your tank: each step for taking the nozzle out of the pump and removing the gas cap, and at what angle to hold the nozzle.

Now let's transfer that analogy to using Visual Basic. If you wanted to show someone the phrase "south-going Zak" on this page, you most likely would not communicate the location of the phrase by describing the dimensions of the book or the kerning of the type or any of the other geographical methods at your disposal. You are much more likely to point your finger at the page and say, "Look here! It's Dr. Seuss in a programming book!" With that example in mind, let's compare programming Windows with the Software Distribution Kit (SDK) to programming in Visual Basic. Using only the SDK, you must describe every action in seemingly minute detail. By contrast, you can achieve the same results in Visual Basic by clicking on an object in the Design environment. Most users of Windows 3.0 or earlier have had experience with a UAE (unrecoverable application error, now known as a GPF or General Protection Fault in Windows 3.1). When you use only the SDK and a C compiler, you will much more likely have more GPFs in your application than you will when using a tool like Visual Basic.

 Tip: *You can change the orientation of the custom control tool box from the standard vertical orientation. Place the tool bar so that part of it extends beyond the screen. Next, delete an existing custom control or add a new ones. The tool bar will resize as shown in Figure 1-1.*

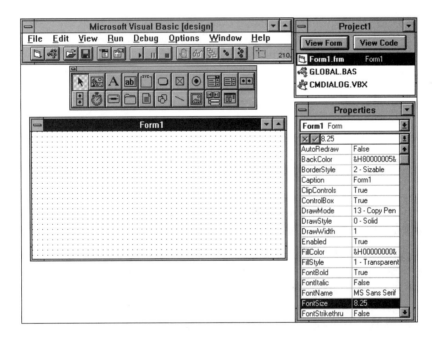

Figure 1-1   *The Visual Basic programming environment.*

In the C-and-SDK-only days, if you wanted to place a dialog box into your application, you had to write the WinMain and MakeProcinstance routines to set up the memory location. Then you had to write the message-handling routines just to get the thing started. After spending a couple of hours, you started writing the actual functionality. Did you need scroll bars? If so, you added another hour—that is, if you had some debugged code you had used elsewhere that you could copy. To place text in the box, you had to do calculations on the font metrics, expressing the location in terms of logical coordinates of whatever display mode you had requested. Then you compiled and ran the program just to see if your guesses and calculations were right.

Visual programming means writing applications by their look and "feel"— exactly the reverse of getting a look and feel by writing the application. Writing a simple Windows shell used to require that you pick and choose among some 450 functions from the API and write about 150 lines of C. With Visual Basic you can do the same thing in about 30 seconds—even throwing in a couple of lines of code if you want to get fancy.

 Note: *Since Visual Basic does not use the Multiple Document Interface, you must do your work against whatever background you loaded—including other tasks that appear minimized.*

Instead of calculating where to place a list box in the dialog, you can click on the list box icon in the tool bar, as shown on the right in Figure 1-1, and put the list box anywhere on the form, dragging it around until you find a location you like. Then, instead of looking through your program editor's list of source files, you can click on the list box object and get the relevant parts of your program matched with the message corresponding to that code. Figure 1-2 shows the code window that pops up when you click on one of the number buttons in the calculator sample program shipped with Visual Basic.

Because so much is done for you in Visual Basic, it's easy to see (no pun intended) what makes visual programming so easy. It does require some orientation to locate the code that you write. However, Visual Basic allows you to print all of the source for a program in one place for easy access. You will be surprised to see how little code you wrote for what your application can do. Listing 1-1 shows a sample of the code printout.

Listing 1-1   *The program listing created by Visual Basic for the code window in Figure 1-2.*

```
' Click event procedure for number keys (0-9).
' Appends new number to the number in the display.
'
```

```
Sub Number_Click (Index As Integer)
    If LastInput <> "NUMS" Then
        Readout.Caption = "."
        DecimalFlag = FALSE
    End If
    If DecimalFlag Then
        ReadOut = ReadOut + Number(Index).Caption
    Else
        Readout = Left(Readout, InStr(ReadOut, ".")-1) + Number(Index).Caption
    End If
    If LastInput = "NEG" Then ReadOut = "-" & ReadOut
    LastInput = "NUMS"
End Sub
```

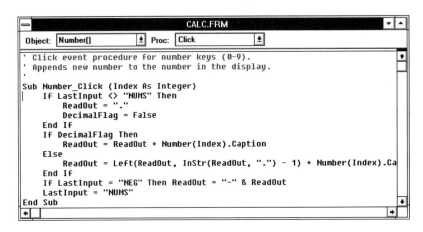

Figure 1-2   *This code window displays the response the program will have to a mouse button click.*

As a program designer, your first step will be to incorporate the event-based nature of Visual Basic. As a program coder, you make the most significant adjustment when you start your programming with visible objects. Traditionally, and especially with Windows programming, it took a lot of code writing before you could see the first thing on the screen. With Visual Basic, the reverse is true. You begin by drawing the program appearance, placing code behind the pictures as a second step. That sequence permits you to use Visual Basic to prototype almost the entire look and feel of an application very quickly.

Visual Basic and Object-Oriented Programming

Is Visual Basic a true object-oriented programming (OOP) tool? No. True OOP languages exhibit three characteristics:

- encapsulation of data and program into one object
- inheritance of characteristics from object or class to object
- polymorphism

The primary distinction between Visual Basic and a true OOP language appears when you see that Visual Basic lacks two of the three main requirements to qualify as a true OOP language. Visual Basic does not support *polymorphism* or true inheritance. In the July 1992 issue of *PC Magazine*, Ray Duncan defines polymorphism as "an object's capability to select the correct internal procedure (method) based on the type of data received in a message." That means a single function or procedure in the program can have the same name as another function or procedure, but can operate differently. For instance, if Visual Basic supported polymorphism, you could have three functions within one form with the same name, each for a different purpose. You could have a set of procedures called Sum. The program would select the correct version of Sum depending on the type of variable passed to it.

To mimic inheritance in Visual Basic, the copying of an "object" from the tool bar to your application roughly parallels creating a descendant to an object or class. In this view, inheritance is creating a new object with characteristics "inherited" from a parent. However, in Visual Basic you are simply creating another instance of a type of object. No true inheritance exists because a change to the parent object (in this case a tool in the bar) would pass through to an existing instance of that object on a form—only to a new instance created after the change. You can emulate OOP behavior in Visual Basic by assembling push buttons as you need to, but that's still not true OOP. Providing that proper variable scoping is involved, you can achieve a similar result by creating multiple copies of a form using the new key word.

The one true aspect of OOP behavior that Visual Basic exhibits is encapsulation. You create a form object and then encapsulate in that object code and possibly data. The two travel together.

Visual Basic Versus Other Basic Languages

Visual Basic derives its foundation from the first BASIC developed at Dartmouth College in the early 1960s. Several variations of BASIC were developed to extend the language before the American National Standards Institute (ANSI) created the first industry standard for BASIC. Microsoft's first Basic, BASIC-80, was the origin of the Visual Basic we have today. Your familiarity with any of the Basic languages, though most especially with Quick Basic, will help you work in Visual Basic in terms of calling on the language itself. Time spent with other languages, like C or a true object-oriented environment, will prepare you better for the overall structure of a Visual Basic program.

Throughout this book, I'll refer to pertinent differences or similarities between other BASICs and Visual Basic. The following is a quick summary of the major differences between Visual Basic and other forms of Basic:

- Prior to Visual Basic 2.0, the Professional Development System (PDS) for Basic 7.0 was the only Basic with native database capability. Visual Basic is the first version of Basic to incorporate the Object Database Connectivity (ODBC) layer as a native database handler. In previous versions of Visual Basic and in most other versions of Basic, you had to construct your own database from the DOS-file access calls for sequential and random-access files. Figure 1-3 shows a PDS 7.0 routine for handling the Indexed Sequential Access Method (ISAM) database native to the character-based PDS compiler.

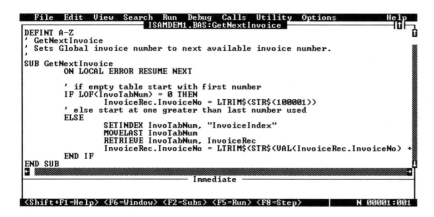

```
  File   Edit   View   Search   Run   Debug   Calls   Utility   Options        Help
                          ISAMDEM1.BAS:GetNextInvoice
DEFINT A-Z
' GetNextInvoice
' Sets Global invoice number to next available invoice number.
'
SUB GetNextInvoice
            ON LOCAL ERROR RESUME NEXT

            ' if empty table start with first number
            IF LOF(InvoTabNum) = 0 THEN
                       InvoiceRec.InvoiceNo = LTRIM$(STR$(100001))
            ' else start at one greater than last number used
            ELSE
                       SETINDEX InvoTabNum, "InvoiceIndex"
                       MOVELAST InvoTabNum
                       RETRIEVE InvoTabNum, InvoiceRec
                       InvoiceRec.InvoiceNo = LTRIM$(STR$(VAL(InvoiceRec.InvoiceNo) +
            END IF
END SUB

                                  Immediate

 <Shift+F1=Help> <F6=Window> <F2=Subs> <F5=Run> <F8=Step>            N 00001:001
```

Figure 1-3   *This code from PDS 7.0 shows a procedure that uses the native ISAM database handler in the PDS.*

- Visual Basic must include parentheses with function calls even when no parameters are passed.
- You cannot define a function by using DEF FN in Visual Basic. Instead, you must use a GoSub or define the function in a separate module.
- There is no equivalent to the QuickBasic sound function in Visual Basic; you must use API calls.
- Visual Basic supports variable length strings in user-defined types but not arrays within those types.
- When you change the name of an object that has code already assigned to it, Visual Basic places that orphaned function into the General code area. The same is true for functions imported from anther Basic.
- GW-BASIC uses all local variables, while Quick Basic and the PDS system use COMMON to allocate global variables. Visual Basic employs three types of variables: (1) implicit and declared local, which are recognized locally; (2) modular which are predefined and visible only locally within the module; and (3) global. Local variables act more like the SHARED type in the QuickBasic and PDS languages.
- The INKEY function for trapping keystrokes in QuickBasic gets replaced by trapping the KeyPress event.
- Visual Basic for DOS does not support real variables where Visual Basic for Windows does.

If you've programmed in other versions of Basic, adjusting to the extra-modular approach of Visual Basic may take a little more work. You cannot simply start at the top of the screen and begin writing code, dimensioning arrays and dropping in functions as you go. It takes a little more planning than that, and you must understand where Visual Basic stores its code and how it reacts to the message traffic in Windows itself.

Chapter 2

The Visual Basic Landscape

Even experienced Basic and Windows programmers need a little orientation before leaping into the Visual Basic environment. If you have worked in other languages, you will recognize a great many of the structures. The If statements operate much like those in the Clarion language, in dBase IV, and in the other Basic languages. The switch statement in C looks very similar to the Select Case statement in Visual Basic. This chapter will take you through the steps of creating your first sample application as a good introduction into the Visual Basic programming tools. If you've read an introductory text or you've already been working in Visual Basic, you may not need to read this chapter. I'll be presenting, in one chapter, an introduction to the environment. After that, I'll move into more advanced application development.

Programming Flow

The operational flow in Windows changed the standard procedural method used by most applications, so it makes sense that a different application development paradigm might go with it. The simple pick lists used in the user interface for mainframe computers, the straight-line path from one function to the next, no longer exist in

Windows. In a Windows application, the programmer loses control over "what the user will do next." That is, programs must respond to the whim of the user by accessing any part of the program at any time. Messages between objects in the environment set up an underground communication system that allows this to happen. The message-passing nature of Windows translates even into the programming environment of Visual Basic. The central problem in describing that paradigm appears when it comes time to tell you where to start your application.

You could begin by creating the file descriptions in the Global module or by writing the special functions you'll need. As a procedural programmer, you might try the traditional approach of writing your way straight through the application, beginning with the opening screen. However, none of those approaches will help you take the most advantage of the Visual Basic application factory.

The diagram in Figure 2-1 shows one of the easiest and most intuitive means for beginning an application. The process really is user-interface driven. You create the look and feel of the program—at least the easy parts—and then begin attaching code.

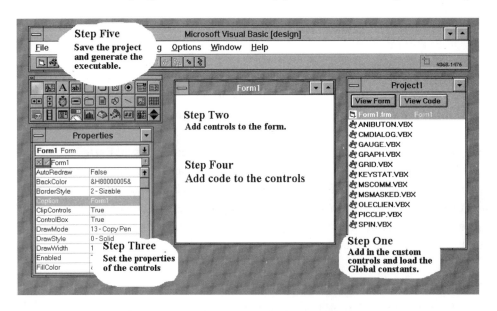

Figure 2-1   *The application development path in Visual Basic.*

The path shown in Figure 2-1 leads you through a rapid assembly of most of the visible elements of your program. The objects you create become the outline you work from to write the code that determines the unique behavior of your application. The steps in Figure 2-1 contain most of the pretty pictures your application presents to users—excluding things like dynamically created buttons, pictures clipped for display, and message boxes and their cousins that pop up at run time. These excluded elements create the unique behavior of your application. Let's look at each step.

Step one: When you first load the Visual Basic environment, it automatically loads the elements of the AUTOLOAD.MAK project file as PROJECT1. AUTOLOAD.MAK is a default project configuration containing a number of custom controls and the first window, which is called **Form1**. You can modify this file to contain the items that you want to appear as defaults. Simply load AUTOLOAD.MAK as a regular project, make your changes, and resave it as AUTOLOAD.MAK. Eliminating all of the custom controls causes the design environment to load a little faster. Form1 won't be editable. It is added by Visual Basic when a new project gets loaded.

Visual Basic ships with a file called CONSTANT.TXT, which contains the more obvious and traditional constant declarations useful in a Visual Basic program-like equating an easy-to-read word with a color. You can create a GLOBAL.BAS file in your application to hold globally declared variables, and load it with CONSTANT.TXT. (You can also make that part of your default project configuration.) Global variables (those set with the Global statement) cannot be declared in a form, but only in a separate procedure, to appear valid in all forms and procedures. Restricting global variables to one default module the way that Visual Basic 1.0 requires you to do can save you time and effort in standardization.

In the Global module, you can load the record definitions for the database files you plan to use and any global memory variables and constants you may need. Remember to do a search for each variable that you place in this file so that you don't step on a definition made in the CONSTANT.TXT file you imported. Also remember that you have only 64K for creating global names.

 Tip: *For Step two, load the Windows File Manager and create a directory for your application. You can then save your project and its many parts in one, easily identifiable place.*

Step two: To give your first form a little more definition than the label, Form1, save it into a file with a descriptive name tied to the function of the form. When you start to save, the default name will appear as FORM#.FRM. Use the directory services in the Save dialog box to change to the new directory for your application and save the form with the new name. Choose a name that you can remember and make it short; you will need it when referring to objects later on. As an option, you can create the other forms you plan to use and name them as well. That will make it easier to build a naming scheme at the form level that you can remember.

Bring up each form that you created, and begin placing the controls roughly where you want them to be in the final application. Don't spend extra time positioning them or adjusting their sizes precisely. As you become accustomed to Visual Basic you will be able to place the controls more precisely the first time. To start with, you'll waste less time if you save the fine finish work for later.

Step three: (last pictured in Figure 2-1): You've spent some time working on your application at this point, so it's a good time to save that work (File/Save file). Here is the point where you set the working name for your application. Since you already saved your form(s) to the new project directory, the default for the directory services are already set. Save the project with a new name you want to use to identify the project and the executable program you will eventually create.

Step four: Go back to the form and begin adding the custom code for operating the application. At this point, you can use the tip for testing the prototype of the application (see the Tip that follows Step six). You can start with the simplest controls for loading and unloading the application, and move on to the more complex data field handlers and form- or module-level declarations you need to make.

Step five: When you decide to save your application, each form will be saved to the same directory as the project. Be careful when saving forms you bring in from another application. Imported forms will save back to their source directory unless you use the "File/Save As . . ." menu selection to give them a separate identity.

Step six: If you have created all of the forms and have already added the controls, then this step is complete. Creating the application becomes a repetition of steps two through five—with a little testing and debugging thrown in for fun.

 Tip: You can easily test your initial program geography after creating the forms and controls for each display. Place two buttons on each form—one to call the next form in the chain and one to quit from the current form. Click on the button to start the next form, and add the statement "Next-Form.Show" in the Click event subroutine (where NextForm is the name *of the form you want to call.) That statement will not only load the next form but display it also. Next, click on the button for leaving the current form, and place the statement "Unload ThisForm" in the click-event subroutine (where ThisForm is the name of the current form.) By using the Unload statement in this quick navigation technique, you remove each form from memory when you click on the Quit button.*

Once you have built the surface interface for your application, it's time to add the deeper levels of functionality that speak, through the interface, to the user. Since you defined your file structures and memory variables in the global CON-STANT.TXT and ran the program in the animation mode, you know that those definitions work. Now you can create the data entry routines. If you defined a record type that uses a foreign (to Visual Basic) Dynamic Link Library (DLL), it's best if you set up a simple entry screen connected to the variables in that record. Even if you plan to verify the entries and set references to multiple files, you should attempt a simple write to the data file to check that link. This verifies that enough space exists in memory to hold the DLL along with the resources you've loaded in the surface interface. Many DLLs will not display their total memory presence until major functions are called by the application. This is true for Visual Basic EXEs as well as in the animation mode of the run time environment. As a simple verification matter, it's a good idea to check the About selection in the Windows Program Manager application to monitor resource usage.

Tip: In Chapter 6, we'll discuss the process for building your own resource monitor.

You could use the Windows SDK and Visual Basic to create a small monitor application, but you can use Program Manager immediately. The real limit you will battle throughout your application development in Visual Basic is the 64K space permitted by Windows for storing your application's resources.

Tip: If you use the Debug version of Windows included with the Windows 3.1 SDK, you will get a false reading on resource use in terms of what your users will get from the normal retail version of Windows 3.1. Anything

over 32K will cause an "out of memory" error. In addition, your application will run much slower than when it runs under the normal version of Windows.

Now you can begin to add the in-depth functionality of your application, secure in the knowledge that your base definitions work. Later, of course, you'll need to do some normal debugging work to repair any errors that you have created by placing data into the wrong type of variable, forgetting to set a required value, or improperly loading or unloading resources. See the section titled "debugging," which appears later in this chapter.

Naming Conventions

If you work in one language, you might be accustomed to a command syntax that looks like the only way to do things. If you work in more than one language, you can get caught mixing statements or syntax. You might be getting an error on a line of code that looks perfectly normal—except, for example, that Visual Basic doesn't permit line continuation characters or an If without a Then.

You should consider a few matters of convention immediately. Visual Basic provides a robust facility for labeling the elements of your program. As with any such capability, you can create a monster if you push the limits. Variable names can become too long, object labels grow cumbersome, and comments can even change the size of your executable program.

Objects in Visual Basic can denote their hierarchy (as in Mother.Son.FootBall), but it's usually not necessary to make the distinction. If you update a label control in a module other than the one in which it appears, it's a good idea to show the sequence—you must if the control name is used in more than one place. The "owner" of a control appears first, then the control itself, and finally the property of the control, as follows:

OwnerForm.Control.Property
as in
MainForm.Quit.Caption

Be sure to consider the lengths of each variable that you establish for file definitions or form objects or function calls. The problem can become acute when you've made a "far" reference to an object in another module and you must assemble all of its parts into one identifier.

To include an identifier in an equation only exacerbates the problems. You would be debugging a very long line of code created by these long variables and by Visual Basic's inability to break a single instruction into two lines.

Just as in C or Pascal, you can create a variable named:

ThisVariableIsTooLongByALot
or
This_Variable_Is_Too_Long

You can create identifiers up to 40 characters long (including underscores) and for each part of an object. That is, you could say

ThisFormLabelIsTooBigToBeUsefulToYou.ThisVariableIsTooLongByALot1234512345123

to describe a command button object in a form. It's fairly obvious that you wouldn't want to do such a thing if you intend to have readable code. Imagine that variable in a simple equation that increments it by a value of one. Since Visual Basic doesn't have the C operator +=, you must spell out the variable twice in the same line.

 Tip: *Underscores can present a small problem, too. When you include them in your variable definitions, they seem to disappear as you highlight that line of code. That effect may hinder your ability to debug a complex statement.*

Another consideration for variable naming concerns the amount of space available for you to store your program in memory. Each level of organization (form, procedure, or module) in your application is allowed 32K for a name and symbol table that contains the actual text of Sub function and Sub procedure names, variable names, line numbers, and line labels, and an additional 4 bytes overhead for each of these names and symbols. (For further information see the Microsoft KnowledgeBase article Q72879—one of the help files included with the Professional edition.) If a form or module exceeds that amount, you'll need to move the resources into a form or module to split them up. If you use up the 32K allowed for the Global module, you have to go back and find places to trim it down, because you can't have multiple global modules.

As with relational database design, if you use one variable in multiple places to do the same thing, it's a good idea to give it the same name. For example, if you use a local variable for counting the repetitions of a loop structure, you should define one variable called counter. (Use the implicit declaration "Counter$" if you plan to declare variables without the use of the Option Explicit or *Deftype* statements.) This method simulates the convenience of a global variable, less the ability to transfer values between objects at incompatible levels, without actually placing it in the Global module. Local definitions are established within procedures and modules with the Const statement for defining a constant, or a *Deftype* statement for setting automatic variable ranges, or a Dim statement for declaring an array. If you use the same variable or constant for several procedures or functions within the same module, make the declaration in the general procedures section for that module.

Message Traffic

The Windows environment operates on the concept of message passing. You create objects, and each object generates messages in response to user actions. If you think of all the objects in the system as receivers of various wavelengths, like short-wave radio, then you can understand how each object "hears" and reacts to the messages it is set to receive. Windows maintains a message receive-and-dispatch utility in the grandparent window of all other window instances you loaded when you started the Windows environment. This utility takes in all of the messages generated in the system, addresses them, and sends them on—much like a post office does. There are general messages, like the one broadcast at system shutdown to which properly written applications respond if they have something to save. There are also specific messages, like those that a mouse generates when you click on the client area of a particular window.

Events drive everything in Windows. If you want to unload a form, you can go to a push-button control, to the Button_Click event, and place the Unload statement as discussed earlier in this chapter in the discussion on building a quick prototype. When you click that button in run mode, a message gets dispatched from your application to the parent window, where it is addressed to go back to your application. Your application receives the message in its own message processing center and executes the Unload statement.

Different messages have different priorities in the Windows message queue, and they carry different data with them, depending on what generated them. Some events create more than one message, thereby affecting more than one application or more than one window within an application. Learning the messaging structure and behaviors will be addressed more completely in Chapter 3.

Debugging

While it is true that Visual Basic does a lot for you, the programs you write can still wind up with bugs. As a result, even with your very first application, you will need some handy tools for tracking down and repairing the defect exhibiting the buggy behavior. Tom Demarco, in his book *Controlling Software Projects*, urges everyone to rename bugs as *defects*:

> A bug is something that crawls of its own volition into your code and maliciously messes things up. It is certainly no reflection on you; it could [have] happen to anyone. But a defect is your own damned fault. Bugs are cute; defects aren't cute at all. Developers sort of like bugs (because developers usually enjoy debugging, which wouldn't be any fun at all without bugs); nobody likes defects. Bugs can be accepted as a fact of life; defects need not be. . . . The first step in trying to develop high-quality software products is to recognize defects for what they are: individual failures to perform. The word *bug* will not appear again in this book. I urge you to banish it from your vocabulary and speak of defects instead.

Demarco's assertion that all developers "usually enjoy debugging" might be going too far. The tools supplied with Visual Basic augmented with those from the Windows Software Development Kit can shorten the process considerably.

Native Visual Basic Tools

The tools native to Visual Basic include the Immediate Window, the Debug statement, and the source code–tracing functions including Watch and the Calls window. Each of these tools works only in the Visual Basic animation or in Run mode, although you can place variables to watch while still in Design mode. You can print the values of variables, change the contents of variables, and even execute lines of code not already written into the running program. The Debug.Print statement works in concert with the Immediate Window to perform the same function as a "watch" variable in debuggers like Codeview (the debugging facility in Microsoft C and the Windows SDK). You can place Debug.Print into your code, attached to a variable, and the value of that variable will print to the Immediate Window each time that statement was called, as shown in Figure 2-2.

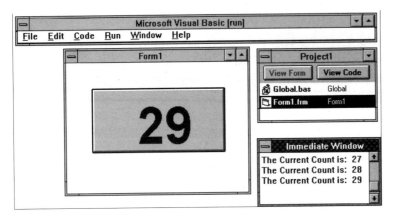

Figure 2-2   *The Immediate Window in the lower right of the diagram shows the repetitions of the counter variable as it increments and then displays in the push button.*

The code in Listing 2-1 shows the Debug statement format placed in the Click event of the push button. Several native Visual Basic techniques appear in the code. Notice the Debug.Print statement, followed by the string of characters that was sent to the Immediate Window. Notice also the change of the caption for the large (and only) push button in the application. You can also use the caption for the form itself as a kind of impromptu Immediate Window, where you can send a changing display to monitor more than one variable at a time: one in the Immediate Window and one in the caption of the form. Especially for push buttons with a static display, this can be handy use of the screen space for your application during the test and de-"defect"-ing (à la Mr. Demarco) of your application.

Listing 2-1   *The program code for printing a value into push-button control as well as for sending the same value, attached to a note, to the Immediate Window.*

```
Sub Counter_Click ()
      Do While Count% <> 30
        Do While Pause% <> 200
          Pause% = Pause% + 1
```

```
      Loop
      Counter.Caption = Str$(Count%)
      Count% = Count% + 1
      Debug.Print "The Current Count is: "; Counter.Caption
    Loop
End Sub
```

Notice also in Listing 2-1 the rather clumsy method used for placing a pause in the display of the numbers in the push button. This would have been a handy place to use the timer control available in the tool bar. Timers monitor the system clock and provide interruptions at the interval you assign it. We could have placed a timer on that application form and replaced the loop structure with a simple If statement based on the timer intervals.

As with more advanced debugging facilities, Visual Basic also provides you with the ability to break execution of the program to perform a number of tasks. You can stop it to type information and test specific statements by using the Immediate Window. You can stop it in the general area of the code where you think your problem exists and then use some of the other methods for tracing through the code. At the point where you request the break manually, you can access the code to place automated breakpoints throughout the code where processing will stop automatically. In case you don't know where to place a breakpoint, you can press the F8 key and step through the code, one line at a time, or press the Shift-F8 key combination to jump to the next procedure called in the program. Once a breakpoint stops the program function, you highlight a selected line of code and then begin execution at that point when the program resumes. To begin execution, you use the Set Next Statement menu selection in the Windows main menu.

The Visual Basic implementation of the Watch tools works like most other language environments. You can ask Visual Basic to monitor a specific variable as it changes state during program execution, and you can interrupt that execution when the contents of the variable meet certain conditions. Each of the debugging facilities will be examined more closely as we discuss the construction of sample applications later in this book.

Useful SDK Tools

Several debugging tools reside in the Windows SDK. Among the most useful are **Heapwalker** and **Spy**. Spy is one of the most educational tools. It lets you set the element of Windows that you want to watch, and then trap the messages passed between the grandparent window and the rest of Windows and your application, as shown in Figure 2-3. Using Spy, you can get an idea of the message traffic relating to each object in your application. This utility becomes especially handy while you are debugging your own DLLs or custom controls, as you will see in Chapter 8. As discussed in Chapter 10, third party products offer more enhanced versions of Spy as in SpyWorks from Desaware.

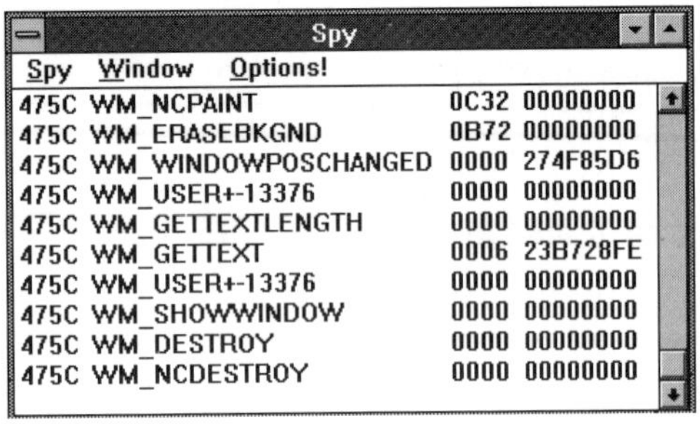

Figure 2-3   *The Spy application included in the Microsoft Windows Software Development Kit lets you watch the messages being processed or relating to a particular window. These are the last of the messages relating to the push button shown in Figure 2-2.*

Heapwalker and the Stress Tester that come with the SDK dive a little deeper into the hardware-based elements of your application by testing and displaying the memory use of your application. Both tools repeat the calls you make in your application and check how much memory you take at the worst times when your user has had your application running for some time. C programmers use this function to make sure they haven't locked memory without releasing it, thereby blocking that area from use by Windows. You can do essentially the same check on the static memory you take by declaring static variables in your modules and procedures.

The Downside

Most programming languages provide some capability that you need for a particular application, as well as a few hurdles that you must find some way to overcome. Exciting new products, in their first incarnations, give you most of a good idea but often leave out a few of the niceties simply to get the product out—the old "shoot the engineers" phase of a project. Visual Basic is no exception. The Microsoft KnowledgeBase available through the CompuServe service contains articles citing different problems with the Visual Basic environment or some aspect of it discovered by Microsoft or by users. Some of those problems relate to how the Windows environment itself handles various situations. Others reflect missing functionality in Visual Basic that the development team must have hated not to fill but chose to delay for a later release. In preparation for your work in Visual Basic, be aware of what you can't do and what you can't do easily, and what you must program against and what you must work around. This chapter will help jump-start you into the world of Visual Basic through its discussion of some of those deficiencies. The following is not a complete list, but it represents the more commonly encountered problems that programmers first find in working with Visual Basic. In later chapters, as we bump up against these problems, as well as others, I'll talk about them at that time also.

Line Breaks

Older versions of Basic and some other languages (like Clarion and the C language) provide a means for splitting a line of one particular instruction into multiple lines. For complex calculations and strings of long names of objects, a line break can be quite convenient. Visual Basic, however, doesn't support line breaks. As a result, you need to be terse when naming variables and objects. Code readability depends on how hard the reader has to work to follow the flow of a program. It's frustrating to try to follow Visual Basic code that wraps many characters to the right side of the editing window. Even with the Home-key quick return to the beginning of a long line, your concentration can break easily regarding the state of variables or what the previous line was doing.

As a Visual Basic programmer, you determine the readability of your program through the intuitive level of your variable names and the cleanness of the structures you create. You can compensate for the lack of line break in Visual Basic if you follow these guidelines:

- Choose short but descriptive variable names.
- Create intermediate variables to hold incremental parts of a long statement that would contain many operators if left intact.

- Create a comment line above an especially long statement. Repeat the actual code in the comment, breaking it into segments. Be careful about doing this frequently, though. Comments use memory, resulting in a larger final EXE in Visual Basic.

Local Variable Messes

If you've written in other languages, you may already practice a tight discipline of variable naming. If you haven't yet learned this discipline, however, Visual Basic can add to your problems by not reporting other problems that can arise. In the C language, if you use a variable local to a function, the compiler will complain if it hasn't been defined anywhere. Visual Basic has a nice feature for defaulting the variable name to be type variant if you haven't used the DEF*type* statement at the top of the module or the implicit symbols $, !, & or %. Let's take one of my favorite examples: UpdateFlag. You can type FirstName and set it up globally, and then cause yourself difficulties in a procedure or function by misspelling it as Updateflag. The compiler goes along its merry way, handling that second spelling as a new variable. (If you have used the Def*type* statement and *type* was Str, then it will default to a string; otherwise Visual Basic 3.D sets up everything as a variant.) You might be depending on that variable for a calculation or a string comparison later in that module, but you keep getting the wrong results. Visual Basic does not check the Global module or the local module to see if you've accurately recalled a variable. To avoid implicit variable directions altogether, place the statement Option Explicit in the Declarations section. This statement forces all variables to be declared.

Device Independence

Part of the magic of Windows was supposed to be that any system running Windows will run your application. Technically, that's usually true. However, if you design your program in a monitor using an 800-by-600 pixel resolution display and you run that program on a monitor operating in standard 640-by-480 mode, all of your carefully arranged windows very likely will be running off the page or else will not be visible. To keep your proportions correct—or at least visible and not inadvertently cropped—you have two choices. You can develop on the same standard resolution as your users have, which will most likely be 640 by 480, or you can use some scaling techniques to reposition and resize the Windows, depending on the device you find.

In Chapter 5 we'll discuss more about controlling your program according to the resident devices. For now, be aware of the physical layout and dimension of your application as it appears on the standard 640-by-480 display.

Visual Basic App as the Shell

A common maneuver with Windows 3.0 was to change the SYSTEM.INI file to list another program as the shell under which Windows starts. Such a move was necessary because the 3.0 version of Program Manager grabbed memory with every icon you displayed when you opened a Program Manager group—memory it never released, so that eventually you ran out of system resources. Often, users will want to load their own application in place of the Program Manager.

A Visual Basic 1.0 application cannot be used as the shell for starting Windows. The VB.EXE does not contain special start-up code that is required by a shell. You can start Windows by using a Visual Basic application listed in the SYSTEM.INI file as the Shell=, but you won't be able to close Windows without rebooting the system.

Visual Basic 2.0 and later versions contain the start-up code necessary for acting as the shell.

64K Segment Limits

The 64K limit applies to the names and symbols tables I talked about earlier in this chapter. Because a grid control was not included when Visual Basic appeared on the market, the grid control was the first thing many programmers tried to create— mostly by clustering buttons into a grid. Unfortunately, those who spent much time clustering buttons discovered that as soon as they hit the 64K ceiling, they were finished adding buttons whether they were ready to be finished or not. (Fortunately, Visual Basic Version 2.0 contained a grid control.)

Using the SDK to write a Dynamic Link Library (DLL), you can create an array that is larger than 64K. Visual Basic 2.0 and later permits you to create an array of controls that share the same file handles. You can create virtual arrays of controls larger than would normally be allowed within the Visual Basic 64K limit. This capability was created by using the global memory allocation functions in the SDK to grab more space than native Visual Basic functions take. You also have the option, of course, of writing your own DLL to handle memory allocation larger than the Visual Basic standard in other ways.

The following shows the limits of memory and various handles within Visual Basic:

Area of Visual Basic	Limits
Forms per application	80 loaded
	230 assigned as variables
Per form, module, or Global module	32K name and symbol table
Global and module name table	64K
Procedures per application	5200 (256K)
Controls in a form	254 names (one array = one name)
Maximum controls in open forms	600 (excluding graphic controls)
Object types per application	256
List and combo boxes	64K
Items in a list box	1K
Text property in a text box	32K (multiline); 255 bytes (single line)
Caption for any control	1K
Tag property of any control	32K
Variable type: Integer	-32,768 to 32,767
Variable type: Long	-2,147,483,648 to 2,147,483,647
Variable type: Single	-3,37E+38 to -1.40E-45 (negative); 1.40E-45 to 3.40E38 (positive)
Variable type: Double	-1.79E308 to -4.94E-324 (negative); 4.94E-324 to 1.79E308 (positive)
Variable type: Currency	-9,22E+14 to 9,244E+14
Variable type: String	64K (except module-level strings)
Nonarray, nonstring data per module	64K
All arrays (not in a DLL)	64K
Local variable stack	16K

Difficult Overlapping Buttons

You cannot successfully overlap buttons on a Visual Basic form without a good deal of effort. If you do, you will get inconsistent and unusual effects in one button or another. An example exists on CompuServe in the MSBasic forum, in a file called VB-TIPS.EXE, for how to "float" one control over the top of another. You must use calls to the API to perform this feat. Here is the example:

Debug event on mouse causes mouse message
and
Access Key causes different event order than clicking

When you use the Debug statement to print a mouse message into the Immediate Window for tracing purposes, that action alone generates a mouse message. If you intend to trace the accurate flow of your application and that part of your application uses the mouse, you cannot use Debug in this manner.

The access key is the single letter in a menu selection that activates that menu selection. Pressing that letter when the menu bar is active *should* result in the same calls and message creation as clicking on the menu with the mouse. However, it doesn't.

These two changes in the expected flow of events in the message traffic demonstrate the vital and very busy conversation going on underneath Windows. You will eventually learn that a mouse movement message has much lower priority in the message queue than other messages; you will also learn how to construct your program to deal with that situation.

Managing Code

The last trouble spot in Visual Basic arises as you manage the code you've written inside your application. Because the Visual Basic paradigm ties the code so closely to objects, you can easily misplace it in your application. For instance, if you create a push button, attach code to its click event, and then rename the button, that code goes to the General Declarations section. If you were to assign to another button the same name as the first name you changed, the code would snap back into the click event for the new control. This can become quite confusing—especially for someone who is more accustomed to looking at procedural code that follows a flow (visually as well as logically) down through an application.

To combat this confusion level at the beginning of your experience in Visual Basic, try printing out all of your code and reviewing it, by procedure, by function, and by module. If you've been careful, no stray code may appear. But you might find code tied to an event that receives a message when you don't expect it, and *that's* why your application behaves as it does.

Chapter 3

Event Management

Events and learning how to manage them make possibly the most interesting aspects of the Windows environment under Visual Basic. Events distinguish Windows from the procedural programming world. As I've already said, you can choose to create pure "procedural" programs even in the Windows world. To do so, though, you will be forced to manage the event message traffic anyway—if only to disable the messages coming in from events in other programs. Your program won't be very popular if, for instance, it prevents display of a warning that should pop up from a personal calendar program about a meeting you scheduled. The trick is to learn what events your application triggers and how it may react to different events in the environment in general.

Events and Their Role in Visual Basic

An event, as the Webster's Ninth New Collegiate dictionary defines it, is "an occurrence, incident, or experience, especially one of some significance." In other words: something that happens—a change of state in the system. In our case, the system is a Visual Basic program running under Windows. The changes might be in the program or might be something in Windows generally—like the message broadcast when a user closes Windows altogether. These changes produce messages. You cannot move the mouse or enlarge a window without generating a message. The messages travel to their destinations, where existing code may trigger other events.

Robotics engineers must program their robots to interpret "pain" as a signal (a message) from the environment about an event involving the robot. Beyond a threshold of "pain" programmed into the robot's operating system, the robot alters its behavior. Think of the elements of a Visual Basic application (including the programming environment) as object robots. The object can be programmed to respond in a certain manner when you send it a certain stimulus. If you don't place your code into the correct event, you won't get the response you expected. The ability to receive messages already exists within Visual Basic. Each "receptor site" within each object activates in response to only one message. Figure 3-1 shows the procedure list for a form in Visual Basic. You cannot change this list, but you can add and delete procedures from the general module within the form.

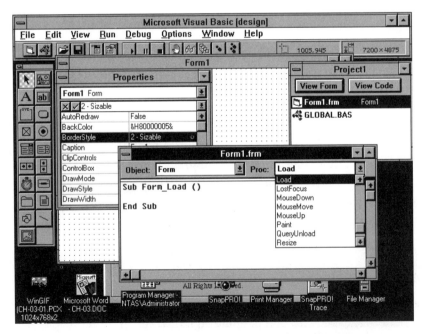

Figure 3-1 *The drop-down list box in the center of the screen shows the "receptor sites," or event procedures where you attach code to process the particular events assigned to them.*

Windows can send approximately 140 messages to a window procedure. A program- or user-initiated action may have more than one impact, also. For instance, if you change the size of a form, both a Form_Resize event and a Form_Paint event execute. In that case, events that add other messages to the queue may fire off code you hadn't intended to access. Windows will use more messages than you can trap in Visual Basic even while it's processing the ones you can trap. For instance, a WM_PAINT message may be initiated by a WM_ERASEBKGND message sent from another window. You can't capture the erase message in unadorned Visual Basic, but you can with a dynamic link library.

Messages

Of the 140 messages that a window can receive , you can trap only 20 of them within a Visual Basic form by using your own Visual Basic code. That doesn't mean the window won't get other messages, but their processing will be handled solely by the Visual Basic runtime libraries and Windows itself unless you intervene with calls to the Windows Application Programming Interface (API). The following table shows all Windows messages (with their identifiers in the SDK file WINDOWS.H) processed explicitly by Visual Basic. (This list does not include the specialized messages for controls.)

Windows Message	Hex ID	Visual Basic Event Procedure
WM_QUIT	0x0012	Form_Unload
WM_SIZE	0005	Form_Resize
WM_PAINT	000F	Form_Paint
WM_ACTIVATE	0006	Form_Activate
WM_SETFOCUS	0007	Form_ or Control_GotFocus
WM_KILLFOCUS	0008	Form_ or Control_LostFocus
WM_KEYDOWN	0100	Form_ or Control_KeyDown
WM_KEYUP	0101	Form_ or Control_KeyUp
WM_CHAR	0102	Form_ or Control_KeyPress
WM_MOUSEMOVE	0200	Form_ or Control_MouseMove
WM_LBUTTONDOWN	0201	Form_ or Control_Click
WM_LBUTTONUP	0202	Form_ or Control_MouseUp

Windows Message	Hex ID	Visual Basic Event Procedure
WM_LBUTTONDBLCLK	0203	Form_ or Control_Click
WM_RBUTTONDOWN	0204	Form_ or Control_MouseDown
WM_RBUTTONUP	0205	Form_ or Control_MouseUp

Processing Paint Messages

Let's take a look at an example of the types of messages your Visual Basic application will handle that you never see. When you cover one window with another and then remove the top window, the bottom window will be repainted. In SDK terms, that means that part of the bottom window has been invalidated. Whenever this situation occurs, the SDK programmer can write code that checks for invalid but visible areas and then repaints them. In Visual Basic this happens automatically, and your application processes the following messages:

1. WM_NC_PAINT [nonclient paint]: The window frame needs repainting.
2. WM_GETTEXT: Copy any related text into a buffer.
3. WM_ERASEBKGND: Prepare an invalidated area for repainting.
4. WM_USER+-16195: (A private message, reserved for Windows use only.)
5. WM_PAINT: Repaint the invalidated area.
6. WM_CTLCOLOR: (Warns the application that one of its controls will be redrawn.)

The fifth message, WM_PAINT, is the one that frequently matters the most to someone doing Visual Basic programming. The event identified as Form_Paint is where you can respond to a WM_PAINT event in Visual Basic. It would be the only one of the six messages that could be easily trapped and used in Visual Basic. Since one action can initiate several messages, you must be certain to take that into account when you trap any particular message and act on it. For instance, when you click on a minimized application, numerous messages are processed by that application, as shown in Figure 3-2. Notice how the low priority of the WM_PAINT message places it almost last—even after the WM_SIZE message.

```
 1. WM_WINDOWPOSCHANGING
 2. WM_WINDOWPOSCHANGED
 3. WM_ACTIVATEAPP
 4. WM_GETTEXT
 5. WM_ACTIVATE
 6. WM_GETTEXT
 7. WM_QUERYDRAGICON
 8. WM_GETTEXT
 9. WM_QUERYOPEN
10. WM_WINDOWPOSCHANGING
11. WM_GETMINMAXINFO
12. WM_GETTEXT
13. WM_ERASEBKGND
14. WM_WINDOWPOSCHANGED
15. WM_MOVE
16. WM_SIZE
17. WM_SETFOCUS
18. WM_ACTIVATE
19. WM_PAINT
20. WM_CTLCOLOR
```

Figure 3-2   *Clicking the mouse on a minimized Visual Basic application to restore it
initiates this list of messages.*

You can build your own "spy" application by using the Debug.Print method and
the Visual Basic Immediate Window. In every event for a form, add a line that
displays the name of the current event, such as: Debug.print "Form_[Event]". Now
when that event is triggered, the Debug.Print method will send the comment in
quotation marks to the Immediate Window. You can resize the form and perform
other actions to find where events will be processed and by what user action. (Using
this test, you can discover that the Debug method causes a problem in Visual Basic
1.0 by causing a second WM_MOUSEMOVE event (Form_MouseMove) when it's
used inside that event itself.)

Dynamic Data Exchange

Dynamic Data Exchange (DDE) works as a form of message in Visual Basic. Though DDE is not a formal message type, you can write your program to use DDE as a means to talk with elements of your program outside of Visual Basic, like Excel or another DDE-aware application. These applications, working as either server or client, can send messages into the Visual Basic application for response by your code.

In addition to carrying the message you intend, DDE that is integrated into your application can trigger other system events also. For instance, if you use the LinkExecute method, in which a Visual Basic application is the server, all Windows events come to a screeching halt until the commands sent to the client using LinkExecute have been completed. If you launch a message box (using the MsgBox statement) or another modal form, you will eventually cause the system to time-out to an error.

You can send messages indirectly throughout your Visual Basic application by performing a task that you believe has nothing to do with DDE. If you change a control capable of DDE, such as a label, Visual Basic checks all valid links and returns errors for invalid links. In the case of any change in the LinkClose event, you create an error—since this event is designed to invalidate the link. Visual Basic believes the link that caused the LinkClose event to fire is partially open, and an error results. The DDE channel that had been open is only partially closed until the LinkClose event finishes completely.

The Message Queue

Most event messages don't travel directly to the event procedure. Instead, the messages go to a message queue. From this queue, Windows or the application itself extracts the messages and processes them. Some Windows messages bypass the queue and go directly to a particular window. (The messages sent under the CreateWindow function in the SDK work that way.)

Each application has a message queue, and Windows itself has a master queue called the **system queue**. All messages pass through the system queue and are dispatched to the message queues of the appropriate application. The Multiple Document Interface discussed in Chapter 8 simulates how Windows itself operates with one master window and subsidiary "children." You load the Windows environment and then start up different applications—each of them a subsidiary to

Windows. Each of these subordinate tasks can converse between themselves or with the **WinMain** task, as the function in the Windows shell program is called. Remember, also, that every object in a Windows program is a window itself, including the button, text, list and other controls. Each window handles its own messages and is capable of sending messages to other windows. For controls included in an array, two controls cannot receive messages simultaneously. Only one control in an array can be accessed at a time.

> **Tip:** *Each application can hold only eight messages in its queue at any one time. The resident messages must be processed, according to their relative priorities, before additional messages can enter the queue. To make a larger queue for an application, you must use the API call to SetMessageQueue. Asynchronous messages—or those sent directly to the Window, bypassing the queue—are an exception to this limit.*

Have you ever noticed that you don't load Windows by itself? You must use a particular application, like Program Manager or File Manager, to act as the "grandparent" Window program or shell. (An application written in Visual Basic 1.0 will not work as a shell under Windows 3.0. Visual Basic 2.0 apps can act as a shell.) That shell provides the message-processing loop (as shown in the C code in Listing 3-1) from the WinMain function of a Windows program that you have written using the bare SDK. The loop receives messages and then sends them back out again to their respective destinations.

Listing 3-1   *The famous Translate/Dispatch loop that exists in all Windows applications for extracting messages from the queue.*

```
/* message polling loop */

while( GetMessage( &msg, 0, 0, 0 ) ) {
  if ( !TranslateAccelerator( hWndMain, hAccelerators, &msg ) ) {
    TranslateMessage( &msg ) ;
    DispatchMessage( &msg ) ;
  }
}
```

When the message arrives at its target window and drops out of the queue and into processing, the target window looks at the six elements of the message before deciding what to do. The six elements include:

- a handle that identifies the window (hwnd)
- a message identifier (msg)
- a 16-bit message specific value (wParam)
- a 32-bit message specific value (lParam)
- the time the message was placed in the queue (double word)
- the mouse coordinates at the time the message was placed in the queue (point structure)

This parameter list summarizes all of the items that may appear within a message. A message may not include all of these items. For instance, only mouse-related messages contain the mouse position coordinates. When we discuss the SDK in greater depth in Chapter 5, the handling of these message elements will take center stage.

When sending messages, you can skip the queue altogether if you like. The Windows SDK provides two important functions for sending messages: **SendMessage** and **PostMessage**. SendMessage transmits the message directly to the Window. In Visual Basic, you can use this function to quickly clear out a list box or to automatically scroll lines in a text box. PostMessage lets you place a message in the queue for processing.

 Tip: The Windows API calls listed in the SDK, such as SendMessage, require special constructions before you can use them in Visual Basic. The methods for using these functions directly will be discussed in Chapter 5.

Even when you use a direct call like SendMessage, a Visual Basic window will have several opportunities to reverse the closing process or to clean up unsaved work. Visual Basic, however, supplies two termination events—Form_Unload and Form_QueryUnload—for each form within an application. To interrupt the shut-down process, you must perform that work in one of these two events. Form_QueryUnload permits you to process a message before the form receives a Form_Unload message. Figure 3-3 shows the simple statements for allowing the user to continue running an application after that application has received and processed the Form_Unload event. The Form_Unload event may derive from the termination of Windows itself, or from a user request by means of that window's control box, to close just that window or the call to the Form_Unload statement for that window from some other place.

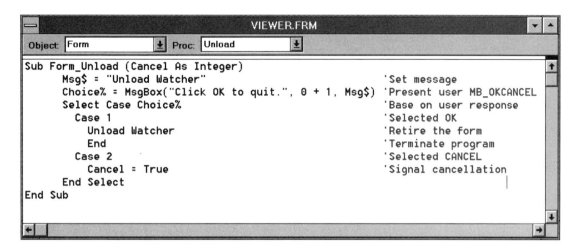

```
┌─────────────────────── VIEWER.FRM ───────────────────────┬─┬─┐
│                                                          │▼│▲│
├──────────────────────────────────────────────────────────┴─┴─┤
│ Object: │Form            │▼│  Proc: │Unload          │▼│       │
├──────────────────────────────────────────────────────────────┤
│Sub Form_Unload (Cancel As Integer)                          │▲│
│     Msg$ = "Unload Watcher"                    'Set message  │█│
│     Choice% = MsgBox("Click OK to quit.", 0 + 1, Msg$) 'Present user MB_OKCANCEL │
│     Select Case Choice%                        'Base on user response │
│        Case 1                                  'Selected OK  │ │
│           Unload Watcher                       'Retire the form │
│           End                                  'Terminate program │
│        Case 2                                  'Selected CANCEL │
│           Cancel = True                        'Signal cancellation │
│     End Select                                               │ │
│End Sub                                                      │▼│
├──────────────────────────────────────────────────────────────┤
│◄│                                                          │►│
└──────────────────────────────────────────────────────────────┘
```

Figure 3-3   *The termination processing of the Message Watcher application shows how to present the user with a message box for choosing to interrupt the closing of the application.*

Mouse Messages

Mouse messages can be skittish, especially with Visual Basic. You may use the MouseDown or MouseUp Visual Basic events, write a DLL, or use an API call to grab the position of the mouse at a certain time. You can get the information through the last parameter of one of the mouse messages, WM_MOUSEMOVE, or through one of the click, double-click, or button up and down messages (see the list of messages displayed earlier in this chapter).

In the Windows SDK, the left button double-click message (WM_LBUTTOND-BLCLK) carries with it the button states as well as the mouse coordinates. Visual Basic's DblClick event does not have any parameters at all, and Visual Basic will not allow you to add them. To get the mouse position for the double-click event, you must attach code to one of the events that does pass coordinate parameters, such as MouseUp, MouseDown, or MouseMove. Figure 3-4 shows a mini-application that demonstrates the tracking of the MouseMove event by using the code in Listing 3-2. The X and Y coordinates of mouse position transfer to global variables (which could also be module level) for processing in the double-click event in the same form.

Listing 3-2   *This code shows the MouseMove event processing for displaying the present position of the mouse.*

```
Sub Label5_MouseMove (Button As Integer, Shift As Integer, X As Single, Y As Single)
     label1.caption = Str$(X) + " x " + Str$(Y)
     MouseX = X
     MouseY = Y
End Sub
```

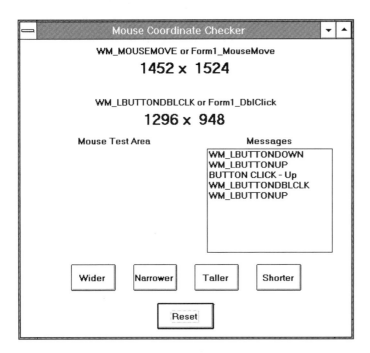

Figure 3-4   *A sample application for testing mouse behavior.*

The top set of coordinates shows the mouse position when the picture in Figure 3-4 was taken, while the second set shows where the last double click of the left button occurred. The list box on the right shows the order of events when you double-click in the Mouse Test Area.

Message Priorities

As your application receives messages into its queue, the Translate/Dispatch loop processes them according to their priority. Don't slip by this point too rapidly, as it can save you hours of debugging time if you take message priorities into account. If you require events to take place in a certain order, you must allow for the vagaries of the queue processing in Windows.

As an example of processing order, take another look at Figure 3-4. The list box at the lower right of the form reports the events as they take place. Figure 3-4 shows the event order for double-clicking the mouse button in the designated Mouse Test Area. Notice that the double click takes place in the midst of other events. Your application may operate differently from the way you expect. Suppose you plan to execute a step on a double click. You might divert processing away from the relevant area simply by using code that launches from a single click or MouseUp event. Notice also in Figure 3-4 that the MouseDown event was not also acknowledged by the Click event.

You can count on the processing order of some messages. As discussed earlier in this chapter, you can set the priority for a message at the highest level (meaning that it is processed immediately) simply by sending the message directly to the form or control. Default processing treats the messages in the order in which they entered the queue. Windows always places the WM_PAINT message (which triggers refreshment of the screen) at the very end of the queue. The paint event (WM_PAINT) is processed last so the screen doesn't flicker from too many repaints before completing all of the changes to be made to it.

Since all messages pass first through the system queue, each application also competes with other applications (or tasks) running at the same time. To reduce the waiting time for any active application, Windows uses a set of algorithms to decide which application should get its messages delivered first. When you create an application that must process real-time input (like a communications product), be sure you create some form of "on hold" technique for handling the delays that will occur when that input falls behind the messages for another application in the queue.

Tip: Windows NT (New Technology—the new operating system from Microsoft) manages queues differently for native NT applications. Each NT application possesses and processes its own message queue, separate from any other application or central system queue. If you load a Windows 3.1 application under NT, that application will share the same system queue as other Windows 3.1 applications. However, that system queue will appear as an application queue under NT.

Property Management

The properties of Visual Basic forms and controls may appear unconnected to the message traffic that your applications will manage. However, the properties play a giant role in how an application responds to the message traffic it receives and in what types of messages it transmits. Figure 3-5 shows the resulting objects when you select items from the Visual Basic Toolbox. Each of these objects has certain properties that control its behavior. Simply by changing one of these properties you can initiate a system message that will affect the application. Simply by changing the properties regulating the size of the form, you can kick off the transmission of paint and size messages. By melding the property settings and the event procedures into a coherent process, you can determine how your application will operate. Messages—your means of speaking to the objects by way of their properties—become the key to controlling your application.

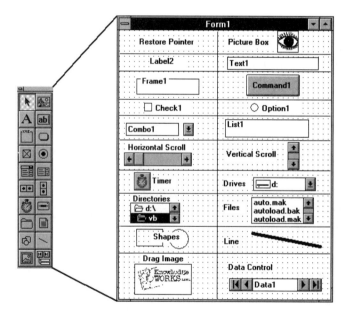

Figure 3-5   *The Toolbox, at the left, is compared to an actual form where each of the tools was placed. The timer control is shown only as a stopwatch and will disappear when the application is run. Each control has a different set of properties.*

All together, for all the controls in standard Visual Basic 3.0 (excluding the Professional Toolkit or other custom controls), there are 199 properties. You can divide the properties for all the controls into four basic groups according to the types of messages each one sends or receives: dimension (size, and position), status (current settings), visibility (images, font specifications, and color), and (contents and ranges). You can divide the properties into other logical groups as shown in the *Visual Basic Language Reference Manual*. (The Language Summary shows the properties organized in a matrix according to the objects that use them.) Each property in the following lists is organized according to the types of messages (that is, the type of action) that the property governs. (These properties lists do not include the custom controls provided in the Professional edition of Visual Basic.)

Dimension-oriented Properties

Align	DrawWidth	MinButton
AutoSize	FixedAlignment	MultiLine
BorderWidth	FontSize	RowHeight
ColAlignment	GridLineWidth	ScaleHeight
ColWidth	Height	ScaleLeft
CurrentX	Left	ScaleWidth
CurrentY	Max	Top
	MaxButton	Width
	Min	

Visibility-oriented Properties

Alignment	ControlBox	FontBold	HighLight
AutoActivate	Count	FontCount	Icon
AutoRedraw	DefaultExt	FontItalic	LeftCol
BackColor	DialogTitle	FontStrikethru	MDIChild
BackStyle	DragIcon	FontTransparent	MousePointer
BorderColor	DrawStyle	FontUnderline	MultiSelect
BorderStyle	FillColor	ForeColor	PasswordChar
Caption	FillStyle	Format	Picture
Checked	Filter	FromPage	Rows
Color	FixedCols	GridLines	ScaleMode
Cols	FixedRows	Hidden	ScaleTop
Columns	Flags	HideSelection	ScrollBars
			Style
			UpdateOption
			Visible

Status-oriented Properties

ActiveControl	EditMode	LinkTopic	PrevInstance	Sorted
ActiveForm	Enabled	ListCount	PrinterDefault	Stretch
ApplsRunning	Exclusive	ListIndex	ReadOnly	TabIndex
AutoVerbMenu	FilterIndex	MaxFileSize	Row	TabStop
Cancel	hDC	MaxLength	SelCount	ToPage
CancelError	HelpCommand	NewIndex	Selected	TopIndex
CellSelected	HelpContext	Normal	SelEndCol	TopRow
ClipControls	HelpKey	ObjectAcceptFormatsCount	SelEndRow	TwipsPerPixelX
Col	hWnd	ObjectGetFormatsCount	SelLength	TwipsPerPixelY
Copies	Index	ObjectVerbFlags	SelStart	Value
DataChanged	InitDir	ObjectVerbsCount	SelStartCol	WindowState
Default	Interval	OleType	SelStartRow	WordWrap
DisplayType	KeyPreview	OleTypeAllowed	Shape	X1,X2,Y1,Y2
DragMode	LargeChange	Page	ShortCut	
DrawMode	LinkMode	Parent	SizeMode	
	LinkTimeout	PasteOK	SmallChange	

Data-oriented Properties

Archive	Drive	HostName	Options
Class	EXEName	Image	Path
Clip	FileName	ItemDir	Pattern
Connect	FileNumber	LinkItem	RecordSet
CtlName	FileTitle	List	RecordSource
Data	FontName	lpOleObject	SelText
Database	Fonts	Name	SourceDoc
DatabaseName	FormName	Object	SourceItem
DataField	HelpContextID	ObjectAcceptFormats	System
DataSource	HelpFile	ObjectGetFormats	Tag
DataText	HelpTextId	ObjectVerbs	Text
			Verb
			WindowList

Designing for EventsFontt

For the remainder of the chapter, I'll focus on the nature of events in light of the knowledge of messages you have now. The emphasis on techniques for managing objects will appear in Chapter Four. If you look at a Windows application as a party, then the objects serve as the guests, food, and location, while the messages represent the music and the conversation. A party doesn't really get interesting until Something Happens—like an event. Once an event has occurred, the messages passing between the guests (or objects) begin to create some movement in the party.

When you design around the events, you must think differently about how your user will approach your application. The user may launch your application, immediately minimize it, and work in a completely different application. If you wrote your program to automatically crunch some data or to do other start-up work, you will slow down the user's work in the other application. Furthermore, you might allow the user to open lots of different input or viewing forms, but then not provide a way for them to be hidden when the user minimizes the application. In either case, you have not planned for the full range of events possible in the life of a Visual Basic application.

Because Windows itself is so intertwined with a Visual Basic application, system events may intrude on your processes. For instance, there is no way for Visual Basic to suppress MouseMove events generated by Windows itself.

In Visual Basic, events may be generated in a different order if you choose a control (such as a button, a check box, or an option box) by using an access or accelerator key rather than the mouse. The events that occur in a different order are Click, LostFocus, and GotFocus. The differing order of events is by design and is not the result of a problem with Visual Basic.

Visual Basic will not by default execute the Paint event for controls or forms of an application with an active message box. When a MsgBox function or statement is active, the Paint event occurs only when the controls and/or forms have the AutoRedraw property set to False.

You can use timer controls to automatically generate an event at predefined intervals. These intervals are specified in milliseconds and can range from 0 to 64767 inclusive. Timer event processing will not be interrupted by new timer events, because of the way that Windows notifies an application that a timer event has occurred. Instead of interrupting the application, Windows places a WM_TIMER message in its message queue. If a WM_TIMER message from the same timer is already in the queue, the new message will be consolidated with the old one.

After the application has finished processing the current timer event, it checks its message queue for any new messages. This queue may have new WM_TIMER messages to process. There is no way to tell if any WM_TIMER messages have been consolidated.

The *Microsoft Visual Basic Language Reference Manual* for version 1.0 states on page 160 that KeyDown and KeyUp events are not generated for the Tab key. This is normally true, but under certain circumstances, the Tab key may generate either or both of these events for a form or control. This errant behavior was removed in Version 2.0.

Writing "Bullet-proof" Code

Writing "bullet-proof" code—that is, a program that causes no errors for the user—is a little more difficult within an event-driven environment than a procedural-only environment. The first step in designing your application is to understand how the events work with each other. I've already shown you one program for watching messages. Now you can look at another one to see the impact of the events in Visual Basic. The Watcher program shown in Figure 3-6 uses every property available to a form.

Figure 3-6   *The Message and Event Monitoring sample application for watching the impact of events in the Visual Basic Environment.*

When you have first loaded Watcher, you can see the use of the MAIN.BAS module, which loads ahead of all other forms and controls in this Visual Basic application. By placing code in that module, you can include a start-up message for the application. The MAIN.BAS module does not exist until you create it—even though it appears as Sub Main in one of the possible defaults for the Start Up Form selectable from the Options main menu selection.

The first event you'll see is the Form_Load event. A message box pops up to let you know that the first event in the first form has executed. Now you can explore the various form events. Try loading Visual Basic itself along with the project file for Watcher so that you can peek at the source code for each procedure you try.

Notice that Watcher first shows that Forms Loaded equals one. This is an example of the DoEvents return value. You won't find code in the procedures for the label that shows the number. Instead, the WM_MOUSEMOVE message or Form_MouseMove event procedure in the Viewer form itself contains the code shown in Listing 3-3:

Listing 3-3 *Polling for MouseMove events in the Form module.*

```
Sub Form_MouseMove (Button As Integer, Shift As Integer, X As Single, Y As Single)
    Static Active%
    If Active% Then Exit Sub        ' Get out if already busy
    Active% = FALSE
    Look.Caption = Str$(DoEvents())  'returns number of forms loaded
    Active% = 0
End Sub
```

Notice the filter that causes the procedure to exit if the static variable Active% remains set. WM_MOUSEMOVE messages signal each twip (twentieth of a point) movement on the screen by the mouse. As a result, thousands of calls to the DoEvents procedure resulting from moving the mouse a few inches causes the error shown in Figure 3-7. This error will always occur when you perform unlimited recursive calls to load a form or control.

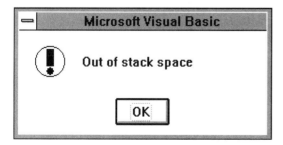

Figure 3-7 *This error results from too many calls to the DoEvents procedure during the processing of a WM_MOUSEMOVE event.*

By grabbing the corner of the form and resizing (enlarging or shrinking) the window, you can see how the form processes the WM_PAINT and WM_SIZE messages. Notice that the WM_PAINT message is not processed when you shrink the window. Try moving another window over the top of Watcher. When you remove it, Watcher processes a paint message. That is because covering part of the form caused the covered portion to become invalid and therefore in need of painting. Next, select Forms from the menu, and choose Form One. When you drag the mouse cursor across the client area below the frame sitting on the form, the DoEvents call in the MouseMove event updates Forms Loaded. Also notice that the GotFocus and LostFocus messages are processed. Now select Dragons and experiment with the Drag Me! button to see the impact of the drag-and-drop messages. If you click the mouse in the Mouse Test Area, you'll see the processing of the MouseDown and MouseUp events. Go to the client area beneath the frame, click the mouse once, and then double-click to see the processing of the Click and DblClick events. Figure 3-8 shows the resulting form after you have experimented with the Mouse Test Area and the drag-and-drop object.

Figure 3-8   *The Drag Me! control was dropped back on itself, and the Mouse Test Area processed a MouseUp event in the Watcher program.*

Finally, close the form by double-clicking on the control box in the upper-left corner of the form. The Unload event allows you to check the user's intentions prior to closing the application. In the case of Watcher, the code in Listing 3-4 shows how to provide an exit choice. You can interrupt the user's exit from an application in the Unload Event, which is preceded by the QueryUnload event. Simply by setting the form cancel property to TRUE, you will abort the exit. The Form_Unload event can be triggered from outside the application, as when Windows itself is closed

Listing 3-4   *The code used to interrupt an exit from a form.*

```
Sub Form_Unload (Cancel As Integer)
    Msg$ = "Unload Watcher"                        'set message to variable
    Choice% = MsgBox("Click OK to quit.", 0 + 1, Msg$) 'launch message box as
MB_OKCANCEL
    Select Case Choice%                            'get user response
      Case 1                                       'user clicked on OK
        Unload Watcher                             'Remove form from memory
        Exit Sub                                   'leave this procedure
        End                                        'terminate the App
      Case 2                                       'user clicked CANCEL
        Cancel = TRUE                              'set flag to TRUE
    End Select
End Sub
```

When you are designing Windows applications with Visual Basic, tracking which events you will respond to and planning which messages to send becomes critical. You can monitor your application by constructing something like the Mouser application discussed earlier, or you can use the SDK tool called Spy to monitor the message traffic. There is no substitute, however, for testing an application under many circumstances—a heavier requirement than single-user, single-mode DOS character–based applications. You must ensure that a system message, unrelated to your application—such as a MouseMove event—doesn't interfere with the operations of your program.

Sample Application: Watcher

Global.Bas

```
'==========================================================================='
' Visual Basic global constant file.                              '
'==========================================================================='
```

Form1

```
Sub Command1_Click ()
    Unload Form1
End Sub
```

Form2

```
Sub Command1_Click ()
    Unload Form2
End Sub
```

Viewer

```
Sub Form_MouseMove (Button As Integer, Shift As Integer, X As Single, Y As Single)
    Static Active%
    If Active% Then Exit Sub      ' Get out if already busy
    Active% = -1
    Look.Caption = Str$(DoEvents()) 'returns number of forms loaded
    Active% = 0
End Sub


Sub One_Click ()
      Form1.Show
End Sub


Sub Two_Click ()
     Form2.Show
End Sub


Sub Three_Click ()
    Const TRUE = -1 ' Define TRUE constant.
    X% = Shell("Calc.exe", 1)    ' Shell the calculator.
    Msg$ = "The calculator has been started.  Do you want to watch "
    Msg$ = Msg$ + "some calculations on the Calculator ?"
    Answer% = MsgBox(Msg$, 4)    ' Display Yes/No message box.
    If Answer% = 6 Then ' 6 = Yes button chosen.
        For I% = 1 To 100    ' Set up counting loop.
            ' Send keystrokes to calculator to add each value of i%
            SendKeys LTrim$(Str$(I%)) + "{+}", TRUE
        Next I%
        SendKeys "=", TRUE  ' Get grand total.
        Msg$ = "Choose OK to close the calculator."
        MsgBox Msg$
    End If
    SendKeys "%{F4}", TRUE   ' Send Alt+F4 to close Calculator.
End Sub


Sub Form_Click ()
    Notes.Caption = "Clicked the Mouse Once"
End Sub
```

```
Sub Form_DblClick ()
    Notes.Caption = "Clicked twice!!"
End Sub

Sub Form_DragOver (Source As Control, X As Single, Y As Single, State As Integer)
    Notes.Caption = "Object dragging across form."
End Sub

Sub Form_DragDrop (Source As Control, X As Single, Y As Single)
     Notes.Caption = "Hey! Object dropped on the form!"
End Sub

Sub Dragon_Click ()
   If DragMe.Visible Then
     DragMe.Visible = False
   Else
     DragMe.Visible = TRUE
   End If
End Sub

Sub DragMe_DragDrop (Source As Control, X As Single, Y As Single)
    Notes.Caption = "Oof! Object Got Dropped."
End Sub

Sub Form_Paint ()
   If Resized Then
      Sizemsg$ = "..and resized!"
      Notes.FontSize = 12
   Else
      Sizemsg$ = ""
      Notes.FontSize = 13.5
   End If
   Notes.Caption = "Watcher was repainted." + Sizemsg$
   Resized = False
End Sub


Sub Form_LostFocus ()
    Notes.Caption = "Watcher lost the focus!"
End Sub

Sub Frame1_DragOver (Source As Control, X As Single, Y As Single, State As Integer)
    Notes.Caption = "Object dragging over frame"
End Sub
```

```
Sub DragMe_DragOver (Source As Control, X As Single, Y As Single, State As Integer)
    Notes.Caption = "Dragging across yourself, dummy!"
End Sub

Sub Form_GotFocus ()
    Notes.Caption = "Watcher got the focus!"
End Sub

Sub MouseTest_MouseDown (Button As Integer, Shift As Integer, X As Single, Y As Single)
    MouseTest.Caption = "Down..."
End Sub

Sub MouseTest_MouseUp (Button As Integer, Shift As Integer, X As Single, Y As Single)
    MouseTest.Caption = "...Up!"
End Sub

Sub ResetAll_Click ()
    MouseTest.Caption = "Mouse Test Area"
    DragMe.Visible = False
    Notes.Caption = "Everything Reset"
End Sub

Sub Form_Resize ()
    If Not Resized Then Resized = TRUE
    Notes.Caption = "Watcher was resized"
End Sub

Sub Form_Unload (Cancel As Integer)
    Msg$ = "Unload Watcher"
    Choice% = MsgBox("Click OK to quit.", 0 + 1, Msg$)
    Select Case Choice%
    Case 1
      Unload Watcher
      Exit Sub
      End
    Case 2
      Cancel = TRUE
    End Select
End Sub

Sub Form_Load ()
    MsgBox "This Message Box was called from the Form_Load event in the Watcher Form."
End Sub
```

```
Sub Form_KeyPress (KeyAscii As Integer)
     DragMe.Caption = Chr$(KeyAscii) + " = " + Str$(KeyAscii)
End Sub


Sub Form_KeyUp (KeyCode As Integer, Shift As Integer)
    DragMe.Caption = "Drag Me!"
End Sub
```

Main.Bas

```
Sub Main ()
    PleaseWait.Show
    PleaseWait.WaitMsg.Caption = "Please Wait, Program Loading..."
    Watcher.Show
    Unload PleaseWait
End Sub
```

WaitMsg

```
Sub Form_Load ()
     WaitMsg.Caption = "Please Wait, Program Loading"
End Sub
```

Sample Application: Mouser

Global.Bas

```
Global MouseX As Integer
Global MouseY As Integer
Global UpOrDown As String
```

Mouse

```
Sub Label5_MouseMove (Button As Integer, Shift As Integer, X As Single, Y As Single)
     Label1.Caption = Str$(X) + " x " + Str$(Y)
     MouseX = X
     MouseY = Y
End Sub


Sub Label5_DblClick ()
     Label2.Caption = Str$(MouseX) + " x " + Str$(MouseY)
     List1.AddItem "WM_LBUTTONDBLCLK"
End Sub


Sub Label5_MouseDown (Button As Integer, Shift As Integer, X As Single, Y As Single)
     List1.AddItem "WM_LBUTTONDOWN"
     UpOrDown = "Down"
End Sub
```

```
Sub Label5_MouseUp (Button As Integer, Shift As Integer, X As Single, Y As Single)
    List1.AddItem "WM_LBUTTONUP"
    UpOrDown = "Up"
End Sub

Sub Label5_Click ()
    List1.AddItem "BUTTON CLICK - " + UpOrDown
End Sub

Sub Wider_Click ()
    Form1.Width = Form1.Width + 100
End Sub

Sub Narrower_Click ()
    Form1.Width = Form1.Width - 100
End Sub

Sub Taller_Click ()
    Form1.Height = Form1.Height + 100
End Sub

Sub Shorter_Click ()
    Form1.Height = Form1.Height - 100
End Sub

Sub Form_Resize ()
    List1.AddItem "WM_SIZE"
End Sub

Sub Form_Paint ()
    List1.AddItem "WM_PAINT"
End Sub

Sub Resets_Click ()
    Form1.Height = 5976
    Form1.Width = 6468
    Label1.Caption = "Label1"
    Label2.Caption = "Label2"
    Do While List1.ListCount
      List1.RemoveItem ListCount
    Loop
End Sub
```

Chapter 4

Object Management

Now that you have studied the ephemeral nature of both events and messages, objects should seem more solid and a bit easier to grasp. You can see a button control or a form on the screen as soon as you have created it. The business of writing a Visual Basic application involves creating the objects and then managing their behavior. In this chapter, I'll discuss techniques for creating applications as we look at each of the object types.

The sample application for this chapter, called Reader, allows the user to import into a Visual Basic database a raw ASCII text file downloaded from CompuServe. Reader is designed to handle files that contain articles from the Microsoft Knowledge Base residing on CompuServe or through Microsoft Online. You can read through the articles sequentially, access an article by using an index created during the import procedure, or jump to an article by using a text search utility. You can also change the display font for the index and the articles. The program saves these settings for your next use. When you print a selected article, the program remembers what directory you used last to access the articles. (Reader also appears in the group project called Lurker, created by Visual Basic users in the MSBASIC forum on CompuServe.) The start-up screen for the Reader application is shown in Figure 4-1.

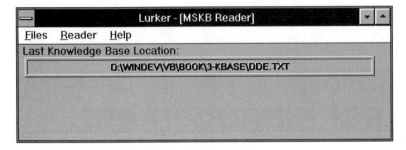

Figure 4-1   *The opening screen for the Reader application shows the last data file accessed by the application.*

Reader uses no API calls to the Windows SDK; it's pure Visual Basic. All of the data file access and manipulation use native Visual Basic, without resorting to the Object Database Connectivity layer (ODBC), which we'll discuss in Chapter 9 or the other database drivers introduced with Visual Basic version 3.0 which will be covered in Chapter 10. You may find simple binary access adequate and fast, and simple even preferable for some uses.

However, I will introduce two new features from Microsoft's Professional Edition for Visual Basic. The two controls used in the Reader, GAUGE.VBX and CMDIALG.VBX, provide a graphic progress bar and access to the common dialog routines in Windows 3.1, respectively. The gauge control was first made available by Microhelp in a third-party product called VBTools. You can access the common dialog functions through direct calls to the Windows 3.1 API. Most of the functionality provided by the two controls is not crucial to the operation of Reader. The common dialog-control file-access functions that are critical can be re-created easily with the device and directory controls included in Visual Basic 1.0.

Programming Notes for Visual Basic

Before we launch into the discussion on objects, a word or two about healthy Visual Basic programming practices is appropriate. Some straightforward rules will help you avoid sticky situations later. Here are a few rules of thumb:

- Determine a policy for variable naming. You can use the Option Explicit statement for forcing type declarations in your code, or you can use the default data type, Def*type*. Both options decrease your chances of inadvertently using a variable type that is incompatible with the current operation. Otherwise, Visual Basic declares each untyped variable as type Variant.

- Keep your code short for each module. The modularity of Visual Basic makes it easy to break operations into smaller chunks. These smaller chunks are easier to debug in the edit windows and your application will behave better.

- Use the On Error statement trap during the design phase in *all* modules. Permitting a module to execute, to generate an error, but then to pass that error into another part of the program makes problems hard to trace. Because the Windows environment changes continually, you may have a problem in one module that appears only intermittently. Regular use of On Error gives you a means for finding the problem each time it occurs.

- If you use the debug version of Windows, test your application in the retail version early in the development process. You create a debug version of Windows by using special files packaged with the SDK. The debug version of Windows also does a better job of stack checking to avoid exhausting the stack capacity in the finished application.

- Keep the number of controls on any one form as low as possible. You read in Chapter 3 about the limits of various areas of Visual Basic, but system performance may degrade before you actually reach those limits. For instance, the Paint message does not always get fully processed when too many controls occupy a form, even though the application will operate without other errors.

- Comment your code, but version 1.0 users should do it sparsely, because this process adds to the size of your EXE. Formatting your code with blank lines and lots of comments will make your EXE program much larger. Each blank line or comment adds a 2-byte overhead to the program. Version 3.0 ignores blank lines and comments when constructing an EXE.

- Use the standard CONSTANT.TXT file in your Global module rather than go to the trouble to invent your own constants.

- Do not use the Debug.Print method in the MouseMove event to test for MouseMove messages in Visual Basic version 1.0. Debug.Print itself triggers a MouseMove event.

- Preload forms for speed, but limit the number of forms loaded to reduce the memory presence. By preloading a form and waiting to display it by means of the Form.Show method, you can load it much faster when you need it. However, you can create too large an application for available memory if you preload everything. Forms loaded into a Multiple Document Interface form cannot be hidden, but only minimized.
- Since each form or control (except these controls in an array) must register its own window class, you can reduce memory requirements by using bitmap graphics to simulate the appearance of objects. If you locate the mouse-click events over this area of the form, you can even trigger events just as you would with a control.
- Each application possesses only one 16K stack which cannot be enlarged. This limit will result in errors most often when your application starts an iterative loop in a form that restarts itself in a subsequent form—a process known as **recursion**.
- If possible, avoid using line numbers or labels to control the flow of your program. Though more often used in other implementations of Basic, the line labels and numbers don't follow the same scoping rules as variables do. You can transfer control only within the current sub or function, and the label must be unique within each of those. Often an error branch uses a label, but a separate generic error response function serves this purpose more effectively.
- Use the Input$ function instead of the Line Input #n statement. The Line Input #n statement strips null characters (CHR$(0)) from input files.
- Decide early on a variable naming scheme to avoid confusion later. The scheme you choose should take into account the scope and type of variable.
- As with each object in Visual Basic, each function, sub, or event procedure is limited to 64K of your source code. Visual Basic 1.0 is limited to approximately 1,300 procedures per application or project, while version 2.0 and 3.0 can handle 5,200 procedures and modules combined. If you try to add more procedures, Visual Basic will take you back to the last procedure you edited, and it might even terminate Visual Basic and return you to Windows.
- For large applications, you can decrease the time it takes for your application to load at start-up by breaking it into smaller EXEs. Visual Basic loads the following into memory at start-up:
    - the start-up form

- the code in all the modules
- the code behind all the forms

- Also, be certain to strip out any unused forms or modules, since the code for these will be loaded during start-up anyway.

Menu Concepts

As disguised objects (because each item appears as part of a menu structure and not separately), menus play an important role in Visual Basic applications. They provide easy access to many functions. Each form is capable of containing a menu. You manage Visual Basic menu structures with properties just as you would any other object. In the Windows SDK and in the days before some of the resource editing programs appeared, you created a menu by typing a structure that looked like the one shown in Listing 4-1.

Listing 4-1 *When using the C language and the Windows SDK, you can create a menu by using this source code.*

```
/*****************************************************/
/*                Resource code for menus           */
/*****************************************************/
MAINMENUBAR MENU
    BEGIN
    POPUP "&File"
        BEGIN
            MENUITEM   "&New...", IDM_New
            MENUITEM   "&Open...", IDM_Open
        END
    POPUP "&Do It!"
        BEGIN
            MENUITEM   "&Practice", IDM_Practice
            MENUITEM   "&The Real Thing", IDM_TheRealThing
        END
    POPUP "&Setup"
        BEGIN
            MENUITEM   "&Beginner", IDM_Beginner
            MENUITEM   "&Intermediate", IDM_Intermediate
            MENUITEM   "&Advanced", IDM_Advanced
            MENUITEM SEPARATOR
            MENUITEM   "&Sound On", IDM_SoundOn
            MENUITEM   "Sound &Off", IDM_SoundOff
```

```
         END
POPUP "\a&Help"
     BEGIN
          MENUITEM    "&Instructions", IDM_Instructions
          MENUITEM    "&About Quick Eyes", IDM_AboutQuickEyes
     END
END
```

You must then use a resource compiler to create the file that eventually will be linked into your Windows program. Notice the use of the ampersand (&) for the hot keys on each menu item in Listing 4-1. These hot keys also work within Visual Basic itself.

Designing menus in Visual Basic takes much less effort than other Windows programming environments. You can set the opening displayed name of the menu selection and its control name, index number, accelerator key combination, and opening state of the menu item (Checked, Enabled, or Visible). At run time, you can reset almost everything associated with a menu selection, including the opening state. Figure 4-2 shows the Menu Design Window for the Reader.

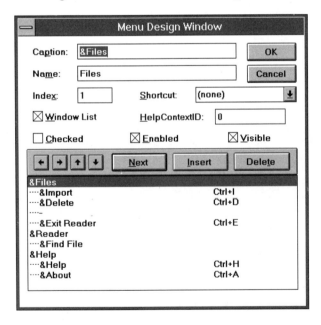

Figure 4-2   *This Menu Design Window shows the menu structure for the Reader application. Notice the HelpContextID for assigning the equate value of a help screen in Windows help.*

You can nest menu selections to five levels below the top menu selection in Visual Basic. Visual Basic does not support some of the native functionality for menus found in the Windows SDK. Features like bitmaps, special fonts, and special breaks require calls to the Windows API for use in Visual Basic. Like icons, cursors, and other controls, menus consume resources. In fact, in design mode you get the same paint problems when more than 50 menu items appear as you get when you have more than 50 controls on a form. Each menu item and each menu gets its own "handle," which means that it has registered its own window class, just the way a regular control does.

Special Menu Considerations

Microsoft recommends that you avoid certain accelerator keys that may activate unexpected parts of your application. It is recommended that you not use the following menu shortcut keys in addition to avoiding shortcut keys used by convention, such as Ctrl-C for copy or Ctrl-V for paste:

ASCII Values	Menu Shortcut Keys	Editing Keys
08	Ctrl+H	Backspace
09	Ctrl+I	Tab
13	Ctrl+M	Enter

If you plan to create an application operable under Windows version 3.0, keep in mind that forms with menus cannot have the BorderStyle property set to Fixed Double. To have menus, a form's BorderStyle property must have one of three settings: None, Fixed Single, or Sizeable.

You can add a separator bar to a menu during run time simply by setting the caption to equal one character of the hyphen ("-"). You can also reconvert this to a selectable menu choice by resetting the caption to ASCII characters other than a dash symbol. Separator bars are best used for drawing a distinction between function groups within the same pull-down menu.

The addition of a menu to a form with no caption, no maximize/minimize buttons, and no control box is not supported in Visual Basic under Windows version 3.0. If you put a menu on a form with no caption bar or associated buttons, the result is a menu bar that does not refresh properly.

If an MDI child window in maximized and contains a frame, and if the window's BorderStyle property is set to None, the window will appear to slip under and be partly covered by the title bar of a parent form that has a menu. An MDI child control with a BorderStyle of None cannot be maximized by the user.

At design time, the cursor control keys do not consistently move through a form's controls. The Right and Down cursor keys should move the focus from one control to another according to the tab index in ascending order. The Left and Up cursor keys should move the focus from one control to another according to the tab index in descending order. For example, look at the Mouse Coordinate Checker sample application in Chapter 3. In design mode, you can't use the cursor keys to move from the button labeled Shorter to the button labeled Reset in one keystroke. The run-time version of the application won't have this problem. While you are in design mode, use the Tab key rather than the control keys to correctly follow the tab index of the controls.

Accelerator Keys

You can provide access to menu functions directly from the keyboard so that the user can pull down a menu without using the mouse. The keystrokes that provide this access are called **accelerators**. Figure 4-3 shows the accelerator keys for the Files menu of the Reader application. Accelerators are not the same as the Alt-<key> combinations you can create by adding an ampersand (&) to a menu selection. The Alt-<key> combinations work only when the menu on which they appear is visible. As you create an interface to your application, be sure to include accelerators in your schemes that allow the user to drive the application without a mouse. Not everyone prefers to use a mouse with Windows applications, and some settings (airliners, for example) make them inconvenient to use.

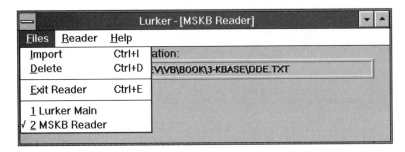

Figure 4-3   *The accelerator keys shown in the pull-down menu can be used to access those menu items even when the menu has not been pulled down.*

When you press an accelerator key combination that corresponds to a menu selection, Windows sends the messages WM_INITMENU, WM_INITMENUPOPUP, and WM_MENUSELECT to the application. These are the same messages that are sent when you access the menu with a mouse.

Programming accelerators in the Windows SDK requires that you place an accelerator table into memory and install an event handler to check for the keystrokes kept in the table. With Visual Basic, however, you simply attach the accelerator keystroke combination to the menu item in the Menu Design Window. With the SDK, you can create accelerator keys from any combination on the keyboard. Visual Basic restricts the eligible list to letters and function keys, so that you use the Control and Shift keys alone or in combination. The SDK also allows you to drive functions other than menu items. It's not possible to use a resource editor like the Windows Resource Editor from Symantec or the Resource Workshop from Borland International to edit the Visual Basic EXE itself. You can directly modify the EXE file for many programs, but not for Visual Basic. The resource tool kit's original purpose was to allow you to edit or copy the resources from within an existing EXE file. Since accelerator keys are resources, you can add them to the EXE just as you would any other resource. In Visual Basic, however, you can make the modifications, but when you try to run Visual Basic it will return an error citing that it found a virus. (Viruses often change the size of the program file, which is what happens when you attempt to add a resource to VB.EXE.) A program created in Visual Basic cannot be edited at all.

The list in Table 4-1 shows the keys available in the Visual Basic programming environment (VB.EXE) as shown by the *Symantec Windows Resource Toolkit*.

Table 4-1   *These hot keys (or accelerators) work inside the Design environment of Visual Basic. The Symantec Windows Resource Toolkit captured this view of the Visual Basic resources for hot keys.*

Type	*Key*	*Code*	*Shift*	*Ctrl*	*Alt*	*Value*	*Invert*
VirtKey	F3	114	No	No	No	32771	No
Virtkey	F3	114	Yes	No	No	32772	No
Virtkey	F5	116	Yes	No	No	1309	No
Virtkey	F5	116	No	No	No	1300	No
Virtkey	F6	117	No	No	Yes	1800	No
Virtkey	F6	117	Yes	No	Yes	1801	No
Virtkey	F7	118	No	No	No	1200	Yes

Table 4-1   *(Continued)*

Type	*Key*	*Code*	*Shift*	*Ctrl*	*Alt*	*Value*	*Invert*
Virtkey	F8	119	No	No	No	1301	No
Virtkey	F8	119	Yes	No	No	1302	No
Virtkey	F9	120	No	No	No	1306	No
Virtkey	F12	123	No	No	No	1009	Yes
Virtkey	F12	123	Yes	No	No	1008	Yes
Virtkey	F12	123	No	Yes	No	1007	Yes
Virtkey	BACK	8	No	No	Yes	1100	No
Virtkey	DELETE	46	Yes	No	No	1101	No
Virtkey	DELETE	46	No	No	No	1103	No
Virtkey	INSERT	45	No	Yes	No	1102	Yes
Virtkey	INSERT	45	Yes	No	No	1105	No

Dynamic Menus

The dynamic nature of Windows and Visual Basic is dramatically evident when you use dynamic menus in your Visual Basic application. Your application can take on an almost infinite depth of functionality. Most character-based applications present a fixed list of selections in each menu. In Visual Basic, you can add new menu selections or simply rename the existing ones based on preceding events initiated by the user or by your Visual Basic application.

Dynamic menus in Visual Basic as shown in Figure 4-4 allow you to replace all or any of the menu selections in an application with text describing another choice. Visual Basic control arrays give you a means to find out which one the user has selected. Since menus are resources, they can be manipulated in control arrays just like push buttons. When you change a menu selection, you must use the Click event for that menu to respond to the user's selection of one of the dynamic menu items. When you load the new menu resource, you attach an index number to it so that you can identify it later. Inside the Click event for the menu itself, you test for which menu item the user has selected, and you respond accordingly. In a menu that you build with permanent selections during the design phase, each menu selection pops up its own click event.

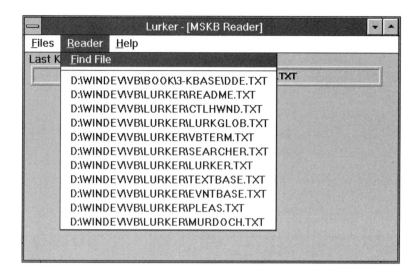

Figure 4-4 *The Reader application scans the last directory accessed for files with the extension "TXT" and places them in the file-access menu (Reader) dynamically. When you choose one of these files, it loads into the Reader.*

In the Reader application, you can use dynamic menus to provide an instantaneous list of text files in the current directory that the Reader can access. No special API calls will be needed, and these selections give the user a quick means to select the text data base to be read without resorting to the common dialog for file access. (The common dialog for changing directories to pick a file will still be available from the Index = 0, or first, menu selection.)

As soon as you add a secondary selection to a menu item, the menu item no longer possesses its own events. You must go to the secondary selections to enter code. In the Reader application, you select the Reader menu choice. That drops down to the one permanently programmed selection called File, which makes a direct call to the common dialog for directory and file access. The File choice is also Index number 0. All of the other menu choices will be spawned from this beginning object.

Tip: *If Visual Basic were a true object-oriented programming environment, then the changes made to the Index=0 object would apply to all of its descendants. However, once the resource or menu item has been loaded, it no longer "inherits" any more characteristics from its parent.*

The first step for creating the dynamic menu occurs in the Form_Load event, where the INI file is checked for the name and location of the last file accessed. The code in Listing 4-2 shows you how to find the file names and how to place them in the menu dynamically.

Listing 4-2   *This code shows the creation of the dynamic menu items shown in Figure 4-4.*

```
StartPath = CurDir$                  'Get current path
PathSettings (Getting)               'Retrieve previous ini (function)

If SavedPath <> "" Then              'Start file list menu
  Load FindFile(1)                   'File list separator
  FindFile(1).Separator = 1          'Separator (undocumented)
  Load FindFile(2)                   'Create file choice
  FindFile(2).Caption = SavedPath
  MenuIndex% = 3                     'Count menu items
Else
  MenuIndex% = 0
End If
TempName$ = RTrim$(CurDir$) + "\" + Dir$("*.TXT") 'Set first entry
If TempName$ <> SavedPath Then                    'match first?
  Load FindFile(MenuIndex%)                       'create menu
  FindFile(MenuIndex%).Caption = TempName$
End If
Do                                                'look for txt files
  TempName$ = Dir$
  If TempName$ = "" Then Exit Do
  MenuIndex% = MenuIndex% + 1
  Load FindFile(MenuIndex%)
  FindFile(MenuIndex%).Caption = CurDir$ + "\" + TempName$
Loop
If SavedPath = "" Then          'Set default if no previous
  SavedPath = StartPath
End If
LastPath.Caption = SavedPath    'Set display
```

It takes two statements to create the finished menu item. A call to the Load statement actually places the resource in memory. Then you set the text of the new resource by setting its Caption property: you use the control name of the master menu item (in this case FileFind) and the index that corresponds to the new menu resource you've created. The following two statements execute:

```
Load FindFile(MenuIndex%)                          'create menu
FindFile(MenuIndex%).Caption = TempName$'set menu item text
```

The application's main window then processes the following sequence of messages:

- WM_WINDOWPOSCHANGING is sent to a window whose dimensions are about to change because of a call to a window management function.
- WM_NCCALCSIZE indicates that the size and position of the window client area needs to be recalculated. In this case, the window is the pop-up menu.
- WM_NCPAINT informs a window that its frame needs to be repainted. ("NC" stands for nonclient.)
- WM_GETTEXT copies text from a buffer into the calling window—the pop-up menu, in this case.
- WM_ERASEBACKGND prepares the candidate window for repainting a region that has been invalidated.
- WM_WINDOWPOSCHANGED is sent to a window whose dimensions have changed because of a call to a window management function.

In the Reader application, the Dir$ and CurDir$ functions do the directory and file-access work. CurDir$ grabs the path of the current directory. Dir$ retrieves file names for the files that match the specification passed to it. Once a specification has been set, though, each call to Dir$ will search sequentially for the next file that matches that specification. In the Reader Form_Load procedure, these successive calls to Dir$ get the file specification that is used to set the caption for the newly created menu resource. As each file is located, the Load statement, placed in a Do loop, creates the next menu resource according to the index number that is assigned when you increment the MenuIndex% local variable.

Visual Basic Objects

Since Visual Basic is *not* a true object-oriented language, as we've discussed, let me introduce you to the ways in which it can emulate object*like* behavior. In Visual Basic you can create objects on the fly, as I'll show when we talk about push buttons and control arrays. Visual Basic 2.0 introduced the idea of forms and controls as objects that can have multiple instances, not just as elements of an array.

Note that in converting Visual Basic 1.0 applications to version 3.0, you may discover functionality disappears where statements using NULL occur. Visual Basic

1.0 permitted API statement calls using the NULL keyword when it had previously been defined as zero. In those cases, you will need to convert the NULL to a zero in the statement.

The object variable introduced in Visual Basic 2.0 gave Visual Basic objects more object behavior. Your ability to create and refer to objects within your code has been increased immensely. In addition to the new flexibility in referring to objects, the object variable permits you to manage memory resources much more closely.

Think of object variables as if they were variable structures. You can set generic (not assigned) or specific (assigned to a particular control type or form) object variables. Each specific object variable contains all of the default information for the object type to which it was set. To use the object variable to the greatest advantage, it is important to understand the following concepts:

- Visual Basic declares implicit object variables and collections for all forms and controls. You can't edit or delete these implicit objects.
- Instances of a form or control can be passed to procedures for operations on the form or control.
- You can create a new instance of a form or control by dimensioning a new variable or by using the Set . . . New statement combination. (Neglecting to include the New statement simply renames the existing form.)
- All new instances of forms or controls occupy memory and resources.
- All form properties and controls with their properties become available to a new instance of a form with controls.
- Child instances of forms and controls not in use and without requirements for retaining values should be set to Nothing to save resources. In the structure example, the Nothing statement clears the variables in the structure and de-allocates the memory used to hold the structure.
- You can detect the current instance for an item by using the Me statement, where "current" means the location of the presently executing code.
- The Controls index tracks controls on the form in reverse order to how they were created. That is, the next control you add to the form will have Controls.Index = 0. That TabIndex property operates separately.

The Controls property, the TypeOf statement, and the Is statement permit you to identify the control types on a form. The sample application shown in Figure 4-5 uses these three features of Visual Basic to inventory the controls on the form. The list box at the bottom of the form shows the controls that appear on the form and their associated Controls.Index number.

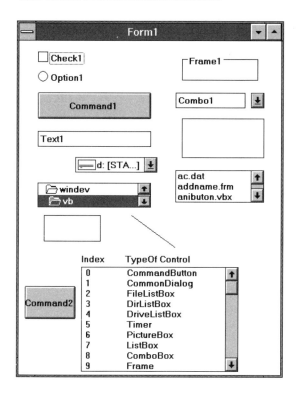

Figure 4-5   *The list box shows the control types and their related Controls index. Even custom control, as in the case of the CommonDialog control, specifies a name by which it can be recognized with the TypeOf statement.*

The code in Listing 4-3 shows all of the stock object types in the only way that you can use to survey all of the control types on a form. The Select structure cannot be used; only the If . . . Then . . . ElseIf . . . Else structure works with the TypeOf and Is statements.

Listing 4-3   *This source code fills a list box with the control types found on a Visual Basic form. The only custom control included in this list is CommonDialog. The rest of the controls are the stock objects supplied with Visual Basic.*

```
For n = 0 To Form1.Controls.Count - 1
    If TypeOf Form1.Controls(n) Is CheckBox Then
```

```
        List1.AddItem Str$(n) + Chr$(9) + "CheckBox"
      ElseIf TypeOf Form1.Controls(n) Is ComboBox Then
        List1.AddItem Str$(n) + Chr$(9) + "ComboBox"
      ElseIf TypeOf Form1.Controls(n) Is CommandButton Then
        List1.AddItem Str$(n) + Chr$(9) + "CommandButton"
      ElseIf TypeOf Form1.Controls(n) Is DirListBox Then
        List1.AddItem Str$(n) + Chr$(9) + "DirListBox"
      ElseIf TypeOf Form1.Controls(n) Is DriveListBox Then
        List1.AddItem Str$(n) + Chr$(9) + "DriveListBox"
      ElseIf TypeOf Form1.Controls(n) Is FileListBox Then
        List1.AddItem Str$(n) + Chr$(9) + "FileListBox"
      ElseIf TypeOf Form1.Controls(n) Is Frame Then
        List1.AddItem Str$(n) + Chr$(9) + "Frame"
      ElseIf TypeOf Form1.Controls(n) Is HScrollBar Then
        List1.AddItem Str$(n) + Chr$(9) + "HScrollBar"
      ElseIf TypeOf Form1.Controls(n) Is Image Then
        List1.AddItem Str$(n) + Chr$(9) + "Image"
      ElseIf TypeOf Form1.Controls(n) Is Label Then
        List1.AddItem Str$(n) + Chr$(9) + "Label"
      ElseIf TypeOf Form1.Controls(n) Is Line Then
        List1.AddItem Str$(n) + Chr$(9) + "Line"
      ElseIf TypeOf Form1.Controls(n) Is ListBox Then
        List1.AddItem Str$(n) + Chr$(9) + "ListBox"
      ElseIf TypeOf Form1.Controls(n) Is Menu Then
        List1.AddItem Str$(n) + Chr$(9) + "Menu"
      ElseIf TypeOf Form1.Controls(n) Is OptionButton Then
        List1.AddItem Str$(n) + Chr$(9) + "OptionButton"
      ElseIf TypeOf Form1.Controls(n) Is PictureBox Then
        List1.AddItem Str$(n) + Chr$(9) + "PictureBox"
      ElseIf TypeOf Form1.Controls(n) Is Shape Then
        List1.AddItem Str$(n) + Chr$(9) + "Shape"
      ElseIf TypeOf Form1.Controls(n) Is TextBox Then
        List1.AddItem Str$(n) + Chr$(9) + "TextBox"
      ElseIf TypeOf Form1.Controls(n) Is Timer Then
        List1.AddItem Str$(n) + Chr$(9) + "Timer"
      ElseIf TypeOf Form1.Controls(n) Is PictureBox Then
        List1.AddItem Str$(n) + Chr$(9) + "PictureBox"
      ElseIf TypeOf Form1.Controls(n) Is VScrollBar Then
        List1.AddItem Str$(n) + Chr$(9) + "VScrollBar"
      ElseIf TypeOf Form1.Controls(n) Is CommonDialog Then
        List1.AddItem Str$(n) + Chr$(9) + "CommonDialog"
      Else
        List1.AddItem Str$(n) + Chr$(9) + "No Control Type"
      End If
    Next n
```

Button Concepts

The ubiquitous button of Visual Basic serves in more roles than most of the other tools. The label may be the next most used control, but buttons can do some things that labels can't do—even things that you would expect labels to do. The same techniques for managing control arrays discussed in the previous section on menus applies to any controls, including buttons. Throughout the rest of the book, the use of indices and control-array management is included within other topics. As with all other controls—except the "lite" graphic controls and controls created in an array— each button must register its own window class, and therefore consumes resources. That is why it's difficult to create a spreadsheet with many cells by simply constructing a grid of adjacent buttons or labels (yes, even labels consume resources).

Note that graphical controls include image, line, shape and label. These controls use few resources because they do not register their own window class and so don't have their own handle.

The Reader application applies several of the more common uses for button controls, including Ok, Cancel, and Print. The Reader also takes advantage of a button control's ability to hide itself until needed and to dynamically change its contents. Labels, for instance, require that the form receive a repaint request before they will display something different from what was shown when the form loaded. (Edit controls work like buttons in this way.) The two controls from the Reader that use this capability include the status display for text searches and the Next and Previous buttons in the article view as shown in Figure 4-6.

In the small sample program in Figure 4-7, notice the effect of leaving the DoEvents() statement out of the loop. A loop without DoEvents() can't process exterior system messages, so the label control never gets repainted. It is the only control that requires interaction with Windows to repaint itself. However, you'll also notice that, with no DoEvents() statement to process events, nothing else in the system will work: you can't terminate the program or go to another Window. This demonstrates the danger of hogging the CPU and not allowing other Windows programs to operate when you forget to include DoEvents() in a CPU-intensive program segment.

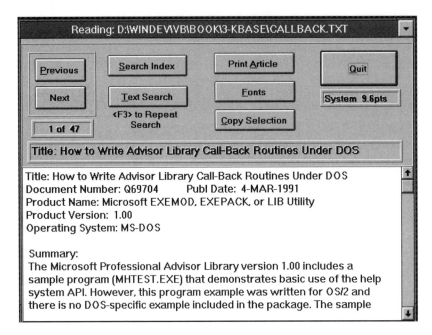

Figure 4-6   *The Next and Previous command buttons (upper left) display the number of bytes the program reads as it searches for the next article to display. In this picture, the Next button was pressed.*

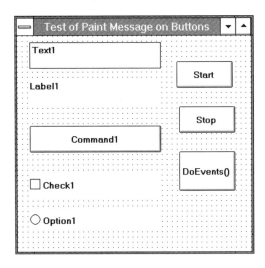

Figure 4-7   *This sample program (DYNFORM.MAK) demonstrates the dynamic updating of labels, edit controls, buttons, option (or radial) buttons, and check-box captions.*

The text search utility in the Reader application lets you hide a button until you need it. The status display button counting the percentage of text searched in the Reader program in Figure 4-6 appears only after the search process begins. Once the search process terminates, the button disappears. In this case, the Visible attribute gets turned off when the control is first loaded, and is set to True when you start the search. If you simply unload the form, you will conserve resources but slow down the application. Generally speaking, you can speed up an application by loading all of the resources at the start, hiding them until you need to display them. (You can even use a hidden list-box control that you never display to re-sort data before you present it.)

 Tip: *A picture-box control can be used as a button. In fact, a picture box offers more events than a button, including Change, DblClick, LinkClose, LinkError, LinkOpen, MouseDown, MouseMove, MouseUp, and Paint. A picture control does not offer the default property available in buttons, however.*

You can use buttons in an array to break code into a new way of conditional branching. In a procedural language, you would create an If or Select Case statement and then branch from there to another If or Select Case statement as the user makes decisions. All of the code would be in one place. You should try to keep your Visual Basic modules as small as possible, and buttons can help you do this.

Suppose you want a button to take on different characteristics depending on the circumstances—like the replaceable menu elements discussed in this chapter. In a procedural language (if it had graphical buttons), you would write a Select Case or If structure where the value passed to the structure would activate a specific set of code in one of the conditions or cases. If you had three different states you wanted the button to assume, you could create such a conditional structure—or you could create three different buttons.

Using Visual Basic, you can load any resource dynamically, including buttons. You can use arrays to spawn new buttons from one "master" button. Figure 4-8 shows a sample application (BUTTONS.MAK) that allows you to create buttons by clicking on the master button. Once you have created a new button, you can drag it to somewhere else on the form. After you've placed the new button, you can click on it and track its behavior as if you had created the button during the design phase.

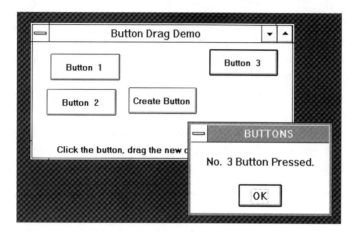

Figure 4-8   *The Button Drag Demo shows how you can create buttons at run time and track their behavior as if you had created them during the design phase.*

   Tip: *When you create buttons—or any other resource—dynamically, they still consume resources at the same rate as if you had created them during the design phase.*

The code in Listing 4-4 shows the handling of the Click event on the master button. That code loads the new button as a unique resource and allows you to drag it around the form. If you click on one of the new buttons, the MsgBox function processes unique behavior for the new button. In this sample, the MsgBox function merely displays a message box, but you can see the purpose of passing the index value for the new array member in the button group on the form.

Listing 4-4   *This code shows what happens in the Click event on the master button in the BUTTONS.MAK program.*

```
Sub Command1_Click (Index As Integer)
        If Index <> 0 Then                              'filter out master
          MessageBox (Index)                            'call unique behavior
          Exit Sub                                      'terminate event
        End If
        ButtonIndex = ButtonIndex + 1                   'increase counter
        Load Command1(ButtonIndex)                      'load new button resource
        TempName$ = "Button " + Str$(ButtonIndex)       'set new caption text
        Command1(ButtonIndex).Caption = TempName$       'set new caption
```

```
      Command1(ButtonIndex).DragMode = 1              'turn off drag mode
      Command1(ButtonIndex).Visible = 1               'make button visible
      Command1(ButtonIndex).DragIcon = LoadPicture(CurDir$ + "\" + "drag.ico")
      Command1(0).Visible = 0                         'disapper master button
End Sub
```

List-Box Concepts

The list-box control in Visual Basic provides a handy tool for displaying multiple instances of one data element or of several data elements grouped into one element. Written with the use of using the plain SDK, list-box behavior gets quite complex to program. Not only must you register a new window class (as with all custom controls), but you must also create the scroll bars and their behavior—and that's just the start. The Windows API includes some handy routines for use in List Boxes, many of which are covered in Chapter 5.

> ***Tip:*** *Since the List() property of a list box gets its own segment in memory, it is limited to holding data totaling no more than 64K or 5440 items, whichever comes first. Any one item in a list box can hold up to 1K of data. When the 64K limit is exceeded, Windows 3.0 causes a UAE, while 3.1 creates trappable errors.*

List boxes appear in several forms throughout Visual Basic. Combo boxes use the list-box structure. The common dialogs used as Professional Edition controls or accessed through the Windows API use a combo box to display the system drive list and list boxes to display files and subdirectories. In addition, the standard Visual Basic Tool Box contains the specialized list boxes that perform these same functions.

Version 1.0 only With the grid alignment option turned on, the list box and the file-list combo box do not resize properly if you draw them too short. Other controls automatically pop to the size of the internal text if you draw them too short.

Setting the List1.Sorted property equal to -1 within the code of a list-box event procedure causes the run-time error "'Sorted' property cannot be set at run time."

Windows 3.0 related only When sorting the contents of a list box with the .Sorted property, the right bracket character ("[") sorts inconsistently. This is not true under Windows 3.1. Windows 3.0 also enforces a 1K limit on the amount of text that can be added to a list box with the AddItem method. When you assign text directly to the List property, Visual Basic allows you to add more than 1K to each string. For the application to remain compatible with Windows 3.0, you must do your own checking of the size of the string.

You will disable the drive list in the drive-list combo-box control if you change the width of the control at run time.

Drive and Directory Combo boxes   In some cases, Visual Basic drive and directory combo boxes do not properly report hardware failures. If you select a floppy drive with no disk, you should and do get Error 68, "Device Unavailable." If you place a floppy disk in that drive and then reselect it, you get updates to the directory or file list boxes in the proper manner. However, if you open the drive and double-click on the directory combo box, Visual Basic does not complain, but neither does it perform any updates. A user could get confused easily, since the system has stopped responding. In the same set of controls, if you change the path property of a directory or file list box to a floppy drive with the door open or with no disk (in the case of 3.5" disks), you get the incorrect Error 68, "Device Unavailable," rather than the more proper Error 71, "Disk Not Ready." Figure 4-9 shows the two types of specialized list boxes you need in order to repeat this problem in the frame titled Disk Drive Error Disappears.

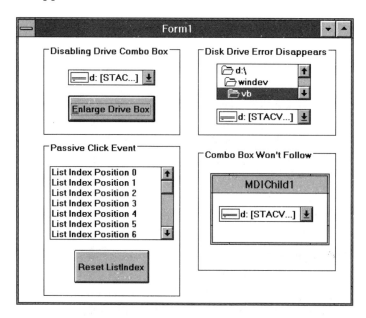

Figure 4-9   *This sample application demonstrates some of the odd behavior of list boxes in Visual Basic.*

Through a programmatic change to the ListIndex property of any Visual Basic list box, you can cause a Click event to be generated. If you select an item in a list box, but then some other part of your program resets the highlight bar to another item in the list box, a Click event will occur. If you have code in the Click event for when a user makes a selection, the same code will execute for the programmatic change.

If you build an application that uses Multiple Document Interface (MDI) child windows, and you place any kind of combo box on it, the list part of the control will not follow the child window if it is moved or resized. It remains operative, but it looks like it just didn't repaint properly.

The ListBox.Sorted property cannot be set at run time. All of the following properties, when you attempt to reset them with code, return Error 382, "Property cannot be set at run time":

ActiveControl	hDC	MultiLine
ActiveForm	hWnd	Parent
BorderStyle (*form and text box only*)	Image	ScrollBars
ControlBox	Index	Sorted
CtlName	List	Style
FontCount	ListCount	Text (*list and combo box only*)
Fonts	MaxButton	Width (*screen only*)
FormName	MinButton	

Sorting List Boxes

Much of the flexibility of Visual Basic comes from dynamically managing the settings for properties. For the most part, the restrictions on the preceding properties fall on object identifiers like FontCount (Fonts installed) and hDC (the handle to the device context of a control). In a few cases, the restrictions include simple behavior modifications to an object—the type of change you become accustomed to making at run time. The .Sorted property of a list box is a good example. You might not want to change anything about a list box except the order in which the contents is displayed. Powerful properties like .Sorted reduce the amount of code you must write. If it's not possible to change the behavior of the list box, you must change what goes into the list box.

You can choose one of two strategies to employ the same list box with different sort orders. In one strategy, you can presort the data in some fashion by using arrays or a search algorithm. Then you read the array into the list box by using the AddItem method and the array index to set the index% parameter of AddItem. (Remember: Your array is limited to 64K unless you use the Professional Edition HugeArray control.) In this strategy, be sure the .Sorted property of the list box is set to False or zero, since adding an item by using the index% parameter out of sequence can prevent the list box from sorting properly.

The other strategy for fooling the list box into displaying data in different orders involves simply changing the item to be sorted. In the case of the Reader application, each of the two sort orders (date and alphanumeric) comes from the positioning of the count% variable in the string passed to AddItem. In date order (the order in which, presumably, the articles were read into the database), the count is added to the beginning of the string. When you use using the Format$ function, zeros fill the empty positions to ensure proper sorting. In the alphanumeric sequence, the count% gets appended to the end of the string, leaving the list box to sort according to the article title. In this strategy, the .Sorted property must be set to True or one, since we want the list box to perform the sort on the strings passed to it. Figure 4-10 shows the index of articles from the Reader application sorted in alphanumeric order.

To distinguish between the two sorting methods, the user first clicks on the Search Index button in the Reader application. Creating two new buttons that are based on the Search Index button and then resized, we can track which sort order the user has requested. Figure 4-11 shows the two buttons that have been created dynamically. The code in Listing 4-5 shows how the buttons are made and how the form that contains the list box is called.

Listing 4-5   *This code responds to a mouse click on the Search Index buttons in two ways: (1) it creates the two new buttons for choosing sort order, and (2) it responds to whichever sort-order button is selected by the user.*

```
Sub Search_Click (Index As Integer)
    If Search(3).Visible = True Then
        '---Create the Date sort order button
        Load Search(20)
        Search(20).Width = Search(3).Width * .6
        Search(20).Left = Search(3).Left - (Search(3).Width * .1)
        Search(20).Caption = "Date"
        '---Create the alphanumeric sort order button
        Load Search(21)
        Search(21).Width = Search(3).Width * .6
        Search(21).Left = Search(3).Left + (Search(3).Width * .6)
```

```
      Search(21).Caption = "Title"
      '---Hide the Search Index button and display the new ones
      Search(3).Visible = False
      Search(20).Visible = True
      Search(21).Visible = True
   Else
      Select Case Index        'Act on the sort order chosen
         Case 20               'Date sort order button clicked
            ListSort = "Num"   'Set global variable
            Load Searcher      'Load form with index list box
            Searcher.Show      'Display the List box
         Case 21               'Alphanumeric sort order chosen
            ListSort = "Alpha"
            Load Searcher
            Searcher.Show
      End Select
   End If
End Sub
```

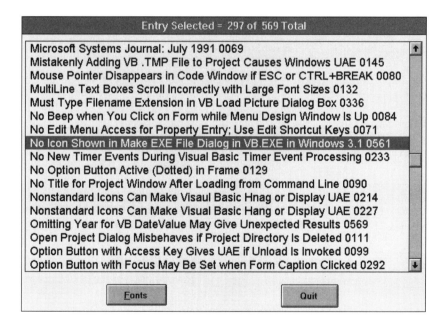

Figure 4-10   *To create this alphanumeric index of articles from the Reader program, the .Sorted property was set to True and the article titles were passed as strings to the AddItem method without a leading numeric counter.*

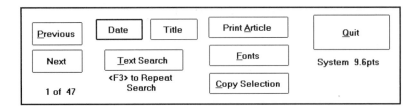

Figure 4-11   *The Date and Title buttons were created dynamically from the Search Index button, which was created at design time.*

As the Form_Load event is processed for the Searcher form (the one containing the index list box), the file with the index entries will be read and the entries added according to the sort type passed in the ListSort global variable. The code in Listing 4-6 shows how the list box gets filled.

Listing 4-6   *This code executes when the Searcher form loads after the user has selected a sort type for viewing the article index in the Reader application.*

```
Sub Form_Load ()
    '--- Fill table with index entries
    On Error GoTo LoadDone
    SavedPtr& = Seek(2)                           'save place in index file
    Seek #2, 1                                    'go to top of index file
    ErrMsg = "Error setting pointer"              'set error message
    Do Until Count& = (LOF(2) / Len(IndexRec))    'read to the end of the file
        Get #2, , IndexRec.IndexEntry             'read the next record
        If IndexRec.IndexEntry = "" Then Exit Do  'stop reading at empty record
        ErrMsg = "Error getting record"           'reset error message
        Count& = Count& + 1                       'increment the counter
        Countr$ = Format$(Count&, "000#")         'format article count
        Title$ = RTrim$(Mid$(IndexRec.IndexEntry, 14)) 'format title
        If ListSort = "Num" Then                  'check for sort type used
            IndexList.AddItem Countr$ + " " + Title$ 'add to the list box
        Else
            IndexList.AddItem Title$ + "   " + Countr$ 'add to the list box
        End If
    Loop
    Seek #2, SavedPtr&                            'reset index pointer in file
    Count& = 0                                    'ensure counter reset
    Searcher.Counter.Caption = Str$(IndexList.ListCount) 'set dialog caption
    IndexList.ListIndex = SavedIndex              'reset pointer in dialog
    '---Retrieve font settings for article display
    F% = FreeFile                                 'get the next valid file number
    FileName$ = StartPath + "\READER.INI"         'set INI file name
```

```
    Open FileName$ For Random As F% Len = 102        'open the file
      Get F%, 9, FSName$                             'get the parameter stored there
      Get F%, 10, FSSize%
      Get F%, 11, FSBold%
      Get F%, 12, FSItalic%
      Get F%, 13, FSUnder%
      Get F%, 14, FSThru%
      Get F%, 15, FSColor&
    Close F%                                         'close the file
      Searcher.IndexList.FontName = FSName$          'set the display of the list box
      Searcher.IndexList.FontSize = FSSize%
      Searcher.IndexList.FontBold = FSBold%
      Searcher.IndexList.FontItalic = FSItalic%
      Searcher.IndexList.FontUnderline = FSUnder%
      Searcher.IndexList.FontStrikeThru = FSThru%
      Searcher.IndexList.ForeColor = FSColor&
    Exit Sub
LoadDone:
    MsgBox ErrMsg + "Error = " + Error$
    Exit Sub
End Sub
```

Notice how the Form_Load procedure chooses the form of AddItem to use based on the value of the global ListSort variable. The Form_load procedure employs several useful practices for filling a list box with data:

- The code loops through the index file after determining how many records the file contains. Count& = (LOF (2) / Len(IndexRec)) uses the LOF function to determine the number of bytes in the file, and divides the result by the size of each record (IndexRec) for a total record count.
- The Get statement does not include a second parameter (recordnumber%). It simply retrieves the next record after the last one that was read.
- The FreeFile function saves you from having to track the correct file number before you open a file. The file holding the defaults will be opened just long enough to retrieve display settings, so there's no need to trap or track the number returned by FreeFile.
- The Windows API contains several calls for managing the INI files. Under Windows, these files hold system- and application-specific default information. The Reader program uses a pseudo-INI file managed with the normal file-access routines from Visual Basic. It retrieves the last file accessed and the font settings for the index and article displays.

A big disadvantage to list boxes becomes evident when you want to create columns of information. The list box does not support tab stops without a call to the Windows API. Figure 4-12 shows the default tab stops that are already embedded in a Visual Basic list box. These "columns" are different from the Columns property of a List box in versions 2.0 and 3.0. This property feeds or snakes data into columns across the list box.

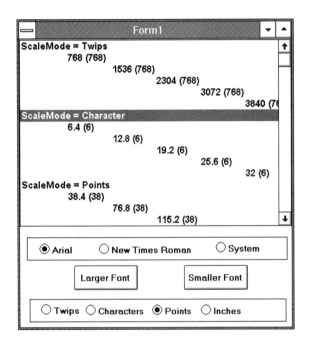

Figure 4-12 *This list box shows the default tab stops in twips, characters, and points. These tab locations cannot be changed except through a Windows API call. The number in parentheses shows the difference between that tab stop and the previous tab stop.*

List boxes can be used to re-sort data, as well. The .Index() property of a list box provides 64K of record buffer in memory. By preloading a list box with the .Sorted property set to True or -1, you can access the items in the list in a different order from the order used in the file. The Reader program uses this technique to strip out duplicate article titles. (The Microsoft KnowledgeBase often contains articles posted more than one time if you regularly use the same search criteria when you download.)

Figure 4-13 shows the bottom of the Searcher form during the design phase. Notice the small box marked ListSort. Although it is not visible to the user (.Visible = False), this is a normal list box that presorts the data that will appear in the index list box just above it. Listing 4-7 shows how the index file is read into the hidden list box called SortList and then transferred to the displayed list box. During the transfer, a filter compares the previous and current titles and skips any titles that match one that is already loaded into the displayed list box.

Figure 4-13   *The controls for the Searcher form at design time reveal the icon for the common dialog control for changing fonts and the hidden list box SortList that presorts the index.*

Listing 4-7   *The first segment of this code reads the index file to load the records into a hidden list box with the .Sorted property turned on. The second segment extracts the records from the hidden list box and places them in the display.*

```
'---fill the hidden list box from the file
Do Until Count& = (LOF(2) / Len(IndexRec))    'read to the end of the file
   Get #2, , IndexRec.IndexEntry              'read the next record
   If IndexRec.IndexEntry = "" Then Exit Do   'stop reading at empty record
   ErrMsg = "Error getting record"            'reset error message
   Count& = Count& + 1                        'increment the counter
   Countr$ = Format$(Count&, "000#")          'format article count
   Title$ = RTrim$(Mid$(IndexRec.IndexEntry, 14))'format title
   If ListSort = "Num" Then                   'check for sort type used
      SortList.AddItem Countr$ + " " + Title$ 'add to the list box
   Else
      SortList.AddItem RTrim$(Title$) + " - " + Countr$    'add to the list box
   End If
Loop
Seek #2, SavedPtr&                            'reset index pointer in file
Count& = 0                                    'ensure counter reset
Searcher.Counter.Caption = Str$(IndexList.ListCount) 'set dialog caption
'---Transfer the sorted contents to the display, skipping duplicates
Do Until Count& = SortList.ListCount          'Fill the display list box
   LastOne$ = Mid$(Last$, 5, Len(Last$) / 2)
   ThisLen% = Len(SortList.List(Count&)) / 2
   ThisOne$ = Mid$(SortList.List(Count&), 5, ThisLen%)
```

```
    If LastOne$ <> ThisOne$ Then 'recycle if the same
        IndexList.AddItem SortList.List(Count&)     'fill list box
        Last$ = SortList.List(Count&)               'save for next time
    End If
    Count& = Count& + 1                             'increment the counter
Loop
```

A Few Words about Icons

Icons take the place of the command prompt in character-based DOS. They launch applications, they display the current path to a file, and they can be used to show other system information. In Visual Basic, as discussed in an earlier section of this chapter, you can simulate the program-launching function of an icon by using picture controls. You add the call to the program in the click event associated with the picture control, then set a picture in the control at design time or use LoadPicture at run time, and you've simulated an icon on the desktop. The Word for Windows icon displays the path and file name for the currently edited file.

 In the same way that you can edit the Prompt command in DOS to show date and time, you can use an icon as shown to display that information and other system events and data. Displaying the system time is one of the easiest ways to use an icon for status display. Add a clock to your application icon by adding a Timer control to your main form and putting the code in Listing 4-8 into the Timer event within the Timer control.

Listing 4-8   *With the Timer Interval property set to 1000 (equals 1 second), setting up the Timer event processing as shown here will update the icon caption when you minimize the application or form containing the timer.*

```
Sub Timer1_Timer ()
    If Main.WindowState = MINIMIZED Then
        Main.Caption = "MSKB Reader" + Chr$(13) + Format$(Now, "hh:mm:ss am/pm")
    End If
End Sub
```

The client area of an application can still be addressed when the application is minimized. If you choose not to use the .Caption property, you can send text and pictures directly to the minimized version of your application. Simply by using the Print method, you can send text with the phrase Print "Text Here" placed in the Form_Resize event. That text, however, disappears when you move the icon. An application processes the following messages when you click the mouse, hold down the button on the icon and move the icon:

WM_QUERYDRAGICON (Sent when no icon is defined.)

WM_WINDOWPOSCHANGING Window size is about to change.

WM_WINPOSCHANGED Window is changed.

WM_WINDOWPOSCHANGING Window size is about to change.

WM_WINPOSCHANGED Window is changed.

WM_MOVE Window was moved.

WM_WINPOSCHANGING Window size is about to change.

WM_NCPAINT Frame around window needs repainting.

WM_ERASEBKGND Client area needs repainting.

WM_GETTEXT Place text in buffer.

WM_GETTEXT

WM_PAINT (Request to repaint.)

WM_ERASEBKND Client area needs repainting.

Notice how the last two messages (WM_PAINT and WM_ERASEBKND) indicate that the screen will repaint. However, a minimized application will never process a Paint event in Visual Basic. That makes it more difficult to place animations or even a clock in the icon. However, you can use scaling methods and the Timer event to make changes. By placing the code from Listing 4-9 in the Timer event, you can create a stopwatch that will track the time since the application (or form) was minimized.

Listing 4-9   *This code turns a minimized application into a stopwatch.*

```
Sub Timer1_Timer ()
      If WindowState = 1 Then                       'when form minimzed
        Cls                                         'clear the screen
        Elapsed = Elapsed + .00001                  'increment the time
        TimeString$ = Format$(Elapsed, "h:m:ss")    'format the time
        Display$ = Mid$(TimeString$, 3)             'crop off the hours
        Print Display$                              'display stopwatch
      Else
        Elapsed = 0                                 'reset the counter
      End If
End Sub
```

As a first step toward making the stopwatch, turn off the icon for the form by adding Form1.Icon = LoadPicture() to the Form_Load event. After that, put a Timer control onto the form and set its .Interval property to 1000 (equals 1 second). Then place in the Timer event the code given in Listing 4-9. Start the application and minimize it. Within one second a clock will begin ticking where the icon normally appears.

Tip: The Now function returns a double precision number where the left side of the decimal contains the date and the right side contains the time. To capture the time only, you must use the Format$ function. To increment the time with implicit double-precision variables (variable#), you must use ".00001" to represent each second.

Label-Control Concepts

Labels provide the simplest window creations within Visual Basic. Labels hold static information, such as field names, and dynamic status information, such as the time or date. With Visual Basic 1.0, labels still involve the registration of a new window class, so they still consume resources. In Windows, each registered window can be identified by its handle—usually referred to as "hWnd." Visual Basic provides the hWnd property for the form but not for the controls in version 1.0. As will be discussed in Chapter 5, you can use the Windows API GetFocus function and the Visual Basic SetFocus method to obtain the hWnd for most Visual Basic controls except for the Label and Frame controls. Version 3.0 provides the window handle (or hWnd) for most controls.

The text within a label is stored within the name-and-symbol table of 32K maximum, which holds all such information for function names, procedure names, variable names, line numbers, line labels, and an additional 4 bytes overhead for each.

Caution: Embedded spaces in a label control will cause the string to wrap too soon.

As discussed earlier in this chapter regarding DoEvents processing, labels require updating from Windows itself. If a process takes over the CPU and does not contain a call to DoEvents for system messages, the displayed contents of a label will not appear after the label caption has been changed.

The Reader application uses labels for the conventional purpose of labeling fields, as with the Text Search entry window shown in Figure 4-14.

Text Search
Type text to Find: [   ]
Start   Quit

Figure 4-14   *The Text Search utility in the Reader application uses a label to present the words "Type test to Find:" as a field label.*

Also, you can use labels as a status display for actions in the program. The Reader application uses a label to display the title of the last article that appeared in the viewer. The contents of the label get updated whenever the contents of the Article text box are changed, as shown in Listing 4-10.

Listing 4-10   *The Change event in the article display changes the .Caption property of a label to display the last article shown in the text box called Article. Notice the use of the Mid$ function to test for the end of the first line in the text box in order to read the article title.*

```
Sub Article_Change ()
    LastText.Caption = Mid$(Article.Text, 1, InStr(1, Article.Text, Chr$(13)))
End Sub
```

> ✓ **Note:** *The Mid$ function could be replaced by the Left$ function, which would require one less parameter (where to start) in this case since it starts with the first character.*

Text-box–Control Concepts

Text boxes do all of the text input and editing work in Visual Basic, including the text manipulation of combo boxes. Single-line edit controls (as text boxes were once referred to in the SDK) perform the data entry field type of text entry. Multiline text boxes appear in editors and other displays that show multiple lines of text other than a list box. Multiline text boxes provide a much more manageable text display than that offered by the TextOut function in the SDK, which is used to spit characters out onto a barren and inanimate client area that must be repainted frequently.

The .Text property of text boxes can hold no more than 64K of text, and the default maximum is 32K. You can increase the default size through a call to the Windows API. This limit is not, however, part of the single 64K segment of text and symbols used by the forms and controls other than text boxes, list boxes, and combo boxes.

While specifying a text box as multiline helps you to properly orient text, it can get you into trouble. Visual Basic expects that any carriage return (Chr$(13)) in a text box will be followed by a line-feed character (Chr$(10)), and strips out whatever character appears there. If you send text to a text box that contains carriage returns without the line feed also, you will lose text.

You can determine the number of lines in a text box through the SendMessage API call, which is discussed in Chapter 5. Without the guarantee of a terminating carriage return or other character at the end of each line, you cannot make the same determination by using only Visual Basic. The code in Listing 4-10 shows how you could detect a carriage return (Chr$(13)) by using the Instr function if each line in the text box were terminated that way.

In the Reader application, the article display and at least one of the status displays use a text box. Since the text box handles issues like line wrap for long text strings, it's handy for dynamic status displays. The font description text box in the Reader application changes size based on the length of the phrase used to describe a font. Listing 4-11 shows the calculation for the size of the text box according to the .Text property when its contents change.

Listing 4-11 *When the contents of the font description text box change, this procedure changes the height of the text box dynamically.*

```
Sub Text1_Change ()
        If TextWidth(Text1.Text) > Text1.Width Then
          Text1.Height = Int(TextHeight(Text1.Text) * 2)
        Else
          Text1.Height = Int(TextHeight(Text1.Text))
        End If
End Sub
```

The long text string will be wrapped automatically, since the text box was designated as a multiline text box at design time. A single-line text box (or edit control) operates much the same way as a label except that it can take focus and therefore user input.

The article display in the Reader application uses a large multiline text box. You place the location of the article in the main file by using the index created by the import routine included with the application. Once the range of bytes in the article is identified, the bytes can be read into the text box in one chunk and the text box will handle line wrapping. The dimensions of the text box can then be changed, and the lines will wrap accordingly. The code in Listing 4-12 shows how the text in the article text box of the Reader application is adjusted when you drag the right edge of the form, as illustrated in Figure 4-15.

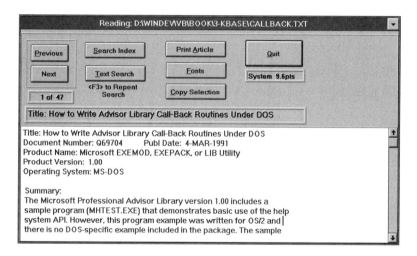

Figure 4-15 *This multiline text box can be enlarged, as shown, and the text will wrap according to the new width when you use the Resize event. The control panel sits inside a frame that does not change with the width of the form.*

Listing 4-12 *This code, placed in the Form_Resize event, allows the user to enlarge the article text box without shrinking it beyond a certain point.*

```
Article.Height = ScaleHeight - Article.Top
If TextBase.Width >= Frame1.Width Then
   Article.Width = ScaleWidth
Else
   TextBase.Width = Frame1.Width
End If
```

Reader Application

GLOBAL.BAS

```
'GLOBALS for Importing
'Constants
Global Const TextBaseSize = 1
Global Const GaugeSize = 2
Global Const Saving = 1
Global Const Getting = 2
Global Const CIS = 1
Global Const ONLINE = 2


'Strings
Global CurrIndex As String * 95
Global TargetFile As String
Global IndexFile As String
Global FilePath As String
Global NextFile As String
Global ReadFile As String
Global LastIndex As String
Global NextLine As String
Global ErrMsg As String
Global TargetText As String
Global SavedPath As String
Global StartPath As String
Global ListSort As String
'Longs
Global Bytes As Long
Global TotBytes As Long
Global ArticleBytes As Long
Global TwipCnt As Long
Global ArticleTop As Long
Global LastSearch As Long
'Integers
Global Pos As Integer
Global FileStart As Integer
Global Steps As Integer
Global FirstTag As Integer
Global TextWide As Integer
Global TBLoaded As Integer
Global SavedIndex As Integer
Global SavedIcon As Integer


' Define the Record for the Index Created in the Import Procedure
Type Record
```

```
        IndexEntry As String * 93
End Type
Global IndexRec As Record


' Define the record for the INI file
Type PathRecord
        SavePath As String * 102
End Type
Global PathRec As Record
```

(include CONSTANT.TXT here)

ABOUT.FRM

```
Sub Form_Load ()
        PText$ = "Reader" + Chr$(13)
        PText$ = PText$ + "for" + Chr$(13)
        PText$ = PText$ + "Microsoft Knowledge Base©"
        Poster.Caption = PText$
        P2Text$ = "Written by Mark S. Burgess, Knowledge Works, Inc." + Chr$(13)
        P2Text$ = P2Text$ + "An Example from Addison Wesley's book: Advanced Visual Basic" +
        ...Chr$(13)
        P2Text$ = P2Text$ + "Part of the LURKER Group Project" + Chr$(13)
        P2Text$ = P2Text$ + "CompuServe, MSBASIC Forum, Section 9"
        Poster2.Caption = P2Text$
End Sub


Sub Okay_Click ()
        Unload AboutBox
End Sub
```

HELPER.FRM

```
Sub Command1_Click ()
        Unload Helper
End Sub


Sub Form_Load ()
        Htext$ = "To use the Compuserve Import facility, dial into CompuServe and"
        Htext$ = Htext$ + " GO MSKB.  Perform your search for articles until you"
        Htext$ = Htext$ + " have the field narrowed to the topic you want.  At the "
        Htext$ = Htext$ + "titles listing when Compuserve asks if you want to "
        Htext$ = Htext$ + "view the articles, type 'S ALL' at the '!' prompt - but "
        Htext$ = Htext$ + "be certain you started a text capture first.  When the "
        Htext$ = Htext$ + "file stops downloading, close the capture file in your"
        Htext$ = Htext$ + "communications program.  This will be the file you will "
```

```
        Htext$ = Htext$ + "import into the reader.  You can import approximately"
        Htext$ = Htext$ + " 680 articles before you will be forced to create another "
        Htext$ = Htext$ + "file." + Chr$(13) + Chr$(13)
        Htext$ = Htext$ + "To use the Microsoft Online import, " + Chr$(13) + "be sure
        ...you export"
        Htext$ = Htext$ + "the articles out of Online in " + Chr$(13) + "sequentially
        ...numbered files"
        Htext$ = Htext$ + " as in '1.txt, 2.txt, 3.txt...  Since " + Chr$(13) + "Online
        ...does not allow"
        Htext$ = Htext$ + " you to save them all to one file, the Reader will automat-
        ...ically"
        Htext$ = Htext$ + "increment to the file name to read to create one large"
        Htext$ = Htext$ + " file and the associated index." + Chr$(13) + Chr$(13)
        Htext$ = Htext$ + "This facility will be part of the Lurker Project and also"
        Htext$ = Htext$ + " appears in Advanced Visual Basic by Mark S. Burgess."
        Helper.HelpText.Caption = Htext$
End Sub
```

IMPORT.FRM

```
Sub Target_Change (Index As Integer)
        TargetFile = Target(1).Text
End Sub


Sub Target_KeyPress (Index As Integer, KeyAscii As Integer)
      'If KeyAscii = KEY_RETURN Then
      '   CisButton(0).SetFocus
      'End If
End Sub


'--------------------------------------------------------
'---- Read the current file and save it to target file
'--------------------------------------------------------
Sub CisButton_Click (Index As Integer)
    OpenFiles'open files for process
    Status.Show                                  'open status display
    Status.CurrentFile(5).Caption = Readfile
    Status.Label1.Caption = "% Complete"
    TwipCalc (GaugeSize)                          'pixels to twips
    Do Until EOF(1)                               'read thru file
      Status.BytesGauge.Value = Bytes / Steps     'set total progress gauge
      Status.Gauge1.Value = ArticleBytes / 100    'set progress gauge
      If Not FirstTag Then FindStart              'strip out garbage characters
      IndexLine (CIS)                             'set index
      ReadLine 1                                  'read a line in raw file
      ArticleBytes = ArticleBytes + Len(NextLine) + 2 'count bytes for this article
```

```
        Pos = InStr(Mid$(NextLine, 1, 14), "KnowledgeBase")'check new article start
        Check% = DoEvents()                              'check system for msgs
    Loop
    NextLine = Chr$(12)                          'set form feed
    Print #2, NextLine                           'write FF to text file
    Close                                        'Close all Files
    Unload Status                                'close status screen
    Unload Import
    Exit Sub
TermCis:                                         'post note & close all
    ErrCheck
End Sub



Sub BytesGauge_Change ()
End Sub

Sub OnlineButton_Click (Index As Integer)
    '--------------------------------------------------------
    '---Prepare the files for reading and writing
    '--------------------------------------------------------
    On Error GoTo Finished
    OpenFiles                                    'open files for process
    Status.CurrentFile(5).Caption = Readfile
    Status.Label1.Caption = "Bytes Total"
    Status.Show
    TwipCalc (GaugeSize)                         'pixels to twips, etc.
    Do
      Bytes = 0
      Pos = 1
      Do Until EOF(1)
        Status.BytesGauge.Value = LOF(2) / 1000  'set progress gauge
        Status.Gauge1.Value = ArticleBytes / 100 'set progress gauge
        IndexLine (ONLINE)
        ReadLine 1
        ArticleBytes = ArticleBytes + Len(NextLine) + 2
        Pos = 0
        Check& = DoEvents()
      Loop
      '--------------------------------------------------------
      '--- Set up the next file to read in
      '--------------------------------------------------------
    Close (1)
    Pos = InStr(Status.CurrentFile(5).Caption, ".")
    Root$ = Mid$(Status.CurrentFile(5).Caption, 1, Pos - 1)
```

```
   NextOne& = Val(Root$) + 1
   If NextOne& < 10 Then
      Nextfile = FilePath + "\" + Format$(NextOne&, "00") + ".TXT"
      Status.CurrentFile(5).Caption = Format$(NextOne&, "00") + ".TXT"
   Else
      Nextfile = FilePath + "\" + LTrim$(Str$(NextOne&)) + ".TXT"
      Status.CurrentFile(5).Caption = LTrim$(Str$(NextOne&)) + ".TXT"
   End If
   ErrMsg = "Problem Opening: " + Nextfile
   Open Nextfile For Input As 1
  Loop
  NextLine = Chr$(12)
  Print #2, NextLine


'-------------------------------------------------------
'---Close all the files and stop processing
'-------------------------------------------------------
Finished:
  Close
  If Not Err Then
    Msg$ = "File Import Complete"
  Else
    Msg$ = "Error: "
  End If
  Msg$ = Msg$ + Str$(Err) + " - " + Error$
  Title$ = "Done Message"
  MsgBox Msg$, 0 + 64, Title$
  Unload Status
  Unload Import
  Exit Sub
End Sub


Sub Command1_Click ()
      Unload Import
End Sub


Sub Label1_DragDrop (Source As Control, X As Single, Y As Single)
      MsgBox "Label Message"
End Sub
```

MAIN.FRM

```
Sub Search_Click (Index As Integer)
     Searcher.Show
End Sub
```

```
Sub Form_Unload (Cancel As Integer)
    Unload Searcher
    Unload TextBase
    Unload Import
    Unload Status
    PathSettings (Saving)
    End
End Sub


Sub ImportProc_Click ()
    On Error GoTo DlgErr
    PickCommon.DialogTitle = "Choose File To Import"
    PickCommon.DefaultExt = "TXT"
    If Dir$(SavedPath) <> "" Then
  PickCommon.InitDir = SavedPath
    End If
    PickCommon.Filter = "Text File (*.TXT)|*.txt|All Files (*.*)|*.*|"
    PickCommon.FilterIndex = 1
    PickCommon.Flags = OFN_FILEMUSTEXIST Or OFN_READONLY
    PickCommon.CancelError = TRUE
    PickCommon.Action = 1
    If Err = FALSE Then
  SavedPath = PickCommon.FileName
  ReadFile = PickCommon.FileTitle
  FilePath = Mid$(PickCommon.FileName, 1, InStr(PickCommon.FileName, ReadFile)- 2)
  Load Import
  Import.Caption = "File Import: " + PickCommon.FileTitle
  TargetFile = PickCommon.FileTitle
  Import.Show
  Import.Target(1).SetFocus
    End If
    Exit Sub
DlgErr:
  If Err = 20477 Then              ' invalid file name passed to dialog
  PickCommon.FileName = ""
  Resume
    End If
    If Err Then MsgBox Error$ + ": " + Str$(Err)
    Exit Sub
End Sub


Sub CloseApp_Click ()
   Unload Main
End Sub
```

```
Sub Form_Load ()
      StartPath = CurDir$           'Get current path
      PathSettings (Getting)        'Retrieve previous ini

      If SavedPath <> "" Then          'Start file list menu
   Load FindFile(1)                 'File list separator
   FindFile(1).Separator = 1        'Separator (undocumented)
   Load FindFile(2)                 'Create file choice
   FindFile(2).Caption = SavedPath
   MenuIndex% = 3                   'Count menu items
      Else
   MenuIndex% = 0
      End If
      TempName$ = RTrim$(CurDir$) + "\" + Dir$("*.TXT") 'Set first entry
      If TempName$ <> SavedPath Then              'match first?
   Load FindFile(MenuIndex%)                      'create menu
   FindFile(MenuIndex%).Caption = TempName$
      End If
      Do                                       'look for txt files
   TempName$ = Dir$
   If TempName$ = "" Then Exit Do
   MenuIndex% = MenuIndex% + 1
   Load FindFile(MenuIndex%)
   FindFile(MenuIndex%).Caption = CurDir$ + "\" + TempName$
      Loop
      If SavedPath = "" Then        'Set default if no previous
   SavedPath = StartPath
      End If
      LastPath.Caption = SavedPath  'Set display
End Sub


Sub Help_Click ()
      Helper.Show Modal
End Sub


Sub Form_Resize ()
      On Error GoTo StartupErr
      Select Case WindowState
   Case NORMAL
         Main.Caption = "MSKB Reader"
         If TBLoaded Then
           TextBase.WindowState = NORMAL
         End If
   Case MINIMIZED
         Main.Caption = Format$(Now, "hh:mm:ss am/pm")
```

```
            If TBLoaded And TextBase.WindowState <> MINIMIZED Then
                TextBase.WindowState = MINIMIZED
                End If
                End Select
                Exit Sub
StartupErr:
    MsgBox "Sizing Error: " + Error$
    Exit Sub
End Sub


Sub Form_GotFocus ()
    LastPath.Caption = SavedPath
End Sub


Sub Delete_Click ()
        On Error GoTo DelErr
        PickCommon.DialogTitle = "Choose Files to Delete"
        PickCommon.DefaultExt = "TXT"
        If Dir$(SavedPath) <> "" Then
PickCommon.InitDir = SavedPath
        End If
        PickCommon.Filter = "Text File (*.TXT)|*.txt|All Files (*.*)|*.*|"
        PickCommon.FilterIndex = 2
        PickCommon.Flags = OFN_FILEMUSTEXIST Or OFN_PATHMUSTEXIST Or OFN_READONLY Or
        ...OFN_ALLOWMULTISELECT
        PickCommon.CancelError = TRUE
        PickCommon.Action = 1
        DgDef% = MB_YESNOCANCEL + MB_ICONQUESTION
        Length% = Len(PickCommon.FileName)
        OldPos% = 1
        If Err = FALSE Then
    Pos% = InStr(OldPos%, PickCommon.FileName, " ")
    If Pos% = 0 Then                        ' DELETE ONE FILE ONLY
      FileMsg$ = PickCommon.FileName
      GoSub DelFile
      Exit Sub
    End If
    Do                                      ' DELETE MULTIPLE FILES
    Pos% = InStr(OldPos%, PickCommon.FileName, " ") ' LOOK FOR A SPACE
    If Pos% = 0 Then                              ' NO SPACE FOUND
      Pos% = OldPos% + Len(Mid$(PickCommon.FileName, OldPos%, Length% - OldPos% + 1))
      ...' MEASURE
    End If
    Toss$ = Mid$(PickCommon.FileName, OldPos%, Pos% - OldPos%)
    If InStr(1, Toss$, "\") = 0 Then     ' DELETE THE NEXT FILE
```

```
      FileMsg$ = Path$ + "\" + Toss$
      GoSub DelFile
    Else
      Path$ = Toss$
    End If
    OldPos% = Pos% + 1
    Loop Until Toss$ = "" Or OldPos% >= Len(RTrim$(PickCommon.FileName))
        End If
        Exit Sub
DelFile:
      Response% = MsgBox(FileMsg$, DgDef%, "Deleting This File?")
      If Response% = IDYES Then
        Kill Path$ + "\" + Toss$
      ElseIf Response% = IDCANCEL Then
        MsgBox "Delete Operation Canceled"
        Exit Sub
      End If
      Return
DelErr:
      If Err = 20477 Then                   ' invalid file name passed to dialog
    PickCommon.FileName = ""
    Resume
      End If
      MsgBox Error$ + ": " + Str$(Err)
      Exit Sub
End Sub


Sub About_Click ()
        AboutBox.Show Modal
End Sub


Sub FindFile_Click (Index As Integer)
        On Error GoTo CancelCheck
        PickCommon.DialogTitle = "Choose Knowledge Base To Browse"
        PickCommon.DefaultExt = "TXT"
        If Dir$(SavedPath) <> "" Then
    PickCommon.InitDir = SavedPath
        Else
    PickCommon.InitDir = CurDir$
        End If
        PickCommon.Filter = "Text File (*.TXT)|*.txt|All Files (*.*)|*.*|"
        PickCommon.FilterIndex = 1
        PickCommon.Flags = OFN_FILEMUSTEXIST Or OFN_PATHMUSTEXIST Or OFN_READONLY
        PickCommon.CancelError = TRUE
```

```
        If Index = 0 Then
    PickCommon.Action = 1
    FileTitle$ = PickCommon.FileTitle
        Else
    PickCommon.FileName = FindFile(Index).Caption
    Path% = Len(RTrim$(CurDir$))
    FullPath% = Len(RTrim$(PickCommon.FileName))
    FileTitle$ = Mid$(PickCommon.FileName, Path% + 2, FullPath% - Path%)
    'MsgBox "File: " + FileTitle$
        End If
        If Err = FALSE Then
    SavedPath = PickCommon.FileName
    ReadFile = FileTitle$
    FilePath = Mid$(PickCommon.FileName, 1, InStr(PickCommon.FileName, ReadFile) - 2)
    TextBase.Show
    TextBase.Quit(4).SetFocus
        End If
        Main.Visible = FALSE
        Exit Sub
CancelCheck:
    If Err = 20477 Then                    ' invalid file name passed to dialog
    PickCommon.FileName = ""
  MsgBox Error$ + ": " + Str$(Err)
  Resume
    'Else
    'MsgBox Error$ + ": " + Str$(Err)
    End If
    Exit Sub
End Sub

Sub Timer1_Timer ()
    If Main.WindowState = MINIMIZED Then
        Main.Caption = Format$(Now, "hh:mm:ss am/pm")
    End If
End Sub
```

SEARCHER.FRM

```
Dim SearcherWide As Long
Dim SearcherHeight As Long
Dim IndexWidthDiff As Long
Dim IndexHeightDiff As Long
Dim Incr As Long

Sub Quit_Click ()
        Unload Searcher
End Sub
```

```
Sub Form_Load ()
    SearcherWidth = Searcher.Width
    SearcherHeight = Searcher.Height
    IndexWidthDiff = SearcherWidth - IndexList.Width
    IndexHeightDiff = SearcherHeight - IndexList.Height
    '--- Fill table with index entries
    On Error GoTo LoadDone
    SavedPtr& = Seek(2)                          'save place in index file
    Seek #2, 1                                   'go to top of index file
    ErrMsg = "Error setting pointer"             'set error message
    '---fill the hidden list box from the file
    Do Until Count& = (LOF(2) / Len(IndexRec))   'read to the end of the file
        Get #2, , IndexRec.IndexEntry            'read the next record
        If IndexRec.IndexEntry = "" Then Exit Do 'stop reading at empty record
        ErrMsg = "Error getting record"          'reset error message
        Count& = Count& + 1                      'increment the counter
        Countr$ = Format$(Count&, "000#")        'format article count
        Title$ = RTrim$(Mid$(IndexRec.IndexEntry, 14))'format title
        If ListSort = "Num" Then                 'check for sort type used
            SortList.AddItem Countr$ + " " + Title$ 'add to the list box
        Else
            SortList.AddItem LTrim$(RTrim$(Title$)) + " - " + Countr$    'add to the list
            ...box
        End If
    Loop
    Seek #2, SavedPtr&                           'reset index pointer in file
    Count& = 0                                   'ensure counter reset
    Searcher.Counter.Caption = Str$(IndexList.ListCount) 'set dialog caption
    '---Transfer the sorted contents to the display, skipping duplicates
    Do Until Count& = SortList.ListCount         'Fill the display list box
        LastOne$ = Mid$(Last$, 5, Len(Last$) / 2)
        ThisLen% = Len(SortList.List(Count&)) / 2
        ThisOne$ = Mid$(SortList.List(Count&), 5, ThisLen%)
        If LastOne$ <> ThisOne$ Then 'recycle if the same
            IndexList.AddItem SortList.List(Count&)    'fill list box
            Last$ = SortList.List(Count&)              'save for next time
        End If
        Count& = Count& + 1                      'increment the counter
    Loop
    IndexList.ListIndex = SavedIndex             'reset pointer in dialog
    F% = FreeFile                                'get the next valid file number
    FileName$ = StartPath + "\READER.INI"        'set INI file name
    Open FileName$ For Random As F% Len = 102    'open the file
        Get F%, 9, FSName$                       'get the parameter stored there
        Get F%, 10, FSSize%
```

```
      Get F%, 11, FSBold%
      Get F%, 12, FSItalic%
      Get F%, 13, FSUnder%
      Get F%, 14, FSThru%
      Get F%, 15, FSColor&
   Close F%                                    'close the file
      Searcher.IndexList.FontName = FSName$    'set the display of the list box
      Searcher.IndexList.FontSize = FSSize%
      Searcher.IndexList.FontBold = FSBold%
      Searcher.IndexList.FontItalic = FSItalic%
      Searcher.IndexList.FontUnderline = FSUnder%
      Searcher.IndexList.FontStrikeThru = FSThru%
      Searcher.IndexList.ForeColor = FSColor&
      Exit Sub
LoadDone:
      MsgBox ErrMsg + "Error = " + Error$
      Exit Sub
End Sub


Sub IndexList_DblClick ()
   '--------------------------------------------------------
   '--- Search text file for selected index entry - read it
   '--------------------------------------------------------
   On Error GoTo Problem
   ErrMsg = "Problem Reading from Index File"
   'If IndexList.ListIndex = 0 And ListSort = "Num" Then
   '  Get #2, 1, IndexRec.IndexEntry     'Get First Index Record
   '  Seek #2, 1                         'Reset pointer to first record
   If ListSort = "Num" Then        'when sorted alphabetically
      Get #2, IndexList.ListIndex + 1, IndexRec.IndexEntry
   Else
      Pos% = Len(IndexList.Text)
      FilePtr% = Val(Mid$(IndexList.Text, Pos% - 4, 5)) - 1
      Get #2, FilePtr%, IndexRec.IndexEntry '
   End If
   SavedIndex = IndexList.ListIndex                'save place in list box
   ArticleTop = Val(Mid$(IndexRec.IndexEntry, 1, 7)) 'get file byte location
   ErrMsg = "Problem Reading from Text File"
   Seek #1, ArticleTop                             'set place in Kbase file
   If ListSort <> "Num" Then FindFF
   ReadArticle                                     'read in the article
   GoBack
   Exit Sub
```

```
Problem:
    If Error$ <> "" Then
      MsgBox ErrMsg + Chr$(13) + "Error: " + Error$
    Else
      MsgBox ErrMsg
    End If
    Exit Sub
End Sub


Sub ReadIt_Click ()
        Call IndexList_DblClick
End Sub

Sub IndexList_Click ()
        Searcher.Caption = "Entry Selected = " + Str$(IndexList.ListIndex + 1) + " of " +
        ...Str$(IndexList.ListCount) + " Total"
End Sub

Sub Command1_Click ()
      Unload Searcher
End Sub

Sub QuitButton_Click ()
        GoBack
End Sub

Sub FontButton_Click ()
      On Error GoTo DlgErr
      FontDialog.DialogTitle = "Choose Display Font"
      FontDialog.Filter = "Text File (*.TXT)|*.txt|All Files (*.*)|*.*|"
      FontDialog.CancelError = TRUE
      FontDialog.Flags = CF_SCREENFONTS Or CF_EFFECTS Or CF_FORCEFONTEXIST
        FontDialog.FontName = Searcher.IndexList.FontName
        FontDialog.FontSize = Searcher.IndexList.FontSize
        FontDialog.FontBold = Searcher.IndexList.FontBold
        FontDialog.FontItalic = Searcher.IndexList.FontItalic
        FontDialog.FontUnderline = Searcher.IndexList.FontUnderline
        FontDialog.FontStrikeThru = Searcher.IndexList.FontStrikeThru
        FontDialog.Color = Searcher.IndexList.ForeColor
      FontDialog.Action = 4
      If Err = FALSE Then
        Searcher.IndexList.FontName = FontDialog.FontName
        Searcher.IndexList.FontSize = FontDialog.FontSize
        Searcher.IndexList.FontBold = FontDialog.FontBold
        Searcher.IndexList.FontItalic = FontDialog.FontItalic
```

```
            Searcher.IndexList.FontUnderline = FontDialog.FontUnderline
            Searcher.IndexList.FontStrikeThru = FontDialog.FontStrikeThru
            Searcher.IndexList.ForeColor = FontDialog.Color
        End If
        Exit Sub
DlgErr:
    If Err Then MsgBox Error$ + ": " + Str$(Err)
    Exit Sub

End Sub


Sub Form_Unload (Cancel As Integer)
        FSName$ = Searcher.IndexList.FontName
        FSSize% = Searcher.IndexList.FontSize
        FSBold% = Searcher.IndexList.FontBold
        FSItalic% = Searcher.IndexList.FontItalic
        FSUnder% = Searcher.IndexList.FontUnderline
        FSThru% = Searcher.IndexList.FontStrikeThru
        FSColor& = Searcher.IndexList.ForeColor
    FileName$ = StartPath + "\READER.INI"
    F% = FreeFile
    Open FileName$ For Random As F% Len = 102
        Put F%, 9, FSName$
        Put F%, 10, FSSize%
        Put F%, 11, FSBold%
        Put F%, 12, FSItalic%
        Put F%, 13, FSUnder%
        Put F%, 14, FSThru%
        Put F%, 15, FSColor&
    Close F%
End Sub


Sub Form_Resize ()
        '---Set the size of the index display
        IndexList.Width = Searcher.ScaleWidth              'use form scale
        IndexList.Height = Searcher.Height - IndexHeightDiff  'base on design spacing
        '---Set the vertical position of the command buttons in non-index area
        FontButton.Top = (IndexList.Top + IndexList.Height) + (FontButton.Height / 2)
        QuitButton.Top = (IndexList.Top + IndexList.Height) + (QuitButton.Height / 2)
        '---Set the horizontal position of the command buttons
        FontButton.Left = Searcher.ScaleWidth * .2
        FontRight& = FontButton.Left + FontButton.Width
        RightSpace& = Searcher.ScaleWidth - FontRight&
        QuitButton.Left = FontRight& + (RightSpace& / 2)
End Sub
```

```
Sub FontButton_DragOver (Source As Control, X As Single, Y As Single, State As Integer)
      MsgBox "Quit control over the top"
End Sub
```

STATUS.FRM

```
Sub AbortButton_Click (Index As Integer)
  Close
  Msg$ = "Aborted File Transfer..."
  Title$ = "Incomplete"
  DegDef& = MB_ICONEXCLAMATION
  Status.Hide
  Import.SetFocus
End Sub
```

TEXTBASE.FRM

```
Sub Command1_Click (Index As Integer)
    Unload TextBase
End Sub


'-------------------------------------------------------
'--- Reads first article from Master File
'-------------------------------------------------------
Sub Form_Load ()
    TBLoaded = TRUE
    TextWide = TextBase.Width
    LastSearch = 0                      'last search
    Bytes = 0                           'zero out import total
     On Error GoTo Problem
     '-----------------------------------------------------
     '--- Name files and set path to files
     '-----------------------------------------------------
    TextBase.Caption = "Reading: " + FilePath + "\" + ReadFile
    FileToRead$ = FilePath + "\" + ReadFile
    Indexfile = FilePath + "\" + Mid$(ReadFile, 1, InStr(ReadFile, ".")) + "idx"
     '-----------------------------------------------------
     '--- Open Files and test for errors
     '-----------------------------------------------------
       ErrMsg = "Problem Opening Source File"
    Open FileToRead$ For Input As 1
       ErrMsg = "Problem Opening Index file"
    Open Indexfile For Random As 2 Len = 93
     '-----------------------------------------------------
     '--- Read first index and article into list box
     '-----------------------------------------------------
```

```
    ErrMsg = "Problem getting index entry"
    Get #2, 1, IndexRec.IndexEntry
    Reader (1)

    '-----------------------------------------------------------
    '--- Reset pointer for next read
    '-----------------------------------------------------------
    ErrMsg = "Problem resetting pointer after read"
    Seek #1, 1
    ErrMsg = "Problem filling the text box - Bytes: " + Str$(Bytes)
    TextBase.Article.Text = Input$((Bytes - 2), #1)
    NextArticle(0).Caption = "Next"
    F% = FreeFile
    FileName$ = StartPath + "\READER.INI"
    Open FileName$ For Random As F% Len = 102
      Get F%, 2, FName$
      Get F%, 3, FSize%
      Get F%, 4, FBold%
      Get F%, 5, FItalic%
      Get F%, 6, FUnder%
      Get F%, 7, FThru%
      Get F%, 8, FColor&
    Close F%
      TextBase.Article.FontName = FName$
      TextBase.Article.FontSize = FSize%
      TextBase.Article.FontBold = FBold%
      TextBase.Article.FontItalic = FItalic%
      TextBase.Article.FontUnderline = FUnder%
      TextBase.Article.FontStrikeThru = FThru%
      TextBase.Article.ForeColor = FColor&
      TextBase.Text1.Text = TextBase.Article.FontName + " " + Str$(TextBase.Article.Font
      ...Size) + "pts"
    Exit Sub
Problem:
    Msg$ = "TextBase Error: " + Error$ + Chr$(13)
    Msg$ = Msg$ + ErrMsg + Chr$(13)
    MsgBox Msg$
    Exit Sub
End Sub

Sub Quit_Click (Index As Integer)
    Unload TextBase
    Unload Searcher
    Main.Visible = TRUE
    Main.WindowState = NORMAL
End Sub
```

```
'------------------------------------------------------------
'--- Reads until form feed for placing next article into window
'------------------------------------------------------------
Sub NextArticle_Click (Index As Integer)
    ResetSearch
    FindFF
    ReadArticle
End Sub


'--------------------------------------------------------
'--- Clear last article & reopen file, reposition to read, read
'--- BYTES passed by memory from last article read: READER()
'--------------------------------------------------------
Sub PreviousArticle_Click (Index As Integer)
    On Error GoTo PrevDone
    ResetSearch
    If (Seek(2) - 1) = 1 Then                    'test for end of file
      ErrMsg = "At top of articles"
      GoTo PrevDone
    End If
    ErrMsg = "Reading Index for current Article"
    Get #2, Seek(2) - 2, IndexRec.IndexEntry      'get displayed index entry
    CurTop = Val(Mid$(IndexRec.IndexEntry, 1, 7))
    ErrMsg = "Reading Start Spot"
    Seek #1, CurTop
    Bytes = 0
    ErrMsg = "Reading Previous Article"
    Reader (2)


    '--------------------------------------------------------
    '--- Resposition and read the article, close the file
    '--------------------------------------------------------
    Seek #1, CurTop
    TextBase.Article.Text = Input$(Bytes - 2, #1)
    PreviousArticle(1).Caption = "&Previous"
    TextBase.Show
    Exit Sub

PrevDone:
    ErrMsg = ErrMsg + Chr$(13) + "Error: " + Error$
    MsgBox ErrMsg
    Exit Sub
End Sub
```

```
Sub Form_Unload (CANCEL As Integer)
     FName$ = TextBase.Article.FontName
     FSize% = TextBase.Article.FontSize
     FBold% = TextBase.Article.FontBold
     FItalic% = TextBase.Article.FontItalic
     FUnder% = TextBase.Article.FontUnderline
     FThru% = TextBase.Article.FontStrikeThru
     FColor& = TextBase.Article.ForeColor
   FileName$ = StartPath + "\READER.INI"
   F% = FreeFile
   Open FileName$ For Random As F% Len = 102
       Put F%, 2, FName$
       Put F%, 3, FSize%
       Put F%, 4, FBold%
       Put F%, 5, FItalic%
       Put F%, 6, FUnder%
       Put F%, 7, FThru%
       Put F%, 8, FColor&
   Close F%
   TBLoaded = FALSE
   Bytes = 0
   Close
   Unload TextFind
   Main.Visible = TRUE
End Sub


Sub CopySelection_Click (Index As Integer)
     ResetSearch
     Clipboard.Clear
     Clipboard.SetText Article.SelText, CF_TEXT
     TextBase.WindowState = MINIMIZED
End Sub

Sub Search_Click (Index As Integer)
   If Search(3).Visible = TRUE Then
     '---Create the Date sort order button
     Load Search(20)
     Search(20).Width = Search(3).Width * .6
     Search(20).Left = Search(3).Left - (Search(3).Width * .1)
     Search(20).Caption = "Date"
     '---Create the alphanumeric sort order button
     Load Search(21)
     Search(21).Width = Search(3).Width * .6
     Search(21).Left = Search(3).Left + (Search(3).Width * .6)
     Search(21).Caption = "Title"
```

```
            '---Hide the Search Index button and display the new ones
            Search(3).Visible = FALSE
            Search(20).Visible = TRUE
            Search(21).Visible = TRUE
            Search(20).SetFocus
        Else
            Select Case Index        'Act on the sort order chosen
                Case 20              'Date sort order button clicked
                    ListSort = "Num"  'Set global variable
                    Load Searcher     'Load form with index list box
                    Searcher.Show     'Display the List box
                Case 21              'Alphanumeric sort order chosen
                    ListSort = "Alpha"
                    Load Searcher
                    Searcher.Show
                    Searcher.IndexList.SetFocus
            End Select
        End If
End Sub


Sub Form_Resize ()
    Select Case WindowState
        Case NORMAL
            TextBase.Caption = "Reading: " + FilePath + "\" + ReadFile
            If Main.WindowState = MINIMIZED Then
              Main.WindowState = NORMAL
              Main.Visible = TRUE
            End If
            Article.Height = ScaleHeight - Article.Top
            If TextBase.Width >= Frame1.Width Then
              Article.Width = ScaleWidth
            Else
              TextBase.Width = Frame1.Width
            End If
        Case MINIMIZED
            TextBase.Caption = RTrim$(Mid$(IndexRec.IndexEntry, 14))
            If Main.WindowState <> MINIMIZED Then
              Main.WindowState = MINIMIZED
              If TextFind.Visible = TRUE Then
                TextFind.Visible = FALSE
              End If
            End If
            Main.Visible = FALSE
    End Select
End Sub
```

```
Sub TextSearch_Click (Index As Integer)
    TextFind.Show
End Sub


Sub Form_KeyDown (KeyCode As Integer, Shift As Integer)
     RepeatSearch (KeyCode)
End Sub


Sub Article_KeyDown (KeyCode As Integer, Shift As Integer)
     RepeatSearch (KeyCode)
End Sub


Sub FontButton_Click ()
     On Error GoTo DlgErr
     ResetSearch
     FontDialog.DialogTitle = "Choose Display Font"
     FontDialog.Filter = "Text File (*.TXT)|*.txt|All Files (*.*)|*.*|"
     FontDialog.CancelError = TRUE
     FontDialog.Flags = CF_SCREENFONTS Or CF_EFFECTS Or CF_FORCEFONTEXIST
       FontDialog.FontName = TextBase.Article.FontName
       FontDialog.FontSize = TextBase.Article.FontSize
       FontDialog.FontBold = TextBase.Article.FontBold
       FontDialog.FontItalic = TextBase.Article.FontItalic
       FontDialog.FontUnderline = TextBase.Article.FontUnderline
       FontDialog.FontStrikeThru = TextBase.Article.FontStrikeThru
       FontDialog.Color = TextBase.Article.ForeColor
     FontDialog.Action = 4
     If Err = FALSE Then
       TextBase.Article.FontName = FontDialog.FontName
       TextBase.Article.FontSize = FontDialog.FontSize
       TextBase.Article.FontBold = FontDialog.FontBold
       TextBase.Article.FontItalic = FontDialog.FontItalic
       TextBase.Article.FontUnderline = FontDialog.FontUnderline
       TextBase.Article.FontStrikeThru = FontDialog.FontStrikeThru
       TextBase.Article.ForeColor = FontDialog.Color
       TextBase.Text1.Text = FontDialog.FontName + " " + Str$(FontDialog.FontSize) +
       ..."pts"
     End If
     Exit Sub
DlgErr:
    If Err = 20477 Then
      MsgBox Error$ + ": " + Str$(Err)
    End If
    Exit Sub
End Sub
```

```
Sub PrintArticle_Click ()
      On Error GoTo PrintErr
      ResetSearch
      TextBase.PrintArticle.Caption = "PRINTING..."
      Printer.FontName = "Modern"
      Printer.FontSize = 12
      Printer.FontBold = TRUE
      Title$ = "Knowledge Base Article - " + Date$
      HWidth = Printer.TextWidth(Title$) / 2
      Printer.CurrentX = Printer.ScaleWidth / 2 - HWidth
      Printer.Print Title$
      Printer.Print
      Printer.Print


      Printer.FontName = TextBase.Article.FontName
      Printer.FontSize = TextBase.Article.FontSize
      Printer.FontBold = TextBase.Article.FontBold
      Length& = Len(Article.Text)
      ReDim ArticleLine(1000) As String
      Posit& = 1
      Do
        NewPos& = InStr(Posit&, Article.Text, Chr$(13)) + 2
        If NewPos& < 3 Then Exit Do
        Count& = Count& + 1
        ArticleLine(Count&) = Mid$(Article.Text, Posit&, (NewPos& - 2) - Posit&)
        Posit& = NewPos&
      Loop
      For I& = 1 To Count&
        Printer.Print Tab(10); ArticleLine(I&)
      Next
      Printer.EndDoc
      TextBase.PrintArticle.Caption = "Print Article"
      Exit Sub
PrintErr:
    MsgBox "Error: " + Error$
    Exit Sub
End Sub

Sub Article_Change ()
    LastText.Caption = Mid$(Article.Text, 1, InStr(1, Article.Text, Chr$(13)))
End Sub

Sub Text1_Change ()
      If TextWidth(Text1.Text) > Text1.Width Then
         Text1.Height = Int(TextHeight(Text1.Text) * 2)
```

```
      Else
        Text1.Height = Int(TextHeight(Text1.Text))
      End If
End Sub
```

TEXTFIND.FRM

```
Sub TextButton_Click (Index As Integer)
      TargetSearch
End Sub


Sub QuitButton_Click (Index As Integer)
      LastSearch = 0
      Unload TextFind
End Sub


Sub Form_Load ()
      SearchMsg.Visible = FALSE
      If TextBase.Article.SelText <> "" Then
        TextFind.FindText.Text = TextBase.Article.SelText
      End If
End Sub


Sub Form_Unload (Cancel As Integer)
      LastSearch = 0
End Sub


Sub FindText_KeyPress (KeyAscii As Integer)
      If KeyAscii = KEY_RETURN Then
        TextButton(0).SetFocus
      End If
End Sub


Sub Form_LostFocus ()
      TextFind.Visible = FALSE
End Sub


Sub Form_GotFocus ()
      TextFind.Visible = TRUE
End Sub
```

PROCESS.FRM

```
Sub ErrCheck ()
  Close
  If ErrMsg = "" Then
```

```
      ErrMsg = "File Import Complete"
    Else
      ErrMsg = ErrMsg + ": " + Error$(Err)
    End If
    Title$ = "Done Message"
    MsgBox ErrMsg, 0 + 64, Title$
    End
End Sub


Sub FindStart ()
'--------------------------------------------------------
'---Read til find first article
'--------------------------------------------------------
    Pos = 0
    Do Until Pos                                'read thru file
      ErrMsg = "Problem Reading from Source File"
      ReadLine 1                                'read a line in raw file
      ArticleBytes = ArticleBytes + Bytes      'count bytes for this article
      Pos = InStr(UCase$(NextLine), "KNOWLEDGE BASE") 'check new article start
    Loop
    'ReadLine 1
End Sub


Sub ReadLine (Rep As Integer)
'--------------------------------------------------------
'---Read a line and save the byte count for CompuServe Import
'--------------------------------------------------------
      Do While Rep <> 0
        Rep = Rep - 1
        Line Input #1, NextLine                 'get the first line
        Bytes = Bytes + Len(NextLine) + 2       'count bytes read
        Status.BytesProcessed(6).Caption = Str$(LOF(2))
      Loop
End Sub


Sub TwipCalc (Place As Integer)
    Select Case Place
      Case GaugeSize
        Pixel& = Status.ScaleWidth              'measure gauge
        ScaleMode = 1                           'reset to Twips
        TwipCnt = Status.ScaleWidth / Pixel&    'calc twips
        Status.BytesGauge.InnerRight = TwipCnt  'set gauge lengths
        Status.Gauge1.InnerRight = TwipCnt
        Bytes = 0
        TotBytes = 0
```

```
            ArticleBytes = 0
            Steps = LOF(1) / 100
        Case TextBaseSize
            Holder& = 1
        End Select
End Sub


Sub OpenFiles ()
  '------------------------------------------------------
  '---Prepare the files for reading and writing
  '------------------------------------------------------
  On Error GoTo TermFiles
  TargetFile = FilePath + "\" + Import.Target(1).Text
  IndexFile = FilePath + "\" + Mid$(Import.Target(1).Text, 1, InStr
  ...(Import.Target(1).Text, ".")) + "idx"
  NextFile = SavedPath    'read CIS file

    ErrMsg = "Problem Opening Source File: " + SavedPath
  Open NextFile For Input As 1

    ErrMsg = "Problem Opening Target File: " + TargetFile
  Open TargetFile For Append As 2

    ErrMsg = "Problem Opening Index File: " + TargetFile
  Open IndexFile For Random As 3 Len = Len(IndexRec.IndexEntry)
  LastRec& = LOF(3) / 93
  If LastRec& <> 0 Then Seek #3, LastRec&
  Exit Sub


TermFiles:
    ErrCheck
End Sub


'------------------------------------------------------
'--- Reads an article after positioned to do so
'--- Looks for a CR, records bytes read and returns
'------------------------------------------------------
Sub Reader (ProcName As Integer)
    Do Until EOF(1)
      Line Input #1, NextLine$                ' read each line
      If Set& <> 1 Then                       ' set caption on first line
        TextBase.Label3.Caption = Str$(Seek(2) - 1) + " of " + Str$(LOF(2) /
Len(IndexRec))
        Set& = 1                              ' mark caption as set
      End If
```

```
      Pos = InStr(NextLine$, Chr$(12))          ' look for form feed
      If Len(NextLine$) = 0 Then                 ' check for no chars
        Bytes = Bytes + 2                        ' account for FF
      ElseIf Pos = 0 Then                        ' when no FF found
        Bytes = Bytes + Len(NextLine$) + 2       ' add length to total
      End If
      If Pos <> 0 Then                           ' when form feed found
        Set& = 0                                 ' reset caption flag
        Exit Do                                  ' if FF found, leave
      End If
      ButtonCount (ProcName)                     ' display counts
      Check& = DoEvents()                        ' poll system
    Loop
End Sub


Sub Gauges (Place As Integer)

End Sub

Sub IndexLine (Mode As Integer)
      If Pos Then                                'if new start
        GoSub FirstTest                          'process first article
        If Mode = CIS Then
            ReadLine 2                           'skip a line to index
        Else
            ReadLine 1
        End If
        IndexRec.IndexEntry = Format$(Seek(2), "0000000") + LTrim$(NextLine)
        Put #3, , IndexRec.IndexEntry            'write to index file
        Print #2, LTrim$(NextLine)               'write title to text file
        ArticleBytes = 0                         'reset article count
      ElseIf FirstTag Then
        ErrMsg = "Problem Writing to File-Main"
        Print #2, NextLine                       'write line to text file
      End If
      Exit Sub

FirstTest:
    If Not FirstTag Then                         'skip form feed at top
      FirstTag = TRUE                            'found the first article
    Else
      NextLine = Chr$(12)                        'set form feed
      Print #2, NextLine                         'write FF to text file
    End If
    Return
End Sub
```

```
Sub ButtonCount (ProcName As Integer)
    '--------------------------------------------------------
    '--- Show counts in Textbase buttons
    '--------------------------------------------------------
    If ProcName = 1 Then                                      ' for Load and Next
      If Bytes > Val(TextBase.NextArticle(0).Caption) + 10 Then    ' when over
      ...10 bytes
        TextBase.NextArticle(0).Caption = Str$(Bytes)              ' display byte
        ...count
      End If
    ElseIf ProcName = 2 Then                                  ' otherwise
    ...for prev
      If Bytes > Val(TextBase.PreviousArticle(1).Caption) + 10 Then ' when over
      ...10 bytes
        TextBase.PreviousArticle(1).Caption = Str$(Bytes)         ' display byte
        ...count
      End If
    End If
End Sub
'

Sub ReadArticle ()
    On Error GoTo NextDone
    '--------------------------------------------------------
    '--- Prevent search beyond the end of the file
    '--------------------------------------------------------
    If Seek(2) > LOF(2) / Len(IndexRec) Then
      ErrMsg = "At The Last Article"
      GoTo NextDone
    End If

    '--------------------------------------------------------
    '--- Set Top, then read the article until carriage return
    '--------------------------------------------------------
      ErrMsg = "Problem finding article pointer"
    ArticleTop = Seek(1)
      ErrMsg = "Problem finding Index pointer"
    CurrRec& = Seek(2)
      ErrMsg = "Problem reading index record"
    Get #2, CurrRec&, IndexRec.IndexEntry
    Bytes = 0

    Reader (1)

    '--------------------------------------------------------
    '--- Resposition and read the article, close the file
    '--------------------------------------------------------
    Seek #1, ArticleTop
```

```
        ErrMsg = "Reached the Last Article"
    TextBase.Article.Text = Input$(Bytes - 2, #1)
    TextBase.NextArticle(0).Caption = "&Next"
    TextBase.Show
    Exit Sub
NextDone:
    If Error$ = "" Then
        ErrorString$ = "End of File"
    Else
        ErrorString$ = Error$
    End If
    ErrMsg = ErrMsg + Chr$(13) + "Error: " + ErrorString$
    MsgBox ErrMsg
    Exit Sub
End Sub


Sub ReadPrevious ()
    On Error GoTo PrevDone
    If (Seek(2) - 1) = 1 Then                    'test for end of file
        ErrMsg = "At The First of Article"
        GoTo PrevDone
    End If
    ErrMsg = "Reading Index for current Article"
    Get #2, Seek(2) - 2, IndexRec.IndexEntry      'get displayed index entry
    CurTop = Val(Mid$(IndexRec.IndexEntry, 1, 7))
    ErrMsg = "Reading Start Spot"
    Seek #1, CurTop
    Bytes = 0
    ErrMsg = "Reading Previous Article"
    Reader (2)


    '-------------------------------------------------------
    '--- Resposition and read the article, close the file
    '-------------------------------------------------------
    Seek #1, CurTop
    TextBase.Article.Text = Input$(Bytes - 2, #1)
    TextBase.PreviousArticle(1).Caption = "&Previous"
    TextBase.Show
    Exit Sub
PrevDone:
    If Error$ = "" Then
        ErrorString$ = "Top of File"
    Else
        ErrorString$ = Error$
    End If
```

```
        ErrMsg = ErrMsg + Chr$(13) + "Error: " + ErrorString$
        MsgBox ErrMsg
        Exit Sub
End Sub

Sub RepeatSearch (KeyCode As Integer)
        If KeyCode = KEY_F3 Then
          TextFind.Visible = TRUE
          TextFind.TextButton(0).SetFocus
          TargetSearch
        End If
End Sub

Sub PathSettings (Mode As Integer)
    FileName$ = StartPath + "\READER.INI"
    Open FileName$ For Random As 1 Len = 102
    Select Case Mode
        Case Saving
            Put #1, 1, SavedPath
        Case Getting
            Get #1, 1, SavedPath
    End Select
    Close #1
End Sub


Sub GoBack ()
   Unload Searcher
   ResetSearch
   TextBase.Show
End Sub

Sub ResetSearch ()
        If TextBase.Search(3).Visible = FALSE Then
          Unload TextBase.Search(20)
          Unload TextBase.Search(21)
          TextBase.Search(3).Visible = TRUE
        End If
End Sub

Sub FindFF ()
    '-------------------------------------------------------
    '--- Position after Carriage Return from Current Article
    '-------------------------------------------------------
      ErrMsg = "Problem locating next form feed"
```

```
      If Seek(2) > 1 Then                'skip this for 1st article
       Do Until EOF(1)
          Char$ = Input$(1, #1)
          If Char$ = Chr$(12) Then
            Seek #1, Seek(1) + 2
            Exit Do
          End If
        Loop
      End If
End Sub


Sub TargetSearch ()
      On Error GoTo SearchError
      TextFind.SearchMsg.Visible = TRUE
      TextFind.TextButton(0).Caption = "Searching"
      TextFind.QuitButton(1).Caption = "&Abort"
      Do Until EOF(2)
        If UCase$(RTrim$(TargetText)) <> UCase$(RTrim$(TextFind.FindText.Text)) Then
          LastSearch = Seek(2)
          TargetText = TextFind.FindText.Text          'SET TARGET VARIABLE
          ErrMsg = "Reading First Index Entry"
        Else
          LastSearch = Seek(2)
          'LastSearch = LastSearch + 1
        End If

        Get #2, LastSearch, IndexRec.IndexEntry         'GET CURRENT INDEX
        ArticleTop = Val(Mid$(IndexRec.IndexEntry, 1, 7))   'READ BYTE LOCATION
        Seek #1, ArticleTop                             'set text spot
        Do Until EOF(1)
          ErrMsg = "Reading to Search"
          ReadLine 1                                    'READ A LINE OF TEXT
          Percent% = (Seek(1) / LOF(1)) * 100
          If Percent% >= OldPercent% + 1 Then
            Progress$ = Format$(Percent%, "###") + "% of File"
            TextFind.SearchMsg.Caption = Progress$
            OldPercent% = Percent%
          End If

          If InStr(NextLine, Chr$(12)) Then             'CHECK FOR FORM FEED
            Exit Do
          End If

          If InStr(UCase$(NextLine), UCase$(LTrim$(TargetText))) Then 'FIND VALUE
            Seek #1, ArticleTop
```

```
        Bytes = 0
        Reader (0)                                      'read article
        Seek #1, ArticleTop
        TextBase.Article.Text = Input$(Bytes - 2, #1)    'fill text box
        TextFind.TextButton(0).Caption = "&Start"
        TextBase.Article.SetFocus

        If Len(TextBase.Article.Text) >= 65535 Then
          MsgBox "Article Too Long to Search"
        Else
          TextBase.Article.SelStart = InStr(UCase$(TextBase.Article.Text),
          ...UCase$(TargetText)) - 1
          TextBase.Article.SelLength = Len(RTrim$(TargetText))
        End If
        TextFind.QuitButton(1).Caption = "&Quit"
        TextFind.SearchMsg.Visible = FALSE
        Exit Sub
      End If
      Result% = DoEvents()
    Loop
  Loop
SearchError:
    If EOF(1) Or EOF(2) Then
      MsgBox "Text Not Found"
      Exit Sub
    End If
    ErrCheck
End Sub
```

Button Drag Demo

BUTTONS.FRM

```
Dim ButtonIndex As Integer

Sub Command1_Click (Index As Integer)
  If Index <> 0 Then                              'filter out master
    MessageBox (Index)                            'call unique behavior
    Exit Sub                                      'terminate event
  End If
  ButtonIndex = ButtonIndex + 1                   'increase counter
  Load Command1(ButtonIndex)                      'load new button resource
  TempName$ = "Button " + Str$(ButtonIndex)       'set new caption text
  Command1(ButtonIndex).Caption = TempName$       'set new caption
  Command1(ButtonIndex).DragMode = 1              'turn off drag mode
  Command1(ButtonIndex).Visible = 1               'make button visible
```

```
   Command1(ButtonIndex).DragIcon = LoadPicture(CurDir$ + "\" + "drag.ico")
   Command1(0).Visible = 0                        'disapper master button
End Sub

Sub Form_DragDrop (Source As Control, X As Single, Y As Single)
     Source.Top = Y - (.5 * Source.Height)
     Source.Left = X - (.5 * Source.Width)
     Command1(0).Visible = 1
     Source.DragMode = 0
End Sub

Sub Form_Resize ()
    Label1.Top = Form1.ScaleHeight - (Label1.Height)
    Label1.Left = (Form1.ScaleWidth / 2) - (Label1.Width / 2)
    Command1(0).Top = (Form1.ScaleHeight / 2) - (Command1(0).Height / 2)
    Command1(0).Left = (Form1.ScaleWidth / 2) - (Command1(0).Width / 2)
End Sub

Sub MessageBox (Index As Integer)
    MsgBox "No." + Str$(Index) + " Button clicked."
End Sub
```

Dynamic Form Demo

GLOBAL.BAS

```
Global Const TRUE = 1
Global Const FALSE = 0
Global RunMode As Integer
Global Events As Integer
```

DYNFORM.FRM

```
Sub Command2_Click ()
     StopForm.Show
     StopForm.Command1.SetFocus
     Form1.Command2.SetFocus
     Do Until RunMode = TRUE
       Counter = Counter + 1
       Text1.Text = "Text: " + Str$(Counter)
       Label1.Caption = "Label: " + Str$(Counter)
       Command1.Caption = "Button: " + Str$(Counter)
       Check1.Caption = "Check: " + Str$(Counter)
       Option1.Caption = "Radial: " + Str$(Counter)
       If Events = TRUE Then
        Check% = DoEvents()
```

```
          End If
        Loop
End Sub

Sub Command3_Click ()
      RunMode = TRUE
End Sub

Sub Command4_Click ()
      If Events = TRUE Then
        Events = FALSE
        Command4.Caption = "DoEvents() Off"
      Else
        Events = TRUE
        Command4.Caption = "DoEvents() On"
      End If
End Sub

Sub Form_Paint ()
        StopForm.Label1.Caption = "Form_Paint Message Received"
        RunMode = FALSE
        If StopForm.Visible Then StopForm.Command1.SetFocus
End Sub

Sub Form_Load ()
    Command4.Caption = "Change" + Chr$(13) + "DoEvents()"
    Events = 1
End Sub
```

STOPFORM.FRM

```
Sub Command1_Click ()
      label1.Caption = ""
      Form1.Command2.SetFocus
End Sub
```

Bug and Feature Demonstration

BUGS.FRM

```
Sub Command1_Click ()
      Drive1.Width = Drive1.Width + 100
End Sub

Sub Command2_Click ()
        List1.ListIndex = 10
End Sub
```

```
Sub Command3_Click ()
     Load MDIChild1
End Sub

Sub Drive2_Change ()
        On Error GoTo Trap
        Dir1.Path = Drive2.Drive
        Exit Sub
Trap:
        Debug.Print Err
        Resume Next
End Sub

Sub Form_Load ()
     For n = 0 To 20
        List1.AddItem "List Index Position " + n
     Next n
End Sub

Sub List1_Click ()
        MsgBox "Click Event Generated in List Box"
End Sub
```

Chapter 5

Working with the SDK

As an event-based environment, Windows communicates through messages. Therefore, you should think of the Application Programming Interface (API) as a system of structured signals. Some of the signals allow you to inform other parts of Windows about what you intend to do or what you have done. Other signals allow you to retrieve information, while the third group of signals lets you talk to yourself (that is, within your own application). You can extend the power of Visual Basic by taking advantage of the API to link your application more closely with Windows.

Because it is almost an operating system, Windows maintains a large amount of information regarding current operations. Not only can you retrieve information about system facilities like fonts and installed devices, but you can get very specific information regarding other applications. You can use functions stored in the Visual Basic EXE and the run-time Dynamic Link Library (VBRUNXXX.DLL) themselves, too. In this chapter, I'll discuss the Windows API and its usefulness in Visual Basic applications. The discussion of printing through the use of API calls appears in Chapter 7. The current chapter will prepare you for Chapter 6, where the discussion turns to actually writing dynamic link libraries.

The Scope of the Windows API

Many of the Windows API functions used by C programmers during the early versions of Windows were implemented as native Visual Basic properties. For instance, each object in Windows has a "handle." That handle represents the unique identity of that object. To draw on a form or paint a picture or change a font, you must know the names of the handles for the objects involved. Handles replace devices like pointers and addresses (the bane of the C language), which refer to the absolute locations of objects in memory. That is because you are no longer responsible for managing memory. Windows does that for you. It provides the handle that you use to refer to the object, but it doesn't require that you know where exactly in memory the object is stored.

> **Tip:** In the earlier versions of Windows, you were forced to lock sections of memory long enough to perform an action where you could be sure of an absolute address. The convention in Windows since then has been to move away from any kind of absolute references. However, if you choose, you can use the Visual Basic API to lock memory with calls like VBLockHsz(hsz), which allows you to lock the location of a string.

As Figure 5-1 shows dramatically, the task of learning all of the Windows API calls would be daunting. (Yet, early Windows programmers using just C and the Windows Software Development Kit were forced to wade through over 450 calls to write a Windows program. That list has grown now to over 800!) To simplify matters for you, I'll discuss the most useful Windows and Visual Basic API calls, the appropriate times to use them, and the calls you should avoid.

A Primer on API Calls

The API supplies a series of function definitions for embedded system capability within the Windows environment. You can't or shouldn't use all of the calls. Often the reason for not using a call is that Visual Basic does not support pointers, not to mention long pointers. The C language, from which Windows was constructed, uses many functions that expect to be passed or to return a long pointer to a value or a string. Some API calls, like GlobalAlloc, interfere with the stated aim of Windows to perform *all* of the memory management. Figure 5-2 dissects the anatomy of a typical API function.

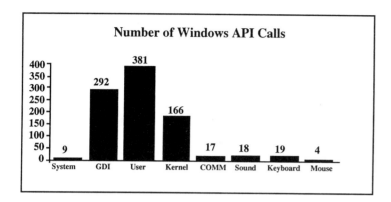

Figure 5-1   *This chart shows the number of API calls in Windows itself*

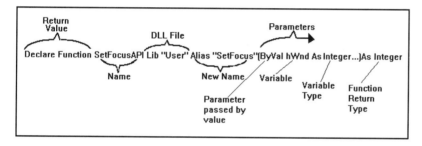

Figure 5-2   *The declaration forms for each of the API calls appear in the WINAPI.TXT supplied in the Professional Edition by Microsoft.*

A large number of functions, however, provide the extensibility that adds significant punch to a Visual Basic programmer's arsenal. To a great extent, if Windows can do it, you can do it in Visual Basic (noting the exceptions just named). Before I begin describing how to use the API, a short discussion of the mechanics will help you take advantage of their functional power.

Function versus Sub Procedures

As with Visual Basic command structures, the API includes both functions (**Function**) and procedures (**Sub**). Both constructs are variations on procedures where a sub does not return anything. When you wish to call them within your program, you must use the Declare statement to tell Visual Basic which form of statement you wish to use. You can declare these procedures locally within a form or in the Global module.

The local declaration must not conflict with any global definitions but follows the same scoping rules as form or modules variables. That means you can use the same name for different declarations in different forms or modules providing that none of them conflict with a global definition. It is not accurate to say that functions return data and procedures do not. Functions return one data item of the declared type, while some procedures and functions may modify the contents of variables in their argument lists—a matter of "returning" data.

Naming the Statement

Each external routine you call from Visual Basic carries with it a specific name as it is identified within its DLL. You must correctly spell the name and not substitute another name, or the Visual Basic interpreter will not be able to locate the function in the DLL.

The Dynamic Link Library or Lib Element

Except for parameter-less functions in Visual Basic, all subs and function declarations must specify the **lib** element or library where the procedure resides. Lib tells Visual Basic the DOS file name for the DLL. Using that name, Visual Basic searches the path for that file in order to tap into the function.

The Alias or Visual Basic Statement

Since you may wind up with two DLLs that have identically named functions, you need some way to distinguish between them. The alias element provides you with a method for resolving that conflict, as well as a means for setting your own naming conventions for external declarations. These are the names by which Visual Basic will know and refer to the functions you intend to use.

The Arguments

The arguments in a declaration may serve two purposes. In functions, they pass information to the DLL for processing. In procedures, they can either pass information to or return new data from the DLL. You also determine the type of data passed back and forth. Table 5-1 shows the matrix for the rules for passing data. "Address to Data" means to use a long integer to act as a pointer.

Table 5-1   *Using these rules, you can select the mode for passing data to a declared function in the Windows API.*

	By Reference	By Value (A copy of the Data)	Address to Data
Pointer to a string	Yes		Yes
Null terminated string			Yes
Numerical value	Yes	Yes	

The parameter list that you pass to the DLL will be checked by Windows. Should there be an invalid parameter, Windows will cause your application to display the General Protection Fault (GPF) error message. Under Windows 3.0, no such parameter checking took place. (In the research conducted before the release of Windows 3.1, Microsoft discovered that over 50 percent of the Unrecoverable Application Errors (UAE) in Windows 3.0 were caused by invalid parameters that were passed to the system by functions—even in their own applications.)

The Statement Type Declaration

For functions only, you must declare the variable type of the data returned to Visual Basic by the external function. You can assign the variable type at the end of the declaration. If you plan to use the procedure to return more than one type of data, then specify the Any variable type, and Visual Basic will interpret the type for you at run time. There are two other ways to declare the return type: you can either use an implicit declaration by attaching the variable declaration character (&,%,$,!,#) to the statement name, or you can rely on the default variable type when you call the function.

Important API Practices

One distinct difference exists between the ways that Visual Basic and the C language handle variables. Visual Basic handles strings differently. C expects that a null termination (Chr$(0)) will appear at the end of the string. If you embed blanks with Chr$(0) and try to pass the resulting string to your function declaration, you will get back the characters only up to the first embedded null character. However, if you try to pass a Visual Basic string to your C function *without* appending the null termination, you will get garbage back also. This is true for all strings except the function arguments that you mean to pass as constants.

A number of API calls will have little or no use to you because those same functions are handled in Visual Basic more easily than through function declarations. Most of those functions handle memory management and graphic interface. For instance, it's much easier to set the title of a form by passing a string into Form1.Caption than it is to make calls to SetWindowText (the API call that sets the title text of a window). Sometimes, however, the line will become somewhat fuzzier. For instance, a Visual Basic application running in the Windows environment should not hog the CPU. When an iterative process starts, you would normally include the DoEvents function in the loop. That allows messages from other applications to be processed. DoEvents performs a function something like the Windows API call PeekMessage, shown here as the C function prototype:

```
BOOL PeekMessage(lpmsg, hwnd, uFilterFirst, uFilterLast, fuRemove)
```

In this call, lpmsg is the message structure for storing the information about the message retrieved, hwnd is the handle of the window whose messages you want to retrieve, uFilterFirst and uFilterLast set the range of messages you seek, and fuRemove sets the parameters for message characteristics. The Visual Basic API declare is as follows (appearing on one line):

```
Declare Function PeekMessage Lib "User" (lpMsg As MSG, ByVal hWnd As Integer, ByVal
...wMsgFilterMin As Integer, ByVal wMsgFilterMax As Integer, ByVal wRemoveMsg As
...Integer) As Integer
```

You may want to work with the system and application message queues but change the way in which DoEvents processes messages. You could use PeekMessage to yield control to the system to process waiting messages that may have a higher priority than any message for the current application. The Windows API also supplies a Yield and a WaitMessage function. A call to Yield suspends the current task to make sure the system message queue is empty. WaitMessage checks the queue when the current task has nothing else to do. You may want to stop the current task and wait for a specific message. The Windows API supplies a function called GetMessage:

```
BOOL GetMessage(lpmsg, hwnd, uMsgFilterMin, uMsgFilterMax)
```

In this call, lpmsg supplies the structure to hold information, hwnd is the handle of the window, and uMsgFilterMin and uMsgFilterMax set the range of messages to retrieve. The Visual Basic API declaration looks like this (appearing on one line):

```
Declare Function GetMessage Lib "User" (lpMsg As MSG, ByVal hWnd As Integer, ByVal
...wMsgFilterMin As Integer, ByVal wMsgFilterMax As Integer) As Integer
```

All of these functions are processed by the Translate/Dispatch loop in the main window, and all of them allow slightly more control over message processing than does the standard Visual Basic DoEvents function. The equivalent call using straight C would look like the code in Listing 5-1.

Listing 5-1   *This C code is roughly equivalent to the DoEvents method in Visual Basic.*

```
If (PeekMessage(&msg,NULL,0,0,PM_REMOVE))
{
/*There is a message to be processed */
TranslateMessage(&msg);

DispatchMessage(&msg);
}
else
/Continue as before */
```

With over 800 API calls, you can augment Visual Basic with API declarations to perform many useful functions not directly supported in Visual Basic. However, you will want to avoid these API calls that clash with Visual Basic or that promote poor Windows programming practices. Most of those types of calls handle memory in a manner incompatible with the good Windows memory management.

The Most Useful Windows API Calls

With 822 API calls, you might get lost while trying to decide which ones to use in your application. To help reduce the time you spend in trying to produce an effect with straight Visual Basic where an API call works more efficiently, this section highlights some of the more common extensions to Visual Basic offered by the API.

Pointers, Strings, and Things

Matching the C language ability to work with pointers to structures and strings with Visual Basic can create the most problems for you of any subject regarding your work with the API. (The other major difficulty involves not closing resources you have opened and unnecessarily consuming memory.)

As mentioned earlier, Windows often passes data in forms that Visual Basic cannot understand. One of the main differences between the native language of Windows itself (a mixture of assembler and C) and Visual Basic is the lack of support for pointers in Visual Basic. For programmers unfamiliar with C, that means that Visual Basic does not support a variable that contains only the information for how to find data and not the actual data. If you examine the contents of a pointer to a string containing someone's name, you don't find the characters of the name.

You can, however, use the API call lstrcpy to handle this situation. In the C language, you copy data by referencing its pointer in an expression such as CopyFunction (Target, Source). The function CopyFunction knows how to handle using the Source pointer to an address to retrieve the data and transfer it into the Target. In the case of finding a string by using a Visual Basic declaration, you first declare the lstrcpy function as (lstr = long pointer to a string):

```
Declare Function lstrcpy Lib "Kernel" (ByVal lpString1 As Any, ByVal lpString2
...As Any) As Long
```

Before making the call to the function, you create a string large enough to hold the text you'll get. Otherwise, Visual Basic truncates the information. Use the Space$ statement to fill a large string with blank spaces, and then make the call to lstrcpy like this:

```
StringVar = lstrcpy(SpaceString$, LongPtrToString)
```

You can retrieve the DOS environment string with the following method. First, declare the API call to retrieve the environment string:

```
Declare Function GetDOSEnvironment Lib "Kernel" () As Long
```

After you have declared the two API calls in the Global module, your code should look like that in Listing 5-2.

Listing 5-2   *This code shows how to retrieve the DOS environment by using two calls, lstrcpy and GetDOSEnviron, from the API.*

```
Dim DosEnv As Long
StringVar$ = Space$(4000)
DosEnv = GetDOSEnvironment()
x& = lstrcpy(StringVar$, DosEnv)
Form1.Text1.Text = StringVar$
```

The GetDOSEnvironment API call actually does less than the Environ$ statement in Visual Basic. This is another example of why you should check the Visual Basic statement, method, and function list before you fold API calls into your application.

The System Monitor Utility

The power of the API becomes evident when you look into what it takes to find out about the inner workings of Windows itself. Visual Basic supplies a few of these functions. For instance, in the MouseMove event, you can retrieve the current position of the mouse hot spot. These coordinates can also be derived from the GetQueueStatus API call. First, you declare the GetQueueStatus function in the Global module of your application as shown in Listing 5-3:

Listing 5-3   *This code is the API declaration in the Global module for the GetQueueStatus function. The flag constants show the types of messages you can examine in the main message queue.*

```
Declare Function GetQueueStatus Lib "User" (ByVal fuFlags As Integer) As Long

' GetQueueStatus flags
Global Const QS_KEY = &H0001
Global Const QS_MOUSEMOVE = &H0002
Global Const QS_MOUSEBUTTON = &H0004
Global Const QS_MOUSE = (QS_MOUSEMOVE Or QS_MOUSEBUTTON)
Global Const QS_POSTMESSAGE = &H0008
Global Const QS_TIMER = &H0010
Global Const QS_PAINT = &H0020
Global Const QS_SENDMESSAGE = &H0040
```

Notice the constant declarations in Listing 5-3. By examining the return value (a long integer) from this function you can find out two things. First, you can find out if a specific message is in the queue—like a WM_PAINT or a WM_TIMER message. Second, you can find out what messages were added to the queue since the last time you called GetQueueStatus, GetMessage, or PeekMessage. This is a fast way to keep an eye on the queue for messages critical to your application.

 Tip: *When a function returns a long integer, the Windows API handles that value by looking at the high-order word and the low-order word, and expects them to carry certain specific information. In rare cases, one or the other of these values comes back empty, or null. If either of these*

*were to contain a pointer to yet another long value—as in a pointer to an
array of other pointers, as occurs inside the Paradox database engine—
you would need to create a dynamic link library to trap that information.
For the most part, however, you can use a bitwise "AND" or "OR" to extract
the value you need.*

After testing for the message by using GetQueueStatus, you call GetMessage to
actually extract the particular message you wanted, and reset the message list
returned in the high-order word of GetQueueStatus.

All of that seems a bit more complicated than simply using the native
MouseMove event in Visual Basic. However, this example shows you how much
work Visual Basic actually does for you. There are functions, however, that you
cannot get access to without a call to the API. The System Monitor utility shows you
several of these functions and how to use them. Figure 5-3 shows the main screen for
the System Monitor utility.

Figure 5-3   *The System Monitor utility demonstrates the API calls that are not native to
Visual Basic for delving into the current status of your Windows environment.*

The API calls used in the System Monitor utility provide functions within a Visual Basic application that the Visual Basic language does not support.

GetWindowsDirectory—retrieve pathname to directory where Windows resides

GetSystemDirectory—retrieve pathname to directory below Windows

The CurDir$ function offered in Visual Basic returns the "current" directory. Suppose that your application requires files to be located in the directory where WIN.COM (the Windows directory) exists. If you required that your application be launched from there, you could use CurDir$ to get the full path name of the Windows directory. However, if you supplied a file and directory dialog (as through the Common Dialogs) and the user changed the default directory settings, CurDir$ would no longer retrieve the directory where your application resided. Using the GetWindowsDirectory and GetSystemDirectory API calls, you can retrieve the Windows directory no matter what changes your user has made to the default subdirectory. These two functions copy a null terminated string into a buffer. To get that C string into a Visual Basic string, you must prepare a receptor before you call the function. The code in Listing 5-4 shows the creation of the PointBuffer$ temporary variable. Calling the Space$ function places 255 spaces in the string. Without those spaces the string returned from GetWindowsDirectory would be truncated improperly.

Listing 5-4 *You can retrieve the name of the directory from which Windows itself was started.*

```
'---Windows Directory
PointerBuffer$ = Space$(255)
LenChars% = GetWindowsDirectory(PointerBuffer$, 255)
SysInfo.Label1(16).Caption = Left$(PointerBuffer$, LenChars%)
```

GetVersion—read version for Windows run time

For some applications, you will rely on functions available in a specific version of Windows. To determine which version might be running your program at a certain time, you can use the GetVersion function. GetVersion returns a long integer with the elements of the version number (left and right sides of the decimal) in the high word and the low word, respectively. To retrieve the correct version number, you must separate the values from the long integer and retranslate them. Listing 5-5 shows how the System Monitor uses GetVersion. Microhelp's VBTools offers a single function called MhWinVersion that returns a single string with version information.

Listing 5-5   *The major version number (to the left of the decimal) appears in the low word of the GetVersion call as the minor version number (to the right of the decimal) appears in the high word.*

```
'---Windows Version
version$ = GetVersion()
LowByte$ = Str$(version% And &HFF)                      'masking off high byte
HighByte$ = LTrim$(Str$((version% And &HFF00) / 256))   'mask of low byte and shift
SysInfo.Label1(13).Caption = LowByte$ + "." + HighByte$ 'combine & display version
```

GetNumTasks—read number of tasks running

The GetNumTasks tells you how many parent tasks Windows is running—with a few exceptions. The return value from GetNumTasks does not include the top-level handle for Windows itself, and it doesn't count the *parent* window of the application that makes the GetNumTasks call. You can use that knowledge to look for another application.

GetWindow—reads Window handles

GetWindowText—reads name of Window referred to by handle

GetWindowTextLength—read length of text in Window's title

GetParent—returns the handle for the parent of a window

Windows keeps track of running applications through their "handles," or the unique name of each instance of each window class. The list created by the Task Manager (which you can load by double-clicking on the background or Desktop of Windows itself) used something like the GetWindow call to locate each window running in the system. As if you were to look through a list of database records, you can scan the task list and create a separate list of the names of all the windows running at any one time.

To make that list, you call GetWindow with the parameter HWND_FIRST to get the first handle on the list. Then you call GetWindowTextLength to find out the length of the title of the window, followed by GetWindowText to actually retrieve the text that identifies the window. (The handle itself is a long integer and is not very descriptive.) You must use the method described earlier for retrieving null terminated strings (C strings) using Visual Basic. You must prepare a variable with ASCII spaces embedded into it by using the Visual Basic Space$ function, and then perform what C programmers call a "string copy" of the text that you retrieved with

GetWindowText. GetWindowTextLength must be used in place of the Visual Basic Len function because the string contains embedded null characters that Visual Basic will interpret as the end of the string and will terminate the string length count incorrectly.

Listing 5-6 shows how the SysInfo application uses these three API calls to take a snapshot of the window handles that are accessible at run time. The user can choose to look at a simulation of the Task Manager list or at a list of all the windows that are running at the time.

Listing 5-6 *The TaskList module of SysInfo reads the list of running tasks when the user selects the type of list. Dimensioning the variables at the beginning reinitializes them.*

```
Sub TaskList (ListType As Integer)
    Dim ThisWnd As Integer
    Dim NameLen As Integer
    Dim ListItem As String

    ThisWnd = GetWindow(SysInfo.hWnd, GW_HWNDFIRST)      'read first handle
    Do Until ThisWnd = 0                                 'more handles in list
     Select Case ListType                               'check request
     Case TopLevel                                      'top level only
       GotParent = GetParent(ThisWnd)                   'look for parent
       If GotParent = NULL Then                         'must be top
         NameLen = GetWindowTextLength(ThisWnd)         'title length
         GoSub ListFiller                               'add to list
       End If
     Case Master                                        'all tasks
       NameLen = GetWindowTextLength(ThisWnd)           'title length
       GoSub ListFiller                                 'add to list
     End Select
     ThisWnd = GetWindow(ThisWnd, GW_HWNDNEXT)          'read next handle
     x = DoEvents()                                     'release CPU
    Loop
                                                         'change list title
    If ListType = Master Then
      SysInfo.TaskLabel.Caption = "Top Level Task List"
    Else
      SysInfo.TaskLabel.Caption = "Master Task List"
    End If
    If SysInfo.Visible = TRUE Then TextSet              'refresh labels
    Exit Sub
```

```
ListFiller:
    ListItem = Space$(NameLen + 2)                         'prep variable
    NameLen = GetWindowText(ThisWnd, ListItem, NameLen + 2)'get title
    ClassName$ = Space$(255)                               'prep variable
    Result = GetClassName(ThisWnd, ClassName$, 255)       'read class
    If NameLen > 0 Then                                   'skip blanks
        NameLen = Len(ListItem)                           'read length
        SysInfo.Combo1.AddItem Mid$(ListItem, 1, NameLen - 2) + " - " + ClassName$
    End If
    Return
End Sub
```

You can choose from several methods for traversing the task list. You can step through the list by passing HWND_NEXT in the second parameter of GetWindow, given in the API declarations, or you can get the first child of a top-level window with the HWND_CHILD parameter. The GetParent call tells you if the window whose handle you've just read through GetWindow has a parent or not. A null return value tells you that this is the top-level window for this particular class of window.

GetClassName—reads the class name of the referenced window

All windows running in the system may have the same name even though they don't have the same handle. (The handle, which is assigned by Windows, must be unique.) However, each window that is not a top-level window has a parent class; that is, the top-level window has registered a class of windows with Windows itself before creating any children. To find out the name of that original class, you can call GetClassName. If you do this with any Visual Basic application, you find out the name that was used by Microsoft to label the project when Visual Basic was in development and was being beta tested: Thunder. Each Visual Basic form is registered under the class name ThunderForm. Figure 5-4 shows the task list of top-level windows that were running at the time the picture was taken.

GetClassName also returns a C string with embedded null characters that will confuse Visual Basic. To use this API call properly, you must prepare a variable with embedded blanks (ASCII spaces), as shown in Listing 5-7.

Listing 5-7 *The ListFiller subroutine (called from the TaskList module in Listing 5-6) shows how to use the GetClassName API call.*

```
ListFiller:
    ListItem = Space$(NameLen + 2)                         'prep variable
    NameLen = GetWindowText(ThisWnd, ListItem, NameLen + 1)'get title
```

```
ClassName$ = Space$(255)                        'prep variable
ClassLen = GetClassName(ThisWnd, ClassName$, 255)   'read class
If NameLen > 0 Then                             'skip blanks
    SysInfo.Combo1.AddItem Mid$(ListItem, 1, NameLen) + " - " + ClassName$
End If
Return
```

SetWindowPos—place the window on the screen

If you load the Clock application that ships with Windows 3.1, you will notice that you can request that the Clock always stay on top of all other applications. That way, no matter what you run, you can still see the clock. Causing your Visual Basic application to work the same way takes one call to the Windows API: SetWindowPos. Listing 5-8 shows the code that causes the SysInfo application to stay on top:

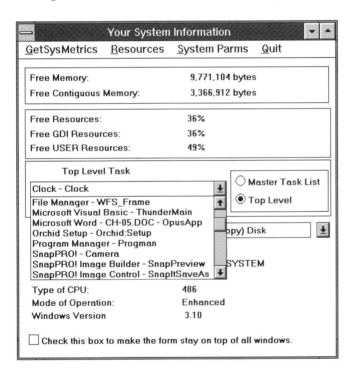

Figure 5-4   *The SysInfo sample program shows the top-level tasks running in Windows. Notice that the Microsoft Visual Basic environment appears as registered to class ThunderMain, its development code name.*

Listing 5-8   *When you click on the check box at the bottom of the SysInfo form, you execute this code and control whether or not SysInfo stays on top of all other applications.*

```
Sub Check1_Click ()
      If Check1.Value = OFF Then
        SysInfo.Combo1.SetFocus
        x% = SetWindowPos(SysInfo.hWnd, HWND_NOTOPMOST, 0, 0, 0, 0, SWP_NOSIZE)
      Else
        SysInfo.Combo1.SetFocus
        x% = SetWindowPos(SysInfo.hWnd, HWND_TOPMOST, 0, 0, 0, 0, SWP_NOSIZE)
      End If
End Sub
```

You should consider two other elements when you use SetWindowPos. First, you should trap the existing location of the Window and restore it when you call SetWindowPos merely to control the stay-on-top element. Second, if this form will call another form, you must allow the second form to appear by turning off the HWND_TOPMOST parameter; otherwise the new form will not be accessible.

GetFreeSpace—read total global memory available

GlobalCompact—read largest contiguous memory block available

Under Windows, retrieving the amount of free memory can be tricky. Windows uses free memory to move objects around so that you can make the optimal use of space. However, to load an application that requires a block of contiguous memory, you must call GlobalCompact. Listing 5-9 shows the two API calls used by the SysInfo application to display free memory information.

Listing 5-9   *You must use these two calls, GetFreeSpace and GlobalCompact, to retrieve both total and free contiguous memory.*

```
'---Free RAM
SysInfo.Label1(1).Caption = Format$(GetFreeSpace(0), "###,###,000") + " bytes"
'---Free Contiguous RAM
SysInfo.Label1(2).Caption = Format$(GlobalCompact(0), "###,###,000") + " bytes"
```

In the preceding code, the integer returned by GetFreeSpace and GlobalCompact must be formatted into something readable through the use of the Visual Basic Format$ function. (In Windows 3.1, the parameter passed in GetFreeSpace is ignored.) As with many API calls, the return value and parameter handling will change for GetFreeSpace, depending on what version of Windows the application uses and what mode the operating system is using. In enhanced mode, the GetFreeSpace call returns the amount of space available to allow an application to load—providing that sufficient resources also exist. In standard mode, GetFreeSpace merely returns the total bytes of memory not allocated to other code segments without regard to memory reserved for non-Windows applications; this can be a hazard when you've shelled out to a character-based program and you've returned to Windows to load another application. You should check both resource level and memory before loading a large application. GlobalCompact not only returns the largest contiguous block of memory, but it discards any discardable objects in memory before it takes a measure. This replicates what Windows will do if you try to load an application that requires all of that space.

GetDriveType—detect fixed, removable or remote disk drive type

When you wish to save data or determine the location of a program, you may need to know the media type for a disk. In the case of a network drive, Windows presents some limits to your access. You can use the GetDriveType to find out two things: (1) the number of drives you have on the system and (2) the drive type for each one. Listing 5-10 shows how you can fill a combo box with the drive types and their assigned letters.

Listing 5-10 *This code shows how to create a list of drives and their corresponding drive types in a combo box in the SysInfo sample application.*

```
'---Get the types of drives in the system
Alpha$ = "ABCDEFGHIJKLMNOPQRSTUVWXYZ"        'set drive letter array
Do
    DriveType% = DriveType% + 1              'count drive types
    Drv$ = Mid$(Alpha$, DriveType%, 1)       'match to letter
    x% = GetDriveType(DriveType% - 1)        'read type of drive
    If x% = 0 And DriveType% <> 2 Then       'exit at end of drive lies
      Combo2.Text = Combo2.List(0)           'set first drive display
      Exit Do
    ElseIf x% = 0 And DriveType% = 2 Then    'skip over B drive if none
      ' MsgBox "No B drive"
    Else
      Select Case x%                         'pick drive type
        Case DRIVE_REMOVABLE
            Msg$ = " Removable (Floppy) Disk"
        Case DRIVE_FIXED
```

```
            Msg$ = " Fixed Disk"
        Case DRIVE_REMOTE
            Msg$ = " Remote or network drive"
        End Select
        Combo2.AddItem "Drive " + Drv$ + ":" + Msg$ 'add to list
      End If
  Loop
```

Notice in the listing that the value of zero returned by GetDriveType must allow for missing drives as it does for the missing B drive.

GetFreeSystemResources—read free total, GDI or USER resources

One of the most critical measures in Windows operations is the amount of system resources consumed by running applications relative to the amount available. You must use GetFreeSystemResources and compare them with the requirements of your application before you can be certain your application will load and that it will not operate irregularly. For instance, if you load more than 50 resources onto a form, it will not repaint properly all of the time. Since Visual Basic supports the creation of controls at run time, a problem can easily result. Listing 5-11 shows the three methods you can use to retrieve system resource measures in your application. No similar command exists in the Visual Basic language.

Listing 5-11 *You can use the GetFreeSystemResources call to find out which type of resource consumption Windows checks when refusing to load an application or a perform function due to insufficient resources.*

```
'---Free Resources Measures
SysInfo.Label1(3).Caption = Str$(GetFreeSystemResources(NULL)) + "%"
SysInfo.Label1(4).Caption = Str$(GetFreeSystemResources(1)) + "%"
SysInfo.Label1(5).Caption = Str$(GetFreeSystemResources(2)) + "%"
```

The GetFreeSystemResources API call returns the lower of either Graphics Device Interface (GDI) or User resources when you pass it the null parameter. If you must unload an application before loading a new one, you can use the other two parameters passed in the preceding code to find out which type of resource (graphics or user-based) is causing the resource deficiency. The availability of resources used in the SysInfo sample application is displayed as follow:

Free Resources:	32%
Free GDI Resources:	32%
Free USER Resources:	44%

GetSystemMetrics—read display information (incl.debugging state)

You can determine a great deal of the display characteristics in Windows with one call to the API: GetSystemMetrics. This call shows its importance when you must display an image and detect the physical bounds of the current display. Figure 5-5 shows the partial list of parameters that GetSystemMetrics can return.

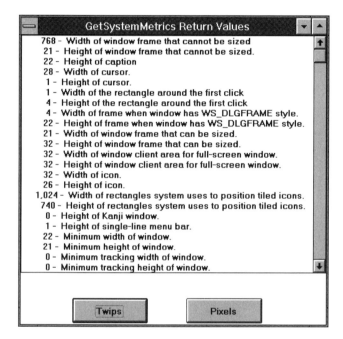

Figure 5-5 *This list box was filled by using return values from the GetSystemMetrics API call.*

Tip: *In the System Monitor sample application used in this chapter, the list boxes that display GetSystemMetrics and SystemInfo Parameters return values were sized automatically to the form by using the following code:*

```
Sub Form_Resize ()
        List1.Width = GetSysMet.ScaleWidth
        List1.Height = GetSysMet.ScaleHeight - (Command1.Height * 2)
        List1.Left = GetSysMet.Scaleleft
        List1.Top = GetSysMet.ScaleTop
End Sub
```

These statements could be replaced with the move mothod as in

```
List1.Move GetSysMet.Scaleleft,
...GetSysMet.GetSysMet.ScaleTop,
...GetSysMet.ScaleWidth,
...GetSysMet.ScaleHeight -
...(Command1.Height * 2
```

GetCurrentTime or GetTickCount—reads milliseconds since Windows started

For creating timed-out demos or for performing functions like automatic saves or automatic back-ups, you can use the GetTickCount API call to get the number of clock ticks since Windows was first started. GetCurrentTime and GetTickCount work identically.

GetWinFlags—reads CPU type and operating mode

When preparing to load an application that requires at least a 386 running in enhanced mode, you can use the Sub Main module to check the computer hardware as it attempts to load the application with the use of GetWinFlags. Listing 5-12 shows how you would use the bitwise AND to extract the CPU type and the mode of operation from the GetWinFlags call.

Listing 5-12 *The GetWinFlags call returns a double word value that must be processed to extract information on the CPU type and the mode of operation.*

```
'---Get CPU Type
Dim dWords As Long
dWords = GetWinFlags()
If (dWords And WF_CPU486) = WF_CPU486 Then
  CPU$ = "486"
ElseIf (dWords And WF_CPU386) = WF_CPU386 Then
  CPU$ = "386"
Else
  CPU$ = "286"
End If
SysInfo.Label1(19).Caption = CPU$
'---Get Mode of Operation
If (dWords And WF_ENHANCED) Then
  SysInfo.Label1(20).Caption = "Enhanced"
Else
  SysInfo.Label1(20).Caption = "Standard"
End If
```

Tip: *The predefined constants for the flags used with GetWinFlags and other API calls appear in the WIN31API.TXT file supplied by Microsoft in the Visual Basic Professional Edition, as well as in the WINDOWS.H file in the standard Windows Software Development Kit.*

SystemParametersInfo—reads parameters of windows environment

You can also determine the state of other physical hardware through the SystemParametersInfo API call. Figure 5-6 shows the types of information you can retrieve with this function.

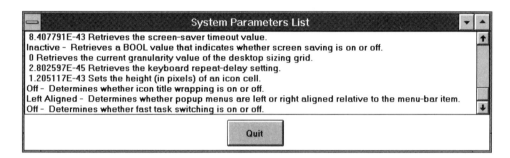

Figure 5-6 *This list box shows some of the system parameters for hardware and debugging that you can retrieve by using the SystemParametersInfo call.*

More Useful API Functions

Once you've grasped the means for using API functions in your Visual Basic applications, you'll want to spend some time looking for useful functions in an SDK reference. To help you get started, the remaining section discusses some of the useful functions that appear in the API and do not have comparable calls in native Visual Basic.

Detecting a Previously Loaded Application

Using the API calls GetModuleHandle and GetModuleUsage, you can find out if an instance of an application you are attempting to load is already running. GetModuleHandle gives you the handle for the program that makes the call. GetModuleUsage returns the number of instances of that application that are running already. Applications like Word for Windows use this method to check whether Share is loaded before allowing another instance of Word to be loaded. A third call, GetModuleFileName, tells you the full path name of the program in which you make the call to that function.

 Tip: *Remember to use a prepared Visual Basic string with any of these three functions, since they return C strings.*

Tracing Focus in Forms

In Visual Basic, forms do not handle focus very well; that is, you cannot manage focus very easily because you can't easily tell when it resides on a form and when it doesn't. A form generates a Lost_Focus event only if there are no controls on the form when it loses focus. To solve that problem, you can do one of the three things: (1) hide all of the controls and then shift the focus, (2) trap the movement to another window by using some sort of variable flag scheme, or (3) use the GetActiveWindow API function. By combining GetActiveWindow with a timer, you can get a handle to the window that presently owns the focus, and compare it with the handle for the form with the timer. (Timers are used often in Visual Basic as "watch dogs" that keep an eye out for a specific event that cannot be trapped in another specific-event procedure.)

Using Visual Basic to Exit Windows

You can create a program that is to be the only Windows program running on a particular machine. You can start the Windows environment and launch your application from the DOS prompt, with a command such as: WIN APP.EXE. However, once you've started Windows, you've lost control over the environment itself. To exit back to the DOS prompt, you'll need a little help. The ExitWindows API function does just the trick. By passing two null parameters in the ExitWindows call, you can close Windows (providing that all other tasks running at the time agree to terminate).

System Modal versus Application Modal

To be **modal** in Windows means to grab the focus and not release it. A user cannot move control to another window until the modal window is closed. Most often forms will be modal, like the form created in the Visual Basic function MsgBox. Once you've opened a message box, you must click on one of the buttons (usually just an OK button) before you can activate any other object in the environment. Such a form is said to be **system modal**. However, you can create the same effect but contain it within an application. If you call up the Open File dialog box in Visual Basic, you'll see that you can switch to other applications, but you can't do anything in another part of Visual Basic until you close that dialog box. That makes the Open File dialog box "application modal."

In Visual Basic, you can add the numeric parameter 1 when you display a form, so that the form becomes "application modal." Creating a system modal form in Visual Basic requires the SetSysModalWindow API Call. Simply declaring SetSysModalWindow in the Global module and calling it with the handle for the form when you load it will not allow the focus to switch to any other place in Windows until that form is unloaded.

Creating a Flashing Title Bar

Many applications in Windows operate with more than one form running at any one time. In those cases, you may want to notify the user when a change in one form affects a change in another form. You can do this by causing the title bar of the form to flash until the responds. The API supplies the FlashWindow function for just this purpose. The FlashWindow function takes a parameter for the window handle of the form to be flashed and an integer that determines if flashing is turned off or on. The function returns a value that tells you the form's state prior to the call to FlashWindow.

Drag-and-Drop an Object and Reset the Parent Window

In Chapter 4 you saw an example that demonstrates how you can spawn new controls from a preexisting parent. In the case of that example, you can click a button and create new buttons that you can drag to a different part of the form. Under those circumstances, each new child control had the same parent—the original button. In some cases, you may want to drop one of those buttons onto another control and have the child "inherit" characteristics of the new control. To do that, you must change the parent of the child control by using the SetParent API function or use the Parent property for those objects that have one. To use the function, you must make the declaration in the Global module and then simply pass the window handle (hWnd) for both the child and the new parent.

Caution: *Improperly restoring a parent to a child can cause Windows to hang.*

Handling List Boxes

SendMessage—general message sending/receiving tool

GetFocus—reads handle of window with focus

SetFocusAPI—resets the focus to a window

List boxes provide a powerful method for displaying collections of data. Unfortunately, the Visual Basic language lacks some important features for manipulating list boxes. For instance, the only way to clear out the items from a list box is to use the RemoveItem method to delete each item, one at a time. For short lists in combo boxes or list boxes, this method works satisfactorily. However, for large collections of data the process just takes too much time.

The API provides a function called SendMessage, which can perform a whole variety of functions, depending on the type of message you pass with it. You can send messages to another window by using SendMessage, just as if the Windows system itself had sent the message. For instance, you can send WM_PAINT messages to repaint a client area of a Window. In this case, you want to send a message that resets the contents of a list box. You perform that reset by sending the LB_RESETCONTENT message, as shown in Listing 5-13:

Listing 5-13 *This code resets the list box referred to by the GetFocus function. The Refresh method performs nearly the same function.*

```
'---GLOBAL.BAS
Const WM_USER = &H400
Const LB_RESETCONTENT = WM_USER + 5
Declare Function GetFocus% Lib "user" ()
Declare Function SendMessage% Lib "user" (ByVal hWnd%, ByVal wMsg%, ByVal wParam%,
...ByVal lParam&)
'---Inside the form
ListBox.SetFocus
x = SendMessage(GetFocus(), LB_RESETCONTENT, 0, 0)
```

The SysInfo sample application uses SendMessage to clear out the combo boxes when listing the master and top-level tasks. The code in Listing 5-14 shows the ComboClear function used in SysInfo.

Listing 5-14 *This function clears out the combo boxes in the SysInfo application to refill with the new data from the task-listing functions.*

```
Sub ComboClear ()
    hWndOld% = GetFocus()
    SysInfo.Combo1.SetFocus
    x = SendMessage(GetFocus(), CB_RESETCONTENT, 0, 0)
    Suc% = SetFocusAPI(hWndOld%)
    If SysInfo.Visible = TRUE Then TextSet
End Sub
```

In Chapter 4, I talked about the inability to set tabs in a list box by using native Visual Basic statements. The list box has a default set of tab stops that you can't change without resorting to the API. Once again, the SendMessage API call provides a means that is unavailable in native Visual Basic. If you pass the message LB_SETTABSTOPS with SendMessage, you can set the number of tab stops and their locations rather easily. You simply specify the number of tab stops you wish to set up, and pass an array with the tab-stop locations, as in this example:

```
Result& = SendMessage(ListBox.hWnd LB_SETTABSTOPS, 3, TabStops(1))
```

TabStops, in this example, is an array of tab positions for the three tabs specified in the third parameter.

You may also want to take advantage of the Visual Basic drag-and-drop feature for dropping text into specified locations within a list box. You can do that providing you use the TextHeight measure to figure out how many lines exist in the list box and then pass the LB_GETTOPINDEX message in the SendMessage function. That message returns a value for the index number of the item at the top of the list-box display. It starts at 0 when the list box first loads, but the user may scroll the display before trying to drop a line of text into the box.

Handling DOS Applications

GetActiveWindow—window handle retrieval

IsWindow—checks for valid window handle

SendKeys—transmit keystrokes to another application

You can start most DOS character mode applications from inside Visual Basic. That permits Visual Basic to operate as a program launcher without limitations. The problem arises, however, in returning complete control to the Visual Basic application. If you don't retake complete control, your Visual Basic application may terminate while the DOS session is still active. Windows itself does not allow itself to be closed while an active DOS application continues to run. Figure 5-7 shows a simple application to launch other applications.

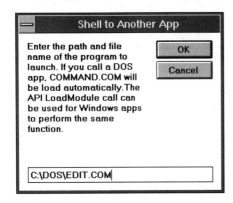

Figure 5-7   *This input box accepts the string to be used by the Shell function to launch an application. Windows applications already in the path (like calc.exe or write.exe) do not need the entire path to be specified.*

Since you cannot pass a message directly to an application that is running in a full DOS window, you must communicate with the DOS window itself. A normal (not maximized or minimized) DOS window permits the use of the SendKeys API call to communicate between DOS and Windows applications where a full screen or maximized DOS window will not—a topic I'll discuss next. You can use the IsWindow and the GetActiveWindow API calls to perform that communication. In Listing 5-14, the Declare statements can be placed in a Global module or simply in the declarations section of a form. You can test the procedure by using a Windows application like notepad.exe. Place the code (except the Declares) in Listing 5-15 into the Click event for a button on a form.

Listing 5-15   *This code ensures that the Visual Basic application does not terminate sooner than an application that it launched by using the Shell function.*

```
Declare Function GetActiveWindow Lib "User" () As Integer
Declare Function IsWindow Lib "User" (ByVal hWnd As Integer) As Integer
```

```
Sub Command1_Click ()
    S1$ = "Enter the path and file name "          'construct instructions
    S2$ = "of the program to launch."
    S3$ = " If you call a DOS app, "
    S4$ = "COMMAND.COM will be load automatically."
    S5$ = "The API LoadModule call can be used for Windows"
    S6$ = " apps to perform the same function."
    Title$ = "Shell to Another App"
    ShelledApp$ = InputBox(S1$ & S2$ & S3$ & S4$ & S5$ & S6$, Title$) 'ask
    If ShelledApp$ = "" Then Exit Sub               'ensure file name given
      OldWin% = GetActiveWindow()                   'get current window handle
      ShellWindowHWnd% = OldWin%                    'save current handle
     x% = Shell(Trim(ShelledApp$), 1)               'call requested app
     While OldWin% = ShellWindowHWnd%               'wait till new app loads
        x% = DoEvents()                             'check for other messages
        Debug.Print "Waiting for Dos APP to load"'immediate window note
        ShellWindowHWnd% = GetActiveWindow()        'get next active window
      Wend
      While IsWindow(ShellWindowHWnd%)              'wait til app terminates
        x% = DoEvents()
      Wend
      MsgBox "Shelled App Terminated", 0, "Program to End"
      End
End Sub
```

The code in Listing 5-15 includes an extra While . . . Wend structure immediately following the launching of an application. An article in the Microsoft Knowledge Base (Q72880, "VB Can Determine When a Shelled Process Has Terminated") presents a solution that works well with other Windows applications but not with DOS applications (which require another command layer to be loaded with COM-MAND.COM). If you begin to test for termination of the shelled application too soon after the Shell statement, the GetActiveWindow call merely retrieves the handle to the Visual Basic program. If you don't enforce the extra While . . . Wend loop to check the current return of GetActiveWindow with the saved value for the Visual Basic program in the case of a DOS application, the Visual Basic program will terminate too early again.

Once you have launched an application, you can pilot it remotely in two ways: either by using Dynamic Data Exchange (DDE) or by sending keystrokes with SendKeys as if they were typed at the keyboard. For applications that respond to DDE, the DDE method is still the best, in most cases. However, for other applications—

especially most DOS programs—SendKeys works. For DOS programs, you must first ensure that Windows is running in 386 enhanced mode and that the DOS program is running in a window and not in full screen. After you have properly launched the application, place on the clipboard the text that you want to send to the DOS program. Then you can paste those characters into the DOS program as if someone had typed them at the keyboard.

Handling Text Boxes

SendMessage—permits instructions to text boxes

The masked edit and text-box controls in Visual Basic 3.0 Professional Edition give you a means for controlling input that was not available in versions prior to of Visual Basic 2.0. For example, where Visual Basic now provides the MaxLength property for masked edit and text-box controls, Visual Basic 1.0 relied upon the SendMessage API call and the EM_LIMITTEXT message to accomplish the same thing. Some capabilities for controlling input that are possible with the API, however, still supplement the masked edit and text-box–control properties.

Figure 5-8 shows how to use the SendMessage routine to talk to a text-box control. The EM_GETLINECOUNT message retrieves the number of text lines in a multiline edit control, and EM_GETLINE retrieves a specific line from the text box. You can use EM_LINEINDEX to find out how many lines exist prior to the current line. Visual Basic 3.0 provides the ItemData property that performs these functions.

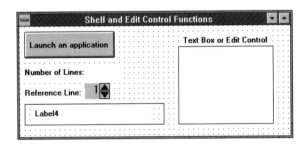

Figure 5-8   *The spin control on the left side of the screen lets you specify which line of text the EM_GETLINE message will retrieve to place in the label control marked Label4. (This figure also shows the push button used in the demonstration of the shell statement, which was discussed in the previous section.*

Handling Graphics

BitBlt—for manipulating bitmaps

Visual Basic provides several means for working with graphic objects as whole objects. If you want to manipulate bitmaps and other objects in smaller components, you have two choices: you can use the Picture Clip control to grab segments of a bit map, or you can use the BitBlt API call. Listing 5-16 shows the sample code for moving a copy of one bitmap into another location by moving only a few pixels at a time.

Listing 5-16 *The Form_Load event prepares the special constants and the graphics mode for using the BitBlt API call to control the scrolling transfer of the bitmap.*

```
Sub Form_Load ()
        HScroll1.Max = 50                    'Set maximum value
        HScroll1.LargeChange = 10            'Cross in 5 clicks
        HScroll1.SmallChange = 1             'Cross in 50 clicks
        Picture1.ScaleMode = PIXEL           'Set graphics mode to pixels
        Picture2.ScaleMode = PIXEL           'Set graphics mode to pixels
        SourceDC = Picture1.hDC              'Get device context: source
        DestDC = Picture2.hDC                'Get device context: destination
        PicWid = Picture2.ScaleWidth         'Calc transfer width
        PicHi = Picture2.ScaleHeight         'Calc same height for both
        RopOps = SRCCOPY                     'Copies source to destination
        SrcLogX = 0
End Sub
Sub HScroll1_Change ()
        Label1.Caption = Str$(HScroll1.Value * 2) + "%"
        SrcLogX = HScroll1.Value: SrcLogY = 0
        DestLogX = SrcLogX: DestLogY = SrcLogY
        PaintWid% = HScroll1.Value
        x% = BitBlt(DestDC, DestLogX, DestLogY, PaintWid%, PicHi, SourceDC,
        ...SrcLogX, SrcLogY, RopOps)
End Sub
```

You must retrieve the device context for both the source and the destination. You can think of the device context as providing a handle to the graphic territory you want to work with. In this sample, the Change event of the scroll bar in Figure 5-9 gives you the means for performing the update of the destination region. The other raster operation codes you can use along with BitBlt to affect the regions include those given in Table 5-2.

Figure 5-9   *By using the scroll bar, you can copy the bitmap on the left into the picture box on the right a few pixels at a time by means of the SRCCOPY raster operation in the BitBlt API call.*

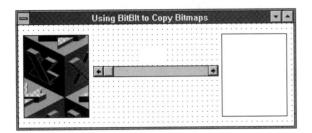

Table 5-2   *The Raster Operations Codes (with the hex values you must use to declare the codes) determine the specific function to be performed on the regions of the screen described by the destination and source device contexts in the BitBlt API call.*

Constant	HEX Value	Operation Description
SRCCOPY	&HCC0020	Copies the source bitmap to the destination
SRCPAINT	&HEE0086	Combines destination and source pixels (OR)
SRCAND	&H8800C6	Combines destination and source pixels (AND)
SRCINVERT	&H660046	Combines destination and source pixels (XOR)
SRCERASE	&H440328	Inverts destination, combines result from SRCAND
NOTSRCCOPY	&H330008	Copies inverted source to destination
NOTSRCERASE	&H1100A6	Inverts result of SRCCOPY (OR)
MERGECOPY	&HC000CA	Combines pattern and source (AND)
MERGEPAINT	&HBB0226	Combines inverted source with destination (OR)
PATCOPY	&HF00021	Copies pattern only to destination
PATPAINT	&HFB0A09	Combines inverted source and pattern (OR) with destination
PATINVERT	&H5A0049	Combines destination with pattern using XOR
DSTINVERT	&H550009	Inverts destination
BLACKNESS	&H42&	Turns destination black
WHITENESS	&HFF0062	Turns destination white

The BitBlt API call exists in the Graphics Device Interface (GDI). BitBlt and the related call StretchBlt, which reshapes bitmaps, condense a large number of graphics operations into one call. Using other API calls, you can add icons to menus (SetMenuItemBitmaps), fill a specified region on the screen with a specific color

(ExtFloodFill), or paint over an object or other region with a special pattern (CreatePatternBrush).

Handling Files:

SetHandleCount—Set maximum file handles for application

One of the dangers you face as a programmer in Visual Basic appears only, it seems, at critical moments. There you are, completing the testing of an application in design mode, when all of a sudden you can't close the application, nor can you exit gracefully from Visual Basic itself by first saving your work. The problem arises from the way that Windows provides handles to your application.

As you open and close files in your application, there is a limited number of file handles at your disposal. If you run out of them but still need one, you're out of luck. This will rarely arise when an application operates after being launched from its executable file. However, in design mode, you have more files open than your application will require, due strictly to Visual Basic. To avoid this pitfall and provide yourself with an easy means to guarantee that you won't lose work, you can employ the SetHandleCount API call. The return value to SetHandleCount is the number of file handles available to an application. Create a simple Visual Basic application with one form containing a label to report the return value from SetHandleCount and an edit control for entering the number of files. Using that application, you can "reserve" file handles by changing the number of file handles available to your programming environment.

You declare the API call in a small utility program for reserving file handles like this:

```
Declare Function SetHandleCount Lib "Kernel" (ByVal wNumber As Integer) As Integer
```

The wNumber parameter of the SetHandleCount indicates the total number of file handles made available to your application. If the value returned by the function is less than what you try to allocate, that means there were fewer handles available within the design (or operating environment) than you requested. You should reexamine the file-handle requirements of your application at that point.

Using the Multimedia Communications Interface API

You can create three kinds of sound with the Windows API functions. Figure 5-10 shows the sample application from which system sound events can be generated.

The code for playing sounds also exists in the file list as shown in Figure 5-10. By double-clicking on the name of a sound file, the DblClick event fires and executes the code in Listing 5-17.

Figure 5-10   *You can launch three types of sound by using three different sound functions in the Windows API. This sample application also uses the multimedia control in the Professional Edition for playing sound, as discussed in Chapter 8.*

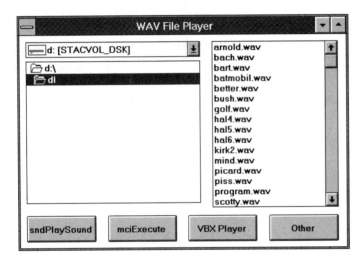

Listing 5-17   *This code declares the sound function, checks to ensure that the file exists on the disk, and then calls the snPLaySound function to play the .WAV file.*

```
'Global DeclarationsSound Declarations
'Multi-Media DLL Driver
Declare Function sndPlaySound Lib "MMsystem" (ByVal lpSound As String, ByVal
...Flags As Integer) As Integer
Sub FileCheck ()
        If File1.FileName <> "" Then
           SoundFile = Dir1.Path + "\" + File1.FileName
        Else
           MsgBox "Please Select A '.WAV' file"
           File1.SetFocus
        End If
End Sub

Sub PlaySound ()
     x% = sndPlaySound(SoundFile, SND_ASYNC)
End Sub
```

You can also play sound file by using the multimedia extensions in the Windows SDK as shown in Listing 5-18.

Listing 5-18 *Using the MCI interface as shown in this code, you can play a sound file.*

```
Sub mciSounds ()
    CmdStr$ = "open " + SoundFile + " type WaveAudio alias mysound"
    mciExecute (CmdStr$)
    mciExecute ("play mysound wait")
    mciExecute ("close mysound")
End Sub
```

The SysInfo Sample Application

Global

```
Global Const FALSE = 0
Global Const TRUE = -1
Global Const OFF = 0
Global Const NULL = 0
Global Const GDI = 1
Global Const USER = 2
Global Const Twips = 0
Global Const Pixels = 3


Type RECT
    left As Integer
    top As Integer
    right As Integer
    bottom As Integer
End Type


Type POINTAPI
    X As Integer
    Y As Integer
End Type


Declare Sub GetCursorPos Lib "User" (lpPoint As POINTAPI)
Declare Sub GetClientRect Lib "User" (ByVal hWnd As Integer, lpRect As RECT)
Declare Sub GetWindowRect Lib "User" (ByVal hWnd As Integer, lpRect As RECT)
Declare Function GetWindowsDirectory Lib "Kernel" (ByVal lpBuffer As String, ByVal
...nSize As Integer) As Integer
Declare Function GetSystemDirectory Lib "Kernel" (ByVal lpBuffer As String, ByVal
...nSize As Integer) As Integer
```

```
Declare Function GetVersion Lib "Kernel" () As Integer
Declare Function GetNumTasks Lib "Kernel" () As Integer


'   SetWindowPos Flags
Global Const SWP_NOSIZE = &H1
Global Const SWP_NOMOVE = &H2
Global Const SWP_NOZORDER = &H4
Global Const SWP_NOREDRAW = &H8
Global Const SWP_NOACTIVATE = &H10
Global Const SWP_DRAWFRAME = &H20
Global Const SWP_SHOWWINDOW = &H40
Global Const SWP_HIDEWINDOW = &H80
Global Const SWP_NOCOPYBITS = &H100
Global Const SWP_NOREPOSITION = &H200
Global Const HWND_TOPMOST = -1
Global Const HWND_NOTOPMOST = -2


Declare Function SetWindowPos Lib "User" (ByVal hWnd As Integer, ByVal hWndInsertAfter
...As Integer, ByVal X As Integer, ByVal Y As Integer, ByVal cx As Integer, ByVal cy
...As Integer, ByVal wFlags As Integer) As Integer


Declare Function GetFreeSpace Lib "Kernel" (ByVal wFlags As Integer) As Long
Declare Function GlobalCompact Lib "Kernel" (ByVal dwMinFree As Long) As Long


Declare Function GetDriveType Lib "Kernel" (ByVal nDrive As Integer) As Integer '0=A,
...1=B...
'   GetDriveType return values
Global Const DRIVE_REMOVABLE = 2
Global Const DRIVE_FIXED = 3
Global Const DRIVE_REMOTE = 4
Global Const DriveA = 0
Global Const DriveB = 1
Global Const DriveC = 2
Global Const DriveD = 3


Declare Function GetFreeSystemResources Lib "User" (ByVal fuSysResource As Integer)
...As Integer


'   GetSystemMetrics() codes
Global Const SM_CXBORDER = 1
Global Const SM_CYBORDER = 2
Global Const SM_CYCAPTION = 3
Global Const SM_CXCURSOR = 4
Global Const SM_CYCURSOR = 5
Global Const SM_CXDOUBLECLK = 6
```

```
Global Const SM_CYDOUBLECLK = 7
Global Const SM_CXDLGFRAME = 8
Global Const SM_CYDLGFRAME = 9
Global Const SM_CXFRAME = 10
Global Const SM_CYFRAME = 11
Global Const SM_CXFULLSCREEN = 12
Global Const SM_CYFULLSCREEN = 13
Global Const SM_CXICON = 14
Global Const SM_CYICON = 15
Global Const SM_CXICONSPACING = 16
Global Const SM_CYICONSPACING = 17
Global Const SM_CYKANJIWINDOW = 18
Global Const SM_CYMENU = 19
Global Const SM_CXMIN = 20
Global Const SM_CYMIN = 21
Global Const SM_CXMINTRACK = 22
Global Const SM_CYMINTRACK = 23
Global Const SM_CXSCREEN = 24
Global Const SM_CYSCREEN = 25
Global Const SM_CXHSCROLL = 26
Global Const SM_CYHSCROLL = 27
Global Const SM_CXVSCROLL = 28
Global Const SM_CYVSCROLL = 29
Global Const SM_CXSIZE = 30
Global Const SM_CYSIZE = 31
Global Const SM_CXHTHUMB = 32
Global Const SM_CYVTHUMB = 33
Global Const SM_DBCSENABLED = 34
Global Const SM_DEBUG = 35
Global Const SM_MENUDROPALIGNMENT = 36
Global Const SM_MOUSEPRESENT = 37
Global Const SM_PENWINDOWS = 38
Global Const SM_SWAPBUTTON = 39

Declare Function GetSystemMetrics Lib "User" (ByVal nIndex As Integer) As Integer

Declare Function GetCurrentTime Lib "User" () As Long
Declare Function GetTickCount Lib "User" () As Long

Declare Function GetWinFlags Lib "Kernel" () As Long

Global Const WF_PMODE = &H1
Global Const WF_CPU286 = &H2
Global Const WF_CPU386 = &H4
Global Const WF_CPU486 = &H8
```

```
Global Const WF_STANDARD = &H10
Global Const WF_WIN286 = &H10
Global Const WF_ENHANCED = &H20
Global Const WF_WIN386 = &H20
Global Const WF_CPU086 = &H40
Global Const WF_CPU186 = &H80
Global Const WF_LARGEFRAME = &H100
Global Const WF_SMALLFRAME = &H200
Global Const WF_80x87 = &H400


Declare Function GetMapMode Lib "GDI" (ByVal hDC As Integer) As Integer


'  GetWindow() Constants
Global Const GW_HWNDFIRST = 0
Global Const GW_HWNDLAST = 1
Global Const GW_HWNDNEXT = 2
Global Const GW_HWNDPREV = 3
Global Const GW_OWNER = 4
Global Const GW_CHILD = 5


Global Const TopLevel = 1
Global Const Master = 2


Declare Function GetWindow Lib "User" (ByVal hWnd As Integer, ByVal wCmd As Integer)
...As Integer
Declare Function GetWindowText Lib "User" (ByVal hWnd As Integer, ByVal lpString As
...String, ByVal aint As Integer) As Integer
Declare Function GetWindowTextLength Lib "User" (ByVal hWnd As Integer) As Integer
Declare Function GetClassName Lib "User" (ByVal hWnd As Integer, ByVal lpClassName As
...String, ByVal nMaxCount As Integer) As Integer



Declare Function SendMessage Lib "User" (ByVal hWnd As Integer, ByVal wMsg As Integer,
...ByVal wParam As Integer, lParam As Any) As Long
Declare Function GetFocus Lib "User" () As Integer
Declare Function SetFocusAPI Lib "User" Alias "SetFocus" (ByVal hWnd As Integer) As
...Integer
Declare Function GetParent% Lib "User" (ByVal hWnd%)
Global Const WM_USER = &H400
Global Const CB_RESETCONTENT = WM_USER + 11
Global Const LB_RESETCONTENT = WM_USER + 5
Global Const ROP_DOWN_LIST = 2


Declare Function SizeofResource Lib "Kernel" (ByVal hInstance As Integer, ByVal
...hResInfo As Integer) As Integer
```

```
Declare Function AccessResource Lib "Kernel" (ByVal hInstance As Integer, ByVal
...hResInfo As Integer) As Integer


'  Predefined Resource Types
Global Const RT_CURSOR = 1&
Global Const RT_BITMAP = 2&
Global Const RT_ICON = 3&
Global Const RT_MENU = 4&
Global Const RT_DIALOG = 5&
Global Const RT_STRING = 6&
Global Const RT_FONTDIR = 7&
Global Const RT_FONT = 8&
Global Const RT_ACCELERATOR = 9&
Global Const RT_RCDATA = 10&


Declare Function SystemParametersInfo Lib "User" (ByVal uAction As Integer, ByVal
...uParam As Integer, lpvParam As Any, ByVal fuWinIni As Integer) As Integer

Global Const SPI_GETBEEP = 1
Global Const SPI_SETBEEP = 2
Global Const SPI_GETMOUSE = 3
Global Const SPI_SETMOUSE = 4
Global Const SPI_GETBORDER = 5
Global Const SPI_SETBORDER = 6
Global Const SPI_GETKEYBOARDSPEED = 10
Global Const SPI_SETKEYBOARDSPEED = 11
Global Const SPI_LANGDRIVER = 12
Global Const SPI_ICONHORIZONTALSPACING = 13
Global Const SPI_GETSCREENSAVETIMEOUT = 14
Global Const SPI_SETSCREENSAVETIMEOUT = 15
Global Const SPI_GETSCREENSAVEACTIVE = 16
Global Const SPI_SETSCREENSAVEACTIVE = 17
Global Const SPI_GETGRIDGRANULARITY = 18
Global Const SPI_SETGRIDGRANULARITY = 19
Global Const SPI_SETDESKWALLPAPER = 20
Global Const SPI_SETDESKPATTERN = 21
Global Const SPI_GETKEYBOARDDELAY = 22
Global Const SPI_SETKEYBOARDDELAY = 23
Global Const SPI_ICONVERTICALSPACING = 24
Global Const SPI_GETICONTITLEWRAP = 25
Global Const SPI_SETICONTITLEWRAP = 26
Global Const SPI_GETMENUDROPALIGNMENT = 27
Global Const SPI_SETMENUDROPALIGNMENT = 28
Global Const SPI_SETDOUBLECLKWIDTH = 29
Global Const SPI_SETDOUBLECLKHEIGHT = 30
```

```
Global Const SPI_GETICONTITLELOGFONT = 31
Global Const SPI_SETDOUBLECLICKTIME = 32
Global Const SPI_SETMOUSEBUTTONSWAP = 33
Global Const SPI_SETICONTITLELOGFONT = 34
Global Const SPI_GETFASTTASKSWITCH = 35
Global Const SPI_SETFASTTASKSWITCH = 36


' SystemParametersInfo flags
Global Const SPIF_UPDATEINIFILE = &H1
Global Const SPIF_SENDWININICHANGE = &H2


Declare Function GetMessageExtraInfo Lib "User" () As Long
Declare Function GetQueueStatus Lib "User" (ByVal fuFlags As Integer) As Long


' GetQueueStatus flags
Global Const QS_KEY = &H1
Global Const QS_MOUSEMOVE = &H2
Global Const QS_MOUSEBUTTON = &H4
Global Const QS_MOUSE = (QS_MOUSEMOVE Or QS_MOUSEBUTTON)
Global Const QS_POSTMESSAGE = &H8
Global Const QS_TIMER = &H10
Global Const QS_PAINT = &H20
Global Const QS_SENDMESSAGE = &H40

Global Const QS_ALLINPUT = &H7F
```

GLOBALSYSME.FRM

```
Sub Form_Resize ()
        List1.Width = GetSysMet.ScaleWidth
        List1.Height = GetSysMet.ScaleHeight - (Command1.Height * 2)
        List1.Left = GetSysMet.Scaleleft
        List1.Top = GetSysMet.ScaleTop
End Sub


Sub ListFill (ModeType As Integer)
        Dim Msg As String
        Dim n As Integer
        Dim Number As String * 10
        ScaleMode = ModeType
        For n = 1 To 35
        Num& = GetSystemMetrics(n)
        Select Case n
          Case SM_CXBORDER
            Msg = " Width of window frame that cannot be sized"
          Case SM_CYBORDER
            Msg = " Height of window frame that cannot be sized."
```

```
Case SM_CYCAPTION
   Msg = " Height of caption"
Case SM_CXCURSOR
   Msg = " Width of cursor."
Case SM_CYCURSOR
   Msg = " Height of cursor."
Case SM_CXDOUBLECLK
   Msg = " Width of the rectangle around the first click"
Case SM_CYDOUBLECLK
   Msg = " Height of the rectangle around the first click"
Case SM_CXDLGFRAME
   Msg = " Width of frame when window has WS_DLGFRAME style."
Case SM_CYDLGFRAME
   Msg = " Height of frame when window has WS_DLGFRAME style."
Case SM_CXFRAME
   Msg = " Width of window frame that can be sized."
Case SM_CYFRAME
   Msg = " Height of window frame that can be sized."
Case SM_CXFULLSCREEN
   Msg = " Width of window client area for full-screen window."
Case SM_CYFULLSCREEN
   Msg = " Height of window client area for full-screen window."
Case SM_CXICON
   Msg = " Width of icon."
Case SM_CYICON
   Msg = " Height of icon."
Case SM_CXICONSPACING
   Msg = " Width of rectangles system uses to position tiled icons."
Case SM_CYICONSPACING
   Msg = " Height of rectangles system uses to position tiled icons."
Case SM_CYKANJIWINDOW
   Msg = " Height of Kanji window."
Case SM_CYMENU
   Msg = " Height of single-line menu bar. "
Case SM_CXMIN
   Msg = " Minimum width of window."
Case SM_CYMIN
   Msg = " Minimum height of window."
Case SM_CXMINTRACK
   Msg = " Minimum tracking width of window."
Case SM_CYMINTRACK
   Msg = " Minimum tracking height of window."
Case SM_CXSCREEN
   Msg = " Width of screen."
```

```
        Case SM_CYSCREEN
            Msg = " Height of screen."
        Case SM_CXHSCROLL
            Msg = " Width of arrow bitmap on horizontal scroll bar."
        Case SM_CYHSCROLL
            Msg = " Height of arrow bitmap on horizontal scroll bar."
        Case SM_CXVSCROLL
            Msg = " Width of arrow bitmap on vertical scroll bar."
        Case SM_CYVSCROLL
            Msg = " Height of arrow bitmap on vertical scroll bar."
        Case SM_CXSIZE
            Msg = " Width of bitmaps contained in the title bar."
        Case SM_CYSIZE
            Msg = " Height of bitmaps contained in the title bar."
        Case SM_CXHTHUMB
            Msg = " Width of thumb box on horizontal scroll bar."
        Case SM_CYVTHUMB
            Msg = " Height of thumb box on vertical scroll bar."
        Case SM_DBCSENABLED
            Msg = " Nonzero if current version of Windows uses double-byte characters."
        Case SM_DEBUG
            Msg = " Nonzero if Windows debugging version."
        End Select
        RSet Number = Format$(Num&, "###,##0")
        List1.AddItem Number + " - " + Msg
    Next n
End Sub


Sub Command1_Click ()
    ListClear
    ListFill (Twips)
End Sub


Sub Command2_Click ()
        ListClear
        ListFill (Pixels)
End Sub


Sub ListClear ()
    hWndOld% = GetFocus()
    List1.SetFocus
    x = SendMessage(GetFocus(), LB_RESETCONTENT, 0, 0)
    Suc% = SetFocusAPI(hWndOld%)
End Sub
```

SYSINFO.FRM

```
Sub TopList_Click ()
     ComboClear
     TaskList (TopLevel)
End Sub

Sub Master_Click ()
      TaskList (Task)
End Sub

Sub MasterList_Click ()
     ComboClear
     TaskList (Master)
End Sub

Sub Form_Click ()
     ComboClear
End Sub

Sub ComboClear ()
     hWndOld% = GetFocus()
     SysInfo.Combo1.SetFocus
     x = SendMessage(GetFocus(), CB_RESETCONTENT, 0, 0)
     Suc% = SetFocusAPI(hWndOld%)
     If SysInfo.Visible = TRUE Then TextSet
End Sub

Sub TextSet ()
     SysInfo.ListCnt.Caption = Str$(SysInfo.Combo1.ListCount)
     If Combo1.ListCount > 0 Then SysInfo.Combo1.ListIndex = 0
     SysInfo.ListCnt.Refresh
     SysInfo.TaskLabel.Refresh
End Sub

Sub TaskList (ListType As Integer)
     Dim ThisWnd As Integer
     Dim NameLen As Integer
     Dim ListItem As String

     ThisWnd = GetWindow(SysInfo.hWnd, GW_HWNDFIRST)    'read first handle
     Do Until ThisWnd = 0                               'more handles in list
      Select Case ListType                              'check request
      Case TopLevel                                     'top level only
        GotParent = GetParent(ThisWnd)                  'look for parent
        If GotParent = NULL Then                        'must be top
```

```
        NameLen = GetWindowTextLength(ThisWnd)           'title length
        GoSub ListFiller                                 'add to list
      End If
    Case Master                                          'all tasks
      NameLen = GetWindowTextLength(ThisWnd)             'title length
      GoSub ListFiller                                   'add to list
    End Select
    ThisWnd = GetWindow(ThisWnd, GW_HWNDNEXT)            'read next handle
    x = DoEvents()                                       'release CPU
  Loop
                                                         'change list title
    If ListType = Master Then
      SysInfo.TaskLabel.Caption = "Master Task List"
    Else
      SysInfo.TaskLabel.Caption = "Top Level Task List"
    End If
    If SysInfo.Visible = TRUE Then TextSet               'refresh labels
    Exit Sub

ListFiller:
    ListItem = Space$(NameLen + 2)                       'prep variable
    NameLen = GetWindowText(ThisWnd, ListItem, NameLen + 1)'get title
    ClassName$ = Space$(255)                             'prep variable
    ClassLen = GetClassName(ThisWnd, ClassName$, 255)    'read class
    If NameLen > 0 Then                                  'skip blanks
        SysInfo.Combo1.AddItem Mid$(ListItem, 1, NameLen) + " - " + ClassName$
    End If
    Return
End Sub


Sub GetMetrics ()
    '---Free RAM
    SysInfo.Label1(1).Caption = Format$(GetFreeSpace(0), "###,###,000") + " bytes"
    '---Free Contiguous RAM
    SysInfo.Label1(2).Caption = Format$(GlobalCompact(0), "###,###,000") + " bytes"
    '---Free Resources Measures
    SysInfo.Label1(3).Caption = Str$(GetFreeSystemResources(NULL)) + "%"
    SysInfo.Label1(4).Caption = Str$(GetFreeSystemResources(1)) + "%"
    SysInfo.Label1(5).Caption = Str$(GetFreeSystemResources(2)) + "%"
    '---Windows Version
    version% = GetVersion()
    LowByte$ = Str$(version% And &HFF)                    ' masking off high byte
    HighByte$ = LTrim$(Str$((version% And &HFF00) / 256)) ' mask off low byte and
    ...shift
```

```
SysInfo.Label1(13).Caption = LowByte$ + "." + HighByte$ ' combine and display
...version
'---Windows Directory
PointerBuffer$ = Space$(255)
LenChars% = GetWindowsDirectory(PointerBuffer$, 255)
SysInfo.Label1(16).Caption = Left$(PointerBuffer$, LenChars%)
'---Windows System Directory
PointerBuffer$ = Space$(255)
LenChars% = GetSystemDirectory(PointerBuffer$, 255)
SysInfo.Label1(17).Caption = Left$(PointerBuffer$, LenChars%)
'---Build Task List
SysInfo.TopList.Value = TRUE
TaskList (Task)
'---Count Tasks Running
SysInfo.Label5.Caption = Str$(GetNumTasks())
'---Time Since Windows Started
GetCount
'---Get CPU Type
Dim dWords As Long
dWords = GetWinFlags()
If (dWords And WF_CPU486) = WF_CPU486 Then
  CPU$ = "486"
ElseIf (dWords And WF_CPU386) = WF_CPU386 Then
  CPU$ = "386"
Else
  CPU$ = "286"
End If
SysInfo.Label1(19).Caption = CPU$
'---Get Mode of Operation
If (dWords And WF_ENHANCED) Then
  SysInfo.Label1(20).Caption = "Enhanced"
Else
  SysInfo.Label1(20).Caption = "Standard"
End If
'---Get the types of drives in the system
Alpha$ = "ABCDEFGHIJKLMNOPQRSTUVWXYZ"          'set drive letter array
Do
    DriveType% = DriveType% + 1                'count drive types
    Drv$ = Mid$(Alpha$, DriveType%, 1)         'match to letter
    x% = GetDriveType(DriveType% - 1)          'read type of drive
    If x% = 0 And DriveType% <> 2 Then         'exit at end of drive lies
      Combo2.Text = Combo2.List(0)             'set first drive display
      Exit Do
    ElseIf x% = 0 And DriveType% = 2 Then      'skip over B drive if none
      ' MsgBox "No B drive"
```

```
        Else
          Select Case x%                      'pick drive type
            Case DRIVE_REMOVABLE
                Msg$ = " Removable (Floppy) Disk"
            Case DRIVE_FIXED
                Msg$ = " Fixed Disk"
            Case DRIVE_REMOTE
                Msg$ = " Remote or network drive"
          End Select
          Combo2.AddItem "Drive " + Drv$ + ":" + Msg$ 'add to list
        End If
    Loop
End Sub


Sub SysMetrics_Click ()
     GetSysMet.Show
End Sub

Sub Command1_Click ()
     GetMetrics
End Sub

Sub Timer1_Timer ()
    GetCount
End Sub

Sub GetCount ()
    SysInfo.Label1(18).Caption = Format$((GetCurrentTime() / 1000000) / 60, "hh:mm:ss")
End Sub

Sub Form_Load ()
     SysInfo.Visible = TRUE
     GetMetrics
End Sub

Sub Quit_Click ()
     Unload SysInfo
End Sub

Sub SystemParms_Click ()
     SysParm.Show
End Sub

Sub Check1_Click ()
```

```
      If Check1.Value = OFF Then
        SysInfo.Combo1.SetFocus
        x% = SetWindowPos(SysInfo.hWnd, HWND_NOTOPMOST, 0, 0, 0, 0, SWP_NOSIZE)
      Else
        SysInfo.Combo1.SetFocus
        x% = SetWindowPos(SysInfo.hWnd, HWND_TOPMOST, 0, 0, 0, 0, SWP_NOSIZE)
      End If
End Sub
```

SYSPARM.FRM

```
Sub Form_Resize ()
        List1.Width = SysParm.ScaleWidth
        List1.Height = SysParm.ScaleHeight - (Command1.Height + (Command1.Height * .05))
        List1.Left = SysParm.Scaleleft
        List1.Top = SysParm.ScaleTop
End Sub


Sub Command1_Click ()
    Unload SysParm
End Sub


Sub Form_Load ()
    'SysParam.Visible = TRUE
    For n = 1 To 35
      Select Case n
        Case SPI_GETBEEP
            Msg$ = "Retrieves a BOOL value that indicates whether the warning beeper
            ...is on or off. "
            u% = SystemParametersInfo(SPI_GETBEEP, NULL, lpiParam, NULL)
            If lpiParam = TRUE Then
              List1.AddItem "On - " + Msg$
            Else
              List1.AddItem "Off - " + Msg$
            End If
        Case SPI_GETMOUSE
            'Msg$ = "Retrieves the mouse speed and the mouse threshold values."
            'u% = SystemParametersInfo(SPI_GETMOUSE, NULL, lpiParam, NULL)
            List1.AddItem Msg$
            List1.AddItem "Threshold 1"
            List1.AddItem "Threshold 2"
            List1.AddItem "Speed"
        Case SPI_GETBORDER
            Msg$ = "Retrieves the border multiplier to determines the width of a
            ...window's sizing border."
```

```
        u% = SystemParametersInfo(SPI_GETBORDER, NULL, lpiParam, NULL)
        List1.AddItem Str$(lpiParam) + " " + Msg$
    Case SPI_GETKEYBOARDSPEED
        Msg$ = "Retrieves the keyboard repeat-speed setting. "
        u% = SystemParametersInfo(SPI_GETKEYBOARDSPEED, NULL, lpiParam, NULL)
        List1.AddItem Str$(lpiParam) + " " + Msg$
    Case SPI_LANGDRIVER
        Msg$ = "Forces the user to load a new language driver."
        u% = SystemParametersInfo(SPI_LANGDRIVER, NULL, lpiParam, NULL)
        List1.AddItem Str$(lpiParam) + " " + Msg$
    Case SPI_ICONHORIZONTALSPACING
        Msg$ = "Sets the height (in pixels) of an icon cell. "
        u% = SystemParametersInfo(SPI_ICONHORIZONTALSPACING, NULL, lpiParam, NULL)
        List1.AddItem Str$(lpiParam) + " " + Msg$
    Case SPI_GETSCREENSAVETIMEOUT
        Msg$ = "Retrieves the screen-saver time-out value. "
        u% = SystemParametersInfo(SPI_GETSCREENSAVETIMEOUT, NULL, lpiParam, NULL)
        List1.AddItem Str$(lpiParam) + " " + Msg$
    Case SPI_GETSCREENSAVEACTIVE
        Msg$ = "Retrieves a BOOL value that indicates whether screen saving is on
        ...or off."
        u% = SystemParametersInfo(SPI_GETSCREENSAVEACTIVE, NULL, lpiParam, NULL)
        If lpiParam = TRUE Then
          List1.AddItem "Active -  " + Msg$
        Else
          List1.AddItem "Inactive -  " + Msg$
        End If
    Case SPI_GETGRIDGRANULARITY
        Msg$ = "Retrieves the current granularity value of the desktop sizing
        ...grid. "
        u% = SystemParametersInfo(SPI_GETGRIDGRANULARITY, NULL, lpiParam, NULL)
        List1.AddItem Str$(lpiParam) + " " + Msg$
    Case SPI_GETKEYBOARDDELAY
        Msg$ = "Retrieves the keyboard repeat-delay setting. "
        u% = SystemParametersInfo(SPI_GETKEYBOARDDELAY, NULL, lpiParam, NULL)
        List1.AddItem Str$(lpiParam) + " " + Msg$
    Case SPI_ICONVERTICALSPACING
        Msg$ = "Sets the height (in pixels) of an icon cell. "
        u% = SystemParametersInfo(SPI_ICONVERTICALSPACING, NULL, lpiParam, NULL)
        List1.AddItem Str$(lpiParam) + " " + Msg$
    Case SPI_GETICONTITLEWRAP
        Msg$ = "Determines whether icon title wrapping is on or off. "
        u% = SystemParametersInfo(SPI_GETICONTITLEWRAP, NULL, lpiParam, NULL)
        If lpiParam = TRUE Then
          List1.AddItem "On - " + Msg$
```

```
            Else
               List1.AddItem "Off -  " + Msg$
            End If
         Case SPI_GETMENUDROPALIGNMENT
            Msg$ = "Determines whether pop-up menus are left or right aligned relative
            ...to the menu-bar item."
            u% = SystemParametersInfo(SPI_GETMENUDROPALIGNMENT, NULL, lpiParam, NULL)
            If lpiParam = TRUE Then
               List1.AddItem "Right Aligned -  " + Msg$
            Else
               List1.AddItem "Left Aligned -  " + Msg$
            End If
         Case SPI_GETFASTTASKSWITCH
            Msg$ = "Determines whether fast task switching is on or off. "
            u% = SystemParametersInfo(SPI_GETFASTTASKSWITCH, NULL, lpiParam, NULL)
            If lpiParam = TRUE Then
               List1.AddItem "On -  " + Msg$
            Else
               List1.AddItem "Off -  " + Msg$
            End If
      End Select
   Next n
End Sub
```

The Player Sample Application

Global

```
Global Const TRUE = -1
Global Const FALSE = 0
Global SoundFile As String


'Sound Declarations
'MultiMedia DLL Driver
Declare Function sndPlaySound Lib "MMsystem" (ByVal lpSound As String, ByVal Flags As
...Integer) As Integer
Declare Sub mciExecute Lib "MMsystem" (ByVal CmdString As String)


'Windows SOUND.DRV Driver
Declare Function StartSound Lib "Sound" () As Integer
Declare Function SetVoiceQueSize Lib "Sound" (ByVal nVoice As Integer, ByVal nBytes As
...Integer) As Integer
Declare Function SetVoiceSound Lib "Sound" (ByVal nVoice As Integer, ByVal lFrequency
...As Long, ByVal nDuration As Integer) As Integer
Declare Function StartSound Lib "Sound" () As Integer
Declare Sub CloseSound Lib "Sound" ()
```

```
'Sound Constants
Global Const SND_SYNC = &H0        ' play synchronously (default)
Global Const SND_ASYNC = &H1       ' play asynchronously
Global Const SND_NODEFAULT = &H2   ' don't use default sound
Global Const SND_MEMORY = &H4      ' lpszSoundName points to a memory file
Global Const SND_LOOP = &H8        ' loop the sound until next sndPlaySound
Global Const SND_NOSTOP = &H10     ' don't stop any currently playing sound
```

VBPLAY.FRM

```
Sub MMControl1_PlayClick (Cancel As Integer)
        MMControl1.DeviceType = "WaveAudio"
End Sub


Sub Form_Load ()
        MMControl1.Enabled = TRUE
        MMControl1.AutoEnable = TRUE
        MMControl1.FileName = SoundFile
        MMControl1.Command = "Open"
End Sub


Sub Form_Unload (Cancel As Integer)
        MMControl1.Command = "Close"
End Sub


Sub Form_Resize ()
        MMControl1.Width = VBXPlay.ScaleWidth
        MMControl1.Left = VBXPlay.Scaleleft
        For n = 1 To 9
          Label1(n).Top = MMControl1.Top + MMControl1.Height
          Label1(n).Left = NextWidth&
          NextWidth& = NextWidth& + MMControl1.Width / 9
          Label1(n).AutoSize = TRUE
        Next
        ReLabel
End Sub


Sub Form_Paint ()
    ReLabel
End Sub


Sub ReLabel ()
        Label1(1).Caption = "Back"
        Label1(2).Caption = "Step"
        Label1(3).Caption = "Play"
```

```
        Label1(4).Caption = "Pause"
        Label1(5).Caption = "Prev"
        Label1(6).Caption = "Next"
        Label1(7).Caption = "Stop"
        Label1(8).Caption = "Record"
        Label1(9).Caption = "Eject"
        x% = DoEvents()
End Sub


Sub Label1_Change (Index As Integer)
        ReLabel
End Sub
```

PLAYER.FRM

```
Sub Drive1_Change ()
        Dir1.Path = Drive1.Drive
End Sub


Sub Dir1_Change ()
    File1.Path = Dir1.Path
End Sub


Sub File1_DblClick ()
    FileCheck
    PlaySound
End Sub


Sub Form_Load ()
    File1.Pattern = "*.WAV"
End Sub


Sub Start_Click (Index As Integer)
        FileCheck
        Select Case Index
            Case 0
                PlaySound
            Case 1
                mciSounds
            Case 2
                VBXPlay.Show
            Case 3
                SoundDriver
        End Select
End Sub
```

```
Sub PlaySound ()
     x% = sndPlaySound(SoundFile, SND_ASYNC)
End Sub

Sub FileCheck ()
        If File1.FileName <> "" Then
          SoundFile = Dir1.Path + "\" + File1.FileName
        Else
          MsgBox "Please Select A '.WAV' file"
          File1.SetFocus
        End If
End Sub


Sub SoundDriver ()

End Sub

Sub mciSounds ()
    CmdStr$ = "open " + SoundFile + " type WaveAudio alias mysound"
    mciExecute (CmdStr$)
    mciExecute ("play mysound wait")
    mciExecute ("close mysound")
End Sub
```

Chapter 6

Dynamic Link Libraries

Executable programs exist in two basic flavors. First is the traditional EXE file extension, which usually serves as the start-up program for most applications. In fact, C-language compilers talk about including "start-up" code along with the "main" statement in the primary executable program. The second form of executable program is called a **dynamic link library** (DLL). Programs of this type carry an extension of EXE when compiled as executable programs and DLL for an extension to the file name when created by means of IMPLIB and LIB.EXE. If you look in the \WINDOWS\SYSTEM subdirectory where you installed Microsoft Windows, you'll see several DLLs with the EXE extension: KERNEL.EXE, USER.EXE, and so on. In Chapter 5, I discussed how to access the functions inside those DLLs. Not to be confused with "import libraries," which resolve calls to an API at link time, DLLs provide new functionality when called upon by an application. In this chapter, we'll explore using DLLs in Visual Basic.

The DLL containing most of the functions for Visual Basic (VBRUNXXX.DLL) is not linked into each program created under Visual Basic. If it were, then those functions would be said to be **static linked** into VB.EXE. In that case, it is likely that each program created with VB.EXE would require those functions to be statically linked in as well, resulting in very large executable programs. Instead, the functions in VBRUNXXX.DLL are loaded into the Windows environment when a Visual Basic program or the programming environment itself loads. The VBRUNXXX.DLL containing the functions unloads when the last of the Visual Basic programs unloads. Table 6-1 shows the 88 functions contained in VBRUNXXX.DLL.

Table 6-1   *These API calls load when you load VB.EXE, an EXE program created in Visual Basic using the Visual Basic Dynamic Link Library (VBRUNXXX.DLL)*

VBAllocPic	VBDirtyForm	VBGetVariantType	VBRestoreFPState
VBAllocPicEx	VBFireEvent	VBGetVariantValue	VBRuntimeError
VBArrayBounds	VBFormat	VBGetVersion	VBScreenToClient
VBArrayElement	VBFreePic	VBInvalidateRect	VBSeekBasicFile
VBArrayElemSize	VBGetAppTitle	VBIsControlEnabled	VBSeekFormFile
VBArrayFirstElem	VBGetCapture	VBIsControlVisible	VBSendControlMsg
VBArrayIndexCount	VBGetClientRect	VBLinkMakeItemName	VBSetCapture
VBCbSaveFPState	VBGetControl	VBLinkPostAdvise	VBSetControlFlags
VBClientToScreen	VBControlHwnd	VBLockHsz	VBSetControlProperty
VBCoerce Variant	VBControlModel	VBMoveControl	VBSetErrorMessage
VBcreateHlstr	VBControlProperty	VBPaletteChanged	VBSetHlstr
VBCreateHsz	VBCOntrolRect	VBPasteLinkOk	VBSetVariantvalue
VBCreateTempHlstr	VBGetDataSourceControl	VBPicFromCF	VBSuperControlProc
VBDefControlProc	VBGetHInstance	VBReadBasicFile	VBTranslateColor
VBDerefControl	VBGetHlstr	VBReadFormFile	VBUnlockHsz
VBDerefHlstr	VBGetHlstrLen	VBRecreateControlHwnd	VBUpdateControl
VBDerefHlstrLen	VBGetHwndControl	VBRefPic	VBWriteBasicFile
VBDerefHsz	VBGetMode	VBRegisterModel	VBWriteFormFile
VBDerefZeroTermHlstr	VBGetModel	VBReleaseCapture	VBXPixelsToTwips
VBDestroyHlstr	VBGetPic	VBRelSeekBasicFile	VBXTwipsToPixels
VBDestroyHsz	VBGetPicEx	VBRelSeekFormFile	VBYPixelsToPixels
VBDialogBoxParam	VBGetRectInContainer	VBResizeHistr	VBYTwipsToPixels
			VBZOrder

Tip: For other DLLs you find, you can locate the function list by using the EXEHDR program included with some versions of Microsoft's compilers. By passing the DLL file name to EXEHDR, you can get a list of the functions available in that DLL.

DLLs provide greater functionality to a program, conserve memory by loading and unloading as required, and reduce disk space: one DLL can be used by several applications. DLLs also serve a handy role in turning existing source code into a Windows-compatible program. By allowing Windows to manage the memory used by the DLL, programs that are otherwise unruly can be made to behave a little better. You can have DLLs, such as those containing the fonts, that do not contain either code or data but yet share resources among Windows applications.

A dynamic link library and an executable Windows program differ in important ways. The Windows program contains an entry point that describes the private stack for that application. A DLL does not own a stack. A Windows program can have multiple instances (depending on the memory model, of course). A DLL can be loaded only once, even though multiple programs may use its functions. Compilers often post a warning regarding local variables with some sort of notice such as "DS != SS"; therefore the local variable definition was assumed. That occurs because DLLs do not have their own stack; they share the stack of the application that called them. DS stands for "data segment," and SS stands for "stack segment." A normal Windows application compiled under the small model (in C) stores data in its own local stack, so DS equals SS.

The Structure of a Dynamic Link Library

Figure 6-1 shows the structure for the code in a dynamic link library. The traditional WinMain statement is replaced by LibMain. For most DLLs, the segments of code for LibMain and the Windows Exit Procedure (WEP) can be included without changing any part—though the WEP segment is often used to perform some sort of clean-up when the DLL unloads from memory.

You must link the LIBENTRY.OBJ file with your DLL or compile the LIBENTRY.ASM file that accompanies the Windows Software Development Kit. When the DLL is called, Libentry actually makes the call to LibMain and returns the success or failure of the call to your Windows. In a normal Windows program, DOS passes variables in registers to the start-up code and uses registers to initialize some global variables (like the environment). Since DLLs don't contain that start-up code, the Libentry module performs that task. In his book *Programming Windows*, Charles Petzold gives a list of the variables that are initialized in this manner and therefore cannot be manipulated by the DLL.

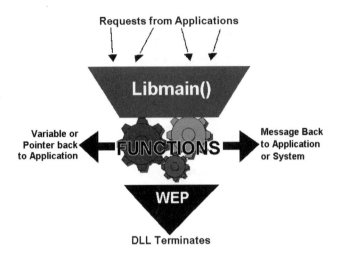

Requests from Applications

Libmain()

Variable or
Pointer back
to Application

FUNCTIONS

Message Back
to Application
or System

WEP

DLL Terminates

Figure 6-1   *The LibMain and WEP procedures provide the framework for the functions contained in a dynamic link library.*

A typical LibMain procedure, as shown in Listing 6-1, contains the information for initializing the DLL. If this function terminates with an error, then the application that calls for the function inside the DLL will be terminated by Windows. If it initializes successfully, then control passes to the function inside the DLL. The call to the Unlock statement in LibMain also determines if the dynamic-link data segment occupied by this DLL will be locked. Notice the variable lpszCmdLine in Listing 6-1. You can pass a string of parameters from the command line to the DLL if you choose.

Listing 6-1   *The LibMain procedure initializes the DLL and returns nonzero if it is successful, otherwise it terminates the DLL and returns null or false.*

```
int FAR PASCAL LibMain (hInst, wDataSeg, cbHeapSize, lpszCmdLine)
unsigned int hInst;
WORD wDataSeg;
WORD cbHeapSize;
LPSTR lpszCmdLine;
        {
        if (cbHeapSize != 0)
            UnlockData(0);
        return 1;
        }
```

The WEP (or Windows Exit Procedure) is the second standard element that must be included in a DLL. Windows calls this procedure when the DLL unloads. The nParameter shown in Listing 6-2 passes the information about whether Windows itself is terminating (SYSTEMEXIT in Borland C++ and WEP_SYSTEM_EXIT in Microsoft C) or if only this DLL is terminating (WEP_FREE_DLL in Microsoft C). You can make decisions about what type of clean-up you wish to do depending on the value passed.

Listing 6-2   *The Windows Exit Procedure gives you a place to perform clean-up for memory or other items when the DLL terminates.*

```
int FAR PASCAL WEP (int nParameter)
    {
    return(1);
    }
```

> **Tip:** *In Borland C++ and some other compilers you need not include an explicit WEP procedure (unless you need to perform special clean-up), because the compiler will include it automatically.*

The third type of file you will need, other than the modules themselves for the functions to be made available in the DLL, is the module definition file, which usually appears as a file with the DEF extension. In Borland C++ you need not create an explicit DEF file, because the IMPDEF utility will create it for you. In fact, due to a pitfall with C++ and mangled names, you can use IMPDEF to troubleshoot by manually creating the DEF file. To do this, you pass IMPDEF the name of your failing DLL.

> **Tip:** *"Mangling" in C++ supports overloading. To differentiate between two identically named functions that return different types, the C++ compilers add identification symbols to each name to allow the compiler to differentiate between the two functions during operation.*

Listing 6-3 shows the DEF file for the first DLL that will be demonstrated in this chapter. For programmers familiar with C, the DEF changes little for DLLs except to change the program to a library. Since multiple instances of a DLL cannot be loaded, the SINGLE key word applies. The STUB specification that appears in C programs for Windows does not appear in a DLL module definition. STUB usually specifies the program to run if someone tries to launch a Windows application from outside Windows. Since DLLs cannot be launched from the command line and will be called only from a program in Windows, this line—though it will compile—will have no effect.

Listing 6-3   *The module definition file for a DLL lists the functions to be exported for use by other applications.*

```
LIBRARY FREEDISK
DESCRIPTION 'DLL to get disk information'
EXETYPE WINDOWS
CODE MOVEABLE DISCARDABLE
DATA MOVEABLE SINGLE
HEAPSIZE 1024
EXPORTS
    WEP                              @1 RESIDENTNAME
    SpaceSpec   @2
```

Caution: *If you name your DLL with the same name as the program from which you will call the DLL, an error will result. When launching an application, Windows checks the module list to see if an instance of the application is already running. If Windows tries to load a DLL with the same name as a program already in the list, the DLL will not load, because you cannot run multiple instances of a DLL. Furthermore, if the DLL is already running when launched by another application, the new application will not load.*

Creating functions not directly supported in Visual Basic serves as one of the most useful roles for DLLs in the Visual Basic environment. It might seem to be the only role, but reproducing some existing functions with slight changes or even creating resource-only DLLs can be done also. The third-party market for custom controls and other DLLs continues to grow with large libraries of functionality from Microhelp, Crescent, Sheridan Software and others. The Professional Edition from Microsoft contains a control that senses the states of the Caps Lock, Num Lock, Insert, and Scroll Lock keys on the keyboard. In the remainder of this chapter, I'll show you how to create four DLLs that will give you functions for your Visual Basic programs that do not appear in the language.

Microsoft Quick C For Windows: Disk Space

Visual Basic does not provide a command or statement to retrieve information on disk space capacity and availability. The API for Windows itself does not supply a single call to get this information, either. You can find out if a drive exists by using the Drive property in a Drive List Box control or by calling the ChDrive statement. The Microsoft C language provides the getdiskfree statement for filling a structure with information regarding disk space. Crescent Software's QuickPac Professional offers two functions: DiskRoom for free space and DiskSize for total space. In this case, Quick C for Windows is the environment used to create the DLL. Figure 6-2 shows how the environment looks when it is loaded with the source files for the DLL.

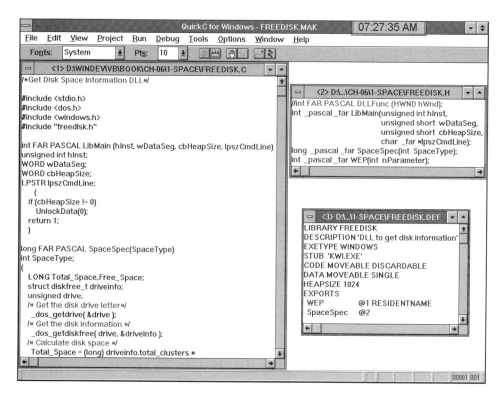

Figure 6-2 *The Quick C for Windows environment shows the source code for creating the disk space DLL that is used in a Visual Basic program.*

To create this DLL, you first create a C source file containing the header references for WINDOWS.H and other libraries from which you will be calling functions. If the DLL function will lend itself to the practice, it's a good idea to write the program as a stand-alone executable that returns a value to the screen, to a file, or to the printer. That will allow you to test and debug the program without leaving the environment. (The debugging utility in Quick C for Windows as well as Microsoft's Codeview, Borland's Turbo Debugger, and Clarion's Topspeed Visual Interactive Debugger will allow you to access a Visual Basic DLL even though the Visual Basic program contains no debugging information.) To compile the Disk Space DLL into an executable, follow these steps:

1. Include in the project the relevant files.
2. Comment out the LibMain and WEP functions.
3. Create a main() function that calls the SpaceSpec function, or comment out the SpaceSpec function (and its prototype in the .H include file) and replace it with a main() statement.
4. Remove the comments surrounding the printf calls.
5. Compile the program without reference to the Libentry module in the link list, and use the DOS EXE compiler defaults.

After you have tested and debugged the function (if possible) as a stand-alone executable, you can reconvert the program to proper DLL format and recompile as a Windows DLL. The source code for the SpaceSpec function appears in Listing 6-4.

Listing 6-4   *The SpaceSpec function returns the total disk space or the free disk space of the default disk drive, depending on the value for the SpaceType variable passed by the Visual Basic caller.*

```
long FAR PASCAL SpaceSpec(SpaceType)
int SpaceType;
{
        LONG Total_Space,Free_Space;
        struct diskfree_t driveinfo;
        unsigned drive;
        /* Get the disk drive letter*/
          _dos_getdrive( &drive );
        /* Get the disk information */
```

```
    _dos_getdiskfree( drive, &driveinfo );
/* Calculate disk space */
  Total_Space = (long) driveinfo.total_clusters *
                      driveinfo.sectors_per_cluster *
                      driveinfo.bytes_per_sector;
  Free_Space = (long) driveinfo.avail_clusters *
                      driveinfo.sectors_per_cluster *
                      driveinfo.bytes_per_sector;
/*Use to test EXE for correct processing inside DLL
  printf("Total Disk Space = %ld\n",Total_Space);
  printf("Free Disk Space = %ld\n",Free_Space);
*/
if (SpaceType == 1)
 return(Total_Space);
else
 return(Free_Space);
```

The SpaceSpec function uses the diskfree_t structure, the dos_getdrive, and dos_getdiskfree functions in Quick C to read the disk space values. By calling dos_getdrive, you get the default disk drive (where the program is running at the time of execution) and supply it to the dos_getdiskfree function. After these calls, the diskfree_t structure called driveinfo contains the information about the disk. The next step is to calculate the total and free disk space based on the values in driveinfo. Finally, the Visual Basic program called the SpaceSpec function and passed it an integer determining which type of information the function should return. Notice that the SpaceSpec function has a return value of a long integer as specified in the function definition:

```
long FAR PASCAL SpaceSpec(SpaceType)
```

As I'll cover in the next example, you cannot physically pass a string back to a Visual Basic program. You must use pointers even though Visual BAsic does not support a pointer itself. In this case, the numeric value contains the information needed. (A long pointer to a string (LPSTR) would require additional conversion.) Now you can write a Visual Basic application to call the function by following these steps:

1. Define the constants TOTAL and FREE, and declare the function in GLOBAL.BAS:

```
Global Const TOTAL = 1
Global Const FREE = 2
Declare Function SpaceSpec Lib "FREEDISK.DLL" (ByVal SpaceAmt As Integer)
...As Long
```

2. Create two labels with descriptions of the values to be shown.

3. Create two labels for displaying the values returned from the function:

```
Sub Form_Load ()
    Label1(0).Caption = Format$(SpaceSpec(TOTAL), "###,###,###,##0") + " bytes"
    Label1(1).Caption = Format$(SpaceSpec(FREE), "###,###,##0") + " bytes"
End Sub
```

After you have properly entered the code for calling the function, you can run the program, which should result in a screen that looks like the one shown in Figure 6-3.

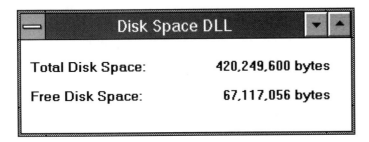

Figure 6-3   *The Disk Space DLL Visual Basic application uses the SpaceSpec function to find total and free disk space. The long return value was formatted with separating commas by means of the Format$ function.*

One advantage of the Quick C for Windows environment appears when you debug your DLL. Visual Basic does not have a compilation and therefore does not contain debugging or symbolic information. However, you can set up the debugger in Quick C for Windows to load the DLL anyway. Simply create an EXE of your Visual Basic program and place the EXE in the Run/Debug selection under Options in Quick C for Windows, along with a reference to your DLL. When you select Go under the Run menu or press F5, the environment will try to load your Visual Basic application and present the dialog shown in Figure 6-4.

Simply click on Yes to continue, and the DLL will load when your application calls it. You can place breakpoints in the DLL code as well as set Watch variables and employ the same methods you would use to debug a normal program written in C.

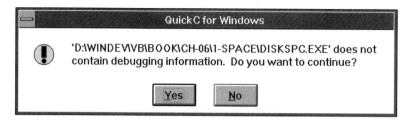

Figure 6-4   *Visual Basic EXE files do not contain debugging information, but you can still debug DLLs called from Visual Basic.*

Borland C++: File Date and Time

Another function not supported in Visual Basic 1.0 was the ability to manage the date-and-time stamp on a file. Visual Basic 2.0 rectified that—at least partially—by providing the FileDateTime function. Using FileDateTime, you can retrieve a file's date or time stamp by passing a file name and then using the Format statement to extract the date or time. As with the disk space DLL, the Windows API won't help Visual Basic 1.0 users at all, and nowhere does Visual Basic support changing the file-date-and-time stamp. In this example, we will look at the use of objects in a C++ DLL as well as introduce the methods for passing strings into and out of a DLL from Visual Basic to retrieve and change the date and time for a file.

The same steps used in the creation of the disk space DLL will be needed for the file information DLL. Borland's C++ environment offers two advantages over Quick C for Windows. Borland's environment does not require that you include the WEP function, because it will be added automatically during the compile. Borland also does not require that you specify a module definition or DEF file, because that also will be created during the link phase. The screen in Figure 6-5 shows the C++ Interactive Development Environment (IDE) from Borland loaded with the file information DLL project.

Figure 6-5 shows most of the OBJECTS.H file used in this example. This file contains the C++ object that will be used to read the file. By default, the variables given just below the Class definition will be private and can be modified only by functions given in the public section. The functions defined in the public section will be used in the main body of the project.

Again, this program includes the code necessary to test the program as a stand-alone executable file. In this case, you can either (1) force defaults on the values to be passed eventually by the Visual Basic program, or (2) enter values at prompts on the screen during the test. Repeat the procedures given in the disk space DLL example for converting the program to using a standard main() entry point for preparing the EXE. When you've debugged the code for any changes you make, you can revert the program to the DLL settings.

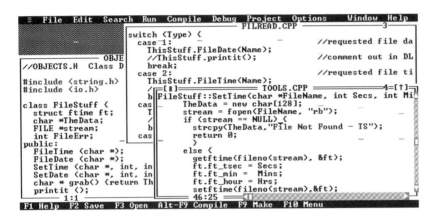

```
≡ File  Edit  Search  Run  Compile  Debug  Project  Options  Window  Help
                              ┌──────── FILREAD.CPP ──────────────3──┐
                     switch (Type) {
                       case 1:
                         ThisStuff.FileDate(Name);          //requested file da
         ──── OBJE       //ThisStuff.printit();            //comment out in DL
//OBJECTS.H  Class D     break;
                       case 2:
#include <string.h>      ThisStuff.FileTime(Name);          //requested file ti
#include <io.h>         /┌─[■]════════════ TOOLS.CPP ═══════════4=[↑]═┐
                       b│FileStuff::SetTime(char *FileName, int Secs, int Mi│
class FileStuff {    cas│   TheData = new char[128];                         │
  struct ftime ft;     T│   stream = fopen(FileName, "rb");                  │
  char *TheData;       /│   if (stream == NULL) {                            │
  FILE *stream;        b│     strcpy(TheData,"File Not Found - TS");         │
  int FileErr;       cas│     return 0;                                      │
public:                 │   }                                                │
  FileTime (char *);    │   else {                                          │
  FileDate (char *);    │     getftime(fileno(stream), &ft);                 │
  SetTime (char *, int, in│   ft.ft_tsec = Secs;                            │
  SetDate (char *, int, in│   ft.ft_min  = Mins;                            │
  char * grab() {return Th│   ft.ft_hour = Hrs;                             │
  printit ();           │     setftime(fileno(stream),&ft);                 │
 ──── 1:1               ═ 46:25 ═╧▓▓▓▓▓▓▓▓▓▓▓▓▓▓▓▓▓▓▓▓▓▓▓▓▓▓▓▓▓▓═┘
 F1 Help  F2 Save  F3 Open  Alt-F9 Compile  F9 Make  F10 Menu
```

Figure 6-5   *The Borland C++ Interactive Development Environment shows the files that have been loaded into the FILREAD project. The object that lets you change the time stamp on a file appears in the lower-right corner and in the selection statements for returning the correct information in the main window for FILREAD.CPP.*

Strings in C and Visual Basic

Visual Basic and C handle strings differently. As a result, you must use long pointers to strings in the DLL to pass information between a DLL and its Visual Basic caller. In C, a string terminates with the appearance of the first null character. C does not consider the string to be terminated until it finds a null, and does not recognize the string unless it is null terminated. Visual Basic, in contrast, terminates the string automatically on its own and does not allow null characters to appear in the string. For example, the phrase "Strings terminate" + Chr$(0) + "with nulls in C" will be recognized in its entirety in Visual Basic, but C will recognize only "Strings terminate" as the valid string, leaving the rest of the phrase hanging out "in mid-air" in memory. Such garbage in memory can easily create an error. This difference in string handling creates a second major problem when you pass a string for modification to a DLL. If the string is not long enough, the DLL cannot extend the length and in some cases will simply write beyond the end of the string and overwrite inappropriate memory locations that might hang the system.

The two answers required to handle the differences in strings between C and Visual Basic involve pointers and prepadding strings. First, you must pass a string to most DLLs by using a variable. If the DLL was not written specifically for Visual Basic, you run the risk of corrupting memory. In fact, to stay on the safe side when writing your own DLLs, you should use pointers. Secondly, when you receive a pointer (or a string itself) from a DLL into Visual Basic, you must either dimension the variable to a fixed length or pad the variable with spaces. Otherwise, Visual Basic may receive a string from the DLL into a variable that is not large enough to hold the string.

File Date and Time

Listing 6-5 shows the main function procedure for FILREAD.DLL written in Borland C++. This example demonstrates how to use C++ objects in a DLL, how to pass strings and read the file date and time, and how to change the file date and time. The first thing to notice about FILREAD is the function declaration. C++ supports a feature called **function overloading**. Essentially, this means that you can use the same function name within the same class providing that it returns a different variable type. In addition, you can use the same function and variable names inside different classes. To distinguish between these like-named items, C++ "mangles" the name—that is, it takes the identifiable part of the name and adds some other identifiers onto it to ensure that the name remains unique. This name mangling can create confusion when you try to call the function from inside Visual Basic. To remove the cause of confusion, you must define the function by using the keywords 'extern "C"'. That permits the export module definition to contain the identifiable function call.

The second thing to notice (or miss, I should say) is the lack of a module definition file at all! Borland C++ does not require that you create a separate module definition. However, you must use the _export keyword just before the function name, as shown in Listing 6-5. That will prompt the library programs IMPLIB and LIB to create the proper declarations for the function.

In these examples, the Visual Basic program that calls the FILREAD DLL passes an integer and a string. The switch statement in Listing 6-5 uses the integer to determine which of the functions to call in the class FileStuff, and the string contains the file name and path that will be passed to the selected function. Notice that the

FileName variable is a far pointer to a string in the Visual Basic program. Then the lstrcpy function moves that data to a local string for operation by the objects in the FileStuff class.

Listing 6-5   *The primary function for the FILREAD.DLL shows how to call C++ objects and return a string to retrieve the date-and-time stamp from a DOS file.*

```
#include <windows.h>
#include <stdlib.h>
#include <iostream.h>
#include <stdio.h>
#include "objects.h"

extern "C" char * FAR PASCAL FilRead (int Type, char *FileName, int SecDay,
...int MinMo, int HrYr); //comment out of exe

char * FAR PASCAL _export FilRead (int Type, char *FileName, int SecDay,
...int MinMo, int HrYr)
//int main(int Type, char *FileName)      //use in EXE instead
{
 FileStuff ThisStuff;
 static char Name[4096];
    lstrcpy(Name,FileName);                //retrieve text of name
                                           //comment out in EXE

    //Use in EXE to test parameters
    //Type == 1;                           //1=date,2=time
    //strcpy(Name,"test.fil");             //force time zone
    //or enter your own
    // cout << "Enter the file info type name: ";
    //    cin >> Type;
    // cout << "Enter the file name: ";
    //    cin >> Name;
    //or comment out up to the blank line for the DLL

  switch (Type) {
    case 1:                                //requested file date
      ThisStuff.FileDate(Name);
      //ThisStuff.printit();               //comment out in DLL
      break;
    case 2:                                //requested file time
      ThisStuff.FileTime(Name);
      //ThisStuff.printit();               //comment out in DLL
      break;
    case 3:                                //change file time
      ThisStuff.SetTime(Name,SecDay, MinMo, HrYr);
```

```
    //ThisStuff.printit();              //comment out in DLL
      break;
    case 4:                             //change file date
      ThisStuff.SetDate(Name,SecDay,MinMo,HrYr);
      //ThisStuff.printit();            //comment out in DLL
      break;
    default:
        //cout << "Wrong Type Passed";
        return (LPSTR) (char *) "Wrong Type Passed";   //comment out of EXE
            }
    //return 0;                         //comment out of DLL
    return (LPSTR) (char *) ThisStuff.grab();          //comment out of EXE
}
```

In C++ the private variable TheTime in the class FileStuff may be modified only by a public function in the same object. The OBJECTS.H file in Listing 6-6 shows the declaration of the functions that appear in TOOLS.CPP in the same listing. The FilRead function used by the Visual Basic application calls these class functions to open the requested file, fill the information structure, and format and return the selected value. Though not strictly necessary, the return values are cast explicitly as long pointers to strings in the FileStuff function called grab (in the "ThisStuff" instance of the object defined by the class FileStuff). The Grab function is used to send the error message "Wrong Type Passed" or to return the requested file data to Visual Basic. The code in Listing 6-5 also contains the statements required for recompiling the program as a stand-alone DOS executable program.

Listing 6-6   *The class called FileStuff defined in OBJECT.H supplies functions (and private variables for them to operate on) in TOOLS.CPP to return values to the exported function of the DLL.*

```
//OBJECTS.H  Class Definition for Times

#include <string.h>
#include <io.h>

class FileStuff {
  struct ftime ft;
  char *TheData;      //The desired info
  FILE *stream;
  int FileErr;
public:
  FileTime (char *);
```

```
FileDate (char *);
SetTime (char *, int, int, int);
SetDate (char *, int, int, int);
char * grab() {return TheData;}
printit ();
};
```

To use FILREAD.DLL, you must retrieve user input (or get the file name and path in some way) to send to the DLL with your selection of either time or date as a return value. Figure 6-6 shows the sample application that lets you access the DLL. The code in Listing 6-7 shows the Visual Basic procedure for calling the DLL. Notice that the variable FileStuff (not related to the class FileStuff in the C++ code) is dimensioned as a fixed-length string variable.

You can test the return value in Figure 6-6 if the incorrect type of date (other than 1 or 2) is passed as well as enter invalid file names to get an error response. You can also change the date-and-time stamp on the selected file used in Figure 6-6.

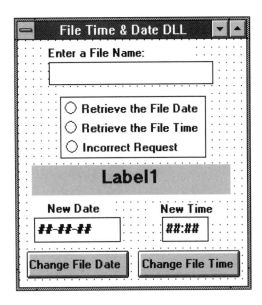

Figure 6-6   *By entering a file name and clicking on a radio button, this example application uses the FILREAD.DLL to retrieve the file's date-and-time stamp.*

Listing 6-7   *This procedure places the file name and path in a fixed-length variable for passing to the DLL function FilRead.*

```
Sub Changer (Kind As Integer)
    Dim LpStrAddress As Long
    Dim FileStuff As String * 255
    FileStuff = LTrim$(RTrim$(Text1.Text))
    Select Case Kind
      Case 3
        Hrs = CInt(Mid$(MaskedEdit2.Text, 1, 2))
        Mins = CInt(Mid$(MaskedEdit2.Text, 4, 2))
        LpStrAddress = FilRead(Kind, FileStuff, 0, Mins, Hrs)
      Case 4
        Months = CInt(Mid$(MaskedEdit1.Text, 1, 2))
        Days = CInt(Mid$(MaskedEdit1.Text, 4, 2))
        Years = (1900 + CInt(Mid$(MaskedEdit1.Text, 7, 2))) - 1980
        LpStrAddress = FilRead(Kind, FileStuff, Days, Months, Years)
    End Select
    LpStrAddress = lstrcpy(FileStuff, LpStrAddress)
    Label1.Caption = FileStuff
End Sub
```

The strings coming from the Masked Edit Controls for date and time in Listing 6-7 are parsed and passed as integer parameters for changing the date and time. The Changer function returns a long integer that points to the address of the string prepared by the C++ code. By declaring the Windows API function lstrcpy in GLOBAL.BAS in Visual Basic, you can bring that variable into the local string FileStuff just as the same API function was used in the C++ code.

Other Parameter-Passing Issues

The Visual Basic approach to parameter passing requires that you compensate for a few other inconsistencies in the environment. You'll encounter a difficulty with passing information to DLLs that require BYTE parameters (which several of the Windows API calls also require). This is easily handled in Visual Basic. Due to the 80x86 architecture, the stack is segmented into word boundaries (a word is two bytes) so that the smallest type pushed onto the stack will be a word. That means you can use a Visual Basic integer (also two bytes) in the place of a BYTE in the parameters passed to the DLL. The integer will be pushed onto the stack in the same way as the BYTE and will take up the same amount of memory.

Another issue in Visual Basic relates to passing monetary values between a DLL and a Visual Basic application. C does not have an equivalent to the Currency type in Visual Basic. To compensate for this, you will need to declare the parameter as a "double" to pass it to the DLL properly. You must then process the double as currency with your own code. Declare "typedef double currency;" in your C code so that you can legally declare a return value for a function as type currency as in "currency FAR ExampleFunc()".

The Module Handler

DLLs, by nature, load into the Windows environment separately from the programs that use them. In fact, the Windows environment itself is run almost entirely by DLLs. As each element or module of Windows (programs, DLLs, and other resources) loads into the environment, Windows assigns it a unique handle. As I write this part of the chapter, the modules listed in Table 6-2 reside in the Windows environment on my computer.

Table 6-2   *This list of currently loaded modules was created by the FreeVB example program.*

Module Name	Module Handle	Path to Library, Driver, Font, or Executable File
ATM	1975	D:\WIN31\SYSTEM\ATM32.DLL
ATMSYS	327	D:\WIN31\SYSTEM\ATMSYS.DRV
AUXDRV	5207	D:\WIN31\SYSTEM\SBPAUX.DRV
CLOCK	4791	D:\WIN31\CLOCK.EXE
COMM	1055	D:\WIN31\SYSTEM\COMM.DRV
COMMDLG	4471	D:\WIN31\SYSTEM\COMMDLG.DLL
COURC	5911	D:\WIN31\SYSTEM\COURC.FON
COURD	5903	D:\WIN31\SYSTEM\COURD.FON
COURE	735	D:\WIN31\SYSTEM\COURE.FON
DCFONT2	2879	D:\WINDOWS\TOOLS\DYNACOM\DCFONT.FON
DCFONT2A	2871	D:\WINDOWS\TOOLS\DYNACOM\DCFONTA.FON
DIALOG	14343	D:\WORD\DIALOG.FON
DISPLAY	487	D:\WIN31\SYSTEM\ORCHIDF.DRV
DRWATSON	7959	D:\WIN31\DRWATSON.EXE
DUCKHOOK	2959	D:\WINDOWS\TOOLS\SNAPPRO\DUCKHOOK.DLL
FILESIZE	8015	D:\WIN31\FILESIZE.DLL
FIXFONTS	1119	D:\WIN31\SYSTEM\8514FIX.FON

Table 6-2   *(Continued)*

Module Name	Module Handle	Path to Library, Driver, Font, or Executable File
FONTS	1079	D:\WIN31\SYSTEM\8514SYS.FON
FREEVB	21855	D:\WINDEV\VB\BOOK\CH-06\3-FREEDL\FREEVB.EXE
GDI	1143	D:\WIN31\SYSTEM\GDI.EXE
GRABBER	2327	D:\WIN31\SYSTEM\CARVGA.GR3
HPPCL	14231	D:\WIN31\SYSTEM\HPPCL.DRV
KERNEL	279	D:\WIN31\SYSTEM\KRNL386.EXE
KEYBOARD	335	D:\WIN31\SYSTEM\KEYBOARD.DRV
MIDI	5239	D:\WIN31\SYSTEM\MIDIMAP.DRV
MMSYSTEM	5439	D:\WIN31\SYSTEM\MMSYSTEM.DLL
MODERN	5943	D:\WIN31\SYSTEM\MODERN.FON
MODLIST	18959	D:\WINDEV\VB\BOOK\CH-06\3-FREEDL\MODLIST.DLL
MOUSE	375	D:\WIN31\SYSTEM\MOUSE.DRV
MSWORD	12263	D:\WORD\WINWORD.EXE
OEMFONTS	1127	D:\WIN31\SYSTEM\8514OEM.FON
OLECLI	10855	D:\WIN31\SYSTEM\OLECLI.DLL
OLESVR	10847	D:\WIN31\SYSTEM\OLESVR.DLL
ORCHID SET	4751	D:\WIN31\ORCHID.EXE
OTRES	6615	D:\WINDOWS\TOOLS\ONTIME\OTRES.DLL
OTWIN	2063	D:\WINDOWS\TOOLS\ONTIME\OTWIN.EXE
PREV	17647	D:\EXCEL\PREV.FON
PROGMAN	1615	D:\WIN31\PROGMAN.EXE
RES	10055	D:\WINDEV\VB\TOOLS\RES\RES.EXE
RESGAUGE	10063	D:\WINDOWS\APPS\RESGAUGE\RESGAUGE.EXE
ROMAN	671	D:\WIN31\SYSTEM\ROMAN.FON
SBFM	5247	D:\WIN31\SYSTEM\SBPFM.DRV
SBPSND	5343	D:\WIN31\SYSTEM\SBPSND.DRV
SCRIPT	687	D:\WIN31\SYSTEM\SCRIPT.FON
SERIFC	5895	D:\WIN31\SYSTEM\SERIFC.FON
SERIFD	5887	D:\WIN31\SYSTEM\SERIFD.FON
SERIFE	751	D:\WIN31\SYSTEM\SERIFE.FON
SHELL	5767	D:\WIN31\SYSTEM\SHELL.DLL
SMALLE	719	D:\WIN31\SYSTEM\SMALLE.FON
SNAPPRO!	2519	D:\WINDOWS\TOOLS\SNAPPRO\SNAPPRO.EXE
SOUND	511	D:\WIN31\SYSTEM\MMSOUND.DRV
SSERIFC	5879	D:\WIN31\SYSTEM\SSERIFC.FON
SSERIFD	5919	D:\WIN31\SYSTEM\SSERIFD.FON

Table 6-2   *(Continued)*

Module Name	Module Handle	Path to Library, Driver, Font, or Executable File
SSERIFE	767	D:\WIN31\SYSTEM\SSERIFE.FON
SYMBOLE	703	D:\WIN31\SYSTEM\SYMBOLE.FON
SYSTEM	367	D:\WIN31\SYSTEM\SYSTEM.DRV
TIMER	5431	D:\WIN31\SYSTEM\TIMER.DRV
TOOLHELP	10263	D:\WIN31\SYSTEM\TOOLHELP.DLL
UNIDRV	14303	D:\WIN31\SYSTEM\UNIDRV.DLL
USER	1159	D:\WIN31\SYSTEM\USER.EXE
VB	12807	D:\WINDEV\VB\VB.EXE
VBRUN100	9935	D:\WIN31\VBRUN100.DLL
WBTRCALL	6831	D:\WINDOWS\TOOLS\ONTIME\WBTRCALL.DLL
WIN87EM	6663	D:\WIN31\SYSTEM\WIN87EM.DLL
WINFILE	4743	D:\WIN31\WINFILE.EXE
WINHELP	22567	D:\WIN31\WINHELP.EXE
WINLD	1007	D:\WIN31\SYSTEM\WINLD.FON

If you study the list in Table 6-2, you will see fonts, DLLs, and programs. Thirteen programs (icons on the desktop) in all were loaded when this list was produced. The FreeVB example program generated this list by using the MODULEENTRY structure in the ToolHelp.DLL, which is shipped with the Windows Software Development Kit. Using the ModuleFirst and ModuleNext functions in ToolHelp.DLL, you can walk the list of module handles resident at the time. Each of these two calls fills the MODULEENTRY structure with the unique information for each module. Listing 6-8 shows the function call in the ModList.DLL example.

Listing 6-8   *The MODULEENTRY structure provides the information on all of the loaded modules when called with ModuleFirst followed by repeating calls to ModuleNext.*

```
void FAR PASCAL ModList(HANDLE hWnd)
{
    MODULEENTRY  ModStuff;
    char szText[128];
    int result;

    ModStuff.dwSize = sizeof (MODULEENTRY);
    result = ModuleFirst(&ModStuff);
```

```
do {
    wsprintf(szText, "%s\t%d\t%s",
                            ModStuff.szModule,
                            ModStuff.hModule,
                            ModStuff.szExePath);
    SendMessage(hWnd, LB_ADDSTRING, 0, (LONG)(LPSTR)szText);
    }
    while (ModuleNext(&ModStuff));
}
```

Listing 6-8 also shows the use of a third method for passing information back to Visual Basic. The Quick C for Windows example for returning disk space statistics discussed earlier in this chapter passed numeric data directly between Visual Basic and the DLL. The Borland C++ example for returning file-date-and-time stamps used a pointer to a string to perform that function. The ModList example in this section uses the SendMessage Windows API call to interface directly with a Visual Basic object—in this case a list box.

To call Modlist, you must first set the focus to the list box. Immediately after that call (List1.SetFocus, for example), you add the statement ModList(GetFocus()). This statement uses the GetFocus API call, which you would have previously declared in the Global module of the Visual Basic program. GetFocus returns the window handle of the list box. SendMessage uses this handle to refer to the list box from within the DLL. Remember that all Visual Basic objects (except for VB 2.0 "lite" controls) register their own Window class. In the case of ModList, looping through the module handles in memory takes place in the DLL, and SendMessage transmits each found handle back to the Visual Basic list-box object. The resulting list appears in Figure 6-7.

Orphan DLLs

The purpose of the list shown in Figure 6-6 goes deeper than merely displaying all of the loaded modules. Very often, when you program a new DLL, the execution of either the DLL or the calling program is interrupted with an error. When this occurs, the DLL may remain in memory but will not be removable, since its caller was terminated by a General Protection Fault. After a few of these failures, you can wind up with unreferenced or orphaned DLLs chewing up memory. In addition, if you try to recompile the DLL on the disk, you will get a sharing error or some other sign of trouble. Borland C++ indicates a fault on the disk drive itself, and Quick C for Windows gets confused.

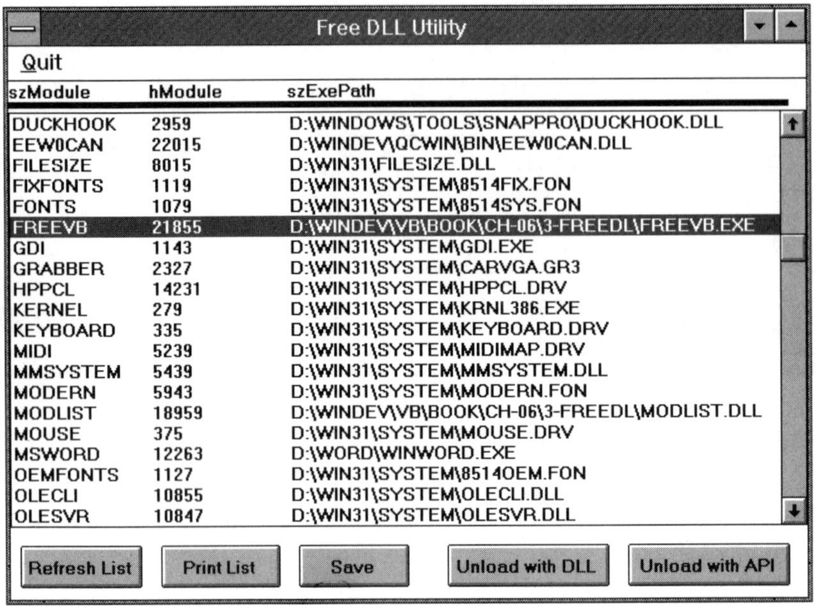

szModule	hModule	szExePath
DUCKHOOK	2959	D:\WINDOWS\TOOLS\SNAPPRO\DUCKHOOK.DLL
EEW0CAN	22015	D:\WINDEV\QCWIN\BIN\EEW0CAN.DLL
FILESIZE	8015	D:\WIN31\FILESIZE.DLL
FIXFONTS	1119	D:\WIN31\SYSTEM\8514FIX.FON
FONTS	1079	D:\WIN31\SYSTEM\8514SYS.FON
FREEVB	21855	D:\WINDEV\VB\BOOK\CH-06\3-FREEDL\FREEVB.EXE
GDI	1143	D:\WIN31\SYSTEM\GDI.EXE
GRABBER	2327	D:\WIN31\SYSTEM\CARVGA.GR3
HPPCL	14231	D:\WIN31\SYSTEM\HPPCL.DRV
KERNEL	279	D:\WIN31\SYSTEM\KRNL386.EXE
KEYBOARD	335	D:\WIN31\SYSTEM\KEYBOARD.DRV
MIDI	5239	D:\WIN31\SYSTEM\MIDIMAP.DRV
MMSYSTEM	5439	D:\WIN31\SYSTEM\MMSYSTEM.DLL
MODERN	5943	D:\WIN31\SYSTEM\MODERN.FON
MODLIST	18959	D:\WINDEV\VB\BOOK\CH-06\3-FREEDL\MODLIST.DLL
MOUSE	375	D:\WIN31\SYSTEM\MOUSE.DRV
MSWORD	12263	D:\WORD\WINWORD.EXE
OEMFONTS	1127	D:\WIN31\SYSTEM\8514OEM.FON
OLECLI	10855	D:\WIN31\SYSTEM\OLECLI.DLL
OLESVR	10847	D:\WIN31\SYSTEM\OLESVR.DLL

Refresh List | Print List | Save | Unload with DLL | Unload with API

Figure 6-7   *The Free DLL utility displays a list of the modules currently loaded into the Windows environment—including the Free DLL module itself (highlighted).*

Removing DLLs from Memory

You have two fairly simple avenues to take care of this situation. (Well, actually you have four, but rebooting the system or restarting Windows are not usually acceptable solutions.) The two avenues, both employed by the FreeVB example program, use the same Windows API call: FreeLibrary. In one case the FreeLibrary call comes from a DLL, and in the second case it is declared in the global section of the Visual Basic program and called directly from Visual Basic. In both cases the module handle identified in the list box by ModList DLL is used to unload the library. Listing 6-9 shows the complete DLL code required to create the FreeDLL dynamic link library when the FreeLibrary call is used.

Listing 6-9   *After you have added a module definition file to the Quick C for Windows project, this code will create a DLL that, when called with the proper module handle, unloads a module from memory.*

```
/*Unload  Dynamic Link Library*/

#include <windows.h>
```

```
#include "freedll.h"

int FAR PASCAL LibMain (hInst, wDataSeg, cbHeapSize, lpszCmdLine)
unsigned int hInst;
WORD wDataSeg;
WORD cbHeapSize;
LPSTR lpszCmdLine;
        {
        if (cbHeapSize != 0)
            UnlockData(0);
        return 1;
        }

int FAR PASCAL FreeDLL(HANDLE Target)
{
        if (GetModuleHandle("FREEDLL.DLL") != Target)
           return FreeLibrary(Target);
        else
          return NULL;
        }

int FAR PASCAL WEP (int nParameter)
    {
    return(1);
    }
```

 Caution: *Unloading modules from the Windows environment can cause Windows itself to become unstable. Even for modules left erroneously in memory, some memory is lost each time you unload the failed module.*

The example code in Listing 6-9 shows you how to make the library call from within a DLL, but this simple example provides little more than the same call made from Visual Basic. Listing 6-10 shows the GLOBAL.BAS declaration and the procedure that you use to make the same call directly from Visual Basic.

Listing 6-10 *Place this code into a button-click procedure in your Visual Basic application to unload a module from memory.*

```
        Pos% = InStr(1, List1.Text, Chr$(9))            'find first tab
        Pos2% = InStr(Pos% + 1, List1.Text, Chr$(9))    'find 2nd tab
        ModuleNum$ = Mid$(List1.Text, Pos%, Pos2% - Pos%)     'grab text in between
        Saved% = List1.ListIndex
```

```
List1.RemoveItem List1.ListIndex
Select Case Index
Case 1
  FreeLibrary (Val(ModuleNum$))
Case 2
  FreeDLL (Val(ModuleNum$))
End Select
List1.SetFocus
retVal& = SendMessage(GetFocus(), LB_RESETCONTENT, 0, 0)
ModList (GetFocus())
List1.ListIndex = Saved%
```

Create a list box, and use the MODLIST.DLL described earlier in this chapter. When you select one of the modules to appear in the list and then click the command button, the FreeLibrary call selected in Case 1 of the code in Listing 6-10 removes the module associated with that handle in memory.

The FREEDLL.DLL example shows you how you can use the DLL to your advantage by performing other API calls or writing your own functions in C. You can use the WEP procedure to clean up memory after removing the module, for example.

Adding Resources through a DLL

Resources constitute a major element of Windows, and DLLs can serve as a primary delivery system of them. Resources contain everything from dialog boxes to cursors to icons and fonts. You can create your own resources easily with a DLL. In fact, writing a custom icon or cursor for loading into Windows might be one of the easiest DLLs you can create.

You use the same WEP and LibMain functions that you use for any DLL, as shown in Listing 6-11. All that remains to create is the resource file itself.

Listing 6-11 *This minimal code and the .RC file compiled with a standard .DEF file will create a DLL with cursor and icon resources.*

```
/*Custom Cursor and Icon DLL*/

#include <windows.h>

int FAR PASCAL LibMain (hInst, wDataSeg, cbHeapSize, lpszCmdLine)
unsigned int hInst;
WORD wDataSeg;
WORD cbHeapSize;
LPSTR lpszCmdLine;
```

```
    {
    if (cbHeapSize != 0)
    UnlockData(0);
    return 1;
    }

int FAR PASCAL WEP (int nParameter)
    {
    return(1);
    }
```

The next step is to create the actual resources you will be using. You can use the image editor in the Windows SDK or any number of shareware bitmap editors that can produce cursors and icons. All that remains to complete the DLL is to create the resource file as shown in Listing 6-12 and compile the DLL.

Listing 6-12 *The resource file specifies the name that will be used in the program to identify the resource, the type of resource, and the file where the compiler can locate each resource.*

moon	CON	moon.ico
stars	ICON	stars.ico
sun	ICON	sun.ico
eye	ICON	eye.ico
bulls	CURSOR	bulls.cur
target	CURSOR	target.cur

In the example program, Resources, the MouseMove event used in two Visual Basic forms changes the cursor as it passes over the form. The system cursor gets restored when you unload the program from memory. Before the cursor can be changed, the MousePointer type must be set to 0 or default; otherwise, the cursor will not change. The LoadLibrary and FreeLibrary calls ensure that the library is properly loaded into memory and removed at the termination of the program. The code in Listing 6-13 shows the Visual Basic code required to load, change, and unload the cursors.

Listing 6-13 *The system cursor shape can be controlled by loading custom cursors from a DLL.*

Executes on start-up of the program:

```
Sub Form_Load ()
        DLLInstance = LoadLibrary("d:\windev\vb\book\ch-06\RESOURCE.DLL")
```

```
        BullsCursHandle = LoadCursor(DLLInstance, "bulls")
        TargetCursHandle = LoadCursor(DLLInstance, "target")
        SysCursHandle = SetClassLong(Form2.hWnd, GCW_HCURSOR, BullsCursHandle)
End Sub
```

Executes when the mouse moves over the primary form:

```
Sub Form_MouseMove (Button As Integer, Shift As Integer, X As Single, Y As Single)
        LastCursor = SetClassLong(Form1.hWnd, GCW_HCURSOR, SysCursHandle)
End Sub
```

Executes when the mouse moves over Form2:

```
Sub Form_MouseMove (Button As Integer, Shift As Integer, X As Single, Y As Single)
      If LastCursor <> BullsCursHandle Then
          LastCursor = SetClassLong(Form2.hWnd, GCW_HCURSOR, BullsCursHandle)
      End If
End Sub
```

Executes when the primary form is unloaded:

```
Sub Form_Unload (Cancel As Integer)
        LastCursor = SetClassLong(Form2.hWnd, GCW_HCURSOR, SysCursHandle)
        LastCursor = SetClassLong(Form3.hWnd, GCW_HCURSOR, SysCursHandle)
        Success = DestroyCursor(WaitCursHandle)
        Success = DestroyCursor(TargetCursHandle)
        Unload Form2
        Unload Form3
        FreeLibrary (DLLInstance)
End Sub
```

Listing 6-13 also shows the clean-up procedures for using the custom cursor DLL called Resources in the examples. If you do not unload the DLL with FreeLibrary, the use counter will be incremented when you load this program the next time. Also, the DLL in the examples contains a number of custom icons. (Listing 6-12 gives their names.) You can access this DLL from Program Manager to give the application a different icon for display on the Windows desktop.

Clarion's TopSpeed Modula-2: All in One

DLLs often collect functions that already exist into a form useful in Windows. The disparate number of languages available today can make that porting job a daunting prospect. Clarion's TopSpeed languages offer the unusual facility of providing a common Windows-compatible development environment for several of the most popular languages: C, C++, Pascal, and Modula-2.

Each of the DLLs in this chapter, including the resource-only DLL, can be combined easily into one DLL in TopSpeed. The TopSpeed project environment can be installed so that it is compatible with all TopSpeed languages or with any one of them.

The first step involves creating the project file. Figure 6-8 shows the project file configuration screen, where you select the type of EXE (DLL in this case), the memory model, and a host of other project-related optimization settings.

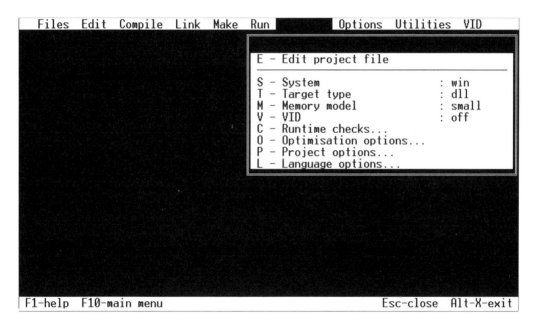

Figure 6-8   *The TopSpeed project-file settings configure the combined project in preparation for compilation.*

The next step is to ensure that the project file (.PR) knows which files to include in the project. Listing 6-14 shows the project file that was used to combine all of the DLLs from this chapter into one.

Listing 6-14   *The TopSpeed project file establishes the list of files to include in the finished product and any special settings, such as win dll.*

```
#system win dll
#model small jpi
```

```
#pragma link_option(case=>off)

#set winmath = 'none'
#compile libmain.mod
#compile modlist.c
#compile freedll.c
#compile tools.cpp
#compile filread.cpp
#compile freedisk.c
#compile objects.rc

#link %prjname
```

In this case, the LibMain and Windows exit procedure (WEP) modules were written in Modula-2 even though the DLL will link together modules written in C++ and straight C. Two modifications were made to the source modules that were used to create the DLLs in the environments described earlier in this chapter. First, the underscores on the keywords FAR and PASCAL in the function prototypes were removed. Second, the keyword "export" was removed. TopSpeed assumes that any function in a DLL will be exported. Listing 6-15 shows the LibMain function as it appears in Modula-2.

Listing 6-15 *The Modula-2 LibMain performs the same function for DLLs as the version discussed earlier in this chapter for other compilers.*

```
IMPLEMENTATION MODULE LibMain;

PROCEDURE LIBMAIN(hInstance: Windows.HANDLE; wDataSeg, cbHeapSize: WORD;
                  lpszCmdLine: Windows.LPSTR): INTEGER;

VAR
  Ret: INTEGER;
BEGIN
  Ret := 1;
  IF hInstance = 0 THEN                   (* Call initialization procedure *)
                                          (* if this is the first instance *)
    IF Windows.LocalInit(wDataSeg, 0, cbHeapSize) = 0 THEN
      Ret := 0;                           (* error *)
    END;
  END;
  RETURN Ret;
END LIBMAIN;

PROCEDURE WEP(nParam: INTEGER) : INTEGER;
```

```
0BEGIN
  IF nParam = Windows.WEP_SYSTEM_EXIT THEN
    RETURN 1;                       (* system exit *)
  END;

  IF nParam = Windows.WEP_FREE_DLL THEN
    RETURN 1;                       (* use count is zero - DLL freed *)
  ELSE
    RETURN 1;                       (* undefined, just return *)
  END;
END WEP;

END LibMain.
```

Modula-2 uses an .EXP file in place of the C .DEF file to define the exports. TopSpeed comes with a utility called TSMKEXP, which examines the object code of a compiled module and defines the exports for you.

Once all of the correct modules appear in the project file, you can compile the DLL and call its functions from your Visual Basic application just as if they were in their separate DLL files as constructed earlier in this chapter.

Free-Module DLL (FREEDLL) and Module Handler DLL (MODLIST)

GLOBAL.BAS

```
Global Const FALSE = 0
Global Const TRUE = -1
Global Const OFF = 0
Global Const NULL = 0
Global Const WM_USER = &H400
Global Const LB_SETTABSTOPS = WM_USER + 19
Global Const CB_RESETCONTENT = WM_USER + 11
Global Const LB_RESETCONTENT = WM_USER + 5
Global Const ROP_DOWN_LIST = 2

Global Tabs(4) As Integer


Declare Sub FreeModule Lib "Kernel" (ByVal hModule As Integer)
Declare Sub FreeLibrary Lib "Kernel" (ByVal hLibModule As Integer)

Declare Sub ModList Lib "d:\windev\vb\book\ch-06\3-freedl\Modlist.dll" (ByVal hWnd
...As Integer)
```

```
Declare Function lstrcpy Lib "Kernel" (ByVal lpString1 As Any, ByVal lpString2 As Any)
...As Long
Declare Sub FreeDLL Lib "d:\windev\vb\book\ch-06\3-freedl\freedll.dll" (ByVal hWnd
...As Integer)

Declare Function GetWindow Lib "User" (ByVal hWnd As Integer, ByVal wCmd As Integer)
...As Integer
Declare Function GetWindowText Lib "User" (ByVal hWnd As Integer, ByVal lpString As
...String, ByVal aint As Integer) As Integer
Declare Function GetWindowTextLength Lib "User" (ByVal hWnd As Integer) As Integer
Declare Function GetClassName Lib "User" (ByVal hWnd As Integer, ByVal lpClassName
...As String, ByVal nMaxCount As Integer) As Integer

Declare Function SendMessage Lib "User" (ByVal hWnd As Integer, ByVal wMsg As Integer,
...ByVal wParam As Integer, lParam As Any) As Long
Declare Function GetFocus Lib "User" () As Integer
Declare Function SetFocusAPI Lib "User" Alias "SetFocus" (ByVal hWnd As Integer)
...As Integer
Declare Function GetParent% Lib "User" (ByVal hWnd%)
```

FREEVB.FRM

```
Sub TaskList ()
    ListClear
    FreeDLL.List1.SetFocus
    ModList (GetFocus())
End Sub

Sub Form_Load ()
    FreeDLL.Visible = TRUE
    FreeDLL.List1.SetFocus
    tabs(0) = 10
    tabs(1) = 50
    tabs(2) = 100
    retVal& = SendMessage(GetFocus(), LB_SETTABSTOPS, 3, tabs(1))
    TaskList
End Sub

Sub Quit_Click ()
    Unload FreeDLL
End Sub

Sub ListClear ()
    hWndOld% = GetFocus()
    FreeDLL.List1.SetFocus
    x = SendMessage(GetFocus(), LB_RESETCONTENT, 0, 0)
    Suc% = SetFocusAPI(hWndOld%)
End Sub
```

```
Sub Form_Resize ()
      If WindowState <> 1 Then
        ListClear
        List1.Width = FreeDLL.ScaleWidth
        List1.Height = FreeDLL.ScaleHeight - (2.5 * Command1(1).Height)
        TaskList
      End If
End Sub

Sub Command1_Click (Index As Integer)
        Pos% = InStr(1, List1.Text, Chr$(9))        'find first tab
        Pos2% = InStr(Pos% + 1, List1.Text, Chr$(9))   'find 2nd tab
        ModuleNum$ = Mid$(List1.Text, Pos%, Pos2% - Pos%)       'grab text in between
        Saved% = List1.ListIndex
        List1.RemoveItem List1.ListIndex
        Select Case Index
        Case 1
          FreeLibrary (Val(ModuleNum$))
        Case 2
          FreeDLL (Val(ModuleNum$))
        End Select
        List1.SetFocus
        retVal& = SendMessage(GetFocus(), LB_RESETCONTENT, 0, 0)
        ModList (GetFocus())
        List1.ListIndex = Saved%
End Sub

Sub Command2_Click ()
        TaskList
End Sub

Sub Command3_Click ()
    PrintMods
End Sub

Sub PrintMods ()
    On Error GoTo ErrorHandler
    Printer.FontName = "Arial"
    Printer.FontSize = 9
    GoSub PageHeader
    For Index% = 0 To List1.ListCount
        Printer.CurrentX = Printer.ScaleWidth - (Printer.ScaleWidth * .9)
        Printer.Print List1.List(Index%)
        Counter% = Counter% + 1
        If Counter% >= 65 Then
```

```
        Counter% = 0
        Printer.NewPage
        GoSub PageHeader
      End If
    Next Index%
    Printer.EndDoc
    Msg$ = "Module printing complete."
    MsgBox Msg$ ' Display message.
    Exit Sub
ErrorHandler:
    MsgBox "Printing Error!"
    Exit Sub
PageHeader:
    Msg$ = "Modules Loaded Page: "
    HWidth = Printer.TextWidth(Msg$) / 2
    Printer.CurrentX = Printer.ScaleWidth / 2 - HWidth
    Printer.Print Msg$ + Str$(Printer.Page) + "."
    Return
End Sub


Sub Command4_Click ()
    NL$ = Chr$(13) + Chr$(10)
    Open "MODULES.DAT" For Output As #1    ' Create a test file
    For Index% = 0 To List1.ListCount
      Print #1, List1.List(Index%)
    Next Index%
    Close #1    ' Close the file
    MsgBox "Save Complete"
End Sub
```

FREEDLL.DLL

FREEDLL.DEF

```
LIBRARY FREEDLL
DESCRIPTION 'DLL to free memory'
EXETYPE WINDOWS
CODE MOVEABLE DISCARDABLE
DATA MOVEABLE SINGLE
HEAPSIZE 1024
EXPORTS
  WEP              @1 RESIDENTNAME
  FreeDLL          @2
```

FREEDLL.H

```
int  _pascal _far LibMain(unsigned int hInst,unsigned short  wDataSeg,unsigned short
...cbHeapSize,char  _far *lpszCmdLine);
int  _pascal _far FreeDLL(HANDLE Target);
int  _pascal _far WEP(int  nParameter);


FREEDLL.C

/*Unload  Dynamic Link Library*/

#include <windows.h>
#include "freedll.h"


int FAR PASCAL LibMain (hInst, wDataSeg, cbHeapSize, lpszCmdLine)
unsigned int hInst;
WORD wDataSeg;
WORD cbHeapSize;
LPSTR lpszCmdLine;
        {
        if (cbHeapSize != 0)
            UnlockData(0);
        return 1;
        }


int FAR PASCAL FreeDLL(HANDLE Target)
{
        if (GetModuleHandle("FREEDLL.DLL") != Target)
          return FreeLibrary(Target);
        else
          return NULL;
        }


int FAR PASCAL WEP (int nParameter)
    {
    return(1);
    }
```

MODLIST.DLL

MODLIST.DEF

```
LIBRARY ModList
DESCRIPTION 'List Active Modules'
EXETYPE WINDOWS
CODE MOVEABLE DISCARDABLE
```

```
DATA MOVEABLE SINGLE
HEAPSIZE 1024
EXPORTS
  WEP            @1 RESIDENTNAME
  ModList        @2
```

MODLIST.H

```
int  _pascal _far LibMain(unsigned int hInst,unsigned short  wDataSeg,unsigned short
...cbHeapSize,char  _far *lpszCmdLine);
int  _pascal _far ModList(int Modet);
int  _pascal _far WEP(int  nParameter);
```

MODLIST.C

```
/*Returns Information on Loaded Modules*/

#include <windows.h>
#include <stdio.h>
#include <toolhelp.h>

int FAR PASCAL LibMain (unsigned int hInst, WORD wDataSeg, WORD cbHeapSize,LPSTR
... lpszCmdLine)
      {
      if (cbHeapSize != 0)
          UnlockData(0);
      return 1;
      }


void FAR PASCAL ModList(HANDLE hWnd)
{
      MODULEENTRY  ModStuff;
      char szText[128];
      int result;

       ModStuff.dwSize = sizeof (MODULEENTRY);
       result = ModuleFirst(&ModStuff);
      do {
          wsprintf(szText, "%s\t%d\t%s",
                                      ModStuff.szModule,
                                      ModStuff.hModule,
                                      ModStuff.szExePath);
        SendMessage(hWnd, LB_ADDSTRING, 0, (LONG)(LPSTR)szText);
        }
      while (ModuleNext(&ModStuff));
}
```

```
int FAR PASCAL WEP (int nParameter)
    {
    return(1);
    }
```

File-Data-and-Time DLL

FORM1.FRM

```
Option Explicit
'Form Level API Declarations
Declare Function FilRead Lib "d:\windev\vb\book\ch-06\2-time\FilRead.DLL" (ByVal TypeT
...As Integer, ByVal FileName As String, ByVal SecDay As Integer, ByVal MinMo As Integer,
...ByVal YrHr As Integer) As Long
'Declare Function FilRead Lib "COMBINED.DLL" (ByVal TypeT As Integer, ByVal FileName
...As String, ByVal SecDay As Integer, ByVal MinMo as Integer, ByVal YrHr As Integer)
...As Long
Declare Function lstrcpy Lib "Kernel" (ByVal lpString1 As Any, ByVal lpString2 As Any)
...As Long
Dim Hrs As Integer
Dim Mins As Integer
Dim Days As Integer
Dim Months As Integer
Dim Years As Integer

Sub Changer (Kind As Integer)
    Dim LpStrAddress As Long
    Dim FileStuff As String * 255
    FileStuff = LTrim$(RTrim$(Text1.Text))
    Select Case Kind
      Case 3
        Hrs = CInt(Mid$(MaskedEdit2.Text, 1, 2))
        Mins = CInt(Mid$(MaskedEdit2.Text, 4, 2))
        LpStrAddress = FilRead(Kind, FileStuff, 0, Mins, Hrs)
      Case 4
        Months = CInt(Mid$(MaskedEdit1.Text, 1, 2))
        Days = CInt(Mid$(MaskedEdit1.Text, 4, 2))
        Years = (1900 + CInt(Mid$(MaskedEdit1.Text, 7, 2))) - 1980
        LpStrAddress = FilRead(Kind, FileStuff, Days, Months, Years)
    End Select
    LpStrAddress = lstrcpy(FileStuff, LpStrAddress)
    Label1.Caption = FileStuff
End Sub

Sub Command1_Click ()
    Changer (4)
End Sub
```

```
Sub Command2_Click ()
    Changer (3)
End Sub

Sub Option1_Click (Index As Integer)
        Reader (Index)
        Label1.Refresh
End Sub

Sub Reader (Pick As Integer)
    Dim LpStrAddress As Long
    Dim FileStuff As String * 255

    FileStuff = LTrim$(RTrim$(Text1.Text))
    If Pick = 3 Then Pick = 5              'set default response
    LpStrAddress = FilRead(Pick, FileStuff, 0, 0, 0)
    LpStrAddress = lstrcpy(FileStuff, LpStrAddress)
    Label1.Caption = FileStuff
End Sub
```

LIBMAIN.CPP

(Use the sample LibMain.cpp, shipped with Borland's C++.)

FILREAD.CPP

```
#include <windows.h>
#include <stdlib.h>
#include <iostream.h>
#include <stdio.h>
#include "objects.h"

extern "C" char * FAR PASCAL FilRead (int Type, char *FileName, int SecDay, int MinMo,
...int HrYr); //comment out of exe

char * FAR PASCAL _export FilRead (int Type, char *FileName, int SecDay, int MinMo,
...int HrYr)
//int main(int Type, char *FileName)     //use in EXE instead
{
 FileStuff ThisStuff;
 static char Name[4096];
    lstrcpy(Name,FileName);                    //retrieve text of name
                                        //comment out in EXE

    //Use in EXE to test parameters
    //Type == 1;                          //1=date,2=time
    //strcpy(Name, "test.fil");            //force time zone
```

```
      //or enter your own
      // cout << "Enter the file info type name: ";
      //   cin >> Type;
      // cout << "Enter the file name: ";
      //   cin >> Name;
      //or comment out up to the blank line for the DLL

  switch (Type) {
    case 1:                              //requested file date
      ThisStuff.FileDate(Name);
      //ThisStuff.printit();             //comment out in DLL
      break;
    case 2:                              //requested file time
      ThisStuff.FileTime(Name);
      //ThisStuff.printit();             //comment out in DLL
      break;
    case 3:                              //change file time
      ThisStuff.SetTime(Name,SecDay, MinMo, HrYr);
      //ThisStuff.printit();             //comment out in DLL
      break;
    case 4:                              //change file date
      ThisStuff.SetDate(Name,SecDay,MinMo,HrYr);
      //ThisStuff.printit();             //comment out in DLL
      break;
    default:
        //cout << "Wrong Type Passed";
        return (LPSTR) (char *) "Wrong Type Passed";   //comment out of EXE
          }
    //return 0;                                //comment out of DLL
    return (LPSTR) (char *) ThisStuff.grab();         //comment out of EXE
}
```

OBJECTS.H

```
//OBJECTS.H  Class Definition for Times

#include <string.h>
#include <io.h>

class FileStuff {
  struct ftime ft;
  char *TheData;    //The desired info
  FILE *stream;
  int FileErr;
public:
  FileTime (char *);
```

```
    FileDate (char *);
    SetTime (char *, int, int, int);
    SetDate (char *, int, int, int);
    char * grab() {return TheData;}
    printit ();
};
```

TOOLS.CPP

```
//GetTimes.cpp  Function for calculating times
#include <time.h>
#include <stdio.h>
#include <io.h>
#include <iostream.h>
#include <errno.h>
#include "objects.h"

FileStuff::printit() {                    //prints to crt in EXE
    cout << TheData;
    return 0;
    }


FileStuff::FileDate(char *FileName) {      //set at init
    TheData = new char[128];
    stream = fopen(FileName, "rb");
    if (stream == NULL) {
        strcpy(TheData,"File Not Found - D");
        return 0;
        }
    else {
      FileErr = getftime(fileno(stream), &ft);
      sprintf(TheData,"%02u/%2u/%04u",ft.ft_month,ft.ft_day,ft.ft_year+1980);
      fclose(stream);
      return 0;
        }
}


FileStuff::FileTime(char *FileName) {              //set at init
    TheData = new char[128];
    stream = fopen(FileName, "rb");
    if (stream == NULL) {
      strcpy(TheData,"File Not Found - T");
      return 0;
        }
    else {
      FileErr = getftime(fileno(stream), &ft);
```

```
        sprintf(TheData,"%02u:%2u:%02u",ft.ft_hour,ft.ft_min,ft.ft_tsec * 2);
        fclose(stream);
        return 0;
    }
}
FileStuff::SetTime(char *FileName, int Secs, int Mins, int Hrs) {          //set at init
    TheData = new char[128];
    stream = fopen(FileName, "rb");
    if (stream == NULL) {
      strcpy(TheData,"File Not Found - TS");
      return 0;
      }
    else {
      getftime(fileno(stream), &ft);
      ft.ft_tsec = Secs;
      ft.ft_min =  Mins;
      ft.ft_hour = Hrs;
      setftime(fileno(stream),&ft);
      strcpy(TheData,"File Time Reset");
      fclose(stream);
      return 0;
    }
}
FileStuff::SetDate(char *FileName, int Day, int Month, int Year) {          //set at init
    TheData = new char[128];
    stream = fopen(FileName, "rb");
    if (stream == NULL) {
      strcpy(TheData,"File Not Found - DS");
      return 0;
      }
    else {
      getftime(fileno(stream), &ft);
      ft.ft_day = Day;
      ft.ft_month = Month;
      ft.ft_year = Year;
      setftime(fileno(stream),&ft);
      strcpy(TheData,"File Date Reset");
      fclose(stream);
      return 0;
    }
}
```

DISKSPACE DLL

GLOBAL.BAS

```
Global Const TOTAL = 1
Global Const FREE = 2
Declare Function SpaceSpec Lib "D:\WINDEV\VB\BOOK\CH-06\1-space\FREEDISK.DLL" (ByVal
...SpaceAmt As Integer) As Long
```

FORM1.FRM

```
Sub Form_Load ()
    Label1(0).Caption = Format$(SpaceSpec(TOTAL), "###,###,###,##0") + " bytes"
    Label1(1).Caption = Format$(SpaceSpec(FREE), "###,###,##0") + " bytes"
End Sub
```

FREEDISK.DEF

```
LIBRARY FREEDISK
DESCRIPTION 'DLL to get disk information'
EXETYPE WINDOWS
STUB  'KWI.EXE'
CODE MOVEABLE DISCARDABLE
DATA MOVEABLE SINGLE
HEAPSIZE 1024
EXPORTS
  WEP           @1 RESIDENTNAME
  SpaceSpec     @2
```

FREEDISK.C

```
/*Get Disk Space Information DLL*/

#include <stdio.h>
#include <dos.h>
#include <windows.h>
#include "freedisk.h"

int FAR PASCAL LibMain (hInst, wDataSeg, cbHeapSize, lpszCmdLine)
unsigned int hInst;
WORD wDataSeg;
WORD cbHeapSize;
LPSTR lpszCmdLine;
      {
      if (cbHeapSize != 0)
          UnlockData(0);
      return 1;
      }
```

```
long FAR PASCAL SpaceSpec(SpaceType)
int SpaceType;
{
        LONG Total_Space,Free_Space;
        struct diskfree_t driveinfo;
        unsigned drive;
        /* Get the disk drive letter*/
          _dos_getdrive( &drive );
        /* Get the disk information */
          _dos_getdiskfree( drive, &driveinfo );
        /* Calculate disk space */
          Total_Space = (long) driveinfo.total_clusters *
                              driveinfo.sectors_per_cluster *
                              driveinfo.bytes_per_sector;
          Free_Space = (long) driveinfo.avail_clusters *
                              driveinfo.sectors_per_cluster *
                              driveinfo.bytes_per_sector;
        /*Use to test EXE for correct processing inside DLL
          printf("Total Disk Space = %ld\n",Total_Space);
          printf("Free Disk Space = %ld\n",Free_Space);
        */
        if (SpaceType == 1)
         return(Total_Space);
        else
         return(Free_Space);
        }


int FAR PASCAL WEP (int nParameter)
    {
    return(1);
    }
```

FREEDISK.H

```
int    _pascal _far LibMain(unsigned int hInst,
long   _pascal _far SpaceSpec(int  SpaceType);
int    _pascal _far WEP(int  nParameter);
```

Resource Only DLL

GLOBAL.BAS

```
Declare Function LoadLibrary Lib "Kernel" (ByVal lpLibFileName As String) As Integer
Declare Function LoadCursor Lib "User" (ByVal hInstance As Integer, ByVal lpCursorName
...As Any) As Integer
Declare Function SetClassLong Lib "User" (ByVal hWnd As Integer, ByVal nIndex As Integer,
...ByVal dwNewLong As Long) As Long
```

```
Declare Function DestroyCursor Lib "User" (ByVal hCursor As Integer) As Integer
Declare Sub FreeLibrary Lib "Kernel" (ByVal hLibModule As Integer)
Global Const GCW_HCURSOR = -12
Global SysCursHandle As Long
Global BullsCursHandle As Long
Global TargetCursHandle As Long
Global LastCursor As Long
Global DLLInstance As Integer
```

FORMONE.FRM

```
Sub Command1_Click ()
        Form2.Show
        Form3.Show
        Form1.Command1.SetFocus
End Sub


Sub Form_Load ()
        DLLInstance = LoadLibrary("d:\windev\vb\book\ch-06\RESOURCE.DLL")
        BullsCursHandle = LoadCursor(DLLInstance, "bulls")
        TargetCursHandle = LoadCursor(DLLInstance, "target")
        SysCursHandle = SetClassLong(Form2.hWnd, GCW_HCURSOR, BullsCursHandle)
End Sub


Sub Form_Unload (Cancel As Integer)
        LastCursor = SetClassLong(Form2.hWnd, GCW_HCURSOR, SysCursHandle)
        LastCursor = SetClassLong(Form3.hWnd, GCW_HCURSOR, SysCursHandle)
        Success = DestroyCursor(WaitCursHandle)
        Success = DestroyCursor(TargetCursHandle)
        Unload Form2
        Unload Form3
        FreeLibrary (DLLInstance)
End Sub


Sub Form_MouseMove (Button As Integer, Shift As Integer, X As Single, Y As Single)
        LastCursor = SetClassLong(Form1.hWnd, GCW_HCURSOR, SysCursHandle)
End Sub


Sub Command2_Click ()
        LastCursor = SetClassLong(Form2.hWnd, GCW_HCURSOR, SysCursHandle)
        LastCursor = SetClassLong(Form3.hWnd, GCW_HCURSOR, SysCursHandle)
        Success = DestroyCursor(WaitCursHandle)
        Success = DestroyCursor(TargetCursHandle)
        Unload Form1
End Sub
```

FORMTWO.FRM

```
Sub Form_MouseMove (Button As Integer, Shift As Integer, X As Single, Y As Single)
    If LastCursor <> TargetCursHandle Then
      LastCursor = SetClassLong(Form3.hWnd, GCW_HCURSOR, TargetCursHandle)
    End If
End Sub
```

FORMTHR.FRM

```
Sub Form_MouseMove (Button As Integer, Shift As Integer, X As Single, Y As Single)
    If LastCursor <> BullsCursHandle Then
        LastCursor = SetClassLong(Form2.hWnd, GCW_HCURSOR, BullsCursHandle)
    End If
End Sub
```

RESOURCE.DEF

```
LIBRARY RESOURCE
DESCRIPTION 'DLL to store custom tools'
EXETYPE WINDOWS
CODE MOVEABLE DISCARDABLE
DATA MOVEABLE SINGLE
HEAPSIZE 1024
EXPORTS
    WEP        @1 RESIDENTNAME
```

RESOURCE.C

```
/*Custom Cursor and Icon DLL*/

#include <windows.h>

int FAR PASCAL LibMain (hInst, wDataSeg, cbHeapSize, lpszCmdLine)
unsigned int hInst;
WORD wDataSeg;
WORD cbHeapSize;
LPSTR lpszCmdLine;
      {
      if (cbHeapSize != 0)
          UnlockData(0);
      return 1;
      }

int FAR PASCAL WEP (int nParameter)
    {
    return(1);
    }
```

OBJECTS.RC

```
moon            ICON            moon.ico
stars           ICON            stars.ico
sun             ICON            sun.ico
eye             ICON            eye.ico
bulls           CURSOR          bulls.cur
target          CURSOR          target.cur
```

Combined DLL

COMBINED.PR

```
#system win dll
#model small jpi
#pragma link_option(case=>off,smart_method=>off)

#set winmath = 'none'
#compile libmain.mod
#compile modlist.c
#compile freedll.c
#compile tools.cpp
#compile filread.cpp
#compile freedisk.c
#compile objects.rc

#link %prjname
```

COMBINED.EXP

```
LIBRARY     Combined

;DESCRIPTION 'Example Combined DLL'

DATA     PRELOAD SINGLE

HEAPSIZE  1024
STACKSIZE 4096

EXETYPE WINDOWS

EXPORTS
    MODLIST         @?
    SpaceSpec       @?
    FreeDLL         @?
    FilRead         @?
    WEP             @?
```

FILREAD.CPP

(See previous FILREAD.CPP.)

FREEDISK.C

```c
/*Get Disk Space Information DLL*/


#include <stdio.h>
#include <dos.h>
#include <windows.h>
#include "freedisk.h"

long FAR PASCAL SpaceSpec(SpaceType)
int SpaceType;
{
        LONG Total_Space,Free_Space;
        struct diskfree_t driveinfo;
        unsigned drive;
        /* Get the disk drive letter*/
          _dos_getdrive( &drive );
        /* Get the disk information */
          _dos_getdiskfree( drive, &driveinfo );
        /* Calculate disk space */
          Total_Space = (long) driveinfo.total_clusters *
                             driveinfo.sectors_per_cluster *
                             driveinfo.bytes_per_sector;
          Free_Space = (long) driveinfo.avail_clusters *
                             driveinfo.sectors_per_cluster *
                             driveinfo.bytes_per_sector;
        /*Use to test EXE for correct processing inside DLL
          printf("Total Disk Space = %ld\n",Total_Space);
          printf("Free Disk Space = %ld\n",Free_Space);
        */
        if (SpaceType == 1)
         return(Total_Space);
        else
         return(Free_Space);
        }
```

FREEDISK.H

```c
//int FAR PASCAL DLLFunc (HWND hWnd);
long  pascal far SpaceSpec(int        SpaceType);
```

FREEDLL.C

```
/*Unload  Dynamic Link Library*/

#include <windows.h>
#include "freedll.h"

int FAR PASCAL FreeDLL(HANDLE Target)
{
        if (GetModuleHandle("FREEDLL.DLL") != Target) {
           FreeLibrary(Target);
           return 1;
           }
        else
           return NULL;
}
```

FREEDLL.H

```
int  pascal far FreeDLL(HANDLE Target);
```

LIBMAIN.MOD

```
IMPLEMENTATION MODULE LibMain;

PROCEDURE LIBMAIN(hInstance: Windows.HANDLE; wDataSeg, cbHeapSize: WORD;
                  lpszCmdLine: Windows.LPSTR): INTEGER;

VAR
  Ret: INTEGER;
BEGIN
  Ret := 1;
  IF hInstance = 0 THEN                  (* Call initialization procedure *)
                                         (* if this is the first instance *)
    IF Windows.LocalInit(wDataSeg, 0, cbHeapSize) = 0 THEN
      Ret := 0;                          (* error *)
    END;
  END;
  RETURN Ret;
END LIBMAIN;


PROCEDURE WEP(nParam: INTEGER) : INTEGER;

BEGIN
  IF nParam = Windows.WEP_SYSTEM_EXIT THEN
    RETURN 1;                    (* system exit *)
  END;
```

```
    IF nParam = Windows.WEP_FREE_DLL THEN
      RETURN 1;                       (* use count is zero - DLL freed *)
    ELSE
      RETURN 1;                       (* undefined, just return *)
    END;
END WEP;


END LibMain.
```

MODLIST.C

```
/*Returns Information on Loaded Modules*/

#include <windows.h>
#include <stdio.h>
#include <toolhelp.h>

void FAR PASCAL ModList(HANDLE hWnd)
{
    MODULEENTRY  ModStuff;
    char szText[128];
    int result;

     ModStuff.dwSize = sizeof (MODULEENTRY);
     result = ModuleFirst(&ModStuff);
    do {
        wsprintf(szText, "\t%d\t%s\t%s",
                                  ModStuff.hModule,
                                  ModStuff.szModule,
                                  ModStuff.szExePath);
      SendMessage(hWnd, LB_ADDSTRING, 0, (LONG)(LPSTR)szText);
      }
      while (ModuleNext(&ModStuff));
}
```

MODLIST.H

```
int  _pascal _far ModList(int Modet);
```

OBJECTS.H

(See previous OBJECTS.H.)

OBJECTS.RC

```
moon            ICON        moon.ico
stars           ICON        stars.ico
sun             ICON        sun.ico
eye             ICON        eye.ico
bulls           CURSOR      bulls.cur
target          CURSOR      target.cur
```

TOOLS.CPP

(See previous TOOLS.CPP.)

Chapter 7

Printing In Visual Basic

The printed output serves as an often forgotten but important element of a user interface. The printed page can influence the user's next step with an application as significantly as online help or other prompts. If what comes out of the printer is not what the user expected, then your user interface work may be going to waste. In Visual Basic, the tools provided for printing are fewer than most other categories of functions. They include the following:

- the Printer object
- the EndDoc method
- the Newpage method
- the Print statement
- the Cls method
- the PrintForm method
- the New Page method
- Print.[properties]

Many of the generic properties, such as the text and positioning tools, overlap with screen manipulation. The graphics functions also fit into this category of dual-purpose tools. The Debug object associates most closely with the printing tools as those tools interact with the screen to display information.

The behavior of the Debug object raises an important point in the world of Windows graphical output. Windows attempts to be device independent. In the context of printed output, that means that the screen and the printer operate as peers: both serve as devices through which the Windows API communicates with the user. Therefore, you should be able to write output code that works generically between the screen and the printer. Practically speaking, this *does* work, but there are exceptions, as I'll discuss in this chapter.

The Windows API contributes a great deal to the facilities for manipulating printers. The small number of printing-specific objects, statements, and functions must be married to the API to control a wide range of output devices. In this chapter, I'll address the most frequently asked questions regarding printing.

The Hardware

After deciding what data to print and how to present that data, the connection to, and manipulation of, the output hardware is the primary difficulty with printed output. Formatting the document to be printed should be a breeze in a device-independent world like Windows. It isn't. The format of the document must take into account, as does the program that sends the document, what the printer looks like: how it's connected, which kind is connected, what mode it's in, and so on.

Device Selection

You can write your own Print Manager by using Visual Basic, if you choose. Most applications include some sort of a printer setup utility. Visual Basic provides the printing object and a few other relevant commands, but it provides little visibility into the hardware for printing. Remember that Windows negotiates with hardware devices through drivers. When you install a new printer, you place its driver into the Windows System directory and plant a reference to it in the initialization files (.INI), where you also indicate which access port that driver will use. From then on, all printing is channeled through those drivers.

In the [windows] section of the WIN.INI file, Windows maintains a reference to which driver you selected as the default printer. That's the first place to begin managing printers with Visual Basic. You will find a reference like "device=HP LaserJet Series II,HPPCL,LPT1:." This line contains the name of the printer as it appears in lists in Print Manager, the name of the driver (in this case, contained in the file HPPCL.DRV), and the port assigned to the printer. You can change this value from inside Visual Basic by using the WriteProfileString API call. Before you change it, though, you'll probably want to know which printer is set as the default. To begin that discussion, let's talk about the implications of accessing a default printer under Windows by using Visual Basic.

When you access a font for display on the screen or the printer, you may format a common-dialog box to permit the user to choose only from the fonts that are compatible with the current printer drivers. The CommonDialog control in the Professional Edition of Visual Basic also provides a common dialog for controlling page output to the printer, as shown in Figure 7-1.

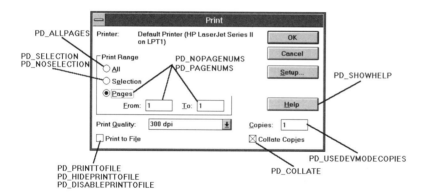

Figure 7-1   *The code in Listing 7-1 creates the print-control dialog from the Common-Dialog control. This screen displays the flags that influence different objects in the dialog.*

The CommonDialog control replaces a whole series of Graphics Device Interface (GDI) calls. In Listing 7-1, the Flag properties provide the greatest capability you can assign to this type of dialog. One of the most useful of them is PD_USEDEV-MODECOPIES, which checks the default printer object for capabilities before permitting the user to change the number of copies to be requested.

Listing 7-1   *By passing a different set of property values to the CommonDialog control, you can create a print-dialog control as shown in Figure 7-1.*

```
          On Error GoTo PrintDlgErr              'Error trapping
          '---Establish property settings for printer dialog
          PrintDialog.Copies = 1
          PrintDialog.Flags = PD_SHOWHELP Or PD_PAGENUMS Or PD_COLLATE Or
          ...PD_USEDEVMODECOPIES'PD_PRINTSETUP
          PrintDialog.FromPage = 1
          PrintDialog.ToPage = 1
          PrintDialog.Min = 1                    'Sets range for page range to print
          PrintDialog.Max = 100
          PrintDialog.PrinterDefault = True      'TRUE resets default printer in WIN.INI
          PrintDialog.Action = 5                 'Call for print dialog
          '---Present message box with results of selections in the dialog
          If Err = False Then
            Result$ = "Copies = " + PrintDialog.Copies + Chr$(13)
            Result$ = Result$ + "From Page = " + PrintDialog.FromPage + Chr$(13)
            Result$ = Result$ + "To Page   = " + PrintDialog.ToPage + Chr$(13)
          End If
          MsgBox Result$, , "Results of Print Settings"
          '---Set the printer to the selections made in the dialog
          Printer.FontName = LabelText.FontName
          Printer.FontSize = LabelText.FontSize
          Printer.FontBold = LabelText.FontBold
          Printer.FontItalic = LabelText.FontItalic
          Printer.FontUnderline = LabelText.FontUnderline
          Printer.FontStrikethru = LabelText.FontStrikethru
          Printer.ForeColor = LabelText.ForeColor
          Printer.Print LabelText
          Printer.EndDoc                         'Release the printer DC
          Exit Sub
PrintDlgErr:
      MsgBox Error$ + ": Print Cancelled"
      Exit Sub
```

Some printers do not permit multiple copies but must be sent independent print requests for each copy. Later in the chapter, I'll talk about PrinterDefault, a powerful property that does some of the work in changing the default printer with WriteProfileString. If you set PrinterDefault to True, the CommonDialog control changes the "device" setting of the [windows] section in WIN.INI to contain the same printer you choose for the print job when you use the print dialog. Except for these notable situations, you must do the work to coordinate your Visual Basic document with the printer. Although you have the correct font selected to display text on the screen—even if it's a True Type font that can be used on the printer or the screen—you must still set the properties for the Printer object.

 Tip: *Whenever you access printer functionality through the Visual Basic Printer object, you must be sure to release the device context (hDC). Otherwise, even API calls you send to change the default printer or to query the current printer capabilities will refer only to the printer first accessed through the Printer object.*

The Printer Browser Utility

As mentioned earlier in this chapter, you can build the ability to review the capabilities of the installed printers right into your applications. The Printer Browser utility does just that. Figure 7-2 shows the opening screen of the Printer Browser. Notice the Common Dialog control in the upper left of the client area. Two menu choices access this control: (1) Change Font allows you to change the font used in the label text shown in the client area by passing a 4 to the Action property (PrintDialog.Action = 4), and (2) Print presents the printer setup dialog by passing 5 to the Action property (PrintDialog.Action = 5). The Printer Data menu selection presents a list of the installed printers and allows you to browse their capabilities.

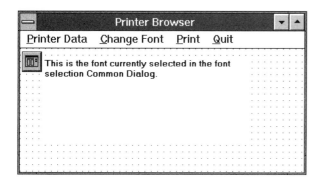

Figure 7-2 *The Printer Browser.*

An Inventory of Installed Printers

By pressing the Printer Data menu selection in the Printer Browser utility, you launch the form called Printers.frm. The Load event for this form uses the GetProfileString API call to perform a two-stage process for retrieving the installed printers. Listing 7-2 shows how the Load event first sets the tab locations for the list box in the Printers form, and then reads the current printer from the [windows] section of the WIN.INI to save it so that it can be restored later.

Listing 7-2   *The Form_Load event reads a list of the installed printers from the WIN.INI file.*

```
Sub Form_Load ()
    '--Set the tabs for the list box
    Static Tabs(2) As Integer
    PrinterForm.Visible = True
    DeviceList.SetFocus
    Tabs(0) = 20      '80
    Tabs(1) = 80      '120
    x% = SendMessage(GetFocus(), LB_SETTABSTOPS, 1, Tabs(1))
    '--Get the current printer
    GetCurrent
    '--Get the list of installed printers with one call
    nSize = 255
    lpRetStr = Space$(nSize)
    AppName$ = "devices"
    x% = GetProfileString(AppName$, ByVal 0&, "Can't Find Section", lpRetStr, nSize)
    OldPos% = 1: Pos% = 1
    Do
      Pos% = InStr(OldPos%, lpRetStr, Chr$(0))
      If Pos% = 0 Then Exit Do
      Device$ = Mid$(lpRetStr, OldPos%, Pos% - OldPos%)
      OldPos% = Pos% + 1
      DeviceList.AddItem Device$
    Loop
    '--Get the ports assigned to the installed drivers
    For NextPrinter = 0 To (DeviceList.ListCount - 2)
      ListedPrinter$ = DeviceList.List(NextPrinter)
      x% = GetProfileString(AppName$, ListedPrinter$, "Can't Find Section", lpRetStr,
      ...nSize)
      Comma% = InStr(lpRetStr, ",")
      ListedPrinter$ = ListedPrinter$ + Chr$(9) + Mid$(lpRetStr, 1, Comma% - 1) +
      ...Chr$(9) + Mid$(lpRetStr, Comma% + 1, 30)
      DeviceList.List(NextPrinter) = ListedPrinter$
    Next NextPrinter
End Sub
```

Lastly, the Form_Load event, reads the [device] list from the WIN.INI file with one call to GetProfileString which passes a Null (By Val &0) in the second parameter. That call returns a list of the printer names. The list of printer names is parsed from the string in the next Do ... Loop, and each name is added to the list box. Now we can read through each entry in [devices] and retrieve the driver name and port for each printer. Finally, we can assemble the finished list-box entry by concatenating the printer information separated by tabs (Chr$(9)) to get the final list box as shown in Figure 7-3.

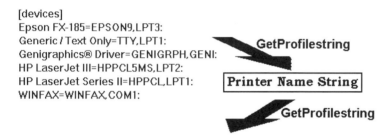

Figure 7-3 *You can read all of the entries of a section of the WIN.INI file with one call to GetProfileString and then, using that information, read the specifics for each individual entry.*

Reading Printer Capabilities

Visual Basic presents the developer with a single printer object. You can't create another instance of this object the way you can duplicate a form. Windows supports only one default printer, and its characteristics pass to the Visual Basic printer object. When you access that printer object, Visual Basic grabs a device context (DC) from Windows. Think of this as if you were marking out a section of a drawing pad. The section you mark contains the characteristics of the default printer, and you hold that section until you release it by using the EndDoc method.

The Printer Browser provides facilities for examining the characteristics of the default printer and for changing the default.

The Printer object doesn't have a properties window such as a form or an edit-control object in Visual Basic. Each of its characteristics—at least the ones with direct Visual Basic control—must be set or viewed programmatically. The Printer Browser provides a quick inventory of these properties with the Settings menu selection, as shown in Figure 7-4.

```
┌─────────────────────────────────────────┐
│        Current Printer Properties        │
├─────────────────────────────────────────┤
│  Fonts    Quit                           │
├─────────────────────────────────────────┤
│ CurrentX:           0                    │
│ CurrentY:           0                    │
│ DrawMode:           13                   │
│ DrawStyle:          0                    │
│ DrawWidth:          1                    │
│ FillColor:          0                    │
│ FillStyle:          1                    │
│ FontBold:           0                    │
│ FontCount:          54                   │
│ FontItalic:         0                    │
│ FontSize:           12                   │
│ FontStrikethru:     0                    │
│ FontTransparent:    -1                   │
│ FontUnderline:      0                    │
│ ForeColor:          80000008H            │
│ hDC:                3650                 │
│ Height:             15840                │
│ Page:               1                    │
│ ScaleHeight:        15120                │
│ ScaleLeft:          0                    │
│ ScaleMode:          1                    │
│ ScaleTop:           0                    │
│ ScaleWidth :        11520                │
│ TwipsPerPixelX:     4.8                  │
│ TwipsPerPixelY:     4.8                  │
│ Width:              12240                │
│ TextHeight(Test):   240                  │
│ TextWidth(Test):    576                  │
│ FontName:           Courier              │
└─────────────────────────────────────────┘
```

Figure 7-4   *Using the Print method and the tabs built into a form, you can easily inspect the property settings for the Printer object.*

The Windows API lets you use the Escape call to inventory the printer capability. Escape employs a "callback" address. That means that a location in memory must be established through which Windows can send a message to the function when locating the printer driver. Visual Basic doesn't support callbacks, so you must place the Escape API call into a Dynamic Link Library (DLL). Listing 7-3 shows the Escape call made from a QuickC for Windows DLL.

Listing 7-3 *Passing the QUERYESCSUPPORT constant in the Escape API call returns True if the printer device context passed in the first parameter supports the capability passed in the third parameter.*

```
int FAR PASCAL GetEscape(PrinterDC, TheEscape)
HDC PrinterDC;
int TheEscape;
{
short   nEscIndex;
int nSendBack;
    nEscIndex = TheEscape;
    nSendBack = Escape(PrinterDC, QUERYESCSUPPORT, sizeof(int), (LPSTR) &nEscIndex,
    ...NULL);
    return(nSendBack);
}
```

Printer escapes, as set through the Escape API call, can manipulate the printer or simply tell you what the current settings on the printer may be. In many cases, the escape may support only PostScript printers, as with GETFACENAME, or it may exist for compatibility with previous versions of Windows, as with GETSETPAPERMETRICS. In the latter case, printer drivers written for Windows 3.0 or later may not even support that escape. The DeviceCapabilities and ExtDeviceMode API functions replace this escape for many functions.

For the items in Table 7-1 that do not appear in the Visual Basic constants, you must define them yourself. In all cases in which a particular escape exists purely for backward compatibility, use the replacement function.

Table 7-1 *When you want to set or determine the capabilities of a particular device, you can use the Escape function to pass the printer escapes to the printer device.*

Escape Constant	Purpose	Recommended Replacement	PS Only
ABORTDOC	Stops current job, erases pending data	AbortDoc function	
BANDINFO	Fills structure with info on whether text or graphics in next band to print	Send text and graphics in each band	
BEGIN_PATH	Opens a path into which drawing primitives are passed to avoid simulating images on device		Yes

Table 7-1   *(Continued)*

Escape Constant	Purpose	Recommended Replacement	PS Only
CLIP_TO_PATH	Supports clipping regions on device		Yes
DEVICEDATA	See PASSTHROUGH escape		
DRAFTMODE	Prints faster with lower quality		
DRAWPATTERNRECT	Creates pattern, gray scale, or solid black on printers supporting HP-PCL		
ENABLEDUPLEX	Determines if device supports duplex ouput	ExtDeviceMode function	
ENABLEPAIRKERNING	Determines if spaces are automatically added between characters (kerning)		
ENABLERELATIVEWIDTHS	Permits length of string to be calculated from one character		
END_PATH	Terminates BEGIN_PATH		Yes
ENDDOCAPI (ENDDOC)	Ends print started with STARTDOC	EndDoc function	
ENUMPAPERBINS	Retrieves info on printer-paper bins	DeviceCapabilities function	
ENUMPAPERMETRICS	Returns paper types and definition on area on page eligible for printing	DeviceCapabilities function	
EPSPRINTING	Suppresses PostScript header-control output so no GDI calls are made		Yes
EXT_DEVICE_CAPS	Supplements GetDeviceCaps to retrieve info on printer		Yes
EXTTEXTOUTAPI	Produces formatted text output	ExtTextOut function	
FLUSHOUTPUT	Clears device buffer		
GETCOLORTABLE	Gets RGB color-table entry		
GETEXTENDEDTEXTMETRICS	Fills buffer with font information		
GETEXTENTTABLE	Gets widths of characters in a group		
GETFACENAME*	Gets name of current physical font		Yes
GETPAIRKERNTABLE	Fill structure with kerning information		
GETPENWIDTH**			
GETPHYSPAGESIZE	Gets physical page size of device		
GETPRINTINGOFFSET	Fills structure with offset from upper left of physical page on device		
GETSCALINGFACTOR	Retrieves scaling factores for x and y axes on device		
GETSETPAPERBINS	Gets number of paper bins and sets the current bin on device	DeviceCapabilities and ExtDeviceMode functions	
GETSETPAPERMETRICS	Sets paper type from a structure	DeviceCapabilities and ExtDeviceMode functions	

Table 7-1 *(Continued)*

Escape Constant	Purpose	Recommended Replacement	PS Only
GETSETPRINTORIENT	Returns or sets current page orientation on device	ExtDeviceMode function	
GETSETSCREENPARAMS*	Returns or sets screen info for rendering halftones on device		
GETTECHNOLOGY	Retrieves specific technology type of device	No substitute, but may not be supported	
GETTRACKKERNTABLE	Fill structure with kerning info on current font		
GETVECTORBRUSHSIZE	Retrieves size of plotter pen used to fill closed figures		
GETVECTORPENSIZE	Retrieves size of plotter pen used to fill closed figures		
MFCOMMENT	Adds a comment to a metafile		
MOUSETRAILS*	Activates mouse blur (trail) for a device		
NEWFRAME	Tells device a page is finished	StartPage, EndPage functions	
NEXTBAND	Tells printer current band is done	Not to be used in metafiles	
PASSTHROUGH	Sends data directly to printer		
POSTSCRIPT_DATA	See PASSTHROUGH escape		
POSTSCRIPT_IGNORE	Sets a flag to ignore or accept output		
QUERYESCSUPPORT	Finds out if capability is supported		
RESTORE_CTM	Restores transformation matrix (see SAVE_CTM)		Yes
SAVE_CTM	Restores previously saved matrix for translating, rotating, and scaling coordinates on device		Yes
SELECTPAPERSOURCE	Chooses bin for paper source	DeviceCapabilities	
SETABORTPROC	Sets Abort flag before StartDoc to cancel job in print buffer	SetAbortProc function	
SETALLJUSTVALUES	Sets all text justification values used for text output in Windows 3.0	ExtTextOut function	
SET_ARC_DIRECTION	Sets direction for drawing elliptical arcs		Yes
SET_BACKGROUND_COLOR	Sets and retrieves current background color on device		
SET_BOUNDS	Sets bounding rectangle for picture		Yes
SET_CLIP_BOX	Sets clipping rectangle or restores previous one		

Table 7-1   *(Continued)*

Escape Constant	Purpose	Recommended Replacement	PS Only
SETCOLORTABLE	Sets an RGB color-table entry or closest equivalent		
SETCOPYCOUNT	Sets number of uncollated copies to print	ExtDeviceMode	
SETCHARSET**			
SETDIBSCALING**			
SETKERNTRACK	Sets specific kerning track for supporting printers		
SETLINECAP(aka SETENDCAP)	Sets cap for each end of line		Yes
SETLINEJOIN	Sets how device will join two intersecting line segments		Yes
SET_MIRROR_MODE**			Yes
SETMITERLIMIT	Sets angle for replacing miter join with bevel join on device		Yes
SET_POLY_MODE	Sets how device will handle Polygon and Polyline functions		
SET_SCREEN_ANGLE	Allows simulation of tilting photo		
SET_SPREAD	Sets slight overlap for filling blank between primitives with white		
STARTDOC	Tells device to start print job	StartDoc function	
STRETCHBLTAPI	Allows scaling of bitmap	StretchBlt function	
TRANSFORM_CTM	Modifies current coordinate transformation matrix		Yes

* Not in WIN31 API constants shipped with Visual Basic 2.0.

** Not in Windows 3.1 SDK manuals but defined in Visual Basic constants.

Using the TextWidth method with the Printer device loads the Print Manager and eventually sends a header (a header for PostScript printers but a form feed for others) to the printer. Use the API call GetTextExtent instead of the TextWidth method, or else use the relevant escape to avoid sending that default.

Any escape sequences sent directly by means of the Visual Basic Print method appear at the top of the output file, ahead of the printer-setup code sent by Visual Basic. The print method sends an ESC+E, which resets the printer to its default power on state; in other words, you lose your settings. If you use the Printer.Form method, the ESCape character gets printed as a graphic.

To send information directly to the printer, bypassing printer drivers to avoid such problems, you can use one of two methods:

- You can simply open the printer port for normal output: open "lpt1" for output as #1. If you want to send an escape, for instance, you execute the following: print #1,chr$(27). Combined with the ASCII 12 value, a form feed can be sent to the printer for printing a document that you don't want to reset with the EndDoc method.
- You can use the Escape API call and the PASSTHROUGH function to send the same data.

Several of the escapes cited in Table 7-1 were moved into functions in Windows 3.1. The GetDeviceCaps function sets or retrieves the printer capabilities involved with these outmoded escapes. You can use escapes or the GetDeviceCaps to determine whether a printer can support graphics.

 Tip: *In Visual Basic design mode, a Printer Error message appears when you try to print a form on a printer with no graphics support. Using the Printer Browser, you can test this. Choose the Printer Data menu selection, and ensure you have the Generic/Text Only printer driver installed. Double-click on Printer Data with the mouse, and click on Yes in the dialog box that pops up to ask if you want to change printers. Go to the Visual Basic design environment and try to print a form. The Printer Error message will be displayed.*

Figure 7-5 shows the calls to GetDeviceCaps when the HP LaserJet Series II laser-printer driver is the current printer, and Figure 7-6 shows the same set of calls when a Generic/Text Only printer driver is the default.

Listing 7-4 shows the GetDeviceCaps procedure used in the Printer Browser to retrieve the device capabilities of the currently loaded printer driver. The constants for these calls appear in the WINDOWS.H file in the Windows SDK, and in the CONST.TXT file, which accompanies Visual Basic. Listing 7-5 shows the function you use to retrieve the proper values from the bits mapped into the return value of GetDeviceCaps. By using a logical AND to relate the return value and the constant, you can mask over the other bits in the return value to extract a finding about each printer capability.

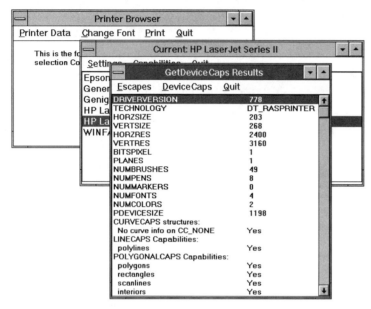

Figure 7-5   *The Printer Browser utility shows the values returned from all of the calls to the GetDeviceCaps function.*

GetDeviceCaps Results	
Escapes DeviceCaps Quit	
DRIVERVERSION	778
TECHNOLOGY	DT_CHARSTREAM
HORZSIZE	215
VERTSIZE	279
HORZRES	1020
VERTRES	66
BITSPIXEL	1
PLANES	1
NUMBRUSHES	0
NUMPENS	0
NUMMARKERS	0
NUMFONTS	6
NUMCOLORS	2
PDEVICESIZE	2196
CURVECAPS structures:	
No curve info on CC_NONE	Yes
LINECAPS Capabilities:	
No Line Info on LC_NONE	Yes
POLYGONALCAPS Capabilities:	
No Polygon Info on PC_NONE	Yes
TEXTCAPS Capabilities:	
EmboldenAbility–DOUBLE	Yes
UnderlineAbility–ABLE	Yes

Figure 7-6   *Each printer driver presents different capabilities. The list box in this figure shows the settings for a Generic/Text Only printer as returned by GetDeviceCaps.*

Listing 7-4 *This code shows part of the much longer procedure in the Printer Browser for polling all of the printer driver capabilities possible to read using the GetDeviceCaps function.*

```
Sub GetDevCaps ()
      EscapeList.Clear
      Dim CapsDev As Integer
      For CapsDev = DRIVERVERSION To COLORRES
        Result% = GetDeviceCaps(Printer.hDC, CapsDev)
        Select Case CapsDev
          Case DRIVERVERSION:        '  Device driver version
            EscapeList.AddItem "DRIVERVERSION" + Chr$(9) + Str(Result%)
          Case TECHNOLOGY:           '  Device classification
            Select Case Result%
              Case DT_PLOTTER: EscapeList.AddItem "TECHNOLOGY" + Chr$(9) +
              ..."DT_PLOTTER"
              Case DT_RASDISPLAY: EscapeList.AddItem "TECHNOLOGY" + Chr$(9) +
              ..."DT_RASDISPLAY"
              Case DT_RASPRINTER: EscapeList.AddItem "TECHNOLOGY" + Chr$(9) +
              ..."DT_RASPRINTER"
              Case DT_RASCAMERA: EscapeList.AddItem "TECHNOLOGY" + Chr$(9) +
              ..."DT_RASCAMERA"
              Case DT_CHARSTREAM: EscapeList.AddItem "TECHNOLOGY" + Chr$(9) +
              ..."DT_CHARSTREAM"
              Case DT_METAFILE: EscapeList.AddItem "TECHNOLOGY" + Chr$(9) +
              ..."DT_METAFILE"
              Case DT_DISPFILE: EscapeList.AddItem "TECHNOLOGY" + Chr$(9) +
              ..."DT_DISPFILE"
            End Select
          Case HORZSIZE:             '  Horizontal size in millimeters
            EscapeList.AddItem "HORZSIZE" + Chr$(9) + Str(Result%)
          Case VERTSIZE:             '  Vertical size in millimeters
            EscapeList.AddItem "VERTSIZE" + Chr$(9) + Str(Result%)
          Case HORZRES:              '  Horizontal width in pixels
            EscapeList.AddItem "HORZRES" + Chr$(9) + Str(Result%)
          Case VERTRES:              '  Vertical width in pixels
            EscapeList.AddItem "VERTRES" + Chr$(9) + Str(Result%)
          Case BITSPIXEL:            '  Number of bits per pixel
            EscapeList.AddItem "BITSPIXEL" + Chr$(9) + Str(Result%)
          Case PLANES:               '  Number of planes
            EscapeList.AddItem "PLANES" + Chr$(9) + Str(Result%)
          Case NUMBRUSHES:           '  Number of brushes the device has
            EscapeList.AddItem "NUMBRUSHES" + Chr$(9) + Str(Result%)
          Case NUMPENS:              '  Number of pens the device has
            EscapeList.AddItem "NUMPENS" + Chr$(9) + Str(Result%)
          Case NUMMARKERS:           '  Number of markers the device has
```

```
          EscapeList.AddItem "NUMMARKERS" + Chr$(9) + Str(Result%)
      Case NUMFONTS:                 '  Number of fonts the device has
          EscapeList.AddItem "NUMFONTS" + Chr$(9) + Str(Result%)
      Case NUMCOLORS:                '  Number of colors the device supports
          EscapeList.AddItem "NUMCOLORS" + Chr$(9) + Str(Result%)
      Case PDEVICESIZE:              '  Size required for device descriptor
          EscapeList.AddItem "PDEVICESIZE" + Chr$(9) + Str(Result%)
      Case CURVECAPS:                '  Curve capabilities
        EscapeList.AddItem "CURVECAPS structures:"
        CheckCap Result%, CC_NONE, "No curve info on CC_NONE"
        CheckCap Result%, CC_CIRCLES, "circles"
        CheckCap Result%, CC_PIE, "pie wedges"
        CheckCap Result%, CC_CHORD, "chord arcs"
        CheckCap Result%, CC_ELLIPSES, "ellipese"
        CheckCap Result%, CC_WIDE, "wide lines"
        CheckCap Result%, CC_STYLED, "styled lines"
        CheckCap Result%, CC_WIDESTYLED, "wide styled lines"
        CheckCap Result%, CC_INTERIORS, "interiors"
      Case ASPECTX:                  '  Length of the X leg
          EscapeList.AddItem "ASPECTX" + Chr$(9) + Str(Result%)
    ...MORE
```

Listing 7-5   *The CheckCap function examines the value returned from the call to GetDeviceCaps in the GetDevCaps procedure of Listing 7-4.*

```
Sub CheckCap (Result%, Cap%, CapStr$)            'Pass in type, item and descr
      CapRes = Result And Cap                    'Shift Bits to read value
      If CapRes And (Cap <> PC_NONE) Then        'Fill list box w/result of item test
        EscapeList.AddItem "  " + Trim$(CapStr) + Chr$(9) + "Yes"  'Send string to
        ...list box
      ElseIf (Cap = PC_NONE) And Result% = 0 Then                 'Same for LC and CC
        EscapeList.AddItem "  " + Trim$(CapStr) + Chr$(9) + "Yes"  'Send no cap string
      End If
End Sub
```

Notice that the constant that tests for the category of return values involved with curve, text, raster, polygon, and line capabilities equates to zero. That means you will need a separate test (as shown in Listing 7-5) to determine when a zero value retrieved from the GetDeviceCaps return variable does not mean that a particular capability exists in the current printer driver. After you have compiled and run the Printer Browser, play around with its abilities to query the capabilities of your printers. You can use the ExtDeviceMode API call to get additional information on the printer driver. ExtDeviceMode allows you to retrieve or to set a printer device. GetDeviceCaps merely retrieves information.

 Tip: *Using any Visual Basic method on the printer device initiates a StartDoc, which must be terminated with an EndDoc before that driver may be released. This is especially troublesome when you attempt to use API calls to change the default printer and a previous method opened, but did not close, the printer device. Simply issue an EndDoc before you make the API call to release the printer driver for changing or reinitializing.*

If you want to send information to a printer that is not the default, you can use the SpoolFile API call. The first parameter of SpoolFile contains the name of the printer. With this method, you can distribute printing jobs to different printers instead of sending them all to the one default printer.

Hardware-Control Tips

You can gather an immense amount of data using the methods we've been discussing. Now we can cover how to control the printing hardware using escapes, API functions and simple Visual Basic syntax.

Printing Color   You can set the colors for output in Visual Basic in one of two ways: through the ForeColor property of the Printer object or through the SetTextColor API call. In Visual Basic 1.0, the ForeColor property did not work and you were forced to use SetTextColor.

The declaration for SetTextColor is as follows:

```
Declare Function SetTextColor Lib "GDI" (ByVal hDC As Integer, ByVal crColor As Long)
...As long
```

To prepare the printer to print in color the next characters it receives, simply call SetTextColor like this: return&=SetTextColor(Printer.hDC,QBColor(ColorChoice)). The next character you send will print according to ColorChoice. You can also use SetTextColor to change the color of a bitmap when moving it from a monochrome to a color-device context.

Printing in Landscape Mode   Some printer settings can be changed with the Escape function used in the Printer Browser application earlier in this chapter. In the Printer Browser, we used the Escape API call to retrieve information about the current printer. That required a callback, and so Escape had to be placed inside a DLL. You can also create a user-defined type patterned after the DEVMODE structure in the SDK and the ResetDC API call to retrieve the orientation of the printer without resorting to a DLL.

To merely send data to the printer, you can use the Escape API call right within your Visual Basic application. For instance, you can set a printer to landscape mode. (If you need to find out the state of the printer first, you must use the Escape DLL.)

Caution: Remember that the printer device context (DC) must be released after you send it instructions.

The Escape API function requires a structure in its fourth parameter, and you can create that construction with a Visual Basic–defined type. First, specify the PageMode structure by placing this code in your form declarations area or your global or local module:

```
Declare Function Escape Lib "GDI" (ByVal hDC As Integer, ByVal nEscape As Integer,
...ByVal nCount As Integer, ByVal lplnData As Any, ByVal lpOutData As Any) As Integer
Type PageMode
        Direction As Long
        lPadding As String * 16
EndType
Const Landscape = 1
Const Portrait = 2
Const GETSETPAPERORIENT = 30
```

If you plan to work with the Escape API call, you should import the section of the WINAPI.TXT file with the Escape constants. Among these constants is one called GETSETPAPERORIENT, which you'll need for the second parameter of the Escape call. Wherever you wish to change the page orientation, call the Escape function as follows:

```
Direction = Landscape
return% = Escape(Printer.hDC, GETSETPAPERORIENT, Len(PageMode),Null)
Printer.EndDoc
```

To handle many different printer types, you should write your application to handle printers in the most adaptable way possible. However, if your application will never use anything other than an HP LaserJet, you can set the page orientation to landscape simply by using an escape character and the proper initialization string as follows:

```
Landscape$ = Chr$(27) + "&l1O"      'Ampersand L, No. 1, Letter O
Portrait$ = Chr$(27) + "&l0O"       'Letter L, number 0, Letter O
open "lpt1" for output as #1
print #1, Landscape$
print #1, Chr$(12)
Close #1
```

Finding the Printable Area   For finding the printable area on a page, don't forget that the Printer.Width method includes unprintable areas. You must use the Printer.ScaleWidth and .ScaleHeight methods to control where you print characters on the page. Using the GetDeviceCaps API from the Printer Browser application described earlier in this chapter will give you the physical dimensions of the printable area of the page so that you can adjust the page precisely.

Laser-Printing Graphs   To print a graph in Visual Basic 1.0, it was necessary to convert the graph to monochrome, size it to cover a form, and then print the form. Setting the DrawMode property to 5 for printing didn't work. That function was fixed in Visual Basic 2.0. Simply setting the DrawMode property causes the form to print (Graph1.DrawMode = 5). However, you must include the specific name of the graph. Simply setting DrawMode = 5 won't work.

Interrupting the Printer

You can interrupt the printing of a document in several ways in your Visual Basic application. George Campbell, in a message found on CompuServe, presented a method that performs essentially the same functions you would perform to stop a print job sent to the Windows Print Manager. The method in Listing 7-6 won't work if the print job has not been sent to the Print Manager.

Listing 7-6   *When you want to activate the Print Manager to shut down a print job, you use the same procedure you would perform manually.*

```
Sub KillPrint_Click  'A command button

On Error GoTo NoPrintMan
```

```
AppActivate "Print Manager"
SendKeys "%{ }{Down 5}%{F4}", 1

Goto EndIt

NoPrintMan:
MsgBox "Print Manager not running, or no active print job!"
Resume EndIt

EndIt:
End Sub
```

You can terminate a print job and leave in the printer what you've already sent. You can prevent the job from appearing in the Print Manager by simply interrupting whatever process you are using to send information to the printer with the Print method. This can be useful for building test logs in which you want the printer to record events but the events aren't contiguous in time. The information won't print (in the case of a laser printer) until the page fills or until you release the printing device context by using the EndDoc method.

Most of the time, when you want to interrupt the printer, you want to prevent the print job (or any trace of it) from reaching the printer. If you are using the Print Manager, you have a better chance of stopping short jobs from printing at all. If you don't use the Print Manager, you can prevent the job from finishing. The code in Listing 7-7 shows you how to achieve both results.

Listing 7-7   *Place this test code into a Visual Basic form with two command buttons to test how to interrupt a print job.*

```
Declare Function ABORTDOC Lib "GDI" (ByVal hDC As Integer) As Integer
Dim GlobalStop As Integer

Sub Command1_Click ()
      GlobalStop = False                 'Reset abort flag
      On Error GoTo PostIt               'Set up error response
      For n% = 1 To 200                  'Perform a series of Prints
        Form1.Print Str$(n%)             'Show the print on the form
        x% = DoEvents()                  'Allow outside events
        Printer.Print Str$(n%) + " -- Test Print"'Send text to the print object
      Next n%                            'Loop again
      If GlobalStop = True Then r% = ABORTDOC(Printer.hDC)'Clear the printer if called
      Printer.EndDoc                     'Release the device context
      MsgBox "Finished"                  'present done message
```

```
        Exit Sub
PostIt:
    MsgBox Error$ & ": Printing Job Aborted"
    Exit Sub
End Sub

Sub Command2_Click ()
    GlobalStop = True                    'Set flag to abort printing
End Sub
```

The AbortDoc API call allows you to remove jobs from the Print Manager even before they are actually printed. Whenever you send a print job that bypasses the Print Manager, AbortProc clears out the Printer object of the remaining elements of the print job. Notice in Listing 7-7 that the call to AbortProc is made before the call to the EndDoc method. If you do this in reverse order, the printing process is not affected. That's because EndDoc has released the handle to the device context used in the printing process, and AbortProc now refers to a completely different printer device context (Printer.hDC).

The Print Process

Maintaining Word Wrap

Managing text sent to the printer is not much different from working with the text as it appears on the screen. For instance, in Chapter 5 we looked at a utility that lets you walk through the lines of text in a text box. Visual Basic doesn't give you any native means to recognize each line, so you must use the SendMessage API call to print the text as it appears. The code in Listing 7-8 fits inside a command button where you can compare the two means of printing: (1) simply sending the text to the Printer object or (2) controlling each line as it goes to the printer, with the opportunity to insert carriage returns and maintain formatting.

Listing 7-8   *The SendMessage API call can retrieve text from a text box line by line, where it can be processed (as with Trim, which deletes unwanted spaces) before it is printed.*

```
Sub Command1_Click (Index As Integer)
    Text1.SetFocus
    Select Case Index
    Case 0:
```

```
      Printer.Print Text1.Text
      Printer.EndDoc
   Case 1:
      Counter& = SendMessage(Text1.hWnd, EM_GETLINECOUNT, 0&, 0&)
      For N& = 0 To (Counter& - 1)
        LoStuff% = MAX_CHARS And (255)
        HiStuff% = Int(MAX_CHARS / 256)
        GotLine$ = Chr$(LoStuff%) + Chr$(HiStuff%) + Space$(MAX_CHARS - 2)
        Text1.SetFocus
        Result = SendMessage(Text1.hWnd, EM_GETLINE, CInt(N&), GotLine$)
        Printer.Print Trim(GotLine$)
        'MsgBox Trim(GotLine$)
      Next N&
      Printer.EndDoc
   End Select
End Sub
```

 Tip: *The SendMessage API call must have a string prepared with the elements to hold the lower word in the lparam as well as the padded spaces to hold the string value. This parameter must be passed by value (ByVal) or you will get a General Protection Fault (GPF). The error occurs as the Sub terminates or the first time Visual Basic attempts to process the GotLine$ string value.*

Printing to an MDI or a Printer Device Context

In early Windows programming, the TextOut function was one of the primary means used to send text to the client area of a window. In Visual Basic 2.0, the Multiple Document Interface (MDI) forms do not have a Print method. To print on an MDI form, you must turn back to the TextOut function. You must retrieve the device context (DC) of the client area of the window, paint the text, and then release the DC. The code in Listing 7-9 shows how you would control output to the MDI window by using the TextOut function.

Listing 7-9   *To properly place the messages in an MDI window, you must calculate their position from the size of the MDI window and its relation to the parent window. MDI windows do not support the x and y positions in the same manner as the other forms.*

```
Sub MDIChild1_MouseDown (Button As Integer, Shift As Integer, X As Single, Y As Single)
   Dim MDIRect As RECT
   Static OldX As Integer
```

```
    Static OldY As Integer
    GetWindowRect MDICHild1.hWnd, MDIRect
    DC% = GetDC(MDICHild1.hWnd)
    MDIWide% = MDIRect.Right - MDIRect.Left
    MDITall% = MDIRect.Bottom - MDIRect.Top
    MouseX& = (MDIWide% / Form1.ScaleWidth) * X
    MouseY& = (MDITall% / Form1.ScaleHeight) * Y
    MDIMsg$ = "X:" + Str$(X) + " Y:" + Str$(Y)
    Result% = TextOut(DC%, MouseX&, MouseY&, MDIMsg$, Len(MDIMsg$))
    Result% = TextOut(Printer.hDC, MouseX&, MouseY&, MDIMsg$, Len(MDIMsg$))
    OldX = X: OldY = Y
    RelDC% = ReleaseDC(MDICHild1.hWnd, DC%)
End Sub
```

To paint text onto the MDI Window, you must first use the GetWindowRect API call to find out the size of the MDI Window. You will need that data to calculate the positioning information from the click messages. Notice in Listing 7-9 that the GetDC/ReleaseDC construction was not necessary to place data into the Printer. The Printer object already presents a DC handle through the Printer.hDC property. Using the function in Listing 7-9, you can replicate on the printer the output on the screen.

If you want to change the font or the color of the text you print out, you can use the GetStockObject API call to grab a new font or to change the color of the text. You simply call GetStockObject to move the intelligence regarding that object into a variable. Then you call SelectObject with the DC you wish to use and the variable information you retrieved about the object. Now, any output you send to that device context will appear with the new characteristics. This process is called *selecting an object into a device context*.

In some cases it's not even necessary to resort to API calls to achieve certain printed looks. You can add superscripts and subscripts to your displayed or printed output merely by manipulating the text height and size information, as follows:

1. Save the current Control.FontSize and Control.CurrentY.
2. Multiply the current FontSize by .5, and make that the current Font-Size.
3. Calculate the distance to move the text by multiplying the TextHeight by .5.
4. Print the text.
5. Restore the old values for FontSize and CurrentY.

Tip: *When you attempt to send data to the printer in one variable that exceeds 32,767 twips (twentieth of a point) on the printing device, you will get an Overflow error message.*

Matching the Screen to the Printed Output

To match the screen display with the printed output, you can use the EnumFonts function to fill the LOGFONT structure with the font you wish to use. The more closely it matches the font you used on the screen, the more similar the results will be on the printer. Get the DC for the printer you want to use, and then convert the lfHeight and lfWidth members of LogFont from screen resolution to printer resolution. Lastly, call the CreatFontIndirect to let Windows construct the font to be used for printing. Now you're ready to use SelectObject to pull that font into your DC and print. Don't forget to release the DC with EndDoc or EndDocAPI. If you don't have printer fonts available to match your screen fonts, you'll be able to achieve only vague resemblance in a manufactured output, and you'll have to calculate the position of each character. Use the data from the TextMetric structure to find out the sizes of the characters you'll be using.

The Printer Browser

PRINTSTAT.FRM

```
Sub Fonts_Click ()
      FontForm.Show
End Sub

Sub Form_Paint ()
    PrintStats.Cls
    PaintForm
End Sub

Sub Form_Resize ()
    PrintStats.Cls
    PaintForm
End Sub

Sub Form_Unload (Cancel As Integer)
      'Release the Printer Object DC
      Printer.EndDoc
End Sub
```

```
Sub PaintForm ()
    '---Printer Object Properties
    Print "CurrentX: "; Tab(20); Printer.CurrentX
    Print "CurrentY: "; Tab(20); Printer.CurrentY
    Print "DrawMode: "; Tab(20); Printer.DrawMode
    Print "DrawStyle: "; Tab(20); Printer.DrawStyle
    Print "DrawWidth: "; Tab(20); Printer.DrawWidth
    Print "FillColor: "; Tab(20); Printer.FillColor
    Print "FillStyle: "; Tab(20); Printer.FillStyle
    Print "FontBold: "; Tab(20); Printer.FontBold
    Print "FontCount: "; Tab(20); Printer.FontCount
    Print "FontItalic: "; Tab(20); Printer.FontItalic
    Print "FontSize: "; Tab(20); Printer.FontSize
    Print "FontStrikethru: "; Tab(20); Printer.FontStrikethru
    Print "FontTransparent: "; Tab(20); Printer.FontTransparent
    Print "FontUnderline: "; Tab(20); Printer.FontUnderline
    Print "ForeColor: "; Tab(20); Hex(Printer.ForeColor) + "H"
    Print "hDC: "; Tab(20); Printer.hDC
    Print "Height: "; Tab(20); Printer.Height
    Print "Page: "; Tab(20); Printer.Page
    Print "ScaleHeight: "; Tab(20); Printer.ScaleHeight
    Print "ScaleLeft: "; Tab(20); Printer.ScaleLeft
    Print "ScaleMode: "; Tab(20); Printer.ScaleMode
    Print "ScaleTop: "; Tab(20); Printer.ScaleTop
    Print "ScaleWidth : "; Tab(20); Printer.ScaleWidth
    Print "TwipsPerPixelX: "; Tab(20); Printer.TwipsPerPixelX
    Print "TwipsPerPixelY: "; Tab(20); Printer.TwipsPerPixelY
    Print "Width: "; Tab(20); Printer.Width
    Print "TextHeight(Test): "; Tab(20); Printer.TextHeight("Test")
    Print "TextWidth(Test): "; Tab(20); Printer.TextWidth("Test")
    Print "FontName: "; Tab(20); Printer.FontName
End Sub

Sub Quitter_Click ()
    Unload PrintStats
End Sub
```

SHOWFONT.FRM

```
Sub About_Click ()
    AboutBox.Show
End Sub

Sub ChgFont_Click ()
    Do
        Pick% = Pick% + 1
```

```
Select Case Pick%
  Case 1:
    PrintDialog.Flags = CF_BOTH Or CF_NOSIMULATIONS
    PrintDialog.DialogTitle = "NOSIMULATIONS"
  Case 2:
    PrintDialog.Flags = CF_BOTH Or CF_FIXEDPITCHONLY
    PrintDialog.DialogTitle = "FIXEDPITCHONLY"
  Case 3:
    PrintDialog.Flags = CF_BOTH Or CF_FORCEFONTEXIST
    PrintDialog.DialogTitle = "FORCEFONTEXIST"
  Case 4:
    PrintDialog.Flags = CF_BOTH Or CF_NOVECTORFONTS
    PrintDialog.DialogTitle = "NOVECTORFONTS"
  Case 5:
    PrintDialog.Flags = CF_BOTH Or CF_PRINTERFONTS
    PrintDialog.DialogTitle = "PRINTERFONTS"
  Case 6:
    PrintDialog.Flags = CF_BOTH Or CF_TTONLY
    PrintDialog.DialogTitle = "TTONLY"
  Case 7:
    PrintDialog.Flags = CF_BOTH Or CF_SCALABLEONLY
    PrintDialog.DialogTitle = "SCALABLEONLY"
  Case 8:
    PrintDialog.Flags = CF_BOTH Or CF_BOTH
    PrintDialog.DialogTitle = "BOTH"
  Case 9:
    PrintDialog.Flags = CF_BOTH Or CF_WYSIWYG Or CF_BOTH Or CF_SCALABLEONLY
    PrintDialog.DialogTitle = "WYSIWYG"
    Pick% = 0
End Select
Result% = MsgBox("Click NO to use a different Setting", MB_YESNOCANCEL +
...MB_ICONQUESTION, PrintDialog.DialogTitle)
Select Case Result%
  Case IDCANCEL:
    Exit Sub
  Case IDYES:
    Exit Do
End Select
Loop
On Error GoTo DlgErr
PrintDialog.Filter = "Text File (*.TXT)|*.txt|All Files (*.*)|*.*|"
PrintDialog.CancelError = True
PrintDialog.FontName = LabelText.FontName
PrintDialog.FontSize = LabelText.FontSize
PrintDialog.FontBold = LabelText.FontBold
```

```
      PrintDialog.FontItalic = LabelText.FontItalic
      PrintDialog.FontUnderline = LabelText.FontUnderline
      PrintDialog.FontStrikethru = LabelText.FontStrikethru
      PrintDialog.Color = LabelText.ForeColor
      PrintDialog.Action = 4
      If Err = False Then
        LabelText.FontName = PrintDialog.FontName
        LabelText.FontSize = PrintDialog.FontSize
        LabelText.FontBold = PrintDialog.FontBold
        LabelText.FontItalic = PrintDialog.FontItalic
        LabelText.FontUnderline = PrintDialog.FontUnderline
        LabelText.FontStrikethru = PrintDialog.FontStrikethru
        LabelText.ForeColor = PrintDialog.Color
      End If
      Exit Sub
DlgErr:
      MsgBox Error$ + ": No Changes Made"
      Exit Sub
End Sub


Sub Command3_Click ()

End Sub


Sub PrinData_Click ()
      PrinterForm.Show
End Sub


Sub PrintDlg_Click ()
      On Error GoTo PrintDlgErr           'Error trapping
      '---Establish property settings for printer dialog
      PrintDialog.Copies = 1
      PrintDialog.Flags = PD_SHOWHELP Or PD_PAGENUMS Or PD_COLLATE Or
      ...PD_USEDEVMODECOPIES 'PD_PRINTSETUP
      PrintDialog.FromPage = 1
      PrintDialog.ToPage = 1
      PrintDialog.Min = 1                 'Sets range for page range to print
      PrintDialog.Max = 100
      PrintDialog.PrinterDefault = True  'TRUE resets default printer in WIN.INI
      PrintDialog.Action = 5             'Call for print dialog
      '---Present message box with results of selections in the dialog
      If Err = False Then
        Result$ = "Copies = " + PrintDialog.Copies + Chr$(13)
        Result$ = Result$ + "From Page = " + PrintDialog.FromPage + Chr$(13)
        Result$ = Result$ + "To Page   = " + PrintDialog.ToPage + Chr$(13)
```

```
        End If
        MsgBox Result$, , "Results of Print Settings"
        '---Set the printer to the selections made in the dialog
        Printer.FontName = LabelText.FontName
        Printer.FontSize = LabelText.FontSize
        Printer.FontBold = LabelText.FontBold
        Printer.FontItalic = LabelText.FontItalic
        Printer.FontUnderline = LabelText.FontUnderline
        Printer.FontStrikethru = LabelText.FontStrikethru
        Printer.ForeColor = LabelText.ForeColor
        Printer.Print LabelText
        Printer.EndDoc                          'Release the printer DC
        Exit Sub
PrintDlgErr:
    MsgBox Error$ + ": Print Cancelled"
    Exit Sub
End Sub


Sub Quitter_Click ()
    End
End Sub
```

FONTFORM.FRM

```
Sub Form_Load ()
    For N = 1 To Printer.FontCount
        FontList.AddItem Printer.Fonts(N - 1)
    Next N
End Sub


Sub Form_Resize ()
        FontList.Left = FontForm.ScaleLeft
        FontList.Top = FontForm.ScaleTop
        FontList.Width = FontForm.ScaleWidth
        FontList.Height = FontForm.ScaleHeight
End Sub


Sub Form_Unload (Cancel As Integer)
        'Release the Printer Object DC
        Printer.EndDoc
End Sub


Sub Quitter_Click ()
    Unload FontForm
End Sub
```

CAPAB.FRM

```
Dim CapRes As Integer
Dim Works As String

Sub CheckCap (Result%, Cap%, CapStr$)              'Pass in type, item and descr
        CapRes = Result And Cap                    'Shift Bits to read value
        If CapRes And (Cap <<>> PC_NONE) Then       'Fill list box w/result of item test
          EscapeList.AddItem "  " + Trim$(CapStr) + Chr$(9) + "Yes"  'Send string to
          ...list box
          ElseIf (Cap = PC_NONE) And Result% = 0 Then            'Same for LC and CC
            EscapeList.AddItem "   " + Trim$(CapStr) + Chr$(9) + "Yes"  'Send no cap string
        End If
End Sub


Sub DevCaps_Click (Index As Integer)
    PrinterStuff (Index)
End Sub


Sub Escapes_Click (Index As Integer)
    PrinterStuff (Index)
End Sub


Sub Form_Load ()
    PrinterStuff (2)'Call for GetDeviceCaps list as default on opening
End Sub


Sub Form_Resize ()
      EscapeList.Move Capabilities.ScaleLeft, Capabilities.ScaleTop,
      ...Capabilities.ScaleWidth, Capabilities.ScaleHeight
End Sub


Sub Form_Unload (Cancel As Integer)
      'Release the Printer Object DC
      Printer.EndDoc
End Sub


Sub GetDevCaps ()
        EscapeList.Clear
        Dim CapsDev As Integer
        For CapsDev = DRIVERVERSION To COLORRES
          Result% = GetDeviceCaps(Printer.hDC, CapsDev)
          Select Case CapsDev
            Case DRIVERVERSION:        '  Device driver version
              EscapeList.AddItem "DRIVERVERSION" + Chr$(9) + Str(Result%)
            Case TECHNOLOGY:           '  Device classification
```

```
    Select Case Result%
      Case DT_PLOTTER: EscapeList.AddItem "TECHNOLOGY" + Chr$(9) + "DT_PLOTTER"
      Case DT_RASDISPLAY: EscapeList.AddItem "TECHNOLOGY" + Chr$(9) +
      ..."DT_RASDISPLAY"
      Case DT_RASPRINTER: EscapeList.AddItem "TECHNOLOGY" + Chr$(9) +
      ..."DT_RASPRINTER"
      Case DT_RASCAMERA: EscapeList.AddItem "TECHNOLOGY" + Chr$(9) +
      ..."DT_RASCAMERA"
      Case DT_CHARSTREAM: EscapeList.AddItem "TECHNOLOGY" + Chr$(9) +
      ..."DT_CHARSTREAM"
      Case DT_METAFILE: EscapeList.AddItem "TECHNOLOGY" + Chr$(9) + "DT_METAFILE"
      Case DT_DISPFILE: EscapeList.AddItem "TECHNOLOGY" + Chr$(9) + "DT_DISPFILE"
    End Select
  Case HORZSIZE:            ' Horizontal size in millimeters
    EscapeList.AddItem "HORZSIZE" + Chr$(9) + Str(Result%)
  Case VERTSIZE:            ' Vertical size in millimeters
    EscapeList.AddItem "VERTSIZE" + Chr$(9) + Str(Result%)
  Case HORZRES:             ' Horizontal width in pixels
    EscapeList.AddItem "HORZRES" + Chr$(9) + Str(Result%)
  Case VERTRES:             ' Vertical width in pixels
    EscapeList.AddItem "VERTRES" + Chr$(9) + Str(Result%)
  Case BITSPIXEL:           ' Number of bits per pixel
    EscapeList.AddItem "BITSPIXEL" + Chr$(9) + Str(Result%)
  Case PLANES:              ' Number of planes
    EscapeList.AddItem "PLANES" + Chr$(9) + Str(Result%)
  Case NUMBRUSHES:          ' Number of brushes the device has
    EscapeList.AddItem "NUMBRUSHES" + Chr$(9) + Str(Result%)
  Case NUMPENS:             ' Number of pens the device has
    EscapeList.AddItem "NUMPENS" + Chr$(9) + Str(Result%)
  Case NUMMARKERS:          ' Number of markers the device has
    EscapeList.AddItem "NUMMARKERS" + Chr$(9) + Str(Result%)
  Case NUMFONTS:            ' Number of fonts the device has
    EscapeList.AddItem "NUMFONTS" + Chr$(9) + Str(Result%)
  Case NUMCOLORS:           ' Number of colors the device supports
    EscapeList.AddItem "NUMCOLORS" + Chr$(9) + Str(Result%)
  Case PDEVICESIZE:         ' Size required for device descriptor
    EscapeList.AddItem "PDEVICESIZE" + Chr$(9) + Str(Result%)
  Case CURVECAPS:           ' Curve capabilities
    EscapeList.AddItem "CURVECAPS structures:"
    CheckCap Result%, CC_NONE, "No curve info on CC_NONE"
    CheckCap Result%, CC_CIRCLES, "circles"
    CheckCap Result%, CC_PIE, "pie wedges"
    CheckCap Result%, CC_CHORD, "chord arcs"
    CheckCap Result%, CC_ELLIPSES, "ellipese"
    CheckCap Result%, CC_WIDE, "wide lines"
    CheckCap Result%, CC_STYLED, "styled lines"
```

```
   CheckCap Result%, CC_WIDESTYLED, "wide styled lines"
   CheckCap Result%, CC_INTERIORS, "interiors"
Case ASPECTX:              '  Length of the X leg
   EscapeList.AddItem "ASPECTX" + Chr$(9) + Str(Result%)
Case ASPECTY:              '  Length of the Y leg
   EscapeList.AddItem "ASPECTY" + Chr$(9) + Str(Result%)
Case ASPECTXY:             '  Length of the hypotenuse
   EscapeList.AddItem "ASPECTXY" + Chr$(9) + Str(Result%)
Case LOGPIXELSX:           '  Logical pixels/inch in X
   EscapeList.AddItem "LOGPIXELSX" + Chr$(9) + Str(Result%)
Case LOGPIXELSY:           '  Logical pixels/inch in Y
   EscapeList.AddItem "LOGPIXELSY" + Chr$(9) + Str(Result%)
Case SIZEPALETTE:          '  Number of entries in physical palette
   EscapeList.AddItem "SIZEPALETTE" + Chr$(9) + Str(Result%)
Case NUMRESERVED:          '  Number of reserved entries in palette
   EscapeList.AddItem "NUMRESERVED" + Chr$(9) + Str(Result%)
Case COLORRES:             '  Actual color resolution
   EscapeList.AddItem "COLORRES" + Chr$(9) + Str(Result%)
Case CLIPCAPS:             '  Clipping capabilities
   EscapeList.AddItem "CLIPCAPS" + Chr$(9) + Str(Result%)
Case LINECAPS:             '  Line capabilities
   EscapeList.AddItem "LINECAPS Capabilities:"
   CheckCap Result%, LC_NONE, "No Line Info on LC_NONE"
   CheckCap Result%, LC_POLYLINE, "polylines"
   CheckCap Result%, LC_MARKER, "markers"
   CheckCap Result%, LC_POLYMARKER, "polymarkers"
   CheckCap Result%, LC_WIDE, "wide lines"
   CheckCap Result%, LC_STYLED, "styled lines"
   CheckCap Result%, LC_WIDESTYLED, "wide styled lines"
   CheckCap Result%, LC_INTERIORS, "interiors"
Case POLYGONALCAPS:        '  Polygonal capabilities
   EscapeList.AddItem "POLYGONALCAPS Capabilities:"
   CheckCap Result%, PC_NONE, "No Polygon Info on PC_NONE"
   CheckCap Result%, PC_POLYGON, "polygons"
   CheckCap Result%, PC_RECTANGLE, "rectangles"
   CheckCap Result%, PC_WINDPOLYGON, "winding polygons"
   CheckCap Result%, PC_TRAPEZOID, "trapezoids"
   CheckCap Result%, PC_SCANLINE, "scanlines"
   CheckCap Result%, PC_WIDE, "wide borders"
   CheckCap Result%, PC_STYLED, "styled borders"
   CheckCap Result%, PC_WIDESTYLED, "wide styled borders"
   CheckCap Result%, PC_INTERIORS, "interiors"
Case TEXTCAPS:             '  Text capabilities
   EscapeList.AddItem "TEXTCAPS Capabilities:"
   CheckCap Result%, TC_OP_CHARACTER, "OutputPrecision-CHARACTER"
```

```
                    CheckCap Result%, TC_OP_STROKE, "OutputPrecision-STROKE"
                    CheckCap Result%, TC_CP_STROKE, "ClipPrecision STROKE"
                    CheckCap Result%, TC_CR_90, "CharRotAbility-90"
                    CheckCap Result%, TC_CR_ANY, "CharRotAbility-ANY"
                    CheckCap Result%, TC_SF_X_YINDEP, "ScaleFreedom-X_YINDEPENDENT"
                    CheckCap Result%, TC_SA_DOUBLE, "ScaleAbility-DOUBLE"
                    CheckCap Result%, TC_SA_INTEGER, "ScaleAbility-INTEGER"
                    CheckCap Result%, TC_SA_CONTIN, "ScaleAbility-CONTINUOUS"
                    CheckCap Result%, TC_EA_DOUBLE, "EmboldenAbility-DOUBLE"
                    CheckCap Result%, TC_IA_ABLE, "ItalisizeAbility-ABLE"
                    CheckCap Result%, TC_UA_ABLE, "UnderlineAbility-ABLE"
                    CheckCap Result%, TC_SO_ABLE, "RasterFontAble-ABLE"
                    CheckCap Result%, TC_VA_ABLE, "VectorFontAble-ABLE"
                    CheckCap Result%, TC_RESERVED, "No Function"
                Case RASTERCAPS:            '  Bitblt capabilities
                    EscapeList.AddItem "RASTERCAPS capabilities"
                    CheckCap Result%, RC_BITBLT, "Can do standard BLT"
                    CheckCap Result%, RC_BANDING, "Device requires banding support"
                    CheckCap Result%, RC_SCALING, "Device requires scaling support"
                    CheckCap Result%, RC_BITMAP64, "Device can support >64K bitmap"
                    CheckCap Result%, RC_GDI20_OUTPUT, "has 2.0 output calls"
                    CheckCap Result%, RC_DI_BITMAP, "supports DIB to memory"
                    CheckCap Result%, RC_PALETTE, "supports a palette"
                    CheckCap Result%, RC_DIBTODEV, "supports DIBitsToDevice"
                    CheckCap Result%, RC_BIGFONT, "supports >64K fonts"
                    CheckCap Result%, RC_STRETCHBLT, "supports StretchBlt"
                    CheckCap Result%, RC_FLOODFILL, "supports FloodFill"
                    CheckCap Result%, RC_STRETCHDIB, "supports StretchDIBits"
            End Select
Skipr:    Next CapsDev
        Capabilities.Caption = "GetDeviceCaps Results"
        'Release the Printer Object DC
        Printer.EndDoc
End Sub

Sub GetEscapes ()
    EscapeList.Clear
    For EscIndex = NEWFRAME To SET_MIRROR_MODE
        x% = GetEscape(Printer.hDC, EscIndex)
        If x% > 0 Then
          Yes$ = "Yes"
          Supported% = Supported% + 1
        Else
          Yes$ = ""
        End If
```

```
Select Case EscIndex
          Case NEWFRAME: EscapeList.AddItem "NEWFRAME" + Chr$(9) + Yes$ ' 1
          Case ABORTDOC: EscapeList.AddItem "ABORTDOC" + Chr$(9) + Yes$     ' 2
          Case NEXTBAND: EscapeList.AddItem "NEXTBAND" + Chr$(9) + Yes$     ' 3
          Case SETCOLORTABLE: EscapeList.AddItem "SETCOLORTABLE" + Chr$(9) +
          ...Yes$     ' 4
          Case GETCOLORTABLE: EscapeList.AddItem "GETCOLORTABLE" + Chr$(9) +
          ...Yes$     ' 5
          Case FLUSHOUTPUT: EscapeList.AddItem "FLUSHOUTPUT" + Chr$(9) +
          ...Yes$     ' 6
          Case DRAFTMODE: EscapeList.AddItem "DRAFTMODE" + Chr$(9) +
          ...Yes$     ' 7
          Case QUERYESCSUPPORT: EscapeList.AddItem "QUERYESCSUPPORT" +
          ...Chr$(9) + Yes$     ' 8
          Case SETABORTPROC: EscapeList.AddItem "SETABORTPROC" + Chr$(9) +
          ...Yes$     ' 9
          Case STARTDOC: EscapeList.AddItem "STARTDOC" + Chr$(9) +
          ...Yes$     ' 10
          Case ENDDOCAPI: EscapeList.AddItem "ENDDOCAPI" + Chr$(9) +
          ...Yes$     ' 11
          Case GETPHYSPAGESIZE: EscapeList.AddItem "GETPHYSPAGESIZE" +
          ...Chr$(9) + Yes$     ' 12
          Case GETPRINTINGOFFSET: EscapeList.AddItem "GETPRINTINGOFFSET" +
          ...Chr$(9) + Yes$     ' 13
          Case GETSCALINGFACTOR: EscapeList.AddItem "GETSCALINGFACTOR" +
          ...Chr$(9) + Yes$     ' 14
          Case MFCOMMENT: EscapeList.AddItem "MFCOMMENT" + Chr$(9) +
          ...Yes$     ' 15
          Case GETPENWIDTH: EscapeList.AddItem "GETPENWIDTH" + Chr$(9) +
          ...Yes$     ' 16
          Case SETCOPYCOUNT: EscapeList.AddItem "SETCOPYCOUNT" + Chr$(9) +
          ...Yes$     ' 17
          Case SELECTPAPERSOURCE: EscapeList.AddItem "SELECTPAPERSOURCE" +
          ...Chr$(9) + Yes$     ' 18
          Case DEVICEDATA: EscapeList.AddItem "DEVICEDATA" + Chr$(9) +
          ...Yes$     ' 19
          Case PASSTHROUGH: EscapeList.AddItem "PASSTHROUGH" + Chr$(9) +
          ...Yes$     ' 19
          Case GETTECHNOLGY: EscapeList.AddItem "GETTECHNOLGY" + Chr$(9) +
          ...Yes$     ' 20
          Case GETTECHNOLOGY: EscapeList.AddItem "GETTECHNOLOGY" + Chr$(9) +
          ...Yes$     ' 20
          Case SETENDCAP: EscapeList.AddItem "SETENDCAP" + Chr$(9) +
          ...Yes$     ' 21
          Case SETLINEJOIN: EscapeList.AddItem "SETLINEJOIN" + Chr$(9) +
          ...Yes$     ' 22
```

```
        Case SETMITERLIMIT: EscapeList.AddItem "SETMITERLIMIT" + Chr$(9) +
        ...Yes$      ' 23
        Case BANDINFO: EscapeList.AddItem "BANDINFO" + Chr$(9) + Yes$       ' 24
        Case DRAWPATTERNRECT:
If x% = 1 Then
  EscapeList.AddItem "DRAWPATTERNRECT - Other" + Chr$(9) + Yes$      ' 25
ElseIf x% = 2 Then
  EscapeList.AddItem "DRAWPATTERNRECT - HP IIP" + Chr$(9) + Yes$      ' 25
Else
  EscapeList.AddItem "DRAWPATTERNRECT - HP IIP" + Chr$(9) + Yes$      ' 25
End If
        Case GETVECTORPENSIZE: EscapeList.AddItem "GETVECTORPENSIZE" +
        ...Chr$(9) + Yes$      ' 26
        Case GETVECTORBRUSHSIZE: EscapeList.AddItem "GETVECTORBRUSHSIZE" +
        ...Chr$(9) + Yes$      ' 27
        Case ENABLEDUPLEX: EscapeList.AddItem "ENABLEDUPLEX" + Chr$(9) +
        ...Yes$      ' 28
        Case GETSETPAPERBINS: EscapeList.AddItem "GETSETPAPERBINS" +
        ...Chr$(9) + Yes$      ' 29
        Case GETSETPRINTORIENT: EscapeList.AddItem "GETSETPRINTORIENT" +
        ...Chr$(9) + Yes$      ' 30
        Case ENUMPAPERBINS: EscapeList.AddItem "ENUMPAPERBINS" + Chr$(9) +
        ...Yes$      ' 31
        Case SETDIBSCALING: EscapeList.AddItem "SETDIBSCALING" + Chr$(9) +
        ...Yes$      ' 32
        Case EPSPRINTING: EscapeList.AddItem "EPSPRINTING" + Chr$(9) +
        ...Yes$      ' 33
        Case ENUMPAPERMETRICS: EscapeList.AddItem "ENUMPAPERMETRICS" +
        ...Chr$(9) + Yes$      ' 34
        Case GETSETPAPERMETRICS: EscapeList.AddItem "GETSETPAPERMETRICS" +
        ...Chr$(9) + Yes$      ' 35
        Case POSTSCRIPT_DATA: EscapeList.AddItem "POSTSCRIPT_DATA" +
        ...Chr$(9) + Yes$      ' 37
        Case POSTSCRIPT_IGNORE: EscapeList.AddItem "POSTSCRIPT_IGNORE" +
        ...Chr$(9) + Yes$      ' 38
        Case GETEXTENDEDTEXTMETRICS: EscapeList.AddItem
        ..."GETEXTENDEDTEXTMETRICS" + Chr$(9) + Yes$      ' 256
        Case GETEXTENTTABLE: EscapeList.AddItem "GETEXTENTTABLE" + Chr$(9)
        ...+ Yes$      ' 257
        Case GETPAIRKERNTABLE: EscapeList.AddItem "GETPAIRKERNTABLE" +
        ...Chr$(9) + Yes$      ' 258
        Case GETTRACKKERNTABLE: EscapeList.AddItem "GETTRACKKERNTABLE" +
        ...Chr$(9) + Yes$      ' 259
        Case EXTTEXTOUTAPI: EscapeList.AddItem "EXTTEXTOUTAPI" + Chr$(9) +
        ...Yes$      ' 512
        Case ENABLERELATIVEWIDTHS: EscapeList.AddItem
        ..."ENABLERELATIVEWIDTHS" + Chr$(9) + Yes$      ' 768
```

```
                     Case ENABLEPAIRKERNING: EscapeList.AddItem "ENABLEPAIRKERNING" +
                     ...Chr$(9) + Yes$     ' 769
                     Case SETKERNTRACK: EscapeList.AddItem "SETKERNTRACK" + Chr$(9) +
                     ...Yes$     ' 770
                     Case SETALLJUSTVALUES: EscapeList.AddItem "SETALLJUSTVALUES" +
                     ...Chr$(9) + Yes$     ' 771
                     Case SETCHARSET: EscapeList.AddItem "SETCHARSET" + Chr$(9) +
                     ...Yes$     ' 772
                     Case STRETCHBLTAPI: EscapeList.AddItem "STRETCHBLTAPI" + Chr$(9) +
                     ...Yes$     ' 2048
                     Case BEGIN_PATH: EscapeList.AddItem "BEGIN_PATH" + Chr$(9) +
                     ...Yes$     ' 4096
                     Case CLIP_TO_PATH: EscapeList.AddItem "CLIP_TO_PATH" + Chr$(9) +
                     ...Yes$     ' 4097
                     Case END_PATH: EscapeList.AddItem "END_PATH" + Chr$(9) +
                     ...Yes$     ' 4098
                     Case EXT_DEVICE_CAPS: EscapeList.AddItem "EXT_DEVICE_CAPS" +
                     ...Chr$(9) + Yes$     ' 4099
                     Case RESTORE_CTM: EscapeList.AddItem "RESTORE_CTM" + Chr$(9) +
                     ...Yes$     ' 4100
                     Case SAVE_CTM: EscapeList.AddItem "SAVE_CTM" + Chr$(9) +
                     ...Yes$     ' 4101
                     Case SET_ARC_DIRECTION: EscapeList.AddItem "SET_ARC_DIRECTION" +
                     ...Chr$(9) + Yes$     ' 4102
                     Case SET_BACKGROUND_COLOR: EscapeList.AddItem
                     ..."SET_BACKGROUND_COLOR" + Chr$(9) + Yes$     ' 4103
                     Case SET_POLY_MODE: EscapeList.AddItem "SET_POLY_MODE" + Chr$(9) +
                     ...Yes$     ' 4104
                     Case SET_SCREEN_ANGLE: EscapeList.AddItem "SET_SCREEN_ANGLE" +
                     ...Chr$(9) + Yes$     ' 4105
                     Case SET_SPREAD: EscapeList.AddItem "SET_SPREAD" + Chr$(9) +
                     ...Yes$     ' 4106
                     Case TRANSFORM_CTM: EscapeList.AddItem "TRANSFORM_CTM" + Chr$(9) +
                     ...Yes$     ' 4107
                     Case SET_CLIP_BOX: EscapeList.AddItem "SET_CLIP_BOX" + Chr$(9) +
                     ...Yes$     ' 4108
                     Case SET_BOUNDS: EscapeList.AddItem "SET_BOUNDS" + Chr$(9) +
                     ...Yes$     ' 4109
                     Case SET_MIRROR_MODE: EscapeList.AddItem "SET_MIRROR_MODE" +
                     ...Chr$(9) + Yes$     ' 4110
             End Select
         Next EscIndex
     Capabilities.Caption = Str$(Supported%) + " of " + Str$(EscapeList.ListCount) +
     ..."Escapes Supported"
     'Release the Printer Object DC
     Printer.EndDoc
End Sub
```

```
Sub PrinterStuff (Index As Integer)
      Screen.MousePointer = 11 'Set mouse pointer to Wait
      Static Tabs(2) As Integer'Set tabs array
      Capabilities.Visible = True    'Ensure the form is visible
      EscapeList.SetFocus       'Ensure focus on list
      Tabs(0) = 30              'Set first tab location
      Tabs(1) = 115            'Set second tab location
      x% = SendMessage(GetFocus(), LB_SETTABSTOPS, 2, Tabs(1)) 'Set tabs
      Select Case Index                  'Respond to menu choice
              Case 1:
         GetEscapes            'Pass printer escapes to list
              Case 2:
         GetDevCaps            'Pass printer capabilities
      End Select
      Screen.MousePointer = 0  'Restore default
      Printer.EndDoc
End Sub

Sub Quitter_Click ()
    Unload Capabilities
End Sub
```

PRINTERS.FRM

```
Dim nSize As Integer
Dim lpRetStr As String
Const WM_WININICANGE = &H1A
Dim NewPrinter As String
Dim OldPrinter As String
Dim Changed As Integer

Sub Capab_Click ()
    Capabilities.Show
End Sub

Sub DeviceList_DblClick ()

    'Parse out the printer string
    Pos% = InStr(DeviceList.List(DeviceList.ListIndex), Chr$(9))
    Pos2% = InStr(Pos% + 1, DeviceList.List(DeviceList.ListIndex), Chr$(9))

    Part1$ = Mid$(DeviceList.List(DeviceList.ListIndex), 1, Pos% - 1)
    Part2$ = Mid$(DeviceList.List(DeviceList.ListIndex), Pos% + 1, (Pos2% - 1) - Pos%)
    Part3$ = Mid$(DeviceList.List(DeviceList.ListIndex), Pos2% + 1, 30)

    NewPrinter = RTrim$(Part1$) + "," + RTrim$(Part2$) + "," + RTrim$(Part3$)
```

```
    'Get existing printer
    GoSub Existing
    OldPrinter = Mid$(lpRetStr, 1, InStr(lpRetStr, Chr$(0)) - 1)

    'Give the user a chance to cancel the printer change
    Pick% = MsgBox("Change: " + Chr$(13) + OldPrinter + Chr$(13) + " to: " + Chr$(13) +
    ...NewPrinter, 1 + 32, "Change This Printer?")
    If Pick% = 2 Then Exit Sub  'Exit if the user chooses CANCEL
    'Release the Printer Object DC
    Printer.EndDoc
    'Write the selected printer in as the new current printer
    Result% = WriteProfileString("windows", "device", NewPrinter)
    x% = SendMessage(&HFFF, WM_WININICHANGE, 0, ByVal "")
    GoSub Existing
    PrinterForm.Caption = "Current: " + Mid$(lpRetStr, 1, InStr(lpRetStr, Chr$(0)) - 1)
    Changed = True
    Exit Sub
```

Existing:

```
    'Get and save current printer setting in WIN.INI
    nSize = 80
    lpRetStr = Space$(nSize)
    Result% = GetProfileString("windows", "device", "Can't Find Default Printer",
    ...lpRetStr, nSize)
    Return
End Sub


Sub Form_Load ()
    'Set the tabs for the list box
    Static Tabs(2) As Integer
    PrinterForm.Visible = True
    DeviceList.SetFocus
    Tabs(0) = 20      '80
    Tabs(1) = 80      '120
    x% = SendMessage(GetFocus(), LB_SETTABSTOPS, 1, Tabs(1))
    'Get the current printer
    GetCurrent
    'Get the list of installed printers
    nSize = 255
    lpRetStr = Space$(nSize)
    AppName$ = "devices"
    x% = GetProfileString(AppName$, ByVal 0&, "Can't Find Section", lpRetStr, nSize)
    OldPos% = 1: Pos% = 1
    Do
```

```
      Pos% = InStr(OldPos%, lpRetStr, Chr$(0))
      If Pos% = 0 Then Exit Do
      Device$ = Mid$(lpRetStr, OldPos%, Pos% - OldPos%)
      OldPos% = Pos% + 1
      DeviceList.AddItem Device$
    Loop
    'Get the ports assigned to the installed drivers
    For NextPrinter = 0 To (DeviceList.ListCount - 2)
      AppName$ = "devices"
      ListedPrinter$ = DeviceList.List(NextPrinter)
      If Mid$(OldPrinter, 1, 5) = Mid$(ListedPrinter$, 1, 5) Then Place% = NextPrinter
      x% = GetProfileString(AppName$, ListedPrinter$, "Can't Find Section", lpRetStr,
      ...nSize)
      Comma% = InStr(lpRetStr, ",")
      ListedPrinter$ = ListedPrinter$ + Chr$(9) + Mid$(lpRetStr, 1, Comma% - 1) +
      ...Chr$(9) + Mid$(lpRetStr, Comma% + 1, 30)
      DeviceList.List(NextPrinter) = ListedPrinter$
    Next NextPrinter
    DeviceList.ListIndex = Place%
End Sub


Sub Form_QueryUnload (CANCEL As Integer, UnloadMode As Integer)
    If Changed Then
      Result% = MsgBox("Do you want to restore the original default?", MB_YESNOCANCEL +
      ...MB_ICONQUESTION, "Restore Default")
    End If
    Changed = False
    If Result% = IDYES Then
     'Release the Printer Object DC
      Printer.EndDoc
      Result% = WriteProfileString("windows", "device", OldPrinter)
      'x& = SendMessage(CDERR_DIALOGFAILURE, WM_WININICHANGE, 0, ByVal "windows")
      x% = SendMessage(&HFFF, WM_WININICHANGE, ByVal 0&, ByVal "")
    ElseIf Result% = IDCANCEL Then
      CANCEL = IDCANCEL
    End If
    OldPrinter = ""
    NewPrinter = ""
End Sub


Sub Form_Resize ()
    PrinterForm.Height = 3216
    DeviceList.Move PrinterForm.ScaleLeft, PrinterForm.ScaleTop,
    ...PrinterForm.ScaleWidth, PrinterForm.ScaleHeight
End Sub
```

```
Sub GetCurrent ()
    nSize = 30
    lpRetStr = Space$(nSize)
    x% = GetProfileString("windows", "device", "No Printer Selected", lpRetStr, nSize)
    If x% > nSize Then MsgBox "Profile String Concatenated", MB_OK +
    ...MB_ICONEXCLAMATION, "WIN.INI"
    Comma% = InStr(1, lpRetStr, ",")
    If Comma% = 0 Then
      MsgBox "Unable to Find 2nd Field in Device", MB_OK + MB_ICONEXCLAMATION,
      ..."WIN.INI"
    Else
      PrinterForm.Caption = "Current: " + Mid$(lpRetStr, 1, Comma% - 1)
    End If
    OldPrinter = lpRetStr
End Sub


Sub Quitter_Click ()
    Unload PrinterForm
End Sub


Sub Settings_Click ()
    PrintStats.Show
End Sub
```

ABOUTBOX.FRM

```
Sub Command1_Click ()
    Unload AboutBox
End Sub


Sub Form_Load ()
    Notes$ = "Created by Mark S. Burgess" + Chr$(13)
    Notes$ = Notes$ + "for Chapter 7 - Printing" + Chr$(13)
    Notes$ = Notes$ + "Advanced Visual Basic" + Chr$(13)
    Notes$ = Notes$ + "published by Addison-Wesley"
    Label2.Caption = Notes$
End Sub
```

GLOBAL.BAS

```
Type RECT
    Left As Integer
    Top As Integer
    Right As Integer
    Bottom As Integer
End Type
```

```
'Functions Unique to This Program
Declare Function GetEscape Lib "D:\WINDEV\VB\BOOK\CH-07\GETESC.DLL" (ByVal hDC As
...Integer, ByVal EscapeCode As Integer) As Integer
Declare Function GetDeviceCaps Lib "GDI" (ByVal hDC As Integer, ByVal nIndex As
...Integer) As Integer
Declare Function Escape Lib "GDI" (ByVal hDC As Integer, ByVal nEscape As Integer,
...ByVal nCount As Integer, ByVal lpInData As Any, ByVal lpOutData As Any) As Integer
Declare Function SendMessage Lib "User" (ByVal hWnd As Integer, ByVal wMsg As Integer,
...ByVal wParam As Integer, lParam As Any) As Long
Declare Function GetFocus Lib "User" () As Integer
Global Const WM_USER = &H400
Global Const LB_SETTABSTOPS = WM_USER + 19
Declare Function GetProfileString Lib "Kernel" (ByVal lpAppName As String, ByVal
...lpKeyName As Any, ByVal lpDefault As String, ByVal lpReturnedString As String,
...ByVal nSize As Integer) As Integer
Declare Function WriteProfileString Lib "Kernel" (ByVal lpApplicationName As String,
...ByVal lpKeyName As String, ByVal lpString As String) As Integer

(--Insert GDI Escapes from WIN31API.TXT--)

(-- Insert Device Parameters for GetDeviceCaps()from WIN31API.TXT--)

(--Insert Device Capability Masks from WIN31API.TXT--)

(--Insert CONST.TXT from WIN31API.TXT--)
```

Chapter 8

Custom Controls

In Chapter 5 we extended Visual Basic through calls directly to the Windows application programming interface (API). In Chapter 6 we got into a completely different set of languages to extend Visual Basic with dynamic link libraries. At the end of this chapter, we'll discuss the possibilities for subclassing Windows (a means of intercepting messages) to combine API calls and dynamic link libraries to extend Visual Basic. For most of this chapter, however, we'll discuss a third major way to add capability to Visual Basic: through **custom controls**.

When you start Visual Basic for the first time, you get a large tool bar with lots of controls. These are the standard controls shipped with Visual Basic in the Standard or Professional editions. You may also have tapped into the large market for third-party constructed controls from Microhelp, Crescent, Sheridan, and others. And yet you may still require capability that you can't buy and that you haven't been able to tap through the standard visual language, a few calls to the API, or a quick DLL. That's where custom controls fit in. You can create a re-usable tool that behaves in a new way but makes itself available through the same toolbox.

The Anatomy of a Custom Control

A custom control is a special form of dynamic link library. All of the learning you did back in Chapter 6 regarding DLLs applies to custom controls. A custom control is merely a stricter form of DLL that requires property, event, and model structures. Depending on your compiler, you must still use the entry (LibMain) and exit code (WEP) peculiar to a DLL. Some compilers, like Borland C++ and Microsoft QuickC for Windows, supply the Windows Exit Procedure (WEP) implicitly. Visual Basic controls also send a final message to a routine called VBTERMCC, where you can perform any cleanup and sign-off chores your application requires without using a WEP function. The diagram in Figure 8-1 shows the primary conceptual flow of a custom control in operation.

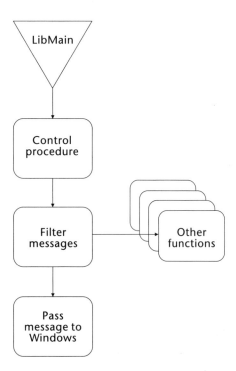

Figure 8-1   *This ABC FlowChart diagram depicts the conceptual elements of a custom control.*

The components of a custom control are as follows:

- .C, .CPP, .TPW (source files)
  - LibMain entry point
  - Control procedure
  - Control registration function
  - Required include file references
- .H (include files)
  - Includes WINDOWS.H and VBAPI.H (from CDK)
  - #defines for bitmaps, properties, and events ⎫
  - Property structure ⎬ application
  - Event structure ⎭ specific
  - Model structure
- .DEF (definition files)
  - Export function names
  - Memory configuration
- .RC (resource files)
  - Dialog definitions
  - Four icon definitions for the toolbox
  - Menu definitions
  - String tables

Creating a Simple Custom Control

To create a simple custom control, we'll look together at how to use Borland C++ for Windows. We won't be using the C++ capabilities this time. Later in the chapter, we'll take a look at creating a custom control by using C++ in Microsoft's Visual C++ package, and I'll describe how you can do the same thing in Borland's package.

Since custom controls follow a specific structure that repeats a great deal of information from control to control, I recommend that you copy the source code from one of the examples in the Microsoft Knowledge Base, the Visual Control Pack, or the Control Development Kit in the Visual Basic Professional edition. First, you need to create a LibMain just as with any other dynamic link library. Listing 8-1 shows the LibMain for the custom control VBCNTRL.VBX. Borland C++ supplies a Windows Exit Procedure (WEP), so it's not necessary to write one out unless you wish to perform some additional cleanup before your control terminates.

Listing 8-1   *Every custom control must include a LibMain function.*

```
/*Initialize library - called when the first client loads the DLL.*/
int FAR PASCAL LibMain
(
    HANDLE hModule,
    WORD   wDataSeg,
    WORD   cbHeapSize,
    LPSTR  lpszCmdLine
)
{
    /*Avoid warnings on unused (but required) formal parameters */
    wDataSeg    = wDataSeg;
    cbHeapSize = cbHeapSize;
    lpszCmdLine = lpszCmdLine;
    hmodDLL = hModule;
    return 1;
}


/*Register custom control when DLL is loaded for use.*/
BOOL FAR PASCAL _export VBINITCC(USHORT usVersion, BOOL fRuntime)
{
    fRuntime  = fRuntime;
    usVersion = usVersion;
    return VBRegisterModel(hmodDLL, &modelVBCntrl); /* Register control(s) */
}
```

Listing 8-1 also shows the VBINITCC function used to register the window for the custom control. Except for the graphic or "lite controls", all custom controls create a window of their own for controlling message traffic. (To create graphical controls, you must use the MODEL_fGraphical flag in the control structure.) This is a departure from a DLL that does not require a separate window to be useful except when you intend to use the DLL for subclassing another window. The important part of the VBINITCC function is the VBRegisterModel function call. Using the window definition in Listing 8-2 from the include files, VBRegisterModel creates the identity for the custom control window. Two parameters, fRunTime and usVersion, grab from Visual Basic the system information that indicates which version of the VBRUNXXX.DLL is in use by the application. The parameters then place that version data into the control window model before the window is registered.

Listing 8-2 *Every custom control uses the MODEL structure in place of the &wndclass structure used with the RegisterClass API call in a standard Windows program.*

```
MODEL modelVBCntrl =
    {
    VB_VERSION,                         /* VB version being used*/
    0,                                  /* MODEL flags*/
    (PCTLPROC)VBCntrlCtlProc,           /* VBCONTRL procedure*/
    CS_VREDRAW | CS_HREDRAW,            /* Class style*/
    WS_BORDER,                          /* Default Windows style*/
    0,                                  /* Size of CIRCLE structure*/
    IDBMP_VBCNTRL,                      /* Palette bitmap ID*/
    "VBControl",                        /* Default VBCONTRL name*/
    "VBCNTRL",                          /* Visual Basic class name*/
    NULL,                               /* Parent class name*/
    VBCNTRL_Properties,                 /* Property information table*/
    VBCNTRL_Events,                     /* Event information table*/
    IPROP_VBCNTRL_BACKCOLOR,            /* Default property*/
    IEVENT_VBCNTRL_CLICK,               /* Default event*/
    -1                                  /* Property representing value of ctl*/
    };
```

All of the functions in this simple custom control appear in Borland's Object Browser list box, as shown in Figure 8-2.

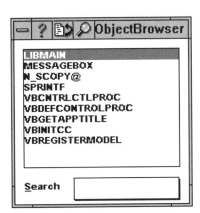

Figure 8-2 *MessageBox, sprintf, and M_SCOPY are not required when you construct a custom control. The other functions shown here must be included.*

The MODEL structure contains the control procedure name (3rd parameter) to process the messages for the control window. Next, the class name and default name identify the control to Windows. The parent-class name entry will be used later when we look at subclassing. Finally, the event and property structure names appear in the 11th and 12th parameters.

The Visual Basic Control Development Kit (CDK) comes with the VBAPI.H include file and the related VBAPI.LIB library file. The LIB file must be included in the make or project file for the custom control.

 Tip: Even though Microsoft encourages you to make dynamic link librar-ies in the large (or far) segment reference model, each custom control must reference its own data segment. That is because several versions of one control may be running at the same time—unlike a dynamic link library, which may be loaded once and may then be referenced multiple times. Therefore, you must either explicitly cast all of the structures and variables as NEAR or use the small or compact model and allow the compiler to help you with variable casting.

Before we jump into processing actions in the control procedure, let's complete the structural work in the custom control. The standard sets of properties and events appear in the CDK. It's not necessary, though, to include all of either group if you want to limit the number of programming options within your control. It would be a bit silly to include properties or events that don't have any associated functionality within your control. The exception to this is if you want to capture user input to those properties for use somewhere else. You can construct the control to provide the property and to store any settings made to it without attaching specific functionality.

If you choose to construct your own properties and events, you have three steps to perform. These steps are discussed later in the chapter, in the section "Using Visual C++."

The last structural code that you must write appears in the resource files. You must include #defines for the four bitmaps you will need to represent the control in the Visual Basic environment. You can pick any number to start defining a bitmap as your icon. The first one (the lowest number) will be the unselected version in the toolbox when you first add the control to your environment. The second bitmap (#define 1 + 1) is the "selected" look of the icon. As a step toward hardware independence for your control, the third bitmap (#define1+3 and +6) creates the icon to be used in monochrome and EGA displays respectively.

Tip: Speaking of independence, you can include code in your custom control for checking the version number of the environment using your control. The MODEL structure holds the version number when you set it with VBINITCC as shown previously in Listings 8-1 and 8-2. You will learn more about this in the forthcoming section on Visual C++.

Add to the include files for your control any string tables, dialogs, or menus you plan to use in your application. It's not necessary for all of these objects to be in the control at the beginning, however.

Lastly, you can call from Visual Basic an external function stored inside the custom control in the same manner that you call any other DLL. If you are using a C++ compiler, you must preface the function prototype with the _extern keyword to prevent name mangling. The function must appear in the Exports list of the .DEF definition file, also. Since you shouldn't cross out of the data segment in a custom control, you can use these exported functions in your Visual Basic program without creating a second DLL. In that manner, you can provide a programmable interface to the functions inside the custom control.

The last, and most active, element of a custom control is the control procedure itself. Listing 8-3 shows the control procedure for the Borland C++ example. This function receives the messages intended for the custom control window and either processes them or passes them on with VBDefControlProc. You can insert whatever message processing you wish.

Listing 8-3   *This simple example of a control procedure demonstrates how to trap and process messages inside a custom control.*

```
/*Control Procedure*/
LONG FAR PASCAL VBCntrlCtlProc(HCTL hctl,      /*Handle to the control*/
                               HWND hwnd,      /*Window handle*/
                               USHORT msg,     /*Inbound message*/
                               USHORT wp,      /*message wParam*/
                               LONG lp)        /*message lParam*/
{
  char szLn1[] = "Design Mode Help requested for SIMPLE.VBX.";
  char szLn2[] = "To call Help, use the API function:";
  char szLn3[] = "BOOL WinHelp(hwnd,             //Handle";
  char szLn4[] = "                 lpszHelpFile,  //File address";
  char szLn5[] = "                 fuCommand,     //Context";
  char szLn6[] = "                 dwData).         //Type of data";
```

```
//Process message passed from Windows thru Visual Basic to Control
switch(msg)
  {
  case WM_RBUTTONDOWN:     //On right mouse button click or
  case WM_RBUTTONDBLCLK:   //double click inside custom control
    {
    //Retrieve title from Visual Basic applcation
    VBGetAppTitle((LPSTR)szTtlBuffer,20);
    //Format a null terminated string for the message box
    retval = sprintf(szMsgBuffer, "%s\n", "Message from the Custom Control");
    //return to the Visual Basic application
    break;
  case VBM_HELP:           //On F1 key while in Design mode
    retval = sprintf(szTtlBuffer, "%s\n", "Help on Simple Control");
    //Format a null terminated string for the message box
    retval = sprintf(szMsgBuffer, "%s\n%s\n%s\n%s\n%s\n%s\n",szLn1,szLn2,
    ...szLn3,szLn4,szLn5,szLn6);
    //return to the Visual Basic application
    break;
    }
  default:
    return VBDefControlProc(hctl, hwnd, msg, wp, lp);
  }
  //Present message box
    MessageBox(hwnd, (LPSTR) szMsgBuffer, (LPSTR) szTtlBuffer, MB_OK);
    return VBDefControlProc(hctl, hwnd, msg, wp, lp);
    // return NULL; Replace to prevent message forwarding
}
```

In the sample for the simple control in Listing 8-3, we are processing two messages: a mouse button and the F1 key. Before you actually grab the messages to process their contents, you might call the VbGetAppTitle function as shown. This retrieves the name of the Visual Basic application in which the control resides and places it into a legal string (according to Visual Basic memory management rules) for the control to process in Visual Basic.

Just as with the string processing concerns in the Windows API, which we discussed in Chapter 5, you must be meticulous in your string handling within a custom control. Since Visual Basic processes all of the messages coming to the control before they arrive at the control, you must be certain that the strings it accesses will not corrupt memory. All of the messages passing through Visual Basic to the control are appended with the control handle (HCTL). This handle remains valid throughout the life of the control even when the window handle (HWND) for that control changes. Therefore, you must use the proper string types (HSTL or HSZ) when handling properties as strings. An HSTL is a Visual Basic string with no embedded nulls, and HSZ is more like a standard C string that supports embedded nulls. You must ensure that you maintain the NEAR variable referencing. And you must be sure that all strings are null terminated. You can use standard C strings inside the custom control, as in the examples using CHAR to create a message box.

The Simple control processes both the single- and double-click states of the mouse button (WM_RBUTTONCLK and WMRBUTTONDBLCLK) inside the control's window area in the Visual Basic application. This does not prevent you from trapping and processing the standard click events from within Visual Basic. You can also trap user keyboard events; for example, pressing the F1 key fires the VBM_HELP message in the sample. To call the help engine, you simply call the WinHelp function at this point in the code. In the sample program, the default message processing passes the F1 keystroke on into Windows and launches the actual help engine in addition to the message box, as shown in Figure 8-3.

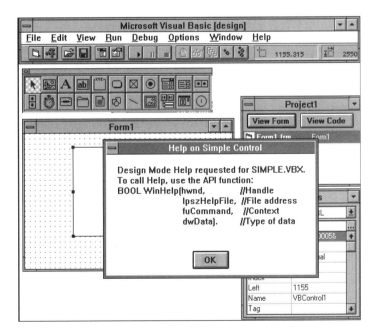

Figure 8-3   *You can trap the F1 key and provide help to the programmer by using your custom control.*

Using Visual C++

Now that you've seen the foundation of control for a custom control, let's take a look at the structures that provide the control's characteristics: events and properties. For this example, I'll use Visual C++ from Microsoft to show how you can use an object-oriented language to create the same structures that you saw in the previous section.

 Tip: You cannot create custom methods *for a Visual Basic custom control. To simulate a method, create DLL-like functions within the control and declare them in Visual Basic as will any API call. Since a custom control contains the entry and exit code of a normal DLL, all you need to create is the function itself. See Chapter 6 for how to handle DLLs.*

The primary benefit you get from creating custom controls in Visual C++ comes with access to the Microsoft Foundation Classes (MFC) and the ability to use the custom control in either Visual C++ or Visual Basic.

Now you must beware of two conditions possible within a Visual C++ custom control: (1) the type of access to the MFC and (2) the level of Visual Basic functions used.

If you want your custom control to be accessible from a Visual C++ application while retaining its ability to run inside a Visual Basic application, you must compile with the USRDLL, instead of the AFXDLL, version of the MFC class library to create the custom control. In the latter version, Visual C++ places the custom control code into a separate stand-alone DLL (MFC200.DLL). This construction makes more efficient custom controls for Visual C++ but makes them unusable in Visual Basic. A custom control created by using AFXDLL is not usable within Visual Basic since it requires the Visual C++-specific DLL MFC200.DLL.

From the Visual Basic side, if you create a custom control with Visual Basic specific functions, you will not be able to use the control in your Visual C++ applications. Table 8-1 lists the Visual Basic custom control functions and their 1.0 alternatives in Visual C++. In most cases for any of the replacements listed, you must first use the VBGetControlHwnd to retrieve the handle of the control.

Table 8-1   *Visual Basic custom control functions are listed here with their 1.0 alternatives in Visual C++.*

Visual Basic 2.0 and later Function	1.0 Alternative for Visual C++ Custom Control
VBCreateTempHlstr	Use the 1.0 version call to VBCreateHlstr and VBDestroyHlstr to do the same thing.
VBDerefHlstrLen	Use VBDerefHlstr or VBGetHlstrLen to do something similar.
VBDerefZeroTermHlstr	Use VBDerefHlstr. (VBDerefZeroTermHlstr is specific to null terminated strings
VBGetHlstr	Use VBDerefHlstr and wsprintf, or VBCreateHlstr and VBSetHlstr to copy data from one buffer to another.
VBResizeHlstr	Use VBCreateHlstr, VBDerefHlstr, wsprintf, and VBSetHlstr.
VBClientToScreen	Use SDK call ClientToScreen.
VBGetCapture	Use SDK mouse functions.
VBGetClientRect	Use SDK GetCapture.
VBGetControl	User SDK GetParent and ToolHelp to walk the module and window-handle list.
VBGetControlRect	Use SDK GetWindowRect.
VBGetRectInContainer	User SDK GetParent and GetWindowRect. (If the control is not subclassed from the container, you will need to know the control handle first.)
VBInvalidateRect	Use SDK InvalidateRect.
VBIsControlEnabled	Use SDK IsWindowEnabled.
VBIsControlVisible	Use SDK IsWindowVisible.
VBMoveControl	Use Window structure setting changes.
VBScreenToClient	Use SDK ScreenToClient.
VBSetControlFlags	No direct substitute.
VBUpdateControl	Issue WM_PAINT message to Window with UpdateWindow.
VBZOrder	No direct substitute.
VBLinkMakeItemName	No direct substitute. (Consider using DdeAccessData and global memory construct).
VBLinkPostAdvise	Use SDK DdePostAdvise.
VBPasteLinkOk	Use SDK DdePostAdvise.
VBCbSaveFPState	No direct substitute.
VBRestoreFPState	No direct substitute.
VBAllocPicEx	Use SDK CreatePalette or AfxSetPict.
VBGetPicEx	Use handle to a bitmap.
VBPaletteChanged	Use checking procedure for PALETTEENTRY structure.
VBTranslateColor	Use SDK SetPaletteEntries.
VBDirtyForm	No direct substitute.
VBGetModel	No direct substitute.

Table 8-1   *(Continued)*

Visual Basic 2.0 and later Function	1.0 Alternative for Visual C++ Custom Control
VBGetVersion	Use the SDK File Installation library (VER.DLL).
VBRunTimeError	Use the CVBControl::mnError public data member.
VBFormat	No direct substitute.
VBArray	No direct substitute.
VBRegisterModel	No direct substitute.
VBPaste	No direct substitute.
VBSetErrorMessage	No direct substitute.
VBSetCapture	No direct substitute.
VBCoerceVariant	No direct substitute.
VBGetVariantType	No direct substitute.
VBGetVariantValue	No direct substitute.
VBSetVariantValue	No direct substitute.

Array access, data conversion, variant access, and error handling are all version 2.0 functions and require various applications of C data typing as substitutes.

To use Visual C++ to build a custom control for Visual Basic, you must first ensure that the lafxdw or lafxdwd library (the latter is the debug version) has been created. Due to the disk space it consumes, neither library is created when you install Visual C++. Table 8-2 shows the final disk space required when you construct each library.

Table 8-2   *Disk space requirements for library files.*

Small Model

LAFXCW.LIB	1,319,641K
LAFXCWD.LIB	2,042,893K

Large Model

LAFXDW.LIB	1,220,621K
LAFXDWD.LIB	1,938,211K

DLLs for Visual C++ Custom Controls Only

MFC200.LIB	365,568K
MFC200D.LIB	584,192K

To construct these libraries, use the NMAKE utility in the Windows SDK or the one that comes with Visual C++. It contains a make file that will properly construct the libraries if you pass them the following parameters:

Debugging version (lafxdwd.lib):

MODEL=L TARGET=W DLL=1 DEBUG=1

Retail version (lafxdw.lib):

MODEL=L TARGET=W DLL=1 DEBUG=0

Linking one of these libraries with the WINDLL standard DLL library will provide the calls to the MFC that you will need. If you use the debugging version, remember to recompile with the retail version before you make final the delivery of the control.

Properties

Although you can't add methods to your Visual Basic control, you can add properties and events. Properties describe the nature of your control, and events describe how that nature is predisposed to behave within an application. Listing 8-4 shows the properties settings given in SIMPLVC.H for the Visual C++ sample application. The last line shows the entries for a new property. (In Visual Basic 1.0, you must insert the property in sorted sequence. Visual Basic 2.0 requires that you place any new property or event at the end of the list.)

Listing 8-4 *This code shows property structures for a custom control.*

```
// Property list
#define IPROP_SIMPL_CTLNAME        0
#define IPROP_SIMPL_INDEX          1
#define IPROP_SIMPL_LEFT           3
#define IPROP_SIMPL_TOP            4
#define IPROP_SIMPL_WIDTH          5
#define IPROP_SIMPL_HEIGHT         6
#define IPROP_SIMPL_VISIBLE        7
#define IPROP_SIMPL_PARENT         8
#define IPROP_SIMPL_DRAGMODE       9
#define IPROP_SIMPL_DRAGICON       10
#define IPROP_SIMPL_TAG            11
#define IPROP_SIMPL_HWND           12
#define IPROP_SIMPL_BOXTYPE        13

//Standard Properties array
PPROPINFO NEAR Simpl_Properties[] =
    {
```

```
        PPROPINFO_STD_CTLNAME,
        PPROPINFO_STD_INDEX,
        PPROPINFO_STD_LEFT,
        PPROPINFO_STD_TOP,
        PPROPINFO_STD_WIDTH,
        PPROPINFO_STD_HEIGHT,
        PPROPINFO_STD_VISIBLE,
        PPROPINFO_STD_PARENT,
        PPROPINFO_STD_DRAGMODE,
        PPROPINFO_STD_DRAGICON,
        PPROPINFO_STD_TAG,
        PPROPINFO_STD_HWND,
        &Property_BoxType,
        NULL
        };
```

To create properties in your custom control, you must first give them names. Well, actually, you must first design the control, determine the property types you'll need and then give them names. Within the include file, you use the #define statement to attach an English word to each property identifier. Then you place each property identifier inside an array that Visual Basic will focus on to construct the properties list. That array is of type PROPINFO. Listing 8-5 shows the PROPINFO structure, in which you give each property its operating characteristics. It's not necessary to include all of the items in the PROPINFO structure—only those you change or place holders.

Listing 8-5   *The PROPINFO structure describes each property.*

```
typedef struct tagPROPINFO
  {
  PSTR npszName;
  FLONG fl;                    // PF_ flags
  BYTE offsetData;             // Offset into static structure
  BYTE infoData;               // 0 or _INFO value for bitfield
  LONG dataDefault;            // 0 or _INFO value for bitfield
  PSTR npszEnumList;           // For type == DT_ENUM, this is
                               // a near ptr to a string containing
                               // all the values to be displayed
                               // in the popup enumeration listbox.
                               // Each value is an sz, with an
                               // empty sz indicated the end of list.
  BYTE enumMax;                // Maximum legal value for enum.
  } PROPINFO;
```

The Visual Basic Control Development Kit comes with several standard properties, already defined. However, your needs may not be met with these standard items. To create more, you simply follow the same procedure used by the standard properties. The difference lies in the fact that the VBAPI.H and VBAPI.LIB files contain the definitions for the standard properties ,while you must write your own in the include file for your application. Listing 8-6 shows the structures required to create a property.

Listing 8-6   *This code shows structures required to define a new property and prepare for storing its settings.*

```
//Macro for calc of position in user structure
#define OFFSETIN(struc, field) ((USHORT)&(((struc *)0)->field))

//Storage for New Property
typedef struct tagBOXTYPE
        {
        char TheBox;
        }BOXTYPE;

typedef BOXTYPE FAR * LPBOXTYPE;

//Enumerated list of property settings
CHAR szBoxFlag[] =      "0 - MB_OK\0"\
                        "1 - MB_OKCANCEL\0"\
                        "2 - MB_ABORTRETRYIGNORE\0"\
                        "3 - MB_YESNOCANCEL\0"\
                        "4 - MB_YESNO\0"\
                        "5 - MB_RETRYCANCEL\0"\
                        "";
//New Property Structure
PROPINFO NEAR Property_BoxType =
        {
        "BoxType",
        DT_ENUM|PF_fGetData|PF_fSetData|PF_fSaveData,
        OFFSETIN(BOXTYPE,TheBox),
        0,
        3,
     (PSTR) szBoxFlag,
        5
        };
```

The new property described in Listing 8-6 creates an entry in the on-screen properties list box with six choices as defined by the szBoxFlag array. This is an "enumerated list" that appears in the next-to-the-last entry in the PROPINFO structure. (Each standard property in the CDK was defined the same way.) After you give the property its on-screen name (BoxType, for example), you specify how that property structure itself will act by setting the flags that determine whether you will save the data as set by the user, retrieve defaults, and so on. In this case, I've written the control to retrieve (PF_fGetData) its settings from an array (DT_ENUM—for enumerated list) stored on the disk (PF_fSaveData). You must type the actual structure in which the data appears, and then point back into by it using the OFFSETIN macro. (No other read or write operations are necessary to permanently store the information on disk.) The result of creating the property in this fashion appears in Figure 8-4.

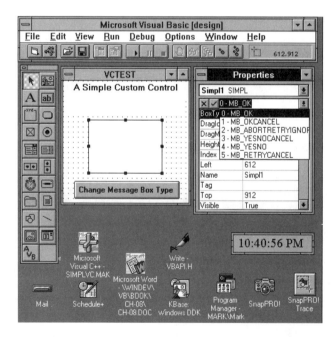

Figure 8-4   *The simple control written in Visual C++ displays the choices presented by the new property settings.*

In Figure 8-4, notice the addition to the toolbar of the initials AVB ("Advanced Visual Basic"). That button provides access to the custom control, which is a box on the form. The pull-down Pick List in the Properties box shows the choices created with the new property BoxType. The sample Visual Basic program using this control permits you to change the property setting that determines which box is displayed. You click on the command button to execute the code shown in Listing 8-7.

Listing 8-7   *This code sets the contents of the property box Pick List.*

```
If Simp11.BoxType <> 5 Then
        Simp11.BoxType = Simp11.BoxType + 1
Else
        Simp11.BoxType = 0
End If
Select Case Simp11.BoxType
        Case 0:
                Label2.Caption = "0 - MB_OK"
        Case 1:
                Label2.Caption = "1 - MB_OKCANCEL"
        Case 2:
                Label2.Caption = "2 - MB_ABORTRETRYIGNORE"
        Case 3:
                Label2.Caption = "3 - MB_YESNOCANCEL"
        Case 4:
                Label2.Caption = "4 - MB_YESNO"
        Case 5:
                Label2.Caption = "5 - MB_RETRYCANCEL"
End Select
```

The process by which a control loads into an application is shown in Figure 8-5. Notice that some properties may apply to the control's window before the window is created. These are known as pre-HWND properties. Some properties, such as BorderStyle or ClipControls require ReCreateControlHwnd if they are not set as pre-HWND. Also, you can force a property to load early by setting the PF_fPreHwnd property flag in its definition.

Events

The next concern, after adding the custom properties, is to add new event types to your custom control. The process for adding new events nearly replicates the process for adding new properties. The standard events are typed within the VB API library in the same manner as the standard properties. As with properties, you can choose to include or exclude whichever items you like. For the cases in which you won't be supporting drag-and-drop facilities, you'll want to remove those events from the standard list to avoid confusing the user of your custom control. Listing 8-8 shows the section of the VBAPI.H that defines the standard events.

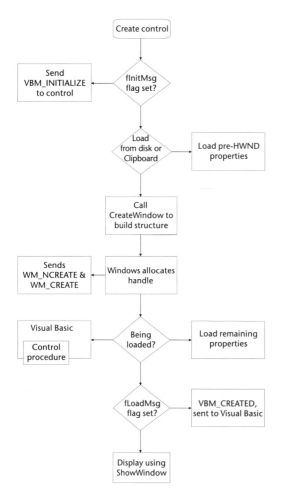

Figure 8-5   *This is the process for loading a control.*

Listing 8-8 *This code shows the standard events and the event structure.*

```
//---------------------------------------------------------------------------
// Control event definitions and structures.
//---------------------------------------------------------------------------
#define EF_fNoUnload  0x00000001L

typedef struct tagEVENTINFO
  {
  PSTR          npszName;       // event procedure name suffix
  USHORT        cParms;         // number of parameters
  USHORT        cwParms;        // # words of parameters
  PWORD         npParmTypes;    // list of parameter types
  PSTR          npszParmProf;   // event parameter profile string
  FLONG         fl;             // EF_ flags
  } EVENTINFO;


//---------------------------------------------------------------------------
// Standard control event list
//---------------------------------------------------------------------------
#define IEVENT_STD_CLICK      0x0000
#define IEVENT_STD_DBLCLICK   0x0001
#define IEVENT_STD_DRAGDROP   0x0002
#define IEVENT_STD_DRAGOVER   0x0003
#define IEVENT_STD_GOTFOCUS   0x0004
#define IEVENT_STD_KEYDOWN    0x0005
#define IEVENT_STD_KEYPRESS   0x0006
#define IEVENT_STD_KEYUP      0x0007
#define IEVENT_STD_LOSTFOCUS  0x0008
#define IEVENT_STD_MOUSEDOWN  0x0009
#define IEVENT_STD_MOUSEMOVE  0x000A
#define IEVENT_STD_MOUSEUP    0x000B
#define IEVENT_STD_LINKERROR    0x000C
#define IEVENT_STD_LINKOPEN     0x000D
#define IEVENT_STD_LINKCLOSE    0x000E
#define IEVENT_STD_LINKNOTIFY   0x000F
#define IEVENT_STD_LINKCHANGE   0x0010
#define IEVENT_STD_NONE       0x0FFF
#define IEVENT_STD_LAST       0x0FFF
```

To create a special event, you simply add your own event structure and include it in the list of custom events for your control. (Remember that you must add the event to the bottom of the list in Visual Basic 2.0 and in sorted order in Visual Basic 1.0.)

Listing 8-9 shows the custom event, FollowUpMsg, added to the event list for the custom control.

Listing 8-9   *The custom event structures are folded into the standard events.*

```
//New Event
EVENTINFO NEAR Event_FollowUpMsg =
        {
        "FollowUpMsg",
        0,
        0,
    NULL,
        NULL
        };


// Event list
#define IEVENT_SIMPL_CLICK          0
#define IEVENT_SIMPL_DRAGDROP       1
#define IEVENT_SIMPL_DRAGOVER       2
#define IEVENT_SIMPL_FOLLOWUPMSG    3

PEVENTINFO NEAR Simpl_Events[] =
    {
    PEVENTINFO_STD_CLICK,
    PEVENTINFO_STD_DRAGDROP,
    PEVENTINFO_STD_DRAGOVER,
    &Event_FollowUpMsg,
    NULL
    };
```

The custom events act as placeholders for code written in Visual Basic. You can affect the manner in which the event responds to information and when it fires. In this case, you can cause the messages processed by the control to determine a condition for when it should fire. You place this code into your control procedure for the custom control and then use the VBFireEvent statement to cause the code stored in this event to fire.

The Visual C++ environment makes it easy to detect messages sent from Windows to your application. Figure 8-6 shows the Class Wizard you can use to add message processing to your custom control procedure. The left button-click message was used in the sample.

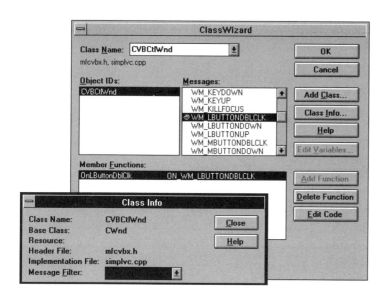

Figure 8-6   *This is the Class Wizard access to processing messages in Visual C++.*

In the case of the FollowUpMsg event in this simple example, you might want to test for the closure of any form in the application and toss a message out for the user to respond to. In that case, you would place this statement at the end of your control procedure:

```
err = VBFireEvent(hctl, IFOLLOWUPMSG,NULL)
```

The third parameter is Null because the event does not have any parameters. You could create the event with a parameter for passing the name of the form that closed.

 Tip: *When you fire an event from within a control and expect to perform additional work inside the control on return, your only protection from crashing the system is to create an error filter at the end of the control. Do that rather than create a simple VBDefControlProc, since the result of the Visual Basic code embedded in the procedure might be to destroy the control.*

If you don't place a VBFireEvent somewhere in your control, the code inside the event will never be executed unless you call for it inside Visual Basic. In that case you are merely calling a subroutine, and the utility for placing the code inside a control is low.

 Tip: *For backward compatibility with older versions of Visual Basic, you can use the definitions provided in the VBAPI.H file for supplying the older structure definitions.*

Now that you have all of the custom structures in your code, you can compile the project in Visual C++ and run it in Visual Basic for debugging. You can use the standard version of CodeView to debug your DLL. In the Program Manager definition for launching CodeView from an icon, place a /L after CVW.EXE and then the name of your custom control and the name of the application that calls it. Now create a Visual Basic application, load the control into the application, and create an EXE. You can't debug your custom control in Visual Basic design mode. When you launch CodeView, it will pop up a message telling you that the program you want to debug has no debugging information within it. That message refers to the Visual Basic application, not your custom control. (You must, of course, have compiled your custom control in debug mode.) Simply click on OK, and the processor will jump to the Visual Basic app or to the line in the custom code initialization where you placed a breakpoint.

Visual C++ uses the same method that QuickC for Windows uses to debug applications. In the Options/Debug menu selection, place the name of the simple Visual Basic application that you wrote. When you want to debug the program, go to the Debug menu selection on the main menu to launch the program, or simply press the F5 key. If you haven't set any breakpoints, you may want to start by pressing the F8 key to begin stepping through the program one line at a time.

A Word about Subclassing

Once you have created a control—or employed someone else's control in your application—you can change the behavior of that control without changing the control itself. Through a process called **subclassing**, you can grab the functional parts of a control and bend that control to your own methods. To subclass—literally to create a control below the class of another control—you must divert the messages intended for a control into your own code. Jeff Simms, a regular on the Visual Basic forums on CompuServe, applied the SetParent call to Windows Write—changing the parent of the control to the form in his Visual Basic application. That moved all of the capabilities of Write into his Visual Basic application. The tricky part of such processing is that you must trap and save the name of the original parent of the target control (Windows itself, in this case) and replace or restore it, or you will cause Windows to generate a General Protection Fault.

It's not wise to subclass one of the standard Visual Basic controls unless you can be certain that the standard control will always load ahead of the attempt to subclass. Otherwise, the name of the standard control is not registered and the attempt to subclass will fail.

Using the API calls GetWindowLong and SetWindowLong, you can subclass the standard Windows controls also. You can do this in one of two ways: (1) using instance subclassing, in which only the messages for a specific window are redirected, or (2) using global subclassing, in which any window manufactured from the WNDCLASS structure will have its messages redirected. Global subclassing uses SetClassLong.

A Borland C++ Custom Control

SIMPLE.C

```
/*Advanced Visual Basic Custom Control*/
#include <windows.h>
#include <vbapi.h>
#include "simple.h"
#include <stdio.h>

/*Global Variables*/
HANDLE hmodDLL;
static char szMsgBuffer[50], szTtlBuffer[50];
static int retval;

/*Control Procedure*/
LONG FAR PASCAL VBCntrlCtlProc(HCTL hctl,    /*Handle to the control*/
                               HWND hwnd,     /*Window handle*/
                               USHORT msg,    /*Inbound message*/
                               USHORT wp,     /*message wParam*/
                               LONG lp)       /*message lParam*/
{
  char szLn1[] = "Design Mode Help requested for SIMPLE.VBX.";
  char szLn2[] = "To call Help, use the API function:";
```

```
char szLn3[] = "BOOL WinHelp(hwnd,                  //Handle";
char szLn4[] = "                    lpszHelpFile,  //File address";
char szLn5[] = "                    fuCommand,     //Context";
char szLn6[] = "                    dwData).         //Type of data";
//Process message passed from Windows thru Visual Basic to Control
switch(msg)
   {
   case WM_RBUTTONDOWN:     //On right mouse button click or
   case WM_RBUTTONDBLCLK:  //double-click inside custom control
     {
     //Retrieve title from Visual Basic applcation
     VBGetAppTitle((LPSTR)szTtlBuffer,20);
     //Format a null terminated string for the message box
     retval = sprintf(szMsgBuffer, "%s\n", "Message from the Custom Control");
     //return to the Visual Basic application
     break;
   case VBM_HELP:          //On F1 key while in design mode
     retval = sprintf(szTtlBuffer, "%s\n", "Help on Simple Control");
     //Format a null terminated string for the message box
     retval = sprintf(szMsgBuffer, "%s\n%s\n%s\n%s\n%s\n%s\n",szLn1,szLn2,
     ...szLn3,szLn4,szLn5,szLn6 );
     //return to the Visual Basic application
     break;
    }
   default:
     return VBDefControlProc(hctl, hwnd, msg, wp, lp);
   }
   //Present message box
     MessageBox(hwnd, (LPSTR) szMsgBuffer, (LPSTR) szTtlBuffer, MB_OK);
     return VBDefControlProc(hctl, hwnd, msg, wp, lp);
     // return NULL; Replace to prevent message forwarding
}


/*Initialize library - called when the first client loads the DLL.*/
int FAR PASCAL LibMain
(
    HANDLE hModule,
    WORD   wDataSeg,
    WORD   cbHeapSize,
    LPSTR  lpszCmdLine
)
{

    /*Avoid warnings on unused (but required) formal parameters */
    wDataSeg  = wDataSeg;
    cbHeapSize = cbHeapSize;
```

```
    lpszCmdLine = lpszCmdLine;

    hmodDLL = hModule;

    return 1;
}


/*Register custom control when DLL is loaded for use.*/
BOOL FAR PASCAL _export VBINITCC(USHORT usVersion, BOOL fRuntime)
{
    fRuntime  = fRuntime;
    usVersion = usVersion;
    return VBRegisterModel(hmodDLL, &modelVBCntrl); /* Register control(s) */
}
/*Non QuickC Win, Microsoft C7 or Borland C++ apps would require a WEP*/
```

SIMPLE.DEF

```
; SIMPLE.def - module definition file for SIMPLE.VBX custom control
LIBRARY         SIMPLE
EXETYPE         WINDOWS
DESCRIPTION     'Visual Basic Custom Control'
CODE            MOVEABLE PRELOAD
DATA            MOVEABLE SINGLE PRELOAD
HEAPSIZE    2048
EXPORTS
        WEP     @1      RESIDENTNAME
```

SIMPLE.RC

```
/* CTRL1.RC */

#include "simple.h"

/* SIMPLE resources for VBCONTRL1 model*/

IDBMP_VBCNTRL BITMAP DISCARDABLE "simplecu.bmp"
IDBMP_VBCNTRLDOWN BITMAP DISCARDABLE "simplecd.bmp"
IDBMP_VBCNTRLMONO BITMAP DISCARDABLE "simplemu.bmp"
IDBMP_VBCNTRLEGA BITMAP DISCARDABLE "simpleeu.bmp"
```

SIMPLE.H

```
/* simple.h */

/* Toolbox bitmap resource IDs numbers.*/
#define IDBMP_VBCNTRL           8000
```

```
#define IDBMP_VBCNTRLDOWN       8001
#define IDBMP_VBCNTRLMONO       8003
#define IDBMP_VBCNTRLEGA        8006

#ifndef RC_INVOKED

/*VBCONTRL Procedure*/
LONG FAR PASCAL VBCntrlCtlProc(HCTL, HWND, USHORT, USHORT, LONG);

/* Property list - Define the consecutive indices for the properties*/
#define IPROP_VBCNTRL_CTLNAME       0
#define IPROP_VBCNTRL_INDEX         1
#define IPROP_VBCNTRL_BACKCOLOR     2
#define IPROP_VBCNTRL_LEFT          3
#define IPROP_VBCNTRL_TOP           4
#define IPROP_VBCNTRL_WIDTH         5
#define IPROP_VBCNTRL_HEIGHT        6
#define IPROP_VBCNTRL_VISIBLE       7
#define IPROP_VBCNTRL_PARENT        8
#define IPROP_VBCNTRL_DRAGMODE      9
#define IPROP_VBCNTRL_DRAGICON      10
#define IPROP_VBCNTRL_TAG           11
#define IPROP_VBCNTRL_HWND          12

PPROPINFO VBCNTRL_Properties[] =
    {               PPROPINFO_STD_CTLNAME,
    PPROPINFO_STD_INDEX,
    PPROPINFO_STD_BACKCOLOR,
    PPROPINFO_STD_LEFT,
    PPROPINFO_STD_TOP,
    PPROPINFO_STD_WIDTH,
    PPROPINFO_STD_HEIGHT,
    PPROPINFO_STD_VISIBLE,
    PPROPINFO_STD_PARENT,
    PPROPINFO_STD_DRAGMODE,
    PPROPINFO_STD_DRAGICON,
    PPROPINFO_STD_TAG,
    PPROPINFO_STD_HWND,
    NULL
    };

/* Event list - Define the consecutive indices for the events*/
#define IEVENT_VBCNTRL_CLICK        0
#define IEVENT_VBCNTRL_DRAGDROP     1
#define IEVENT_VBCNTRL_DRAGOVER     2
```

```
PEVENTINFO VBCNTRL_Events[] =
    {
    PEVENTINFO_STD_CLICK,
    PEVENTINFO_STD_DRAGDROP,
    PEVENTINFO_STD_DRAGOVER,
    NULL
    };


/* Model struct - Define the VBCONTRL model (using the event and property
...structures).*/
MODEL modelVBCntrl =
    {
    VB_VERSION,                      /* VB version being used*/
    0,                               /* MODEL flags*/
    (PCTLPROC)VBCntrlCtlProc,        /* VBCONTRL procedure*/
    CS_VREDRAW | CS_HREDRAW,         /* Class style*/
    WS_BORDER,                       /* Default Windows style*/
    0,                               /* Size of CIRCLE structure*/
    IDBMP_VBCNTRL,                   /* Palette bitmap ID*/
    "VBControl",                     /* Default VBCONTRL name*/
    "VBCNTRL",                       /* Visual Basic class name*/
    NULL,                            /* Parent class name*/
    VBCNTRL_Properties,              /* Property information table*/
    VBCNTRL_Events,                  /* Event information table*/
    IPROP_VBCNTRL_BACKCOLOR,         /* Default property*/
    IEVENT_VBCNTRL_CLICK,            /* Default event*/
    -1                               /* Property representing value of ctl*/
    };


#endif  /* RC_INVOKED */


Visual C++ Custom Control
```

SIMPLEVC.CPP

```
// Simple Visual C++ Custom Control


#define _USRDLL                      // Export "C" interface
#include <afxwin.h>
extern "C"                           // handle "C" name mangling
{
#include <vbapi.h>
#include "simplvc.h"                 // VB Property, Event & MODEL defs
}
#include "mfcvbx.h"                   // MFC Class definitions
```

```
//////////////////////////  CWinApp Object functions
////////////////////////////////////////////////
CVBDLL theApp;                          // MFC initializations & call LibMain()

BOOL CVBDLL::InitInstance()             // One time intializations
{return TRUE;}

int  CVBDLL::ExitInstance()             // One time cleanup object cleanup
{return 0;}

CVBCtlWnd::CVBCtlWnd(HWND hwnd)         //Constructor For class CVBCtlWnd
{
    Attach(hwnd);
    m_hCtl = ::VBGetHwndControl(hwnd);
}

void CVBCtlWnd::OnLButtonDblClk(UINT Flag, CPoint pt)//Respond to mouse click
{
    char buf[25];                                   //Receives formatted text
    int nBox;                                       //Receives property setting
    LPBOXTYPE lpbox;                                //Property data structure
    wsprintf(buf,"Point = (%d,%d)",pt.x,pt.y);      //Format message text
    lpbox = (LPBOXTYPE)VBDerefControl(CVBCtlWnd::m_hCtl);//Get Property settings
    nBox = lpbox->TheBox;                           //Get property data
    switch (nBox)
        {
      case 0:
        MessageBox(buf,"MB_OK",MB_OK);
        break;
      case 1:
        MessageBox(buf,"MB_OKCANCEL",MB_OKCANCEL);
        break;
      case 2:
        MessageBox(buf,"MB_ABORTRETRYIGNORE",MB_ABORTRETRYIGNORE);
        break;
      case 3:
        MessageBox(buf,"MB_YESNOCANCEL",MB_YESNOCANCEL);
        break;
      case 4:
        MessageBox(buf,"MB_YESNO",MB_YESNO);
        break;
      case 5:
        MessageBox(buf,"MB_RETRYCANCEL",MB_RETRYCANCEL);
        break;
      default:
```

```
        MessageBox(buf,"No Box Type Selected",MB_OK);
    }
    VBFireEvent(CVBCtlWnd::m_hCtl,IEVENT_SIMPL_FOLLOWUPMSG, NULL); //Launch custom
    ...event
}

//-------------------- Default Window Procedure
LRESULT CVBCtlWnd::DefWindowProc(UINT msg,WPARAM wp,LPARAM lp)
{
    return ::VBDefControlProc(m_hCtl,m_hWnd,msg,wp,lp);// Control on last message
}

////////////////////////// Message Map of CVBCtlWnd Class
///////////////////////////////////////////
BEGIN_MESSAGE_MAP(CVBCtlWnd, CWnd)                       //Message Map CVBCtlWnd Class
    //{{AFX_MSG_MAP(CVBCtlWnd)
    ON_WM_LBUTTONDBLCLK()                               // Act on left double click
        //}}AFX_MSG_MAP
END_MESSAGE_MAP()

//-------------------- Control Procedure
extern "C" LONG FAR PASCAL _export SimplCtlProc(HCTL hctl,HWND hwnd,USHORT msg,USHORT
...wp,LONG lp)
{
    if(hwnd == FALSE)
      return ::VBDefControlProc(hctl,hwnd,msg,wp,lp); // Exit when no valid window  handle
    theApp.OnIdle(0L);                                 // Garbage collection on temp objects
    CVBCtlWnd* pCtl = (CVBCtlWnd*)CWnd::FromHandlePermanent(hwnd);
    if(pCtl == NULL)                                   // Only one instance of Control.
      pCtl = new CVBCtlWnd(hwnd);
    return (pCtl->WindowProc(msg,wp,lp));              // call default
VBDefControlProc()
}

extern "C" BOOL FAR PASCAL _export VBINITCC(USHORT,BOOL) // Register the Control Class
{
    return ::VBRegisterModel(AfxGetInstanceHandle(), &modelSimpl);
}
```

SIMPLEVC.H

```
// Resource Information
#define IDBMP_SIMPL        8000
#define IDBMP_SIMPLDOWN    8001
#define IDBMP_SIMPLMONO    8003
#define IDBMP_SIMPLEGA     8006
```

```
#ifndef RC_INVOKED
//Macro for calc of position in user structure
#define OFFSETIN(struc, field) ((USHORT)&(((struc *)0)->field))

//New Property
typedef struct tagBOXTYPE
        {
        char TheBox;
        }BOXTYPE;

typedef BOXTYPE FAR * LPBOXTYPE;

CHAR szBoxFlag[] =      "0 - MB_OK\0"\
                       "1 - MB_OKCANCEL\0"\
                       "2 - MB_ABORTRETRYIGNORE\0"\
                       "3 - MB_YESNOCANCEL\0"\
                       "4 - MB_YESNO\0"\
                       "5 - MB_RETRYCANCEL\0"\
                       "";

PROPINFO NEAR Property_BoxType =
        {
        "BoxType",
        DT_ENUM|PF_fGetData|PF_fSetData|PF_fSaveData,
        OFFSETIN(BOXTYPE,TheBox),
        0,
        3,
    (PSTR) szBoxFlag,
        5
        };

// Control Procedure
LONG FAR PASCAL _export SimplCtlProc(HCTL, HWND, USHORT, USHORT, LONG);
// Model struct
// Property list
#define IPROP_SIMPL_CTLNAME      0
#define IPROP_SIMPL_INDEX        1
#define IPROP_SIMPL_LEFT         3
#define IPROP_SIMPL_TOP          4
#define IPROP_SIMPL_WIDTH        5
#define IPROP_SIMPL_HEIGHT       6
#define IPROP_SIMPL_VISIBLE      7
#define IPROP_SIMPL_PARENT       8
#define IPROP_SIMPL_DRAGMODE     9
#define IPROP_SIMPL_DRAGICON    10
#define IPROP_SIMPL_TAG         11
#define IPROP_SIMPL_HWND        12
#define IPROP_SIMPL_BOXTYPE     13
```

```
//Standard Properties array
PPROPINFO NEAR Simpl_Properties[] =
    {
    PPROPINFO_STD_CTLNAME,
    PPROPINFO_STD_INDEX,
    PPROPINFO_STD_LEFT,
    PPROPINFO_STD_TOP,
    PPROPINFO_STD_WIDTH,
    PPROPINFO_STD_HEIGHT,
    PPROPINFO_STD_VISIBLE,
    PPROPINFO_STD_PARENT,
    PPROPINFO_STD_DRAGMODE,
    PPROPINFO_STD_DRAGICON,
    PPROPINFO_STD_TAG,
    PPROPINFO_STD_HWND,
    &Property_BoxType,
    NULL
    };

//New Event
EVENTINFO NEAR Event_FollowUpMsg =
        {
        "FollowUpMsg",
        0,
        0,
    NULL,
        NULL
        };

// Event list
#define IEVENT_SIMPL_CLICK          0
#define IEVENT_SIMPL_DRAGDROP       1
#define IEVENT_SIMPL_DRAGOVER       2
#define IEVENT_SIMPL_FOLLOWUPMSG    3

PEVENTINFO NEAR Simpl_Events[] =
    {
    PEVENTINFO_STD_CLICK,
    PEVENTINFO_STD_DRAGDROP,
    PEVENTINFO_STD_DRAGOVER,
    &Event_FollowUpMsg,
    NULL
    };

//Model Structure
char NEAR szSimplvc[] = "Simpl";
char NEAR szSimpl[] = "SIMPL";
```

```
MODEL NEAR modelSimpl =
    {
    VB_VERSION,              // VB version being used
    0,                       // MODEL flags
    (PCTLPROC)SimplCtlProc,  // Control procedure
    CS_VREDRAW | CS_HREDRAW, // Class style
    WS_BORDER,               // Default Windows style
    0,                       // Size of SIMPL structure
    IDBMP_SIMPL,             // Palette bitmap ID
    szSimplvc,               // Default control name
    szSimpl,                 // Visual Basic class name
    NULL,                    // Parent class name
    Simpl_Properties,        // Property information table
    Simpl_Events,            // Event information table
    IPROP_SIMPL_HEIGHT,      // Default property
    IEVENT_SIMPL_CLICK,      // Default event
    -1                       // Property representing value of ctl
    };
                             // RC_INVOKED
#endif
```

SIMPLEVC.RC

```
//Microsoft App Studio generated resource script.
//
#include "RESOURCE.h"

#define APSTUDIO_READONLY_SYMBOLS
/////////////////////////////////////////////////////////////////////////////
//
// Generated from the TEXTINCLUDE 2 resource.
//
#include "afxres.h"
#include "SIMPLVC.h"


/////////////////////////////////////////////////////////////////////////////////
#undef APSTUDIO_READONLY_SYMBOLS


/////////////////////////////////////////////////////////////////////////////
//
// Bitmap
//

IDBMP_SIMPL            BITMAP  DISCARDABLE     "SIMPLCU.BMP"
IDBMP_SIMPLDOWN        BITMAP  DISCARDABLE     "SIMPLCD.BMP"
```

```
IDBMP_SIMPLMONO          BITMAP  DISCARDABLE     "SIMPLMU.BMP"
IDBMP_SIMPLEGA           BITMAP  DISCARDABLE     "SIMPLEU.BMP"
#ifdef APSTUDIO_INVOKED
/////////////////////////////////////////////////////////////////////////
//
// TEXTINCLUDE
//

1 TEXTINCLUDE DISCARDABLE
BEGIN
    "RESOURCE.h\0"
END

2 TEXTINCLUDE DISCARDABLE
BEGIN
    "#include ""afxres.h""\r\n"
    "#include ""SIMPLVC.h""\r\n"
    "\0"
END

3 TEXTINCLUDE DISCARDABLE
BEGIN
    "\r\n"
    "\0"
END


/////////////////////////////////////////////////////////////////////////
#endif    // APSTUDIO_INVOKED


#ifndef APSTUDIO_INVOKED
/////////////////////////////////////////////////////////////////////////
//
// Generated from the TEXTINCLUDE 3 resource.
//


/////////////////////////////////////////////////////////////////////////
#endif    // not APSTUDIO_INVOKED
```

SIMPLVC.DEF

```
; Simplvc.def - for SIMPLVC.VBX custom control
;-------------------------------------------
LIBRARY         SIMPLVC
EXETYPE             WINDOWS
```

```
DESCRIPTION 'Visual Basic Simple Custom Control'
CODE           PRELOAD MOVEABLE
DATA           PRELOAD MOVEABLE SINGLE
HEAPSIZE    4096
EXPORTS
    WEP @1   RESIDENTNAME
SEGMENTS
    WEP_TEXT FIXED
```

RESOURCE.H

```
//{{NO_DEPENDENCIES}}
// App Studio generated include file.
// Used by SIMPLVC.RC
//

// Next default values for new objects
//
#ifdef APSTUDIO_INVOKED
#ifndef APSTUDIO_READONLY_SYMBOLS

#define _APS_NEXT_RESOURCE_VALUE        101
#define _APS_NEXT_COMMAND_VALUE         40001
#define _APS_NEXT_CONTROL_VALUE         1000
#define _APS_NEXT_SYMED_VALUE           101
#endif
#endif
```

MFCVBX.H

```
// Control Classes for SIMPLVC
class CVBCtlWnd : public CWnd
{
public:
    HCTL m_hCtl;
    CVBCtlWnd(HWND hwnd);
    LRESULT DefWindowProc(UINT msg,WPARAM wp,LPARAM lp);
    void PostNcDestroy(){delete this;}
    LRESULT WindowProc(USHORT msg,WPARAM wp,LPARAM lp)
      {    return   CWnd::WindowProc(msg,wp,lp);        }
protected:
    //{{AFX_MSG(CVBCtlWnd)
    afx_msg void OnLButtonDblClk(UINT nFlags, CPoint point);
    afx_msg void OnRButtonDblClk(UINT nFlags, CPoint point);
        //}}AFX_MSG
    DECLARE_MESSAGE_MAP()
};
```

```
//Initialize MFC and call LibMain()
class CVBDLL : public CWinApp
{
public:
        //{{AFX_MSG(CVBDLL)
    BOOL InitInstance();
    int  ExitInstance();
    //}}AFX_MSG
};
```

A Visual Basic Test Program

Add to CONTANT.BAS with CONST.TXT

```
Type RECT
     Left As Integer
     Top As Integer
     Right As Integer
     Bottom As Integer
End Type


Global lpRect As RECT
```

VCTEST.FRM

```
Sub Command1_Click ()
     If Simpl1.BoxType <> 5 Then
       Simpl1.BoxType = Simpl1.BoxType + 1
     Else
       Simpl1.BoxType = 0
     End If
     Select Case Simpl1.BoxType
       Case 0:
           Label2.Caption = "0 - MB_OK"
       Case 1:
           Label2.Caption = "1 - MB_OKCANCEL"
       Case 2:
           Label2.Caption = "2 - MB_ABORTRETRYIGNORE"
       Case 3:
           Label2.Caption = "3 - MB_YESNOCANCEL"
       Case 4:
           Label2.Caption = "4 - MB_YESNO"
       Case 5:
           Label2.Caption = "5 - MB_RETRYCANCEL"
     End Select
End Sub
```

Chapter 9

Integrating Visual Basic with Other Applications

Connectivity sits at the heart of the Windows environment. The messaging architecture leads easily to *inter*application as well as *intra*application communications. You could use API calls such as SendMessage to talk with other applications, including all of the calls to find a Window, and then stuff messages into its queue and try to parse the system message queue and the foreign application message queue to see the reaction. However, Dynamic Data Exchange (DDE) and Object Linking and Embedding (OLE) perform those functions much more efficiently and easily. Beginning with version 2.0, Visual Basic presented controls and forms integrated with DDE and OLE. OLE appeared as a separate custom control, and DDE was integrated into controls and forms as properties. Visual Basic 3.0 enhanced both services to empower the applications programmer.

Many other books discuss the techniques and application-specific reasons for linking Visual Basic to various programs. I'll discuss some of those methods for a couple of programs, but the emphasis in this chapter will be on the underlying support provided by Windows for DDE and OLE. We'll take a look at the API calls for coding DDE- and OLE-capable applications and the elements of the Windows architecture you'll be using.

I assume most readers have used DDE in other Windows application. The Primer in the next section only serves to speed your acquaintance with Visual Basic's implementation of DDE. According to the Microsoft standard for DDE entity names, "servers" supply data on request from "clients."

A Visual Basic DDE Primer

Before launching into the internals of DDE and how they work, I want to spend a short time with a simple review of the DDE facilities in Visual Basic. As a start, we'll step through the process for creating first a server and then a client application, that talk to each other with DDE.

The Services

As with most Visual Basic services but different from most implementations of DDE, Visual Basic's version of DDE is run through a combination of properties and statements. Prior to the execution of your program, the ability to carry on DDE conversations may or may not be already located inside the other program. You can set the LinkMode, LinkTopic, LinkItem, and LinkTimeout properties while you're in design mode, and these will initiate calls to the DDEML when your application starts. (More about the DDEML in the subsection "Connecting by Using a Module Name.") If you set LinkMode to "Source," a conversation can be opened between your application and someone else's with no further coding on your part. The range of facilities for managing DDE under Visual Basic is shown in Table 9-1.

Table 9-1   *Notice that LinkExecute is both a method and an event in Visual Basic DDE*

Events	Methods	Properties
LinkClose	**LinkExecute**	LinkItem
LinkError	LinkPoke	LinkMode
LinkExecute	LinkRequest	LinkTimeout
LinkNotify	LinkSend	LinkTopic
LinkOpen		

It's not necessary to monitor the events in Visual Basic DDE unless you have a specific reason to do so. You can carry on a conversation by simply manipulating the properties and using standard On Error calls to test for error conditions. For instance, if you wanted Excel to supply a total from a column of numbers to a Visual Basic text control, you could set the LinkMode, LinkTopic, and LinkItem properties, and—providing Excel was running and the spreadsheet was loaded—the data would be made available as planned. The art and science of DDE with Visual Basic involve all of the maneuvering you must do to stay in touch with your sometimes fragile conversations in the Windows environment, which cannot guarantee a stable and dependable situation.

A Quick Example

You can try a quick example to prove that you can implement DDE this easily within Visual Basic. Open a new project in Visual Basic, and place an edit control (text box) on the form. Now set the form's LinkMode property to Source to create a DDE server. That's it. You've just created a DDE-aware application capable of responding to a DDE client. Compile that into an executable program and launch it.

Now it's time to create the DDE workhorse: the destination application or client.

 Tip: *For this sample, the edit controls for both server and client applications will be called Text1 and will have the multiline property set to True. You can dress up the application later if you like. These instructions provide the minimum to make this simple demonstration work properly.*

Open a new project and place an edit control on the default form. Then place five option buttons on the form by placing one and then copying it and posting four more as part of a control array. Next, click on one of the option buttons, and place the code in Listing 9-1 into the Click event. Listing 9-1 also shows how the client identifies its source via the LinkTopic setting in the LinkData subroutine.

Listing 9-1   *By creating a control array, you can easily see the means for controlling DDE events within a Visual Basic application.*

```
Select Case Index
  Case NOLINK                        'Hide when no link
    Text1.LinkMode = NOLINK          'Turn off existing links
    Option3D1(3).Visible = False
    Option3D1(4).Visible = False
```

```
        Case LINK_AUTOMATIC                'Set Auto DDE Link
          GoSub LinkData
          Text1.LinkMode = LINK_AUTOMATIC
        Case LINK_MANUAL                   'Set manual DDE link
          GoSub LinkData
          Text1.LinkMode = LINK_MANUAL
        Case LINK_NOTIFY                   'Get Data from source
          Text1.LinkRequest
        Case LINK_POKE                     'Send data to source
          Text1.LinkPoke
      End Select
      Exit Sub
LinkData:
      Text1.LinkMode = NOLINK              'Turn off existing links
      Option3D1(3).Visible = True          'Show new options
      Option3D1(4).Visible = True
      Text1.LinkTopic = "Source|Form1"     'Set linking data
      Text1.LinkItem = "Text1"
      Return
```

As shown in Listing 9-1, managing DDE links with the descriptive comments makes the code much more readable. You can save yourself some work by adding CONSTANT.TXT to the project file list. I normally label this GLOBAL.BAS to ensure that it remains with the rest of the module source code for an application. The segments of CONSTANT.TXT that apply to DDE conversations appear in Listing 9-2.

Listing 9-2   *The constant values specified in CONSTANT.TXT make your DDE transaction code much easier to read.*

```
' ErrNum (LinkError)
Global Const WRONG_FORMAT = 1
Global Const DDE_SOURCE_CLOSED = 6
Global Const TOO_MANY_LINKS = 7
Global Const DATA_TRANSFER_FAILED = 8
' LinkMode (forms and controls)
' Global Const NONE = 0              ' 0 - None
Global Const LINK_SOURCE = 1        ' 1 - Source (forms only)
Global Const LINK_AUTOMATIC = 1 ' 1 - Automatic (controls only)
Global Const LINK_MANUAL = 2        ' 2 - Manual (controls only)
Global Const LINK_NOTIFY = 3        ' 3 - Notify (controls only)
' LinkMode (kept for VB1.0 compatibility, use new constants instead)
Global Const HOT = 1       ' 1 - Hot (controls only)
Global Const SERVER = 1 ' 1 - Server (forms only)
Global Const COLD = 2    ' 2 - Cold (controls only)
```

To make this example work, you must add two more constant definitions: "Const NOLINK = 0" and "Const LINK_POKE = 4". These are not included in CON-STANT.TXT. Finally, to get things started off right, preset the option button control array to No Link at the beginning. Since the control array contains the code that you require for getting the options at run time set properly, you need to merely set the .Value property of the array to True for the first element, No Link, and that selection will simulate a click on the option.

When you run the application, you will be using the highest level of control for DDE and relying on Visual Basic to do the rest. The first step is to create an automatic link. Figure 9-1 shows the destination application as it links to the source application.

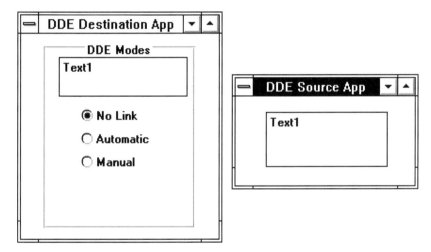

Figure 9-1   *The simple DDE sample as it looks on program start-up.*

The moment you choose the automatic link, the DDE channel between the two applications is opened and any change to the source will appear in the destination. Notice also that the two modes of forcing data between the applications become enabled.

When working with DDE, several programs exist for watching the message traffic created by the exchange. The Windows Software Development Kit (SDK) contains a useful program called DDESPY.EXE. We discussed plain old SPY.EXE in prior chapters. DDESPY.EXE watches DDE messages exclusively. Listing 9-3 shows DDESPY displaying the message traffic when the two sample applications open up an automatic link.

Listing 9-3   *Using the sample DDE application, DDESPY records this log of the DDE transaction for opening an automatic link.*

```
Task:0x348f, Time:678191341, String Handle Created: c14a(DEST)
Task:0x35af Time:678191432 Callback:
        Type=Register, fmt=0x0("?"), hConv=0x0, hsz1=0xc14a("DEST")
        hsz2=0x5760c14a("DEST:(5760)"), hData=0x0, dwData1=0x0, dwData2=0x0
        return=0x0
Task:0x1ff7 Time:678191492 Callback:
        Type=Register, fmt=0x0("?"), hConv=0x0, hsz1=0xc14a("DEST")
        hsz2=0x5760c14a("DEST:(5760)"), hData=0x0, dwData1=0x0, dwData2=0x0
        return=0x0
Task:0x348f, Time:678191567, String Handle Destroyed: c14a(DEST)
Task:0x348f, Time:678191619, String Handle Created: c14e(Form1)
Task:0x348f, Time:678191669, String Handle Created: c11f(SOURCE)
Task:0x35af Time:678191773 hwndTo=0xf0c Message(Sent)=Initiate:
        hwndFrom=0x5830, lParam=0xc14ec11f
        App=0xc11f("SOURCE")
        Topic=0xc14e("Form1")
Task:0x63f Time:678191918 hwndTo=0xecc Message(Sent)=Initiate:
        hwndFrom=0x5830, lParam=0xc14ec11f
        App=0xc11f("SOURCE")
        Topic=0xc14e("Form1")
[..additional attempts to initiate to other controls on the form.]
Task:0x36a7 Time:678194312 hwndTo=0x517c Message(Sent)=Initiate:
        hwndFrom=0x5830, lParam=0xc14ec11f
        App=0xc11f("SOURCE")
        Topic=0xc14e("Form1")
Task:0x36a7 Time:678194452 Callback:
        Type=Connect, fmt=0x0("?"), hConv=0x0, hsz1=0xc14e("Form1")
        hsz2=0xc11f("SOURCE"), hData=0x0, dwData1=0x347f021e, dwData2=0x0
        return=0x1
        Context = (wFlags=0, wCountryID=0, iCodePage=1004, dwLangID=0, dwSecurity=0)
Task:0x348f Time:678194567 hwndTo=0x5830 Message(Sent)=Ack:
        hwndFrom=0x58c0, lParam=0xc14ec11f
        App=0xc11f("SOURCE")status=c11f(fAck fBusy )
        Topic=Item=0xc14e("Form1")
Task:0x36a7 Time:678194717 Callback:
        Type=Connect_confirm, fmt=0x0("?"), hConv=0x858c0, hsz1=0xc14e("Form1")
        hsz2=0xc11f("SOURCE"), hData=0x0, dwData1=0x0, dwData2=0x0
        return=0x1
Task:0x348f, Time:678194774, String Handle Created: c152(Text1)
Task:0x36a7 Time:678194831 hwndTo=0x58c0 Message(Posted)=Advise:
        hwndFrom=0x5830, lParam=0xc15232cf
        status=32cf(fAckReq ) fmt=0x1("CF_TEXT")
        Item=0xc152("Text1")
```

```
Task:0x36a7 Time:678195118 Callback:
        Type=Advstart, fmt=0x1("CF_TEXT"), hConv=0x858c0, hsz1=0xc14e("Form1")
        hsz2=0xc152("Text1"), hData=0x0, dwData1=0x0, dwData2=0x0
        return=0x1
Task:0x348f Time:678195179 hwndTo=0x5830 Message(Posted)=Ack:
        hwndFrom=0x58c0, lParam=0xc1528000
        App=0x8000("#32768")status=8000(fAck )
        Topic=Item=0xc152("Text1")
Task:0x348f Time:678195327 Callback:
        Type=Xact_complete, fmt=0x1("CF_TEXT"), hConv=0x65830, hsz1=0xc14e("Form1")
        hsz2=0xc152("Text1"), hData=0x30c76cda, dwData1=0x10060, dwData2=0x8000
        return=0x0
Task:0x348f Time:678195387 Error: #4006 = Invalidparameter
        Input data is inaccessible.
Task:0x348f, Time:678195484, String Handle Destroyed: c152(Text1)
Task:0x348f, Time:678195536, String Handle Created: c152(Text1)
Task:0x36a7 Time:678195591 hwndTo=0x58c0 Message(Posted)=Request:
        hwndFrom=0x5830, lParam=0xc1520001
        fmt=0x1("CF_TEXT")
        Item=0xc152("Text1")
Task:0x36a7 Time:678195760 Callback:
        Type=Request, fmt=0x1("CF_TEXT"), hConv=0x858c0, hsz1=0xc14e("Form1")
        hsz2=0xc152("Text1"), hData=0x0, dwData1=0x0, dwData2=0x0
        return=0x31e701a0
        Output data=
        "Text1"
Task:0x348f Time:678195906 hwndTo=0x5830 Message(Posted)=Data:
        hwndFrom=0x58c0, lParam=0xc1523fe7
        status=3000(fRelease fRequested ) fmt=0x1("CF_TEXT")
        Data=
        "Text1"
        Item=0xc152("Text1")
Task:0x348f Time:678196050 Callback:
        Type=Xact_complete, fmt=0x1("CF_TEXT"), hConv=0x65830, hsz1=0xc14e("Form1")
        hsz2=0xc152("Text1"), hData=0x30c76cbe, dwData1=0x20060, dwData2=0x0
        return=0x0
        Input data=
        "Text1"
Task:0x348f, Time:678196202, String Handle Destroyed: c152(Text1)
Task:0x348f, Time:678196252, String Handle Destroyed: c14e(Form1)
Task:0x348f, Time:678196304, String Handle Destroyed: c11f(SOURCE)
```

A manual link permits you to have a bit more control over the DDE transactions. When speed counts, an automatic link and its continuous updating of the destination may slow your application to an unacceptable level. With a manual link, you can control when the destination receives data. You can use the LinkRequest method to retrieve data only when the destination wants to receive it. Conversely, you can use the LinkPoke method to send data from the destination back to the source application.

If the application you are trying to control with DDE supports some sort of command or macro syntax, you can use the LinkExecute method to control it remotely. If the other application is a Visual Basic app, you can't use LinkExecute; you must instead resort to the SendKeys statement to control the application. If you want to transmit pictures, LinkSend permits you to send data as do many of the other DDE methods, except that it specializes in handling pictures. Its sole purpose for life is to update a destination. Visual Basic updates text boxes and labels automatically in an automatic link, but not pictures. The DDE elements that track the status of the DDE conversation are LinkError, LinkClose, LinkOpen, and the related LinkTimeOut. These respond to changes in the state of the DDE conversation, with the exception of LinkTimeOut. LinkTimeOut should be used to set the amount of time you are willing to hold up any process dependent upon a DDE transaction which is waiting for another application responsible for one side of the transaction to wake up and respond. You can monitor the other three events to handle matters like controlled sign-off or writing out configuration data to an INI file.

The "Other" Application

As you can probably tell, it matters a lot in DDE whether both applications in a conversation are running at the same time. There's no such thing as a stored DDE conversation, since the responses by both sides may not go the same way twice in a row as you respond to LinkError and other changes in each application during the session. So, finding or making sure the other application is running—not the one in which you are writing Visual Basic code, but your target—becomes an issue.

You have several tools at your disposal for making certain contact with another application. Of course, you can always simply toss a message at whatever application you want to contact and then assume it's not available when an error comes back, but this is not a very elegant nor an effective means for making the first contact. If you have control over the environment and you are therefore certain that the application will not be running, you can use the SHELL statement to launch the second application. If you need a higher degree of control, you may want to write a short DLL and use the WINEXEC function to launch the application.

On the other extreme, if you know that the other application is already running, either because you have launched it explicitly or you are tracking it by some other means, you can use the AppActivate statement to make certain it is still available.

A non–Visual Basic method called FindWindow is used in the following DLL example. You can use the FindWindow API call to search the open Windows for you. Lastly, you can use a DLL to search through the module list to find out which applications are already running. This method is used also in the remaining examples in this chapter.

The System Topic

No generally accepted published standards exist for what services an application that supports DDE conversations should include. However, Microsoft recommends that certain facilities be supported, and one of those facilities is the system topic. If this were a book on how to write applications by using C, we would have to delve into the mysteries of trapping the DDE message traffic in the system and the application queue for initiating a conversation or sensing when another application wants to connect. With Visual Basic, it's a simple matter of setting properties and using a few commands. However, in the applications you might want to link to, the matter gets a little more complex. To address that issue, I've created a DLL that will survey the applications on your system and determine which application can support the system topic.

The DDE Survey Program

In surveying your system for an unknown number of applications, you must read through the module list much like the MODLIST DLL we created in Chapter 6 except that we'll use those same Windows API calls within Visual Basic.

The first step is to fill the list box with the modules that represent each application. To do that, you must retrieve the Window handle of each Window in the system. Since even most controls have a Window handle, you have to sort through the child windows until you locate the parent for one application. Using GetWindow(DDE-Form.hWnd, GW_HWNDFIRST), you get the first window in the list. GetParent(ThisWnd%) gives you the handle for the parent of the window handle you have found. If no parent exists (and one must exist for all Windows in an application except the parent for the application), you move on to extract the information you need for the DDE transaction.

Now that we have the handle for the correct window to identify the application, we need to separate the instances of that application, since several versions of the same application may be running. GetWindowWord(ThisWnd%, GWW_HIN-STANCE) provides the instance, and GetModuleFileName(ThisInst%, ModName$, 255) provides the full path and file name for the application, as in C:\WORD\WINWORD.EXE. It's necessary to trim the .EXE before we can use this as a module name for the DDE calls.

For this sample, the next step that the application takes isn't really necessary; we know the application is running, since we have its module name. However, in other applications, you might be looking for a particular application to connect to using DDE. As mentioned earlier in this chapter, several means exist for ensuring that an application is running. You can simply launch the application by using the Visual Basic function call Shell(), walk the module list as I just described, or use the FindWindow API call to test for the existence of an application. Since we've already determined that the current window is a parent window, we can use GetWindowTextLength(ThisWnd%) and GetWindowText(ThisWnd%, ListItem$, NameLen% + 1) to retrieve the title text for the window. Finally, you can use the GetClassName(ThisWnd%, ClassName$, 255) call to retrieve the class name of the application window. Either the class name or the window title can be used separately with FindWindow to locate the window in question. In this case, we are retrieving those artifacts from the windows themselves, so we already know they exist.

Connecting by Using a Module Name

At the end of all of this retrieval of windows, the code in Listing 9-4 shows the actual attempt to connect to the application. Since list boxes themselves don't' support DDE, it's necessary to place a picture, edit control, or label on the form to perform the DDE connection. In this sample, we're using a label named Status that can be moved off the visible part of the form but can be kept enabled (visible) to operate the DDE connection.

Listing 9-4   *As soon as valid module information can be located for an application, this code attempts to connect by means of DDE to that application.*

```
'-------Attempt to link to system topic
If hWnds <> 0& Then
  If Trim(ModName$) <> "" Then                'When valid module
    x% = DoEvents()                           'Process Events
```

```
    Status.LinkMode = NONE                          'Turn off link
    Status.LinkTopic = ModName$ & "|System"         'Set topic
    x% = DoEvents()                                 'Process Events
    Status.LinkMode = AUTOMATIC                      'Try to link
  End If
End If
```

The first step in the connection process permits other applications to perform their work. (We've dominated the CPU since we began this module.) Then we ensure a clear link by turning off any existing links for this application. Now we use the module name we retrieved and append to it the system topic. Normally, you would also have a LinkItem property to set, but we won't know which application we're connecting, and the type of LinkItem changes for different applications. For instance, you connect to bookmarks in Word for Windows, but you connect to a single spreadsheet cell in Excel and to a control in another Visual Basic application.

Finally, we set the LinkMode to AUTOMATIC for the label named Status, and Visual Basic attempts to create the link to the application described in the ModName$ variable, giving the path and root file name. Without a LinkItem, this will generate an error. The errors supported by the LinkError event cover a rather limited number of subjects, most of which refer to DDE conversations already in progress. These errors include the following:

> Listed in the CONSTANT.TXT file:
>> Global Const DDE_SOURCE_CLOSED = 6
>> Global Const TOO_MANY_LINKS = 7
>> Global Const DATA_TRANSFER_FAILED = 8

> Others:
>> Other application requested wrong data format (1)
>> Not enough memory for DDE (11)

In the WINDOWS.H file, the following error codes are included by means of the DDEML.H file in all Windows applications that support DDE:

DMLERR_NO_ERROR	0
DMLERR_FIRST	0x4000
MLERR_ADVACKTIMEOUT	0x4000
MLERR_BUSY	0x4001
MLERR_DATAACKTIMEOUT	0x4002

MLERR_DLL_NOT_INITIALIZED	0x4003
MLERR_DLL_USAGE	0x4004
MLERR_EXECACKTIMEOUT	0x4005
MLERR_INVALIDPARAMETER	0x4006
MLERR_LOW_MEMORY	0x4007
MLERR_MEMORY_ERROR	0x4008
MLERR_NOTPROCESSED	0x4009
MLERR_NO_CONV_ESTABLISHED	0x400a
MLERR_POKEACKTIMEOUT	0x400b
MLERR_POSTMSG_FAILED	0x400c
MLERR_REENTRANCY	0x400d
MLERR_SERVER_DIED	0x400e
MLERR_SYS_ERROR	0x400f
MLERR_UNADVACKTIMEOUT	0x4010
MLERR_UNFOUND_QUEUE_ID	0x4011
DMLERR_LAST	0x4011

The 2XX series of errors within Visual Basic include these values from the DDEML.H error codes as well as others:

281	No More DDE Channels
282	No foreign application responded to a DDE initiate
283	Multiple applications responded to a DDE initiate
284	DDE channel locked
285	Foreign application won't perform DDE method or operation
286	Timeout occurred while waiting for DDE response
287	User pressed ESC key during DDE operation
288	Destination is busy
289	Data not provided in DDE operation
290	Data in wrong format
291	Foreign application quit
292	DDE conversation closed or changed
293	DDE method invoked with no channel open
294	Invalid DDE link format
295	Message queue filled; DDE messages lost
298	DDE requires DDEML.DLL

In the sample application, the value returned after an attempt to connect indicates the ability of the connect candidate application to support the system topic. If the application does not understand the system topic, it returns error 282, "No foreign application responded to a DDE initiate." Otherwise you get error 285, "Foreign application won't perform DDE method or operation." It won't perform the DDE method because we didn't pass anything in the LinkItem property so that it would to know what to perform.

Under Windows for Workgroups, with several applications running, the DDE Survey application appears, as shown in Figure 9-2. Each application consumes several lines in the list box.

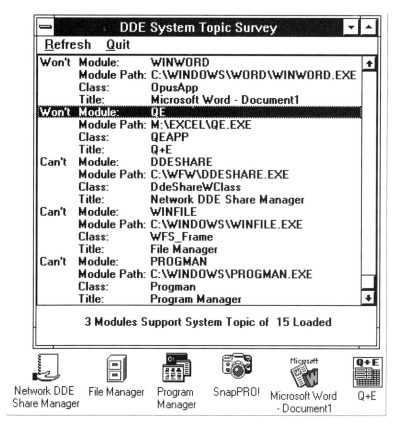

Figure 9-2   *When the DDE Survey program is run or the Refresh Menu item is selected, it displays all of the modules running in Windows.*

In Figure 9-2, notice that applications you might think would support DDE—like Program Manager and File Manager—do not so so as well as you might expect. That does not mean they won't support DDE (in fact, both of those applications do), but you cannot poll them with a program like Survey to discover what topics they support. That is why support for the system topic should be provided in an application; it permits other applications to interact more effectively by enabling them to get a list of the topics your application supports.

Along those lines, when you choose the "service" name (the first part of the topic address) that your C application offers up for DDE conversation, you should limit your application to one service with the same name as the application. This permits other applications to guess what service to address when they attempt to create a DDE link. In Visual Basic you are restricted to one service name, which will always be the name of the application.

Retrieving the Topic List

Now that the DDE Survey program has provided a means to access the applications that support the system topic, we'll go on to get a list of those topics. In the case of the sample program, DDE Survey, we will establish a DDE conversation in the DLL to take advantage of the ability to place a callback routine in a DLL. As with all DLLs, this will contain a LibMain and a WEP function. Because this sample was prepared in Borland C++ version 3.1, a WEP is not needed and, while a sample module definition file is included in the source listings, Borland supplies a default that works.

The flow of functions to retrieve the list is depicted in Figure 9-3. The first step, creating the connection, is necessary for two reasons: we need to reconnect to the module after placing it in the list in the test of system topics, and we need to create the handles to strings for functions used later in the DLL.

The two critical pieces of information required for requesting a list of topics and displaying them are the module or service name for the application serving as the DDE source, and the handle of the list box in the Visual Basic application. The instance handle must have been derived from a prior call to Ddeinitialize, and cannot be garnered from within Visual Basic because Visual Basic cannot process a callback function. Even though Visual Basic makes things easy, data like the instance handle of a DDE conversation is not available.

The first list box in the DDE Survey program presents the module name we'll need to start the conversation. The code in Listing 9-5 shows how the Survey program

grabs that information when you double-click on the correct line in the entry for each
running application.

Figure 9-3   *Once you have called the DLL from within Visual Basic, API calls are
responsible for managing the DDE conversation.*

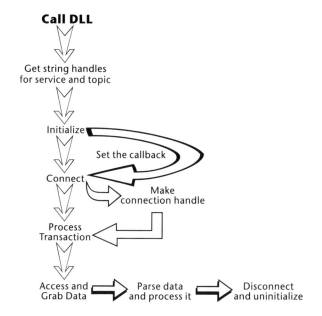

Call DLL

Get string handles
for service and topic

Initialize

Set the callback

Connect

Make
connection handle

Process
Transaction

Access and
Grab Data

Parse data
and process it

Disconnect
and uninitialize

Listing 9-5   *Double-clicking on the correct line for a module executes this code to establish
the DDE connection before calling the DLL to get the topics list.*

```
Sub RunList_DblClick ()
        On Error GoTo BadOne
        Target$ = RunList.List(RunList.ListIndex)
        If InStr(Target$, "Module:") = 0 Then
           MsgBox "Click on first line of entry"
           Exit Sub
        Else If InStr(Target$, "Won't") = 0 Then
           MsgBox "This application doesn't support the System Topic.
           Exit Sub
        End If
        Md% = InStr(Target$, ":")
        TopicMod = Mid$(Target$, Md% + 2, Len(Target$) - Md%)
        Status.LinkMode = NONE                          'Turn off other link
```

```
        Status.LinkTopic = TopicMod & "|System"          'Set topic
        Status.LinkItem = ""
        x% = DoEvents()                                  'Process Events

        Status.LinkMode = MANUAL                         'Try to link as check
        MsgBox "Link Created Successfully", MB_OK, "DDE"
        Status.LinkMode = NONE        'Cancel link
        Topics.Show
        Exit Sub
BadOne:
    If Err Then
        MsgBox Str$(Err) & ": " & Error$, MB_OK, "Connection Error"
    End If
    Exit Sub
End Sub
```

The code in Listing 9-5 also shows initiating a link with the module selected. Since the list is not maintained dynamically, this step ensures that the application is still running before the call to the Dynamic Link Library. The intelligence for calling the DLL—including the actual function call and the function declaration—lives in the Topics.Frm module. The code in Listing 9-6 displays the final step within Visual Basic before the DLL takes over.

Listing 9-6   *The function call DDEList passes the module name (TopicMod) the handle for the list box to be filled (TopicList.hWnd) and the actual topic to be used (Topic$).*

```
        Topic$ = "System"
        Msg$ = "Calling the DLL with:" & Chr$(13)
        Msg$ = Msg$ & "   1) List Box Handle: " & Str$(TopicList.hWnd) & Chr$(13)
        Msg$ = Msg$ & "   2) Module: " & TopicMod & Chr$(13)
        Msg$ = Msg$ & "   3) Topic: " & Topic$
        ret% = MsgBox(Msg$, MB_OKCANCEL, "Get Topics Supported")
        If ret% = IDCANCEL Then Exit Sub
        'Inst and handle for main window with module name
        x% = DDEList(TopicMod, TopicList.hWnd, Topic$)
        Select Case x%
          Case 1: Result$ = "Succeeded"
          Case 0: Result$ = "Failed"
        End Select
        MsgBox Result$, MB_OK, "DDEList call Result"
```

This part of the DDE Survey utility allows you to pass various topics to the DLL to check support of that topic by the server targeted by the TopMod variable contents. Figure 9-4 shows the message box that displays the values to be passed to the DLL.

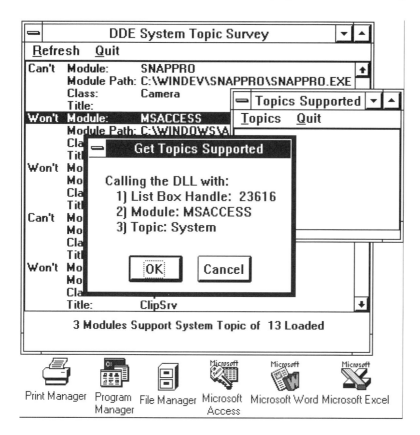

Figure 9-4   *Microsoft Access is the subject for the query about to be issued to the DLL for checking its support for the system topic.*

Once you have selected OK, the DDE Survey program uses the message box shown in Figure 9-4 to call the DDELIST.DLL library. The program uses the following declaration in the general declarations for the Topics.Frm module (all on one line):

Declare Function DDEList Lib "DDElist.dll" (ByVal TopMod As String, ByVal ListhWnd As Integer, ByVal Topic As String) As Integer

The return value for the DLL signifies whether the function has returned after completing its tasks successfully or whether it has exited prematurely or under the wrong circumstances.

Inside the DLL

The primary reason for resorting to a DLL in this program is that DDE operates by using a callback function. Callbacks work like an answering machine. You publish the number of your answering machine, turn it on, and now others can contact you by placing messages on the answering machine tape. You establish a callback function as a global memory object where other applications can place information in response to DDE transactions. Listing 9-7 shows the callback function for the DDELIST.DLL

Listing 9-7   *The callback function in DDELIST.DLL used in the DDE conversation.*

```
// Callback function for DDE messages
HDDEDATA CALLBACK DDECallback(UINT wType,
                              UINT wFmt,
                              HCONV hConv,
                              HSZ hsz1,
                              HSZ hsz2,
                              HDDEDATA hDDEData,
                              DWORD dwData1,
                              DWORD dwData2)
{
 switch (wType)
 {
 default:
sprintf(TestVar,"wType:%d\nwFmt:%d\nhConv:%d\nhsz1:%d\nhsz2:%d\nhDDEData:%d\ndwData1:
...%d\ndwData2:%d\n", wType,wFmt,hConv,hsz1,hsz2,hDDEData,dwData1,dwData2);
        UserMsg(TestVar,"Callback Data", NULL); //not used, prevents warnings
           return NULL;
     }
}
```

Since Visual Basic does not support pointers to the strings containing the information about module and topic, the DDEList function passes them in by value (ByVal). To use them in the C code, you must move them into character strings by using lstrcpy.

Tip: *This DLL uses the UserMsg function to mark the progress of processing inside the DLL. With your compiler's debugging utility, you can comment out these calls and simply step through the program. You lose only the interpretation of the error return codes offered by UserMsg.*

The next step is to register the conversation with the DDEML and initialize the callback structure with the following code:

```
// Initialize DDEML and callback structure
   ui = DdeInitialize(&dwDDEInst,
                   (PFNCALLBACK)DDECallback,
                   CBF_FAIL_ALLSVRXACTIONS,      //suppress server recv
                   0L);
```

The constant, CBF_FAIL_ALLSVRACTIONS, tells the DDEML that you will not accept requests to become a server for other applications. The SDK documentation provides the other qualifying constants that you may use here. In the DdeInitialize statement, the variable dwDDEInst contains the instance handle for the conversation that you will need later. If the initialization fails, this value will be NULL.

The DdeConnect function requires that you use handles to the service and topic strings (the module name and system topic in this case), so you must use the DdeCreateStringHandle API call, which returns the handle and associates the strings with this conversation. If you make this call with two identical values from two separate DLLs, you will get the same handle in return. If you are processing transactions inside the callback function in a generic server or client program, you will need to issue the DdeKeepStringHandle call to hold onto that handle, because it won't last once you leave the callback function. Since we are initiating this use of the handle and will use it and destroy it ourselves, we don't need to hold onto it with DdeKeepStringHandle. However, it will be necessary to issue the DdeFree-StringHandle call before exiting the DLL.

Now it's possible to connect the conversation to the server with the following code:

```
       hConv = DdeConnect(dwDDEInst, hszTopMod, hszSystem, 0);
```

The hConv variable contains the handle to the DDE conversation established with the DdeConnect call.

The next step is to carry out the first transaction in this conversation with the following statement:

```
hDDEData = DdeClientTransaction(NULL,
                                0,
                                hConv,
                                hszItem,
                                CF_TEXT,
                                XTYP_REQUEST,
                                    1000, // ms timeout
                                &dwResult);
```

The DdeClientTransaction addresses the DDEML with the identification of the specific DDE conversation to be used, the handle to the string of system items to be queried, information on the timeout value to be allowed, and what clipboard format (CP_TEXT) the results should be returned within. If hDDEData in the callback structure fills with information, then the transaction has succeeded. To retrieve that information, you must use the DdeAccessData call to fill a byte array with pointers to the actual information. This is the point where we really leave the DDE side of operations in this example and perform some generic C work. To parse that array, this example leans heavily on an example by Herman Rodent aka Nigel Thompson in the Microsoft Knowledge Base for how to parse the string of topics as returned from DDEML in response to the DdeClientTransaction call.

We use the SendMessage API call and the window handle of the Visual Basic list box that was passed into the function at the beginning to place the parsed topic strings directly into the list box. This prevents having to process return values of strings back from the DLL function call inside Visual Basic. The resulting topic list for a query of support of the system topic by Word for Windows appears in Figure 9-5.

Finally, we must disconnect the conversation and release the global memory object (the callback function) before exiting the DLL.

Error Processing

At any time during a DDE conversation, you can use the DdeGetLastError call to find out what the last error produced by a DDE transaction may be. The DDEML.H defines the error returns, and the SDK help facility provides an explanation for each error and what may have produced it. The UserMsg module in DDELIST.DLL formats these return values to be presented in message boxes, as shown in Figure 9-6. The code in Listing 9-8 shows a large switch statement for selecting the particular message box to present.

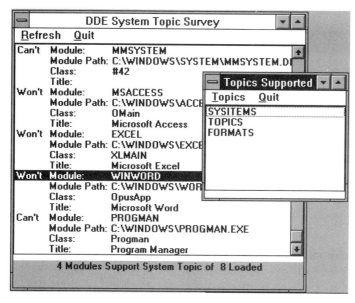

Figure 9-5   *A successful query of an application that supports the system topic yields the type of support available.*

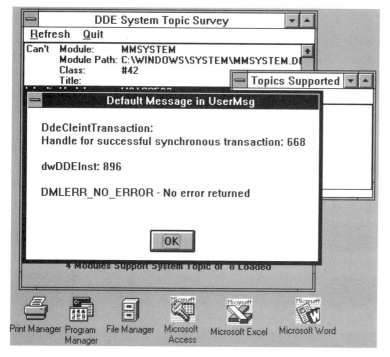

Figure 9-6   *This message box shows that no DDE transaction to this point (specifically the call to DdeConnect) has generated an error.*

Listing 9-8   *For debugging purposes, this function returns the error explanation for the*
last error generated in a DDE conversation.

```
switch(DdeGetLastError(dwDDEInst))
    {
    case DMLERR_NO_ERROR:
      sprintf(Note,"%s\n%s\n",UserNotes,"DMLERR_NO_ERROR - No error returned");
      break;
    case DMLERR_ADVACKTIMEOUT:
      ln1 = "DMLERR_ADVACKTIMEOUT - A request for a";
      ln2 = "synchronous advise transaction has timed out.";
      sprintf(Note,"%s\n%s\n%s\n",UserNotes,ln1,ln2);
      break;
    case DMLERR_BUSY:
      ln1 = "DMLERR_BUSY - The response to the transaction";
      ln2 = "caused the DDE_FBUSY bit to be set.";
      sprintf(Note,"%s\n%s\n%s\n",UserNotes,ln1, ln2);
      break;
    case DMLERR_DATAACKTIMEOUT:
      ln1 = "DMLERR_DATAACKTIMEOUT - A request for a";
      ln2 = "synchronous data transaction has timed out.";
      sprintf(Note,"%s\n%s\n%s\n",UserNotes,ln1,ln2);
      break;
    case DMLERR_DLL_NOT_INITIALIZED:
      ln1 = "DMLERR_DLL_NOT_INITIALIZED - A DDEML API was";
      ln2 = "called without first calling the DdeInitialize";
      ln3 = "function. An invalid IdInst parameter was passed to an API.";
      sprintf(Note,"%s\n%s\n%s\n%s\n",UserNotes,ln1, ln2, ln3);
      break;
    case DMLERR_DLL_USAGE:
      ln1 = "DMLERR_DLL_USAGE - An application initialized as";
      ln2 = "APPCLASS_MONITOR has attempted to perform a DDE transaction,";
      ln3 = "or an application initialized as APPCMD_CLIENTONLY";
      ln4 = "has attempted to perform server transactions.";
      sprintf(Note,"%s\n%s\n%s\n%s\n%s\n",UserNotes,ln1,ln2,ln3,ln4);
      break;
    case DMLERR_EXECACKTIMEOUT:
      ln1 = "DMLERR_EXECACKTIMEOUT - A request for a synchronous";
      ln2 = "execute transaction has timed out.";
      sprintf(Note,"%s\n%s\n%s\n",UserNotes,ln1,ln2);
      break;
    case DMLERR_INVALIDPARAMETER:
      ln1 = "DMLERR_INVALIDPARAMETER - A parameter failed to be validated by the
      ...DDEML:";
      ln2 = "- wrong item-name handle used?";
      ln3 = "- wrong clipboard data format used?";
```

```
  ln4 = "- client-side handle used with server-side function or vice versa?";
  ln5 = "- used a freed data handle or string handle?";
  ln6 = "- More than one instance of the application used the same object?";
  sprintf(Note,"%s\n%s\n%s\n%s\n%s\n%s\n%s\n",UserNotes,ln1,ln2,ln3,ln4,ln5,ln6);
  break;
case DMLERR_LOW_MEMORY:
  ln1 = "DMLERR_LOW_MEMORY - A DDEML application has created a prolonged race";
  ln2 = "condition (where the server application outruns the";
  ln3 = "client), causing large amounts of memory to be consumed.";
  sprintf(Note,"%s\n%s\n%s\n%s\n",UserNotes,ln1,ln2,ln3);
  break;
case DMLERR_MEMORY_ERROR:
  sprintf(Note,"%s\n%s\n",UserNotes,"DMLERR_MEMORY_ERROR - A memory allocation failed.");
  break;
case DMLERR_NO_CONV_ESTABLISHED:
  ln1 = "DMLERR_NO_CONV_ESTABLISHED - client's attempt to";
  ln2 = "establish a conversation has failed.";
  sprintf(Note,"%s\n%s\n%s\n",UserNotes,ln1,ln2);
  break;
case DMLERR_NOTPROCESSED:
  sprintf(Note,"%s\n","DMLERR_NOTPROCESSED - A transaction failed.");
  break;
case DMLERR_POKEACKTIMEOUT:
  ln1 = "DMLERR_POKEACKTIMEOUT - A request for a synchronous poke";
  ln2 = "transaction has timed out.";
  sprintf(Note,"%s\n%s\n%s\n",UserNotes,ln1,ln2);
  break;
case DMLERR_POSTMSG_FAILED:
  ln1 = "DMLERR_POSTMSG_FAILED - An internal call to the PostMessage";
  ln2 = "function has failed.";
  sprintf(Note,"%s\n%s\n%s\n",UserNotes,ln1,ln2);
  break;
case DMLERR_REENTRANCY:
  ln1 = "DMLERR_REENTRANCY - An application instance with a synchronous transaction";
  ln2 = "already in progress attempted to initiate another";
  ln3 = "synchronous transaction, or the DdeEnableCallback";
  ln4 = "function was called from within a DDEML callback function.";
  sprintf(Note,"%s\n%s\n%s\n%s\n%s\n",UserNotes,ln1,ln2,ln3,ln4);
  break;
case DMLERR_SERVER_DIED:
  ln1 = "DMLERR_SERVER_DIED - A server-side transaction was attempted on a";
  ln2 = "conversation that was terminated by the client, or the";
  ln3 = "server terminated before completing a transaction.";
  sprintf(Note,"%s\n%s\n%s\n%s\n",UserNotes,ln1,ln2,ln3);
  break;
```

```
case DMLERR_SYS_ERROR:
    ln1 = "DMLERR_SYS_ERROR - An internal error has occurred in the DDEML.";
    sprintf(Note,"%s\n%s\n",UserNotes,ln1);
    break;
case DMLERR_UNADVACKTIMEOUT:
    ln1 = "DMLERR_UNADVACKTIMEOUT - A request to end an advise transaction has timed
    ...out.";
    sprintf(Note,"%s\n%s\n",UserNotes,ln1);
    break;
case DMLERR_UNFOUND_QUEUE_ID:
    ln1 = "DMLERR_UNFOUND_QUEUE_ID - An invalid transaction identifier was passed";
    ln2 = "to a DDEML function. Once the application has returned";
    ln3 = "from an XTYP_XACT_COMPLETE callback, the transaction";
    ln4 = "identifier for that callback is no longer valid.";
    sprintf(Note,"%s\n%s\n%s\n%s\n%s\n",UserNotes,ln1,ln2,ln3,ln4);
    break;
default:
    sprintf(Note,"%s\n%s\n",UserNotes,"No last error reported by DdeGetLastError");
}
MessageBox(NULL,Note,"Default Message in UserMsg", MB_OK);
}
```

The DdeGetLastError function tells only of the last error for the DDE work in the application identified in the dwDDEInst handle, and not for multiple conversations that one application might be operating. In this example, only one conversation is started, however.

Application Linking

A wide variety of applications of DDE exist, including those associated with NETDDE and with Object Linking and Embedding. The remainder of this chapter is devoted to various techniques and notes for linking to applications.

The following comparison shows the commonalties between the function calls in each application as compared to Visual Basic. (Each of these applications has more commands than are listed.)

Table 9-2   *These Windows applications support DDE statements as shown.*

Excel	WinWord	Procomm	Dynacomm	PowerBuilder	Visual Basic
INITIATE	DDEInitiate	ddeinit	ACCESS	OpenChannel	LinkMode = *type*
REQUEST	DDERequest	dderequest	REQUEST	GetRemote	LinkRequest method

Table 9-2 *(Continued)*

Excel	WinWord	Procomm	Dynacomm	PowerBuilder	Visual Basic
POKE	DDEPoke	ddepoke	POKE	SetRemote	LinkPoke method
EXECUTE	DDEExecute	ddeexecute	INSTRUCT	ExecRemote	LinkExecute method
TERMINATE	DDETerminate	ddeterminate	ACCESS CANCEL	CloseChannel	LinkMode = None
SHELL	SHELL	run	LAUNCH		SHELL

As you can see, the syntax for each application does not adhere to any kind of special standard. In the case of Dynacomm for Windows, Visual Basic–like events can also be handled during a DDE conversation. Dynacomm provides a series of "WHEN"-prefaced commands that activate when the DDE channel sends particular messages:

- WAIT SIGNAL suspends processes until the next DDE message is received.
- WHEN ADVISE prepares Dynacomm to provide information on request.
- WHEN EXECUTE prepares Dynacomm to service an execute statement.
- WHEN INITIATE fires an event when a new conversation is established.
- WHEN POKE, WHEN REQUEST responds to messages from other applications.
- WHEN TERMINATE resembles Visual Basic's Link_Close event.

In other applications, like SuperProject for Windows and Procomm for Windows, the DDE server facilities operate automatically with paste links. SuperProject supplies a menu selection in "Inter Project Connections," where you get one dialog to fill in for establishing SuperProject as a client and another dialog for setting it up as a server. It will respond to the native syntax of other applications for managing DDE conversations. Other applications that support DDE focus on only one side of the conversation. Teleform from Cardiff Software (a forms creation and optical character-recognition fax software) doesn't modify data that is sent to it, so it operates primarily as a client. In Teleform, the module name is always TeleMgr, the topic is always AnyForm, and it supports four link items:

- LINK sends no headers, but the data is processed before the conversation is suspended.
- LINKH includes headers, and the data is processed before the suspense.

- SUSP holds the data until the suspense processing is complete (without headers).
- SUSPH holds the data (including headers) until the suspense processing is complete.

In the case of PowerBuilder from Powersoft, the statements you use change according whether PowerBuilder will serve as client or server. For instance, StartServerDDE is the same as the connection initiation functions in other applications, but StartHotLink initiates the connection where PowerBuilder is the client.

Linking to Word for Windows: Excel and Q+E

To link to Microsoft Word for Windows, you must include a BookMark in the document, and the document must be open. To ensure a successful link, it's a good idea to check for the existence of Word with a function like FindWindow, and launch it if it is not presently running. Figure 9-7 shows a simple application for connecting to Word for Windows and using it as both a server and a client.

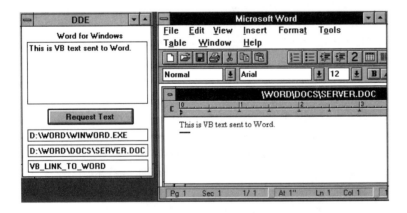

Figure 9-7   *A simple application shows how to poke information into a server application.*

The simple application shown in Figure 9-7 asks for the name of the application to launch, the path to the document to be used, and the name of the specific locus for the DDE transaction, which for Word is the name of a bookmark. Listing 9-9 shows the processing of the button control for controlling the DDE operations between the sample Visual Basic application and Word for Windows. The program assumes that you will launch a copy of Word to get at the document with the bookmark armed for DDE.

Listing 9-9   *By pressing this control and entering text into the edit control, you can send and receive text from Word for Windows.*

```
Select Case Command1.Caption
  Case "Launch Word"
    z% = Shell(Text2.Text & Space$(1) & Text3.Text, 1)
    x% = DoEvents()
    Text1.LinkMode = NONE
    x% = DoEvents()
    Text1.LinkTopic = "WINWORD|" & Mid$(Text3.Text, 3, InStr(Text3.Text, ".") - 3)
    Text1.LinkItem = Text4.Text
    x% = DoEvents()
    Text1.LinkMode = LINK_AUTOMATIC
    Command1.Caption = "Request Text"
  Case "Poke Text"
    Text1.LinkPoke
    Command1.Caption = "Request Text"
  Case "Request Text"
    Text1.LinkRequest
    Command1.Caption = "Poke Text"
End Select
```

To include the entire document in the scope of the DDE transaction, you can assign one bookmark name to the entire document. Follow these steps:

1. Open the document.
2. Place the cursor in row one, column one.
3. Press CTRL+SHIFT+END.
4. Assign the bookmark.

You can take this remote control of Word or other applications even further. The example just given presupposes that you have a document with the bookmark already saved into it. Using the LinkExecute command, you can operate Word for Windows transparently. Anything you can do from the keyboard to operate Word—accessing menus, typing, setting styles, or running macros—you can do remotely from Visual Basic. Simply launch Word, set the DDE link to the default Document1 (winword|document1 for the topic), set a time-out value long enough to permit Word enough time to do the work, and then begin sending LinkExecute statements. For example, if you have a Word macro that loads a report and prints it, you can run that macro from within Visual Basic by establishing the DDE connection and then sending Form.Control.LinkExecute[wordmacro]. Also, if you write a program in another language that allows you to interface to DDE, you can fire the LinkExecute event from outside Visual Basic by establishing a link to the Visual Basic application (or vice versa) and then sending a DDEexecute statement.

 Tip: *Some dialog boxes in Word for Windows may not respond within your original time-out settings. Don't assume that the system has hung up.*

Links to Excel change from the preceding techniques for Word only in that you link to a particular cell in Excel rather than to Word's bookmark. Also, use Excel's default document sheet1 as the right half of the LinkTopic. Q+E can also support DDE. In that case, you use the database file as the right side of the LinkTopic (QE|QUERY1) for default start-up definition, but you use the same cell definition as Excel with the LinkItem. Take note, however, that attempting to LinkPoke to Q+E from Visual Basic when the Allow Editing option is off will cause the program to crash and result in a "Foreign application won't perform DDE method or operation" error message.

 Tip: *When processing DDE data sends from Excel, be sure to strip the trailing carriage-return line feed from the string sent by Excel.*

You can close an application by using DDE, but you run the risk of having to wait for the DDE link to time-out before you get control of the application that sends the closing instructions. Instead, you can terminate the link properly and then make API calls to close the remote application using SendMessage as in the code given in Listing 9-10.

Listing 9-10 *You can close a remote application from outside DDE by passing the WM_CLOSE and WM_SYSCOMMAND messages to it.*

```
Declare Function SendMessage Lib "User" (ByVal hWnd As Integer, ByVal wMsg
...As Integer, ByVal wParam As Integer, lParam As Any) As Long

Const WM_CLOSE = &H10
Const WM_SYSCOMMAND = &H112
Const SC_CLOSE = &HF060

dword& = SendMessage(myhWnd, WM_CLOSE, NULL, NULL)
 x& = SendMessage(myhWnd, WM_SYSCOMMAND, SC_CLOSE, NULL)
```

In closing an application, keep in mind your dependency on how much control you may or may not have. If the user started the application and left a document unsaved, your application won't know that and will be unable to complete the closing procedure.

Even though, as shown earlier, Program Manager doesn't offer support for the system topic, it does support DDE. You can manipulate its groups just like a user does by using these commands:

- CreateGroup(GroupName,GroupPath)
- ShowGroup(GroupName,ShowCommand)
- AddItem(CommandLine,Name,IconPath,IconIndex,XPos,YPos)
- DeleteGroup(GroupName)
- ExitProgman(bSaveState)

These statements used as strings in LinkExecute with a link to Program Manager opened (LinkMode = MANUAL), you can manage user icons and even groups. For a little fun as well as a demonstration, place the controls as shown in Figure 9-8 and place the code from Listing 9-11 into the timer and button as shown to create the "Dancing Groups" application. (The group windows pop open and close rapidly.)

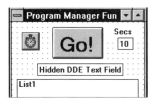

Figure 9-8 *The screen on the left shows the controls in Design mode, and the screen on the right shows the program running.*

This program activates Program Manager and ensures that it's in full-screen mode by using the SendKeys command prior to the opening of the DDE link. Then, a timer is enabled with an interval setting of one tenth of a second. Following that, the DDE channel is opened and the Program Manager PROGMAN topic is used to grab a list of the groups in Program Manager. These are placed in a list box. Now, when the user presses the Go! button, the timer that launches the code is enabled. That code uses the open DDE channel, the Program Manager DDE interface, and a random-number generator to alternately open and then minimize the groups in Program Manager. The user can set the length of time that the display will carry on with its antics before the Go! button is pressed.

Listing 9-11 *The source code for creating the "Dancing Groups" example.*

```
Dim Start As Integer

Sub Form_Load ()
    On Error GoTo ErrMsg
    Form1.Show
    HidnTxt.LinkTopic = "ProgMan|Progman"
    HidnTxt.LinkItem = "PROGMAN"
    x% = DoEvents()
    HidnTxt.LinkMode = LINK_MANUAL
    HidnTxt.LinkRequest         'Get list of the groups
    HidnTxt.LinkMode = NONE
    Last% = 1
    Do
       This% = InStr(Last%, HidnTxt.Text, Chr$(13))
       If This% = 0 Then Exit Do
       List1.AddItem Mid(HidnTxt.Text, Last%, This% - Last%)
       Last% = This% + 2
    Loop
    Exit Sub
ErrMsg:
    MsgBox Str$(Err) & Error$
    End
End Sub

Sub Go_Click ()
    AppActivate "Program Manager"
    SendKeys "%{ }{Enter}", True
    HidnTxt.LinkTopic = "ProgMan|Progman"
```

```
    HidnTxt.LinkMode = LINK_MANUAL
    Timer1.Interval = 100   ' Set Interval to 1 sec
    Timer1.Enabled = True    'Launch the timer
    Start = Timer
End Sub

Sub Timer1_Timer ()
  Static Last As Integer
  Randomize
  n% = Int((List1.ListCount - 3) * Rnd)
  HidnTxt.LinkExecute "[ShowGroup(" & List1.List(Last) & ", 6)]"
  HidnTxt.LinkExecute "[ShowGroup(" & List1.List(n%) & ", 1)]"
  Last = n%
  If Timer >= Start + Text1.Text Then
    Timer1.Enabled = False
    SendKeys "%{ }{Down 3}{Enter}", True     ' Minimize Progman
  End If
End Sub
```

Network DDE

Because of an agreement in May 1992 between Wonderware in Irvine, California, and Microsoft, you can now remotely operate applications across a network by using network DDE in Windows for Workgroups and Windows NT–based networks. Wonderware created the first version of NetDDE. The primary difference between NetDDE and regular DDE involves some bookkeeping on each system and some additional information passed in the LinkTopic. Three steps are involved in establishing a network DDE link:

> 1. Add an item to the Windows SYSTEM.INI file that identifies the link-topic information for the DDE source. To do this, you must call the NDdeShareAdd function from the Windows SDK. The function declaration is as follows (all on one line):

```
Declare Functionion NDdeShareAdd Lib "NDDEAPI.DLL" (Server As Any, ByVal
...LEvel As Integer, ShareINfo As NDDESHAREINFO, ByVal nSize As Long) As
...Integer
```

And the structure for holding the share information looks like this:

```
Type NDdeShareInfo
    szShareNameAs String * MAX_NDDESHARENAME+1 'char
    lpszTargetApp As Long'LPSTR  name of application
    lpszTargetTopic As Long'LPSTR  name of topic
    lpbPassword1 As Long 'LPBYTE read-only password
    cbPassword1 As Long  'sDWORD  ize of password
    dwPermissions1 As Long'DWORD  read-only permissions
    lpbPassword2 As Long 'LPBYTE full-access password
    cbPassword2 As Long  'DWORD  size of password, in bytes
    dwPermissions2 As Long'DWORD  full-access permissions
    lpszItem As Long     'LPSTR  name of permitted item
    cAddItems As Long    'LONG   count of additional items
    LPNDDESHAREITEMINFO lpNDdeShareItemInfo As Long' array of items
End Type
```

You can also use the Registry program in Windows NT or the Share Manager in the Windows for WorkGroups Resource Kit.

2. Create a DDE source application with a DDE link topic corresponding to the information in the SYSTEM.INI file.

3. Establish a DDE destination link that references the network computer name and the SYSTEM.INI link-topic description.

Using a LinkTopic that looks like

"RemoteComputer\NDDE$ | VBDDESource$"

you can query the RemoteComputer and attempt to set up a conversation. Your client application opens a channel to the NETDDE.EXE program, which then queries a copy of itself on the machine you've addressed. That remote copy of NETDDE.EXE then checks the SYSTEM.INI to see if a registered share exists and also checks for the proper password if one is required. If the share exists, you get a DDE conversation as if both applications were on the same computer. You can use the settings of the normal Visual Basic DDE properties to conduct the conversation. The only additional difference is that you should reference the NDDEAPI.H include file with WorkGroup-compatible software development kits for retrieving the processing errors constants.

 Tip: *for Windows NT users: The application instance thrown back from a call to DdeInitialize to attach to the DDEML is thread local. That means that only the applications interfaced to that thread can access that conversation. You can launch the conversation, but you must be sure to terminate it (DdeUnInitialize) from within the same thread or the conversation will not terminate properly.*

Other TidBits about DDE

If you need to pass a set of quotation marks through DDE, you must use the Chr$(34) in the LinkExecute command. For example, to send a "Hello," you would encapsulate the other portions of the string in double quotation marks.

If you need to pass the (") character to your application as part of the string, be sure to create the string by using CHR$(34) for the LinkExecute command in place of the quotation marks.

You can maintain only eight links to Microsoft Excel at any one time.

DDELIST

DDELLIST.C

```
/*Returns Information on Loaded Modules*/
#include <windows.h>
#include <ddeml.h>
#include <stdio.h>
#include "ddelist.h"

static char TestVar[4096];                //for error messages

// Callback function for DDE messages
HDDEDATA CALLBACK DDECallback(UINT wType,
                             UINT wFmt,
                             HCONV hConv,
                             HSZ hsz1,
                             HSZ hsz2,
```

```
                    HDDEDATA hDDEData,
                    DWORD dwData1,
                    DWORD dwData2)
{
 switch (wType)
 {
 default:
  sprintf(TestVar,"wType:%d\nwFmt:%d\nhConv:%d\nhsz1:%d\nhsz2:%d\nhDDEData:%d\ndwData1:
...%d\ndwData2:%d\n",
        wType,wFmt,hConv,hsz1,hsz2,hDDEData,dwData1,dwData2);
        UserMsg(TestVar,"Callback Data", NULL); //not used, prevents warnings
        return NULL;
    }
}

BOOL FAR PASCAL _export DDELIST(char *TopMod, HWND ListhWnd, char *szSystem)
{
    DWORD dwDDEInst = 01;
    UINT ui;
    HSZ hszTopMod,hszSystem,hszItem;
    HCONV hConv;
    HDDEDATA hDDEData;
    DWORD dwResult, dwLength, dwIndex;
    BYTE FAR *pData;
    static char ModName[4096],SysName[128];

    //Move strings passed into local variables
    lstrcpy(ModName,TopMod);
    lstrcpy(SysName,szSystem);

    //Check for errors - confirm no conversation in progress
    sprintf(TestVar,"%s - %s\n",ModName,SysName);
    UserMsg(TestVar,"Module name - no connect yet", dwDDEInst);

    // Initialize DDEML and callback structure
    ui = DdeInitialize(&dwDDEInst,
                    (PFNCALLBACK)DDECallback,
                    CBF_FAIL_ALLSVRXACTIONS,    //suppress server recv
                    0L);
    //Check for errors
    sprintf(TestVar,"%s %d\n%s %d\n","Return: ",ui,"dwDDEInst:",dwDDEInst);
    UserMsg(TestVar,"DdeInitialize", dwDDEInst);
    if (ui != DMLERR_NO_ERROR) {
        UserMsg("Did not get DMLERR_NO_ERROR","At DdeInitialize", dwDDEInst);
        return FALSE;
    }
    //Get pointers to the service and topic
```

```
lstrcpy(szSystem,"System");
hszSystem = DdeCreateStringHandle(dwDDEInst,SysName,CP_WINANSI);
hszTopMod = DdeCreateStringHandle(dwDDEInst,ModName,CP_WINANSI);

//Check for Errors
sprintf(TestVar,"%s\n%d\n%d\n","hszTopMod,hszSystem: ",hszTopMod,hszSystem);
UserMsg(TestVar,"DdeCreateStringHandle", dwDDEInst);

// Initiate a conversation
hConv = DdeConnect(dwDDEInst,
                   hszTopMod,
                   hszSystem,
                   0);
//Check for Errors
sprintf(TestVar,"%s%d\n","hConv: ",hConv);
UserMsg(TestVar,"DdeConnect", dwDDEInst);

// Free the HSZ now
DdeFreeStringHandle(dwDDEInst, hszTopMod);
DdeFreeStringHandle(dwDDEInst, hszSystem);

//Respond to a failed connect by termination
if (!hConv) {
   UserMsg("Failed to fill hConv","DdeFreeStringHandle", dwDDEInst);
   return FALSE;
}

// Try to get the topic list in CF_TEXT format
hszItem = DdeCreateStringHandle(dwDDEInst,
                                SZDDESYS_ITEM_SYSITEMS, //SZDDESYS_ITEM_TOPICS
                                CP_WINANSI);            //Topics supported
//Check for errors                                     //like path and doc
sprintf(TestVar,"%s\n%d\n%d\n","hszTopMod,hszSystem: ",hszTopMod,hszSystem);
UserMsg(TestVar,"Retrieving the string handles", dwDDEInst);

//Establish active conversation
hDDEData = DdeClientTransaction(NULL,
                                0,
                                hConv,
                                hszItem,
                                CF_TEXT,
                                XTYP_REQUEST,
                                   1000, // ms timeout
                                &dwResult);
//Check for errors
//Asynchronous returns true/false, Synchronous return null or handle
switch (hDDEData)
{
```

```
        case TRUE:   sprintf(TestVar,"%s%d\n","hDDEData - TRUE: ", hDDEData);
        case FALSE: sprintf(TestVar,"%s%d\n","hDDEData - FALSE: ", hDDEData);
        default:
          sprintf(TestVar, "%s%d\n", "Handle for successful synchronous transaction:
          ...",hDDEData);
         }
      UserMsg(TestVar,"DdeCleintTransaction", dwDDEInst);

      //Free handles used for retrieving the item support list
      DdeFreeStringHandle(dwDDEInst, hszItem);
      if (hDDEData)
         {
          sprintf(TestVar,"hDDEData contained data(dwLength): %d\n",&dwLength);
          MessageBox(NULL,TestVar,"List Parser",MB_OK);
           // Lock the data so we can parse it
          pData = DdeAccessData(hDDEData, &dwLength);
          sprintf(TestVar,"Data locked for parsing (ListhWnd): %d",ListhWnd);
          UserMsg(TestVar,"DdeAccessData", dwDDEInst);
          // The topics list is tab delimited and has a NULL terminator
          AddItemsToList(ListhWnd, pData);
          UserMsg("Done adding items to list","Function Complete", dwDDEInst);
          // Done with the data
           DdeUnaccessData(hDDEData);
           DdeFreeDataHandle(hDDEData);
          }
      // Disconnect the conversation
      DdeDisconnect(hConv);
      DdeUninitialize(dwDDEInst);
      MessageBox(NULL,"Completed disconnect and uninitialize","Leaving DLL",MB_OK);
      return TRUE;
}


//List of System Topics
static char *szSysItems[] = {
    SZDDESYS_TOPIC,
    SZDDESYS_ITEM_TOPICS,
    SZDDESYS_ITEM_SYSITEMS,
    SZDDESYS_ITEM_RTNMSG,
    SZDDESYS_ITEM_STATUS,
    SZDDESYS_ITEM_FORMATS,
    SZDDESYS_ITEM_HELP,
    SZDDE_ITEM_ITEMLIST,
    NULL
    };
```

```c
//Checks for item in the string
BOOL IsSystemItem(LPSTR lpszItem)
{
    char **pp;

    MessageBox(NULL,"Checking for System Item", "IsSystemItem",MB_OK);
    pp = szSysItems;
    while (*pp) {
        if (!lstrcmp(lpszItem, *pp)) {
            return TRUE;
        }
        pp++;
    }
    return FALSE;
}

//String Parser
void AddItemsToList(HWND ListhWnd, BYTE FAR *pData)
{
    char szItem[128];
    LPSTR pItem;

    MessageBox(NULL,"Entered String Parser","AddItemsToList",MB_OK);
    // Replace \t with \0 and count them
    // then add the counted words
    lstrcpy(szItem, "");
    pItem = szItem;
    while (*pData)
        {
        if (*pData == '\t')
          {
            // Add the current topic to the list
            *pItem = '\0';
            if (lstrlen(szItem))
              {
                // See if we want system topics and if not
                 // check to ensure this isn't one
                if (!IsSystemItem(szItem) || bShowSystemItems)
                  {
                   MessageBox(NULL,"Sending string to list box","Test", MB_OK);
                  SendMessage(ListhWnd,
                            LB_ADDSTRING,
                            (WPARAM) 0,
                            (LPARAM) (LPSTR) szItem);
                  }
              }
          }
```

```
            pData++;
            pItem = szItem;
            *pItem = '\0';
        }
        else
        {
            *pItem++ = *pData++;
        }
    }
}
*pItem = '\0';
// Add the last topic to the list
if (lstrlen(szItem))
    {
      if (!IsSystemItem(szItem) || bShowSystemItems)
        {
        MessageBox(NULL,"Adding last topic","Test",MB_OK);
        SendMessage(ListhWnd,
                    LB_ADDSTRING,
                    (WPARAM) 0,
                    (LPARAM) (LPSTR) szItem);
        }
    }
}
```

UserMsg.C

```
//Error processing module for DDE transactions
#include <windows.h>
#include <ddeml.h>
#include <stdio.h>
#include "ddelist.h"
void UserMsg(LPSTR Note, LPSTR Title, DWORD dwDDEInst)
{
    static char UserNotes[100], *ln1, *ln2, *ln3, *ln4, *ln5, *ln6;

    sprintf(UserNotes,"%s: \n%s\ndwDDEInst: %d\n",Title,Note,dwDDEInst);
    switch(DdeGetLastError(dwDDEInst))
    {
    case DMLERR_NO_ERROR:
      sprintf(Note,"%s\n%s\n",UserNotes,"DMLERR_NO_ERROR - No error returned");
      break;
    case DMLERR_ADVACKTIMEOUT:
      ln1 = "DMLERR_ADVACKTIMEOUT - A request for a";
      ln2 = "synchronous advise transaction has timed out.";
      sprintf(Note,"%s\n%s\n%s\n",UserNotes,ln1,ln2);
      break;
```

```
case DMLERR_BUSY:
  ln1 = "DMLERR_BUSY - The response to the transaction";
  ln2 = "caused the DDE_FBUSY bit to be set.";
  sprintf(Note,"%s\n%s\n%s\n",UserNotes,ln1, ln2);
  break;
case DMLERR_DATAACKTIMEOUT:
  ln1 = "DMLERR_DATAACKTIMEOUT - A request for a";
  ln2 = "synchronous data transaction has timed out.";
  sprintf(Note,"%s\n%s\n%s\n",UserNotes,ln1,ln2);
  break;
case DMLERR_DLL_NOT_INITIALIZED:
  ln1 = "DMLERR_DLL_NOT_INITIALIZED - A DDEML API was";
  ln2 = "called without first calling the DdeInitialize";
  ln3 = "function. An invalid IdInst parameter was passed to an API.";
  sprintf(Note,"%s\n%s\n%s\n%s\n",UserNotes,ln1, ln2, ln3);
  break;
case DMLERR_DLL_USAGE:
  ln1 = "DMLERR_DLL_USAGE - An application initialized as";
  ln2 = "APPCLASS_MONITOR has attempted to perform a DDE transaction,";
  ln3 = "or an application initialized as APPCMD_CLIENTONLY";
  ln4 = "has attempted to perform server transactions.";
  sprintf(Note,"%s\n%s\n%s\n%s\n%s\n",UserNotes,ln1,ln2,ln3,ln4);
  break;
case DMLERR_EXECACKTIMEOUT:
  ln1 = "DMLERR_EXECACKTIMEOUT - A request for a synchronous";
  ln2 = "execute transaction has timed out.";
  sprintf(Note,"%s\n%s\n%s\n",UserNotes,ln1,ln2);
  break;
case DMLERR_INVALIDPARAMETER:
  ln1 = "DMLERR_INVALIDPARAMETER - A parameter failed to be validated by the
  ...DDEML:";
  ln2 = "- wrong item-name handle used?";
  ln3 = "- wrong clipboard data format used?";
  ln4 = "- client-side handle used with server-side function or vice versa?";
  ln5 = "- used a freed data handle or string handle?";
  ln6 = "- More than one instance of the application used the same object?";
  sprintf(Note,"%s\n%s\n%s\n%s\n%s\n%s\n%s\n",UserNotes,ln1,ln2,ln3,ln4,ln5,ln6);
  break;
case DMLERR_LOW_MEMORY:
  ln1 = "DMLERR_LOW_MEMORY - A DDEML application has created a prolonged race";
  ln2 = "condition (where the server application outruns the";
  ln3 = "client), causing large amounts of memory to be consumed.";
  sprintf(Note,"%s\n%s\n%s\n%s\n",UserNotes,ln1,ln2,ln3);
  break;
```

```
case DMLERR_MEMORY_ERROR:
   sprintf(Note,"%s\n%s\n",UserNotes,"DMLERR_MEMORY_ERROR - A memory allocation
   ...failed.");
   break;
case DMLERR_NO_CONV_ESTABLISHED:
   ln1 = "DMLERR_NO_CONV_ESTABLISHED - client's attempt to";
   ln2 = "establish a conversation has failed.";
   sprintf(Note,"%s\n%s\n%s\n",UserNotes,ln1,ln2);
   break;
case DMLERR_NOTPROCESSED:
   sprintf(Note,"%s\n","DMLERR_NOTPROCESSED - A transaction failed.");
   break;
case DMLERR_POKEACKTIMEOUT:
   ln1 = "DMLERR_POKEACKTIMEOUT - A request for a synchronous poke";
   ln2 = "transaction has timed out.";
   sprintf(Note,"%s\n%s\n%s\n",UserNotes,ln1,ln2);
   break;
case DMLERR_POSTMSG_FAILED:
   ln1 = "DMLERR_POSTMSG_FAILED - An internal call to the PostMessage";
   ln2 = "function has failed.";
   sprintf(Note,"%s\n%s\n%s\n",UserNotes,ln1,ln2);
   break;
case DMLERR_REENTRANCY:
   ln1 = "DMLERR_REENTRANCY - An application instance with a synchronous
   ...transaction";
   ln2 = "already in progress attempted to initiate another";
   ln3 = "synchronous transaction, or the DdeEnableCallback";
   ln4 = "function was called from within a DDEML callback function.";
   sprintf(Note,"%s\n%s\n%s\n%s\n%s\n",UserNotes,ln1,ln2,ln3,ln4);
   break;
case DMLERR_SERVER_DIED:
   ln1 = "DMLERR_SERVER_DIED - A server-side transaction was attempted on a";
   ln2 = "conversation that was terminated by the client, or the";
   ln3 = "server terminated before completing a transaction.";
   sprintf(Note,"%s\n%s\n%s\n%s\n",UserNotes,ln1,ln2,ln3);
   break;
case DMLERR_SYS_ERROR:
   ln1 = "DMLERR_SYS_ERROR - An internal error has occurred in the DDEML.";
   sprintf(Note,"%s\n%s\n",UserNotes,ln1);
   break;
case DMLERR_UNADVACKTIMEOUT:
   ln1 = "DMLERR_UNADVACKTIMEOUT - A request to end an advise transaction has
   ...timed out.";
   sprintf(Note,"%s\n%s\n",UserNotes,ln1);
   break;
```

```
    case DMLERR_UNFOUND_QUEUE_ID:
      ln1 = "DMLERR_UNFOUND_QUEUE_ID - An invalid transaction identifier was passed";
      ln2 = "to a DDEML function. Once the application has returned";
      ln3 = "from an XTYP_XACT_COMPLETE callback, the transaction";
      ln4 = "identifier for that callback is no longer valid.";
      sprintf(Note,"%s\n%s\n%s\n%s\n%s\n",UserNotes,ln1,ln2,ln3,ln4);
      break;
    default:
      sprintf(Note,"%s\n%s\n",UserNotes,"No last error reported by DdeGetLastError");
    }
    MessageBox(NULL,Note,"Default Message in UserMsg", MB_OK);
}
```

DDELIST.H

```
/*Function definitions for DDELIST*/
void AddItemsToList(HWND, BYTE FAR *pData);
BOOL IsSystemItem(LPSTR lpszItem);
static bShowSystemItems;
extern BOOL FAR PASCAL DDELIST(char *TopMod, HWND ListhWnd, char *szSystem);
void UserMsg(char far *Note, LPSTR Title, DWORD dwDDEInst);
```

DDELIST.DEF

```
LIBRARY DDELIST
DESCRIPTION 'Lists Topics Supported'
EXETYPE WINDOWS
CODE MOVEABLE DISCARDABLE
DATA MOVEABLE SINGLE
HEAPSIZE 1024
EXPORTS
  WEP             @1 RESIDENTNAME
  DDELIST         @2
  DDECallback     @3
```

DDE Survey

DDEFORM.FRM

```
'  GetWindow() Constants
Const GW_HWNDFIRST = 0
Const GW_HWNDLAST = 1
Const GW_HWNDNEXT = 2
Const GW_HWNDPREV = 3
Const GW_OWNER = 4
Const GW_CHILD = 5
```

```
Const TopLevel = 1
Const Master = 2

Const GWW_HINSTANCE = (-6)
Const WM_USER = &H400
Const LB_SETTABSTOPS = (WM_USER + 19)

Declare Function GetWindow Lib "User" (ByVal hWnd As Integer, ByVal wCmd As Integer)
...As Integer
Declare Function GetWindowText Lib "User" (ByVal hWnd As Integer, ByVal lpString As
...String, ByVal aint As Integer) As Integer
Declare Function GetWindowTextLength Lib "User" (ByVal hWnd As Integer) As Integer
Declare Function GetClassName Lib "User" (ByVal hWnd As Integer, ByVal lpClassName As
...String, ByVal nMaxCount As Integer) As Integer
Declare Function GetParent% Lib "User" (ByVal hWnd%)
Declare Function FindWindow Lib "User" (ByVal lpClassName As Any, ByVal lpWindowName
...As Any) As Integer
Declare Function GetModuleFileName Lib "Kernel" (ByVal hModule As Integer, ByVal
...lpFilename As String, ByVal nSize As Integer) As Integer
Declare Function SendMessage Lib "User" (ByVal hWnd As Integer, ByVal wMsg As Integer,
...ByVal wParam As Integer, lParam As Any) As Long
Declare Function GetWindowWord Lib "User" (ByVal hWnd As Integer, ByVal nIndex As
...Integer) As Integer

Sub Form_LinkClose ()
    MsgBox "Link Closed"
End Sub

Sub Form_LinkError (LinkErr As Integer)
      Select Case LinkErr
      Case 1
        MsgBox "The other app requested data in wrong format"
      Case 6
        MsgBox "Destination app attempted to continue"
      Case 7
        MsgBox "All the source links are in use"
      Case 8
        MsgBox "Auto link or LInkRequest failed for destination"
      Case 11
        MsgBox "No enough memory for DDE"
      Case Else
        MsgBox Str$(LinkErr) & ": Undocumented link error"
      End Select
End Sub

Sub Form_LinkOpen (Cancel As Integer)
      MsgBox "Link Open"
End Sub
```

```
Sub Form_Load ()
    Dim RetVal As Long
    Static Tabs(4) As Integer
    DDEForm.Visible = True
    DDEForm.RunList.SetFocus
    Tabs(0) = 10
    Tabs(1) = 25
    Tabs(2) = 70
    Tabs(3) = 160
    RetVal = SendMessage(DDEForm.RunList.hWnd, LB_SETTABSTOPS, 4, Tabs(1))
    TaskList
End Sub

Sub Form_Resize ()
    RunList.Move DDEForm.ScaleLeft, DDEForm.ScaleTop, DDEForm.ScaleWidth,
    ...DDEForm.ScaleHeight - Status.Height
    Status.Left = DDEForm.ScaleLeft
    Status.Width = DDEForm.ScaleWidth
    Status.Top = DDEForm.ScaleHeight - Status.Height
End Sub

Sub Quit_Click ()
    End
End Sub

Sub RefreshList_Click ()
    RunList.Clear
    TaskList
End Sub

Sub RunList_DblClick ()
    On Error GoTo BadOne
    Target$ = RunList.List(RunList.ListIndex)
    If InStr(Target$, "Module:") = 0 Then
        MsgBox "Click on first line of entry"
        Exit Sub
    ElseIf InStr(Target$, "Won't") = 0 Then
        MsgBox "This application doesn't support the System Topic."
        Exit Sub
    End If
    Md% = InStr(Target$, ":")
    TopicMod = Mid$(Target$, Md% + 2, Len(Target$) - Md%)
    Status.LinkMode = NONE                      'Turn off other link
    Status.LinkTopic = TopicMod & "|System"     'Set topic
    Status.LinkItem = ""
```

```
        x% = DoEvents()                                'Process Events
        Status.LinkMode = MANUAL                       'Try to link
        MsgBox "Link Created Successfully", MB_OK, "DDE"
        x% = DoEvents()
        Status.LinkItem = NONE
        Topics.Show
        Exit Sub
BadOne:
    If Err Then
        MsgBox Str$(Err) & ": " & Error$, MB_OK, "Connection Error"
    End If
    Exit Sub
End Sub

Sub TaskList ()
    On Error GoTo Trapper
    DDEForm.Show
    ThisWnd% = GetWindow(DDEForm.hWnd, GW_HWNDFIRST)    'read first handle
Top: Do Until ThisWnd% = 0                              'more handles in list
        GotParent% = GetParent(ThisWnd%)               'look for parent
        If GotParent% = 0 Then                         'must be top
          '-------Get the executable path name
          ThisInst% = GetWindowWord(ThisWnd%, GWW_HINSTANCE) 'Get instance
          ModName$ = Space$(255)                        'Prep variable
          ModBytes% = GetModuleFileName(ThisInst%, ModName$, 255)' Get path
          ModPath$ = Mid$(ModName$, 1, ModBytes%)       'Trim null term
          If ModPath$ <> "" Then                        'When path found
            Do                                          'Loop through path
              Last% = This%                             'Save last spot
              This% = InStr(This% + 1, ModPath$, "\")   'Find \
            Loop Until This% = 0                        'Go til no more \
            ModName$ = Mid$(ModName$, Last% + 1, InStr(ModName$, ".") - (Last% + 1))
          End If                                        'construct full name
          '-------Get the text of the related window
          NameLen% = GetWindowTextLength(ThisWnd%)      'title length
          ListItem$ = Space$(NameLen% + 2)              'prep variable
          NameLen% = GetWindowText(ThisWnd%, ListItem$, NameLen% + 1)'get title
          AppTitle$ = Mid$(ListItem$, 1, NameLen%)       'Trim null term
          '-------Get the class name
          ClassName$ = Space$(255)                       'prep variable
          ClassLen% = GetClassName(ThisWnd%, ClassName$, 255)'read class
          CName$ = Mid$(ClassName$, 1, ClassLen%)        'Trim null term
          '-------Ensure Window is available
          hWnds = FindWindow(CName$, 0&)
          '-------Attempt to link to system topic
          Select Case Trim(ModName$)
```

```
          Case "DDEML", "USER", "DDEFORM", "VB", "NETDDE", ""
            ThisWnd% = GetWindow(ThisWnd%, GW_HWNDNEXT)
            GoTo Top
        End Select
        If hWnds <> 0& Then
          If Trim(ModName$) <> "" Then                      'When valid module
            Status.LinkMode = NONE                          'Turn off link
            Status.LinkTopic = ModName$ & "|System"         'Set topic
            x% = DoEvents()                                 'Process Events
            Status.LinkMode = AUTOMATIC                     'Try to link
            ctr% = ctr% + 1
          End If
        End If
        '-------Fill the list box
        If ModName$ = "" Then ModName$ = "--No Module Name--"
        If AppName$ = "" Then AppName$ = "--No App Title--"
        DDEForm.RunList.AddItem SysLink$ & Chr$(9) & "Module:" & Chr$(9) & ModName$
        DDEForm.RunList.AddItem Chr$(9) & "Module Path:" & Chr$(9) & ModPath$
        DDEForm.RunList.AddItem Chr$(9) & "Class:" & Chr$(9) & CName$
        DDEForm.RunList.AddItem Chr$(9) & "Title:" & Chr$(9) & AppTitle$
      End If
      '-------get the next Window
      SysLink$ = "Can't"
      ThisWnd% = GetWindow(ThisWnd%, GW_HWNDNEXT)
    Loop
    Status.Caption = Str$(does%) & " Modules Support System Topic of " & Str$(ctr%) &
    ..." Loaded"
    Status.LinkMode = NONE
    Exit Sub
Trapper:
    x% = Err
    If x% = 282 Then
      SysLink$ = "Can't"
      'MsgBox Error$
    ElseIf x% = 285 Then
      SysLink$ = "Won't"
      'MsgBox Error$
      does% = does% + 1
    Else
      Msg$ = Chr$(13) & "APP: " & Trim(AppName$) & Chr$(13) & "Class: " & Trim(CName$) &
      ...Chr$(13) & "Module: " & Trim(ModName$)
      MsgBox Msg$, MB_OK, Str$(Err) & ": " & Error$
    End If
    Resume Next
End Sub
```

TOPICS.FRM

```
Declare Function DDEList Lib "DDElist.dll" (ByVal TopMod As String, ByVal ListhWnd As
...Integer, ByVal Topic As String) As Integer
Declare Function GetWindowWord Lib "User" (ByVal hWnd As Integer, ByVal nIndex As
...Integer) As Integer
Const GWW_HINSTANCE = (-6)


Sub Form_Resize ()
  TopicList.Move Topics.ScaleLeft, Topics.ScaleTop, Topics.ScaleWidth,
  ...Topics.ScaleHeight
End Sub

Sub GetTopic_Click ()
        Topic$ = "System"
        Msg$ = "Calling the DLL with:" & Chr$(13)
        Msg$ = Msg$ & "    1) List Box Handle: " & Str$(TopicList.hWnd) & Chr$(13)
        Msg$ = Msg$ & "    2) Module: " & TopicMod & Chr$(13)
        Msg$ = Msg$ & "    3) Topic: " & Topic$
        ret% = MsgBox(Msg$, MB_OKCANCEL, "Get Topics Supported")
        If ret% = IDCANCEL Then Exit Sub
        'Inst and handle for main window with module name
        x% = DDEList(TopicMod, TopicList.hWnd, Topic$)
        Select Case x%
          Case 1: Result$ = "Succeeded":Topics.Caption = "Topics: " & TopMod
          Case 0: Result$ = "Failed"
        End Select
        MsgBox Result$, MB_OK, "DDEList call Result"
End Sub


Sub ListTopics_Click ()

End Sub


Sub QuitDDEList_Click ()
   Unload Topics
End Sub
```

Chapter 10

Managing Visual Basic Development

This final chapter is a collection of techniques and examples that display more of Visual Basic's capabilities as they contribute to your product and your development process. The third-party tools referenced in this chapter by no means represent the complete stable of tools that you will develop. I have chosen the collection described here because each tool represents a particular group of tools. Visual Basic itself can create tools to help you. The primary example in this chapter, Bug Stomper, shows off the database and reporting facilities of Visual Basic version 3.0.

Changes, Changes

Almost from the moment that you begin to create Visual Basic applications, you will need to track changes and mistakes. Here's a good example:

  1. Open Visual Basic and expose the default form (Form1).

2. If the CMDIALOG.VBX control is not already in the project, place it there.

3. Place the common dialog symbol on the form.

4. Place a command button at the bottom of the form.

5. Place a picture control at the top left of the form.

6. Place next to the picture a label control that stretches across the top of the form.

7. Insert a list box that stretches across the width of the form.

8. In the click event of the command button, place the following lines of code:

```
CMDialog1.Filter = "Icons (*.ico)|*.ico|Pictures(*.bmp)|*.bmp"
CMDialog1.Action = 1
List1.AddItem CMDialog1.FileName
```

9. In the double-click event of the list box, place the following code:

```
Picture1.Picture = LoadPicture()
Label1.Caption = List1.List(List1.ListIndex)
Picture1.Picture = LoadPicture(Label1.Caption)
```

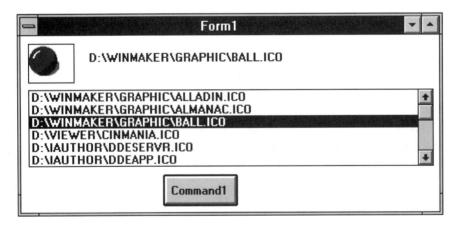

Figure 10-1   *Only six lines of code are required to create this simple application.*

After you've created dynamic link libraries and databases and have used API calls, it's nice to see so much power wrapped in so little code. But, take a close look at this simple application, as illustrated in Figure 10-1. Isn't that command button just a little off center? And isn't the picture box just a little larger than the icon? And what about choosing more than one file to go into the list box when you select file names from the File Open common dialog that pops up? Ah, changes. Sounds like a good introduction to Bug Stomper.

Bug Stomper

The Bug Stomper application includes many of the facilities we've already discussed in this book. New to this chapter are the native database capabilities and the Crystal Report writer. Stomper is a multiple document interface (MDI) application that presents two datafiles in an Access 1.1 database. Figure 10-2 shows the opening screen for Stomper. The Projects file accessible through the File menu contains the project name and project identification number that you use to relate to the second file. The second file contains information on defects and enhancements. Any deletions in the project file are carried to the bug file using a structured query language (SQL) call. The database itself is created using Visual Basic's dynamic array management to provide for creating databases on the fly.

Figure 10-2   *The opening screen for the Stomper program is a MDI form that calls the MainMenu form, which contains the menus shown.*

Opening a Database

The Reports menu selection is disabled because no database (called a **bugbase** in the program) is open. Embedded in this form are two controls that are not visible: the Crystal Reports custom control and the common dialog control. Once the program is started, you can use the File menu selection to call up the common dialog box and select the database you want to use, or to create a new one. The code in Listing 10-1 shows the FileMgr procedure, which is called from the main menu, for opening the common dialog and creating the database.

 Tip: *Most of the code for Stomper resides in the TOOLS.BAS file as procedures and functions that are called from inside objects throughout the program.*

Listing 10-1 *Using the common dialog (File Open) launched in this procedure, the user selects a file or enters a new file name to create a new bugbase.*

Set up the common dialog parameters:
```
MainMenu.Logo.Visible = False   'Retire copyright screen
'Chooses type of dialog and sets characteristics
On Error GoTo DlgErr
If Index = 1 Then           'on Open
   MainMenu.DBFiles.DialogTitle = "Choose Project Bug File to Open"
Else
   MainMenu.DBFiles.DialogTitle = "Choose Path For New File Name"
End If
MainMenu.DBFiles.DefaultExt = "BUG"
If Dir$(SavedPath) <> "" Then
   MainMenu.DBFiles.InitDir = SavedPath
End If
MainMenu.DBFiles.Filter = "Access File (*.MDB)|*.MDB|All Files (*.*)|*.*|"
MainMenu.DBFiles.FilterIndex = 1
If Index = 1 Then
   MainMenu.DBFiles.Flags = OFN_FILEMUSTEXIST Or OFN_READONLY
Else
   MainMenu.DBFiles.Flags = OFN_CREATEPROMPT
End If
MainMenu.DBFiles.CancelError = True
MainMenu.DBFiles.Action = 1
```

After the common dialog completes and the user selects a file, parse out the path and file name:
```
If Err = False Then
   SavedPath = MainMenu.DBFiles.Filename
```

```
BugFIle = MainMenu.DBFiles.Filetitle
BugFilePath = Mid$(MainMenu.DBFiles.Filename, 1,
...InStr(MainMenu.DBFiles.Filename, BugFIle) - 2)
```

Create the database, field, file, and index objects:

```
If Index = 0 Then                                'When creating
  Dim IndexFields() As String                    'Array of indexes
  ReDim NewTable(2)                              'Set number of tables
  CreateBugBase (BugFIle)                        'Build data file
  ReDim NewField(2)                              'Set number of fields
  ReDim IndexFields(1)                           'Set no of index fields
  ReDim NewIndex(1)                              'Set no of indexes
  NewTable(1).Name = "Projects"                  'New Project Table
    FieldNo = 1: IndexNo = 1                     'Reset counters
    CreateField 1, "ProjNum", DB_INTEGER, 0      'Build new field
    CreateField 1, "ProjName", DB_TEXT, 25
    IndexFields(1) = "ProjNum"                   'Build new indexes
    CreateIndex 1, "BY_ProjNum", IndexFields()
    db.TableDefs.Append NewTable(1)              'Add table to defs
  NewTable(2).Name = "Bugs"                      'New bug table
    ReDim NewField(8)                            'Reset no. of fields
    ReDim IndexFields(2)                         'Reset no. of index fields
    ReDim NewIndex(1)                            'Reset no. of indexes
    FieldNo = 1: IndexNo = 1                     'Reset counters
    CreateField 2, "ProjNum", DB_INTEGER, 0      'Build new fields
    CreateField 2, "BugNum", DB_INTEGER, 0
    CreateField 2, "BugTitle", DB_TEXT, 25
    CreateField 2, "DateIn", DB_DATE, 0
    CreateField 2, "Status", DB_BOOLEAN, 0
    CreateField 2, "Type", DB_INTEGER, 0
    CreateField 2, "Priority", DB_INTEGER, 0
    CreateField 2, "Notes", DB_MEMO, 5000
    IndexFields(1) = "ProjNum"                   'Choose index fields
    IndexFields(2) = "BugNum"
    CreateIndex 2, "BY_ProjNum", IndexFields()   'Build new index
    db.TableDefs.Append NewTable(2)              'Add New Table
  db.Close                                       'Close database
End If
```

Create the use variables for accessing the new database or open the selected, existing database:

```
Set db = OpenDatabase(BugFIle)                   'Reopen data base
Set td = db.TableDefs                            'Get table defs
Set tb = db.OpenTable("Projects")                'Focus on projects
```

Set the form captions and move to the top of the data file to fill in the Projects list box:

```
        MainMenu.Reports.Enabled = True
        Main.Caption = "BugBase"             'Caption of MDI form
        'MainMenu.Caption = BugFIle          'Caption of main menu
        ProjForm.Caption = BugFIle           'Caption of projects
        ProjForm.Show                        'Display projects
        tb.MoveFirst                         'Go to first item
        FillProjList                         'Display project list
        ProjForm.ProjList.ListIndex = 0
    Else
        MsgBox "Error Opening File Dialog"
    End If
    Exit Sub
```

Process errors for common dialog and for the following database activity:

```
DlgErr:
    If Err = 20477 Then               ' invalid file name passed to dialog
        MainMenu.DBFiles.Filename = ""
        Resume
    ElseIf Err Then
        MsgBox Error$ + ": " + Str$(Err)
    End If
    Exit Sub
End Sub
```

The third segment of code in Listing 10-1 bears further examination. It calls several generic routines for creating various elements of the database. The Global module contains the handles used by the rest of the application to reference the database that was opened in the FileMgr procedure. The database object names are shown in Listing 10-2.

Listing 10-2 *These are the database objects used in Stomper.*

```
Global db As Database        'Holds data base path
Global td As TableDefs       'Holds table definitions
Global tb As Table           'Holds table
Global bugtb As Table        'Holds second table
Global ds As Dynaset         'Holds dynaset
Global dsort As Dynaset      'Holds second dynaset
Global NewTable() As New TableDef 'Creates new objects
Global NewField() As New Field
Global NewIndex() As New Index
```

After you have retrieved the file name, the first step in creating a new database is to use the Dim and Redim statements to create the arrays of indexes, tables, and fields that you will assemble into the final database. You can make these values programmatically replaceable if you want to vary the elements of the database. By creating editable variables, the user could enter values for the number of databases, tables, fields, and indexes to be created. (The Data Manager in the Visual Basic environment represents one interface to such an approach.) You can also pass in variables for the names and types of the field and index objects created through the Create*type* functions that appear in TOOLS.BAS, as shown in Listing 10-3.

Listing 10-3 *These three statements, CreateBugBase, CreateField and CreateIndex, accept variables that create (1) the database file, (2) fields, and (3) indexes in a bugbase.*

This statement creates the database shell in Access 1.1:
```
Sub CreateBugBase (BugFIle As String) 'Create new databas
  'Bulds new database at path
  Set db = CreateDatabase(BugFIle, DB_LANG_GENERAL)
  'Warns user if anything failed
  If db Is Nothing Then MsgBox "Could Not Create BugBase"
End Sub
```

After the NewTable function creates the target table, this NewField function creates each field according to its type and places them it into the associated table:
```
Sub CreateField (TableNo As Integer, FieldName As String, FieldType As Long, FieldLen
As Integer)
  NewField(FieldNo).Name = FieldName      'Create new data field
  NewField(FieldNo).Type = FieldType      'Set variable type
  If FieldLen Then                        'Depending on field type
    NewField(FieldNo).Size = FieldLen     'Set length
  End If
  NewTable(TableNo).Fields.Append NewField(FieldNo)'Add field to tabledef
  FieldNo = FieldNo + 1                    'Increment field number
End Sub
```

This statement uses the NewIndex function to add the new fields just created and then places the index into the associated table:
```
Sub CreateIndex (TableNo As Integer, IndexName As String, IndexFields() As String)
      On Error GoTo Trap
      NewIndex(IndexNo).Name = IndexName             'New Index
      For n% = 1 To UBound(IndexFields)              'For items in array
        NewIndex(IndexNo).Fields = IndexFields(n%)  'Add field to index
      Next n%
```

```
            NewTable(TableNo).Indexes.Append NewIndex(IndexNo)      'Add Index to table
            IndexNo = IndexNo + 1
            Exit Sub
Trap:
        MsgBox Error$ & ": " & Str$(Err)
        Exit Sub
End Sub
```

Adding Records to the Project Table

Stomper has two files, Projects and Bugs, that use the functions in Listing 10-3 to create their internal structure. Once into the database, you are presented with the Projects list, as shown in Figure 10-3. The error messages that precede the appearance of the Projects list show that no records exist in that table in the database. You can press the Insert key or click on the Add menu selection to get the input form for adding, editing, and deleting records, also as shown in Figure 10-3. The action of the form is determined before it appears, based on which menu selections or keystrokes you have made.

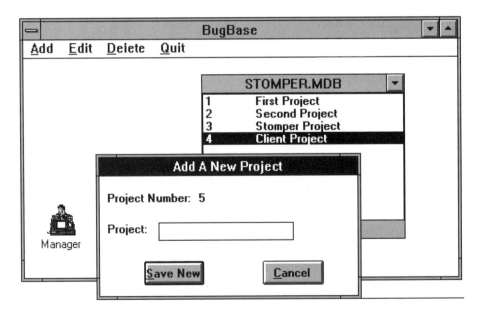

Figure 10-3 *The non-MDI window entry form adds new projects to the list and numbers them automatically.*

The Manager icon shown in Figure 10-3 represents the underlying MDI window that contains the start-up menu. The menus change from the start-up group to those related to projects when the project list appears. The keyboard interface for the projects list appears in Listing 10-4 in the KeyDown event.

Listing 10-4 *The forms involved in repetitive data entry require a keyboard interface. The Keys procedure provides a generic function that is usable throughout the program.*

```
Sub ProjList_KeyDown (KeyCode As Integer, Shift As Integer)
    If KeyCode = KEY_F2 Then ProjList_DblClick: Exit Sub
    If KeyCode = KEY_ESCAPE Then Unload ProjForm: Exit Sub
    Keys KeyCode, ProjMode
End Sub
Sub Keys (KeyStroke As Integer, Src As Integer)
 Select Case KeyStroke
   Case KEY_INSERT:
     CallNew Adding, Src          'Mode, Project or Bug
   Case KEY_DELETE:
     CallNew Deleting, Src
   Case KEY_RETURN:
     CallNew Editing, Src
 End Select
End Sub
```

Since the same entry form is used for adding, editing, and deleting, a function called CallNew exists for determining which characteristics to use in any one instance. In fact, CallNew also distinguishes between the project entry form and the bug detail entry form. In that way, you can standardize how you handle the entry forms. You process CallNew by passing to it the access mode and the form that you want to call, as shown in Listing 10-5.

Listing 10-5 *This procedure prepares the entry forms for both projects and bugs.*

```
Sub CallNew (Mode As Integer, Src As Integer)
    Select Case Mode
    Case Adding:
      EditMode = Adding
      If Src = 1 Then ' Project Edit
        NewProj.AddProjBtn(0).Caption = "&Save New"
        NewProj.Caption = "Add A New Project"    'Set form caption
      Else
```

```
        BugForm.AddBugBtn(0).Caption = "&Save New"
        BugForm.Caption = "Add A New Bug"    'Set form caption
      End If
    Case Deleting:
      EditMode = Deleting
      If Src = 1 Then ' Project Edit
        NewProj.AddProjBtn(0).Caption = "&Delete"
        NewProj.Caption = "Delete This Project?"'Set form caption
      Else
        BugForm.AddBugBtn(0).Caption = "&Delete"
        BugForm.Caption = "Delete This Bug?"    'Set form caption
      End If
    Case Editing:
      EditMode = Editing
      If Src = 1 Then ' Project Edit
        NewProj.AddProjBtn(0).Caption = "&Save"
        NewProj.Caption = "Edit This Project"    'Set form caption
      Else
        BugForm.AddBugBtn(0).Caption = "&Save"
        BugForm.Caption = "Edit This Bug"    'Set form caption
      End If
    End Select
    If Src = 1 Then
      NewProj.Visible = True
    Else
      BugForm.Visible = True
    End If
End Sub
```

Once the form is loaded (in Adding mode, which is a constant defined in the Global module), the MoveLast database function goes to the last record in the projects table (tb), as shown in Listing 10-6. There it reads the last project number, adds a project number to the table, and uses that as the new project number. That means you can never assign a project an old number, an important constraint for both database integrity and the maintenance of project history.

Listing 10-6 *When the project edit form loads, it responds to the editing mode that is passed to it to prepare the project record for processing using FindRec and FillProjRec.*

```
Sub Form_Load ()
    Select Case EditMode              'Depending on access
        Case Adding:                  'When adding
            On Error GoTo SetRec      'Process errors
```

```
            tb.MoveLast                            'Go to last record
            np = tb("ProjNum") + 1                 'Increment project
            ProjNumber = "Project Number: " & Str$(np)'Display new number
        Case Deleting:                             'When deleting
            FindRec                                'Find selected project
            FillProjRec                            'Display its data
        Case Editing:                              'When changing
            FindRec                                'Find selected record
            FillProjRec                            'Display its data
            tb.Edit                                'Go to edit mode
    End Select
    Exit Sub
SetRec:
  If Err = 3021 Then np = 1                        'When no records
  Resume Next                                      'start at one
End Sub
Sub FindRec ()
    tb.MoveFirst                         'Go to top of list
    'Grab project number of selected item
    np = CInt(Mid$(ProjForm.ProjList.List(ProjForm.ProjList.ListIndex), 1, 2))
    Do Until tb("ProjNum") = np          'Read through list til find
      tb.MoveNext                        'Go to next record
    Loop
End Sub
Sub FillProjRec ()
    NewProj.ProjNumber = "Project Number: " & tb("ProjNum") 'Display number
    NewProj.NewProjName.Text = tb("ProjName")               'Display title
End Sub
```

The FindRec and FillProjRec functions, used in Listing 10-4 during the project Form_load event, locate the record requested by the user (in edit and delete mode) and then fill the form accordingly. FindRec moves to the top of the table this time and parses out the project number from the list selection that the user has chosen. Then FindRec locates the selected project entry by looping through the table, using MoveNext to get a record for comparison. Once the record matches, the appropriate slots in the project form are filled.

The next step in processing a project record programmatically occurs when the user presses one of the two buttons on the form. These are placed in a control array, and the contents of the button designated Index = 0 change according to the editing mode. Listing 10-7 shows the code that is called when the user presses one of the two buttons.

Listing 10-7 *This program performs postprocessing for the projects edit form responding to how the user chose to close the form.*

```
Sub AddProjBtn_Click (Index As Integer)
    On Error GoTo ErrProc:
    ListPos = ProjForm.ProjList.ListIndex
    Select Case EditMode              'Add,Edit or Delete?
    Case Adding:                      'In Add Mode
        Select Case Index             'Cancel or Save pressed?
        Case 0                        'Save pressed
            GoSub CheckBlank          'Ensure data in the field
            tb.AddNew                 'Open a new record
            tb("ProjNum") = np        'Set new project number
            tb("ProjName") = NewProjName.Text 'Transfer project name
            tb.Update                 'Set the new record
            ListPos = ProjForm.ProjList.ListCount 'Go to bottom of the list
            FixList                   'Empty, refill list and set highlight
        Case 1                        'Cancel pressed
            'MsgBox "Add Cancelled"
        End Select                    'End Cancel or Save Button Index
    Case Editing:                     'In Edit Mode
        Select Case Index             'Cancel or Save pressed?
        Case 0                        'Save pressed
            GoSub CheckBlank          'Ensure data in the field
            tb("ProjName") = NewProjName 'Set new project name
            np = tb("ProjNum")        'Save record number
            tb.Update                 'Set the record
            FixList                   'Empty, refill list and set highlight
        Case 1                        'Cancel pressed
            'MsgBox "Edit Cancelled"
        End Select                    'End Cancel or Save Button Index
    Case Deleting:                    'In Delete mode
        Select Case Index             'Cancel or Save pressed?
        Case 0                        'Save pressed
            np = ProjForm.ProjList.ListIndex + 1 'Save spot in list
            tb.Delete                 'delete current record
            'Relational Delete for Projects to Bugs
            Dim BugD As QueryDef
            Set BugD = db.OpenQueryDef("Bug Delete")
            SQL$ = "DELETE FROM Bugs WHERE ProjNum = " & tb("ProjNum")
            BugD.SQL = SQL$
            BeginTrans
                BugD.Execute          'Attempt deletion
                If Err Then           'If something fails
                    Rollback          'Reverse transaction
```

```
                 Fatal Err, Error$      'Post the error
              Else
                 CommitTrans              'finalize delete
                 MsgBox "Delete Processed" 'Note completion
           End If
                 BugD.Close              'Close the query
                 db.DeleteQueryDef "Bug Delete" 'Delete query
              FixList                    'Empty, refill list and set highlight
           Case 1                        'Cancel pressed
              'MsgBox "Delete Cancelled"
         End Select                      'End Cancel or Save Button Index
      End Select                         'End EditMode
      Unload NewProj                     'Exit record maintenance mode
      Exit Sub
ErrProc:
   Fatal Err, Error$
   If Err = 3167 Then      'Record is deleted
      FixList
      Unload NewProj
      Exit Sub
   ElseIf Err = 3011 Then
      Set BugD = db.CreateQueryDef("Bug Delete")
   End If '3012 Then 'Object "Bug Delete" already exists
   Resume Next
CheckBlank:
   If NewProjName.Text = "" Then      'For a blank record
      MsgBox "Must Provide Project Name"
      NewProjName.SetFocus             'Reset cursor
      Exit Sub
   End If
   Return
End Sub
```

Listing 10-7 includes several important concepts that involve using the Access 1.1 engine and the Visual Basic interface for database management. For adding records to a database, the record must be created first with the AddNew method. At that point, the process is no different from that of editing a record: you place values into the fields for the record and use the Update method to save them in the file. Since the on-screen list box doesn't know when the database changes unless you tell it, the FixList function maintains your place in the list and keeps the list current with the contents of the file. To ensure that blank records aren't added to the data, the CheckBlank subroutine checks the field for data.

Deleting Records with SQL

When you want to delete records, especially project records, the link to the bug detail in the bugs file becomes an issue. If you delete the project header and that project had associated bugs in the bug file, the bug file will grow with "orphaned" records. To prevent that, some rudimentary referential integrity can be enforced rather easily. The Access engine supports an extended version of the structured query language (SQL). We could have used SQL throughout the data access parts of Stomper to fill lists and update them rather than use the navigational methods of MoveLast, MoveNext and so on.

The advantage of SQL in this situation is that you can assemble one string statement, either by programming it or by embedding it in the code. That statement, actuated by the Execute method, will read through all of your referenced files, looking for each relationship you have specified and performing actions that would take many lines of code to re-create. The major disadvantage of this approach is the lack of debugging facilities for locating problems in your SQL statement. One means of getting a little help is to use the compatibility between Microsoft Access and your Visual Basic Access database. You can open the database with Access, use the Access graphical tools for creating the query and then paste the query into Visual Basic, as shown in Figure 10-4. Also you can use queries created in Access from both Access and Visual Basic if you create static queries from Access—by static, I mean they are not editable from Visual Basic. Conversely, you can check SQL statements you created by hand in Visual Basic by pasting them into the SQL Text window in Access. Access will create a QBE (Query by Example) sample to check the syntax and you won't be able to close the SQL Text window until the syntax is correct. One final note: some incompatibilities exist between the SQL queries generated in Access and the useable syntax in Visual Basic. Be sure to audit the results.

 Tip: *The Microsoft Access application can read and write the database you create in Visual Basic. However, queries created in Visual Basic cannot be operated from Access. They are visible to Access, but when you try to run them, you get an error message:* "Query must contain at least one table or query."

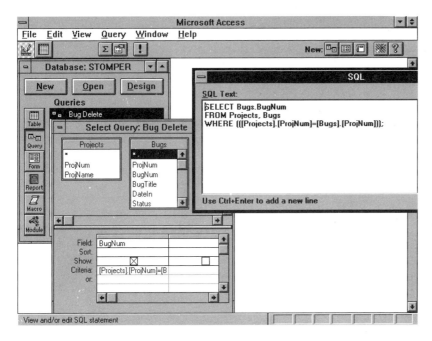

Figure 10-4 *Microsoft Access translates a graphically constructed query into the comparable SQL statement.*

The SQL statement shown in Figure 10-4 shows the creation of a SELECT statement and not a DELETE statement as is needed in this part of the Stomper program. You can test your query first by using a retrieval query (SELECT) to see if you're getting the right data.

In Stomper, the delete function for projects begins by deleting the target project, using tb.Delete: that is, it deletes the current record from the project table object tb. This function can be combined with the SQL query if you choose. You create the query object by first declaring the object "Dim BugD As QueryDef" and then attempting to access the object in the database with "Set BugD = db OpenQueryDef("Bug Delete")". If this call fails because the query doesn't exist in the database, the error routine jumps to the error procedure where several errors can be processed. In the case that the target records in the Bugs file were already deleted (Error 7167), the process simply terminates. If the query does not yet exist (Error 3012), it is created with "Set BugD = db.CreateQueryDef("Bug Delete")". At this point, you must create a string with the SQL statement. You can get the query from Access, or assemble it in your program, or simply embed it in the code.

To perform the query, you have several options. You could use several of the Access database objects: you could create a Dynaset (CreateDynaset) or a snapshot (CreateSnapshot) as the query. The example in Listing 10-7 uses the Execute method. If this were a process to be performed on an external database through ODBC's SQLPassThrough functions, you could use the Execute SQL statement, which does not require that you first create a QueryDef.

The call to Execute is framed within a transaction. You could use the transaction processing in Visual Basic for any file-access processes in Visual Basic. The BeginTrans function opens the frame. If execution of the deletion returns an error, then you can call for Visual Basic to roll back the transaction; otherwise, a call to CommitTrans makes the changes permanent. Version 2.0 of Visual Basic included a set of methods for use with ODBC (Object Database Connectivity) that used the same names as version 3.0 for transaction processing.

Entering the Bug Detail

The bug list and entry form require several other Visual Basic facilities, including masked input, memos, and database field processing. The display of the list uses the API SendMessage call to set the tab spacing between columns, and shows how you can reset a variable's contents prior to display. (This practice of using SendMessage to set tab steps in a list box, which native Visual Basic does not support, is discussed further in Chapter 5.) This is useful for storing selections numerically but then displaying the choice in words. Figure 10-5 shows the entry screen for the bugs file.

The date field in the bug entry field uses a display mask that is different from an input mask. The input mask uses MM/DD/YY but displays the date as DD-MMM-YY. This field uses the masked edit control (MSMASKED.VBX).

For Stomper to access the project table in the database you use the table object. In an Access database, a table object in memory reflects the changes made by anyone who might be changing that object. A table object cannot be sorted, although you can use indexes. You access the bug table in Stomper by creating a dynaset, as shown in Listing 10-8, which can be sorted. In addition, the dynaset can be tailored to contain only the records that apply to the project that was selected earlier. You build the dynaset with CreateDynaset and then apply the filter method to trim the records that were not requested and the sort method to determine the order. By reissuing the

CreateDynaset method with an empty parameter set, you rebuild the dynaset with the new records in the new order.

Figure 10-5   *The Bug Stomper program includes this entry form for recording the bug detail.*

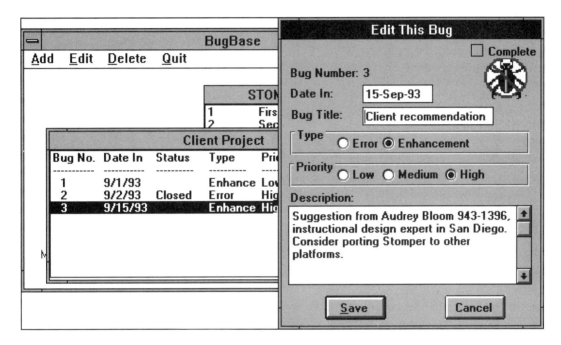

Listing 10-8   *You can sort a list by using a Dynaset.*

```
On Error GoTo Startup                      'Error processor
'Set MDI caption
Proj$ = Mid$(ProjForm.ProjList.List(ProjForm.ProjList.ListIndex), 3)
Bugs.Caption = Proj$                       'Set caption
Set ds = db.CreateDynaset("Bugs")          'Instead of Table
criteria$ = "[ProjNum] = " & ProjNo        'Set Filter spec
ds.Filter = criteria$                      'Get This project only
ds.Sort = "BugNum"                         'Sort in bug no order
Set dsort = ds.CreateDynaset()             'rebuild sorted dynaset
FillBugList                                'Display in list
BugList.ListIndex = 2
Exit Sub                                   'Leave
```

When the user requests a record to delete or edit it the BugFillRec procedure places the values from the file into the display, as shown in Listing 10-9.

Listing 10-9 *The object dsort is a dynaset that contains the sorted values.*

```
Sub FillBugRec ()
    BugForm.BugNumber = "Bug Number: " & dsort("BugNum")   'Set bug number
    BugForm.NewBugTitle.Text = dsort("BugTitle")            'Set bug title
    BugForm.DateIn.Text = dsort("DateIn")                   'Set date display
    If dsort("Status") Then BugForm.Status.Value = 1        'Show Status
    BugForm.Type(dsort("Type")).Value = True                'Show Type
    BugForm.Priority(dsort("Priority")).Value = True        'Show Priority
    If dsort("Notes") <> "" Then                            'Ensure notes
       BugForm.Notes.Text = dsort("Notes")                  'Show notes
    End If
End Sub
```

When the user completes a bug entry and presses the Save button, the values in the data fields have to be moved from the screen objects into the field values before they are written out to the disk file. The fields in this screen could be bound to the fields and the database, but then the database could not be changed at run time, which would defeat the dynamic database creation discussed earlier in this chapter. The code in Listing 10-10 shows the manner in which each field is processed.

Listing 10-10 *This is the subroutine used for completing the edit of a bug record.*

```
Settings:        'Save settings of various radio, check, and other buttons
  dsort("ProjNum") = ProjNo                    'Project Number
  dsort("BugTitle") = NewBugTitle.Text         'Move bug name
  dsort("DateIn") = DateIn.FormattedText       'Move date value
  'Save Status
  If Status.Value = 1 Then                     'If Box checked
     dsort("Status") = True                    'Save -1 (True)
  Else
     dsort("Status") = False                   'Save 0 (False)
  End If
  'Save Type
  If BugForm.Type(0).Value = True Then         'Error
     dsort("Type") = 0
  Else
     dsort("Type") = 1                         'Enhancement
  End If
  'Save Priority Setting
```

```
If BugForm.Priority(0).Value = True Then   'Low
  dsort("Priority") = 0
ElseIf BugForm.Priority(1).Value = True Then 'Medium
  dsort("Priority") = 1
Else
  dsort("Priority") = 2                      'High
End If
dsort("Notes") = Notes.Text                  'Set notes
Return
```

If the fields in the bug screen were bound to the database, this translation would not be necessary. However, if the field values differed from what you wanted to display, you would still have to perform the translation.

Opening a Bugbase from the Command Line

Using the command-line start-up supported by Visual Basic, you can set up an icon in Program Manager to launch Stomper directly into an existing database. The AutoLaunch function in Stomper, working in concert with the AutoOpen function, grabs the command line passed at program start-up, and attempts to open it. If the opening fails, the user gets a chance to either enter a new path and file name or cancel the request for starting with a default and continue on into the program. Listing 10-11 shows the two functions responsible for parsing the string entered at the command, attempting to open the database, using the InputMsg to grab a response from the user, and then trying again when an error occurs the first time.

Listing 10-11 *The AutoLaunch procedure and the AutoOpen function process the input command line.*

```
Sub AutoLaunch ()
  Const BadFile = 0, NoFile = 1
  On Error GoTo LaunchErr                    'Error processing
  MainMenu.Logo.Visible = False              'Retire copyright screen
  'Used in other parts of the program for path names
  SavedPath = Command                        'Save command path
  Do Until x%                                'Go til good
    x% = AutoOpen(SavedPath)                 'Try to open file
    If x% = NoFile Then Exit Sub             'When no file
  Loop
  Set td = db.TableDefs                      'Get table defs
  Set tb = db.OpenTable("Projects")          'Focus on projects
```

```
    Main.Caption = "BugBase"                    'Caption of MDI form
    'MainMenu.Caption = BugFile                  'Caption of main menu
    ProjForm.Caption = BugFIle                  'Caption of projects
    MainMenu.Show                               'Ensure Menu shows
    ProjForm.Show                               'Display projects
    tb.MoveFirst                                'Go to first item
    FillProjList                                'Display project list
    ProjForm.ProjList.ListIndex = 0            'Set cursor
    Exit Sub
LaunchErr:
    If Err = 3021 Then
      Fatal Err, Error$
      Exit Sub
    Else
      Fatal Err, Error$: End
    End If
End Sub
Function AutoOpen (SavedPath As String) As Integer
    On Error GoTo OpenErr
    If InStr(SavedPath, ".") = 0 Then           'Is an extension there?
      SavedPath = Trim$(UCase(SavedPath)) & ".MDB" 'Add the Access 1.1 ext
    End If
    ext% = InStr(UCase(SavedPath), ".MDB")      'Get length of path
    For n = 1 To ext%: lastslash% = InStr(n, SavedPath, "\"): Next n 'find \
    BugFIle = Mid$(SavedPath, lastslash% + 1, (ext% + 4) - lastslash%)'get name
    BugFilePath = Mid$(SavedPath, 1, lastslash%)    'Grab path only
    Set db = OpenDatabase(SavedPath)            'Reopen data base
    AutoOpen = 2                                'Opened request file
    Exit Function                              'Leave
OpenErr:
    If Err = 20477 Or Err = 3044 Then           ' invalid file name passed to dialog
      Prompt$ = Error$ & " Please enter a valid path and file name. "
      Prompt$ = Prompt$ & "Press CANCEL or leave blank to start normally."
      SavedPath = InputBox$(Prompt$, "Error: " & Str$(Err), SavedPath)
      If SavedPath = "" Then                    'When no file picked
        AutoOpen = 1                            'Tell AutoLaunch
        Exit Function                          'leave
      Else
        AutoOpen = 0                            'Open failed
        Exit Function
      End If
    ElseIf Err Then
      Fatal Err, Error$: End                    'Exit Program
    End If
End Function
```

At design time, to simulate the same effect achieved by the code in Listing 10-11 at runtime, you can use the Command Line Argument in the Options\Project Options menu selection.

Programming Assistance

Visual Basic is a rich programming environment, as much for its internal capabilities as for the hooks that it provides for third-party tools to be connected and used within a Visual Basic program. Functions contained in a DLL can be called from within Visual Basic. Custom controls, loaded into the Design environment, can be used to add lots of functionality to the run-time application, as well as to provide facilities within the design environment.

VBAssist

VBAssist from Sheridan Software Systems is a good example of a custom control that provides additional capability within the design environment. Figure 10-6 shows VBAssist loaded into Visual Basic.

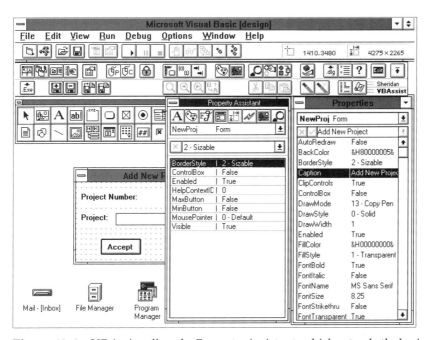

Figure 10-6   *VBAssist offers the Property Assistant, which extends the basic properties box available in Visual Basic.*

Every application that you purchase is someone's idea of how to do work in that subject area. Visual Basic offers a competent programming environment, and applications like VBAssist or Project Archiver from Young Software Works provide other means, another opinion, about how to do the same work. The Property Assistant in VBAssist makes a small change to the standard properties box in Visual Basic by providing a means to collect all of the properties for working with a form. For instance, properties like WindowState, a control box and borders, as shown in Figure 10-6, so that you don't have to search the entire properties box for them. In addition, VBAssist provides form templates, a way to synchronize properties between controls and forms and other access to features throughout the program.

SpyWorks

Another useful program for working with Visual Basic applications expands the SPY.EXE facility that is shipped with the Windows SDK. In testing dynamic link libraries and watching the message traffic while your application operates, SpyWorks (from Desaware) provides a useful look into memory and message activity specifically for Visual Basic. Figure 10-7 shows how you can monitor the messages for the module monitoring utility that we built in Chapter 6. Visual Basic does not provide explicit support for all Windows messages. You can use SpyWorks to track down those messages not included in order to build in API calls and other facilities to respond to them.

In Figure 10-7, notice the repetitive appearance of the LB_ADDSTRING message. This message was sent from the MODLIST.DLL that we built in Chapter 6. The SendMessage function transferred the string containing the module information directly to the list box in the FREEVB program. SpyWorks was set specifically to trap and display those messages as they travel into the application. Notice also that a WM_SIZE message was the last message processed before the LB_ADDSTRING messages started.

In addition to the message monitoring utilities in SpyWorks, you can also use its SpyMem utility to take a more detailed look at memory and to learn a great deal about how your application and Windows in general uses memory. Figure 10-8 shows the tool bar from Visual Basic as a bitmap that is moveable in memory.

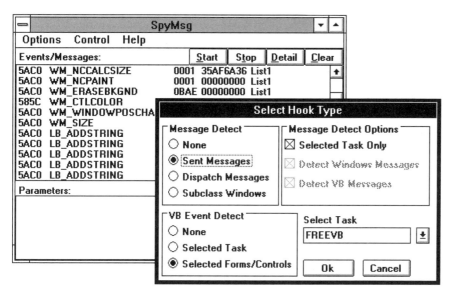

Figure 10-7   *SpyWorks shows the dialog box used for choosing which messages you want to monitor.*

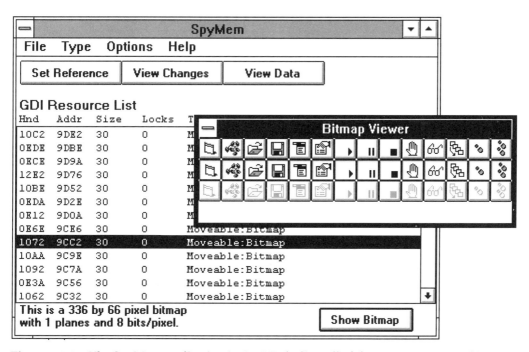

Figure 10-8   *The SpyMem application in SpyWorks lists all of the current memory objects for browsing.*

You may recall that in Chapter 8 we discussed how you must specify three bitmaps to serve as the icons for your custom control. In Figure 10-8, SpyMem displays the bitmaps used by Visual Basic to show the active state of the bitmaps in the tool bar. If you browse further into memory, you'll notice that the other pictures displayed in the Visual Basic interface appear either as groups of bitmaps or singly.

New Functionality

Some of the third-party products that you can procure for use with Visual Basic add functionality to the environment so that you can pass that new functionality on to your program. The early versions of Visual Basic were greatly enhanced and continue to benefit from two groups of controls in particular: the QuickPak Professional for Windows, from Crescent, and VBTools and VBMuscle, from Microhelp. Both products come from programming firms with extensive backgrounds in the BASIC languages. In fact, both of these tool sets have character-based BASIC cousins.

VBTools has more than thirty-seven VBX or custom-control files in its 2.5 version, with more to appear in the version compatible with Visual Basic version 3. Faced with that many controls, you would not want to go through the File\Add File...\Common Dialog path to add each one to your project. To review them quickly, simply create a test project, add one control from VBTools to it, and save it as SAMPLE.MAK. (Be sure to set the preferred format for saving files to Text in the Environment menu choice in Visual Basic.) Then, at the DOS prompt and inside the VBTOOLs directory, type DIR *.VBX>TEMP. Edit the temp file, removing everything but the file names. Then bring the SAMPLE.MAK file into your text editor and paste in or insert the TEMP file after the first control that is already in the list and that uses the same path. If you save that file and then load the project back into Visual Basic, all of the controls will be loaded into the Project window and the resulting tool box will look like the one shown in Figure 10-9.

As with VBTools, the Crescent QuickPak product comes with a barnful of custom controls that add capability to Visual Basic. In the case of QuickPak, you also get the source code for each control so that you can modify a particular control if it isn't performing some of the functions you require. A sample application that comes with QuikPak Professional shows off all of the calendar functions you can make available to your Visual Basic program. The sample application is shown in Figure 10-10.

Figure 10-9   *The Visual Basic Toolbox with the VBTools custom controls added all at once.*

Databases

In the first two versions of Visual Basic, the only native file or database facility you had was through ASCII or unstructured binary files. A true database capability did not exist in the product and could be added only through third-party controls. As a result, the market for third-party database controls is loaded with powerful tools that you can add to your Visual Basic application. The database tools cover the range of formats from dBase and third party custom formats in the case of Agility/VB from Apex Software (one of the early players) to Q+E Multilink/VB, which handles connections to twenty databases.

The database links to Visual Basic appear in DLLs and custom controls. You can get a very robust implementation of SQL through the Quadbase-SQL for Windows from Quadbase Systems. As you did with the DLLs we built in Chapter 6 and the

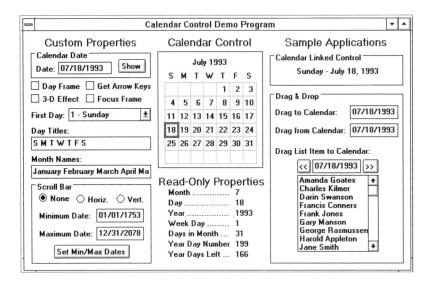

Figure 10-10 *QuickPak Professional provides many ways in which you can manipulate the calendar through the controls in the product.*

API calls we used in Chapter 5, you load into a Global module the Declares for the Quadbase system, and then you can use those statements to perform your SQL database maintenance.

In the case of Q+E MultiLink/VB and Agility/VB, you load a custom control into the Visual Basic project and then add the query and connect tools in the same manner as you would other custom controls. Figure 10-11 shows how you configure the drivers and the environment to read the twenty databases supported by Multilink. These include ACII text files; Btrieve; dBASE-compatible; Excel worksheets (with a database section marked); IBM DB2, IBM OS/2 Database Manager, AS/400, and SQL/DS; INFORMIX; INGRES; Novell's NetWare SQL; Oracle; Paradox; PROGRESS; SQLBase; Sybase and Microsoft SQL Server Products; and Tandem's NonStop SQL and XDB.

As with earlier versions of the Q+E product, you add the query tool to the form and then establish the connection. Agility/VB and Multilink both provide controls that can be bound to a database and a particular field just as the Access engine permits controls to be bound in Visual Basic 3.0. Figure 10-12 shows the properties list for the Connect control in Multilink.

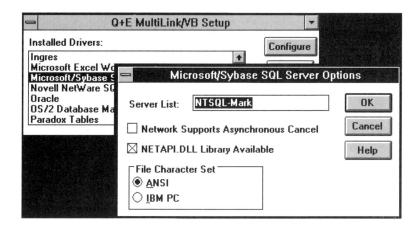

Figure 10-11 *This is the configuration utility for Q+E MultiLink/VB.*

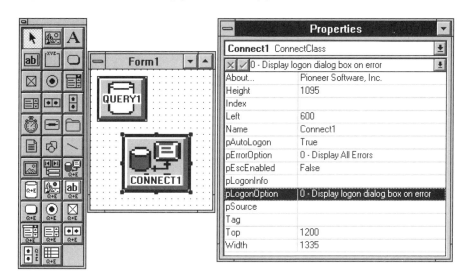

Figure 10-12 *By adding Q+E Multilink/VB controls to a form, you can manipulate the database settings through the Properties window.*

Many more databases exist for Visual Basic, and the number is climbing even though native database facilities are being added in Visual Basic itself. As with the standard controls, improvements and expansions continue to make the Visual Basic programming environment a rich and well-supported place to create applications.

For further reference, see "Add Database Libraries to Visual Basic" by Kenn Nesbitt in the July/August '92 issue of *BASIC/Pro* magazine for a profile of 19 tools; also see Microsoft's ODBC Driver Catalog and "Choosing the Right Addons for Visual Basic: 70 application development tools" in *Data Based Advisor*, January 1993 issue.

Bug Stomper

STOMPER.MAK

```
MAINMENU.FRM
D:\WINNT\SYSTEM\CMDIALOG.VBX
D:\WINNT\SYSTEM\CRYSTAL.VBX
D:\WINNT\SYSTEM\MSMASKED.VBX
D:\WINNT\SYSTEM\THREED.VBX
GLOBAL.BAS
TOOLS.BAS
BUGS.FRM
MDIFORM1.FRM
BUGFORM.FRM
ABOUT.FRM
PROJFORM.FRM
NEWPROJ.FRM
ProjWinSize=0,434,205,323
ProjWinShow=2
IconForm="Main"
Title="STOMPER"
ExeName="STOMPER.EXE"
```

ABOUT.FRM

```
Sub Command1_Click ()
    Unload About
End Sub
```

BUGFORM.FRM

```
Sub AddBugBtn_Click (Index As Integer)
  ListPos = Bugs.BugList.ListIndex      'Save list position
  Select Case EditMode                  'Add,Edit or Delete?
  Case Adding:                          'In Add Mode
    Select Case Index                   'Cancel or Save pressed?
      Case 0                            'Save pressed
        GoSub CheckBlank                'Ensure data in the field
        dsort.AddNew                    'Open a new record
        dsort("BugNum") = np            'Move new bug number
        GoSub Settings                  'Move choices
```

```
         dsort("Notes") = BugForm.Notes.Text     'Save notes
         dsort.Update                             'Set the new record
         ListPos = Bugs.BugList.ListCount         'Go to bottom of the list
         FixBugList                               'Empty, refill & set highlight
       Case 1                                     'Cancel pressed
         'MsgBox "Add Cancelled"
     End Select                                   'End Cancel or Save Button Index
   Case Editing:                                  'In Edit Mode
     Select Case Index                            'Cancel or Save pressed?
       Case 0                                     'Save pressed
         GoSub CheckBlank                         'Ensure data in the field
         np = dsort("BugNum")                     'Save record number
         GoSub Settings                           'Move choices
         dsort.Update                             'Set the record
         FixBugList                               'Empty, refill & set highlight
       Case 1                                     'Cancel pressed
         'MsgBox "Edit Cancelled"                 'Inform user
     End Select                                   'End Cancel or Save Button Index
   Case Deleting:                                 'In Delete mode
     Select Case Index                            'Cancel or Save pressed?
       Case 0                                     'Save pressed
         np = Bugs.BugList.ListIndex + 1          'Save spot in list
         dsort.Delete                             'delete current record
         FixBugList                               'Empty, refill & set highlight
       Case 1                                     'Cancel pressed
         'MsgBox "Delete Cancelled"               'Inform user
     End Select                                   'End Cancel or Save Button Index
   End Select                                     'End EditMode
   Unload BugForm                                 'Exit record maintenance mode
   Exit Sub                                       'Leave
CheckBlank:
   If NewBugTitle.Text = "" Then                  'For a blank record
     MsgBox "Must Provide Project Name"           'Warn user
     NewBugTitle.SetFocus                         'Reset cursor
     Exit Sub                                     'Leave
   End If
   Return                                         'Go back to this proc
Settings:        'Save settings of various radio, check, and other buttons
   dsort("ProjNum") = ProjNo                      'Project Number
   dsort("BugTitle") = NewBugTitle.Text           'Move bug name
   'dsort("DateIn") = Format(DateIn.Text, "mm/dd/yy")       'Move date value
   dsort("DateIn") = DateIn.FormattedText         'Move date value
   'Save Status
   If Status.Value = 1 Then                       'If Box checked
     dsort("Status") = True                       'Save -1 (True)
```

```
      Else
        dsort("Status") = False               'Save 0 (False)
      End If
      'Save Type
      If BugForm.Type(0).Value = True Then     'Error
        dsort("Type") = 0
      Else
        dsort("Type") = 1                      'Enhancement
      End If
     'Save Priority Setting
      If BugForm.Priority(0).Value = True Then  'Low
        dsort("Priority") = 0
      ElseIf BugForm.Priority(1).Value = True Then 'Medium
        dsort("Priority") = 1
      Else
        dsort("Priority") = 2                  'High
      End If
      dsort("Notes") = Notes.Text              'Set notes
      Return
End Sub


Sub AddBugBtn_KeyDown (Index As Integer, KeyCode As Integer, Shift As Integer)
      If KeyCode = KEY_ESCAPE Then Unload BugForm
End Sub


Sub DateIn_KeyDown (KeyCode As Integer, Shift As Integer)
      If KeyCode = KEY_ESCAPE Then Unload BugForm
End Sub


Sub DateIn_ValidationError (InvalidText As String, StartPosition As Integer)
      MsgBox "Date entered not valid", MB_OK, "Position: " & StartPosition
      DateIn.SetFocus
End Sub


Sub Form_Load ()
      BugForm.Show                             'Enable SetFocus in Load
      Select Case EditMode                     'Act on type of editing
        Case Adding:                           'Adding a bug
            On Error GoTo SetRec               'Error processor
            dsort.MoveLast                     'Go to bottom of list
            np = dsort("BugNum") + 1           'increment bug counter
            BugNumber = "Bug Number: " & Str$(np)'Show new bug number
            DateIn.SetFocus                    'Activate cursor on title
            AddBugBtn(0).Caption = "Add"       'Set save caption
            Exit Sub                           'Go to keyboard
```

```
        Case Deleting:                          'Deleting a bug
            dsort.FindFirst "[BugNum] = " & CInt(Mid$(Bugs.BugList.List-
            ...(Bugs.BugList.ListIndex), 2, 2))
            FillBugRec                          'Fill the list
            AddBugBtn(0).Caption = "Delete"     'Set save caption
            AddBugBtn(0).SetFocus
        Case Editing:                           'Changing a bug
            dsort.FindFirst "[BugNum] = " & CInt(Mid$(Bugs.BugList.List-
            ...(Bugs.BugList.ListIndex), 2, 2))
            FillBugRec                          'Display record contents
            DateIn.SetFocus                     'Activate cursor on title
            dsort.Edit                          'Go to edit mode
            AddBugBtn(0).Caption = "Save"       'Set save caption
    End Select
    Exit Sub
SetRec:
  If Err = 3021 Then                            'When no records in data
    np = 1                                      'Start at first bug
  Else
    MsgBox Error$ & ": " & Str$(Err)            'Warn user of error
  End If
  Resume Next                                   'Keep on in this proc
End Sub


Sub NewBugTitle_KeyDown (KeyCode As Integer, Shift As Integer)
    If KeyCode = KEY_ESCAPE Then Unload BugForm
End Sub


Sub Notes_KeyDown (KeyCode As Integer, Shift As Integer)
    If KeyCode = KEY_ESCAPE Then Unload BugForm
End Sub


Sub Priority_KeyDown (Index As Integer, KeyCode As Integer, Shift As Integer)
    If KeyCode = KEY_ESCAPE Then Unload BugForm
End Sub


Sub Type_KeyDown (Index As Integer, KeyCode As Integer, Shift As Integer)
    If KeyCode = KEY_ESCAPE Then Unload BugForm
End Sub
```

BUGS.FRM

```
Sub AddProj_Click ()
  CallNew Adding, BugMode 'Editing
End Sub
```

```
Sub BugList_DblClick ()
   CallNew Editing, BugMode 'Editing
End Sub

Sub BugList_KeyDown (KeyCode As Integer, Shift As Integer)
    If KeyCode = KEY_ESCAPE Then
      Unload Bugs
      ProjForm.SetFocus
    End If
    Keys KeyCode, BugMode
End Sub

Sub DelProj_Click ()
   CallNew Deleting, BugMode 'Editing
End Sub

Sub Edit_Click ()
   CallNew Editing, BugMode 'Editing
End Sub

Sub Form_Load ()
        On Error GoTo Startup               'Error processor
        'Set MDI caption
        Proj$ = Mid$(ProjForm.ProjList.List(ProjForm.ProjList.ListIndex), 3)
        Bugs.Caption = Proj$                'Set caption
        Set ds = db.CreateDynaset("Bugs")   'Instead of Table
        criteria$ = "[ProjNum] = " & ProjNo 'Set Filter spec
        ds.Filter = criteria$               'Get This project only
        ds.Sort = "BugNum"                  'Sort in bug no order
        Set dsort = ds.CreateDynaset()      'rebuild sorted dynaset
        FillBugList                         'Display in list
        BugList.ListIndex = 2
        Exit Sub                            'Leave
Startup:
    MsgBox Error$ & ": " & Str$(Err) & " - "  'Warn user
    Exit Sub
End Sub

Sub Form_Resize ()
   'match list box dimensions to form
   BugList.Move Bugs.ScaleLeft, Bugs.ScaleTop, Bugs.ScaleWidth, Bugs.ScaleHeight
End Sub

Sub ProjList_DblClick ()
   Bugs.Show       'Display Bug list
End Sub
```

```
Sub Quit_Click ()
      Unload Bugs        'Retire bug list for current project
      ProjForm.Show      'Display projects list
End Sub
```

GLOBAL.BAS (Parts Not Included in CONSTANT.TXT and DATACONS.TXT)

```
' Data Access constants
Global db As Database            'Holds data base path
Global td As TableDefs           'Holds table definitions
Global tb As Table               'Holds table
Global bugtb As Table            'Holds second table
Global ds As Dynaset             'Holds dynaset
Global dsort As Dynaset          'Holds second dynaset
Global NewTable() As New TableDef 'Creates new objects
Global NewField() As New Field
Global NewIndex() As New Index

Global EditMode As Integer       'Access type
Global Const Adding = 1
Global Const Editing = 2
Global Const Deleting = 3
Global Const ProjMode = 1
Global Const BugMode = 2

Global np As Integer             'For counting bugs and projects
Global ListPos As Integer        'Maintains position in list
Global FieldNo As Integer        'List of fields in record
Global IndexNo As Integer        'List of indexes in record
Global ProjNo As Integer         'Saves project number
Global SavedPath As String       'Path for 1st database
```

MAINMENU.TXT

```
Sub BugRep_Click (Index As Integer)
  Const WINDOW = 0, PRINTER = 1, FILE = 2
  Select Case Index
    Case 0:
      BugReport.Action = 1
    Case 2:
      BugRep(2).Checked = True
      BugRep(3).Checked = False
      BugRep(4).Checked = False
      BugReport.Destination = WINDOW
    Case 3:
      BugRep(2).Checked = False
      BugRep(3).Checked = True
```

```
      BugRep(4).Checked = False
      BugReport.Destination = PRINTER
    Case 4:
      BugRep(2).Checked = False
      BugRep(3).Checked = False
      BugRep(4).Checked = True
      BugReport.Destination = FILE
  End Select
End Sub


Sub Form_GotFocus ()
    If WindowState = MINIMIZED Then ProjForm.SetFocus
End Sub


Sub Form_KeyDown (KeyCode As Integer, Shift As Integer)
    If KeyCode = KEY_ESCAPE Then
      result% = MsgBox("Do you want to quit stomping?", MB_YESNO, "Leaving...")
      If result% = 6 Then End
    End If
End Sub


Sub Form_Load ()
    If Command <> "" Then AutoLaunch
    Reports.Enabled = False
End Sub


Sub Form_Resize ()
    LogoMove          'Tools - positions logo on Mainmenu
End Sub


Sub Help_Click ()
      About.Show      'Display credits
End Sub


Sub MainQuit_Click ()
    result% = MsgBox("Do you want to quit stomping?", MB_YESNO, "Leaving...")
    If result% = 6 Then End
End Sub


Sub New_Click (Index As Integer)
    MainMenu.WindowState = MINIMIZED
    MainMenu.Caption = "Manager"
    FileMgr (Index)         'Call dialog box
End Sub
```

```
Sub Open_Click (Index As Integer)
    MainMenu.WindowState = MINIMIZED
    MainMenu.Caption = "Manager"
    FileMgr (Index)                'Call dialog box
End Sub
```

MDIFORM1.FRM

```
Sub MDIForm_Load ()
  MainMenu.Visible = True                'Launch main manu form
  'ProjForm.Show                         'Bring list to front
  'If ProjForm.ProjList.ListCount > 0 Then
  '  ProjForm.ProjList.ListIndex = 0  'Set cursor
  'End If
End Sub
```

NEWPROJ.FRM

```
Sub AddProjBtn_Click (Index As Integer)
      On Error GoTo ErrProc:
      ListPos = ProjForm.ProjList.ListIndex
      Select Case EditMode                'Add,Edit or Delete?
       Case Adding:                       'In Add mode
          Select Case Index               'Cancel or Save pressed?
            Case 0                        'Save pressed
              GoSub CheckBlank            'Ensure data in the field
              tb.AddNew                   'Open a new record
              tb("ProjNum") = np          'Set new project number
              tb("ProjName") = NewProjName.Text 'Transfer project name
              tb.Update                   'Set the new record
              ListPos = ProjForm.ProjList.ListCount 'Go to bottom of the list
              FixList                     'Empty, refill list, and set highlight
            Case 1                        'Cancel pressed
              'MsgBox "Add Cancelled"
          End Select                      'End Cancel or Save Button Index
       Case Editing:                      'In Edit mode
          Select Case Index               'Cancel or Save pressed?
            Case 0                        'Save pressed
              GoSub CheckBlank            'Ensure data in the field
              tb("ProjName") = NewProjName 'Set new project name
              np = tb("ProjNum")          'Save record number
              tb.Update                   'Set the record
              FixList                     'Empty, refill list, and set highlight
            Case 1                        'Cancel pressed
              'MsgBox "Edit Cancelled"
          End Select                      'End Cancel or Save Button Index
```

```
      Case Deleting:                      'In Delete mode
          Select Case Index               'Cancel or Save pressed?
            Case 0                        'Save pressed
              np = ProjForm.ProjList.ListIndex + 1 'Save spot in list
              tb.Delete                   'delete current record
             'Relational Delete for Projects to Bugs
              Dim BugD As QueryDef
              Set BugD = db.OpenQueryDef("Bug Delete")
              SQL$ = "DELETE FROM Bugs WHERE ProjNum = " & tb("ProjNum")
              BugD.SQL = SQL$
              BeginTrans
                BugD.Execute              'Attempt deletion
                If Err Then               'If something fails
                  Rollback                'Reverse transaction
                  Fatal Err, Error$       'Post the error
                Else
                  CommitTrans             'finalize delete
                  MsgBox "Delete Processed" 'Note completion
                End If
                BugD.Close                'Close the query
                db.DeleteQueryDef "Bug Delete" 'Delete query
              FixList                     'Empty, refill list, and set highlight
            Case 1                        'Cancel pressed
               'MsgBox "Delete Cancelled"
          End Select                      'End Cancel or Save Button Index
      End Select                          'End EditMode
      Unload NewProj                      'Exit record maintenance mode
      Exit Sub
ErrProc:
    Fatal Err, Error$
    If Err = 3167 Then      'Record is deleted
      FixList
      Unload NewProj
      Exit Sub
    ElseIf Err = 3011 Then
      Set BugD = db.CreateQueryDef("Bug Delete")
    End If '3012 Then 'Object "Bug Delete" already exists
    Resume Next
CheckBlank:
    If NewProjName.Text = "" Then      'For a blank record
      MsgBox "Must Provide Project Name"
      NewProjName.SetFocus             'Reset cursor
      Exit Sub
    End If
    Return
End Sub
```

```
Sub AddProjBtn_KeyDown (Index As Integer, KeyCode As Integer, Shift As Integer)
    If KeyCode = KEY_ESCAPE Then Unload NewProj
End Sub

Sub Form_Load ()
    Select Case EditMode                            'Depending on access
      Case Adding:                                  'When adding
          On Error GoTo SetRec                      'Process errors
          tb.MoveLast                               'Go to last record
          np = tb("ProjNum") + 1                    'Increment project
          ProjNumber = "Project Number: " & Str$(np)'Display new number
      Case Deleting:                                'When deleting
          FindRec                                   'Find selected project
          FillProjRec                               'Display its data
      Case Editing:                                 'When changing
          FindRec                                   'Find selected record
          FillProjRec                               'Display its data
          tb.Edit                                   'Go to edit mode
    End Select
    Exit Sub
SetRec:
  If Err = 3021 Then np = 1                         'When no records
  Resume Next                                       'start at one
End Sub

Sub NewProjName_KeyDown (KeyCode As Integer, Shift As Integer)
    If KeyCode = KEY_ESCAPE Then Unload NewProj
End Sub
```

PROJFORM.FRM

```
Sub AddProj_Click ()
  CallNew Adding, ProjMode 'Editing project
End Sub

Sub DelProj_Click ()
  CallNew Deleting, ProjMode     'Set access type for project
End Sub

Sub Edit_Click ()
  CallNew Editing, ProjMode    'Set access type for project
End Sub

Sub Form_Load ()
  ProjForm.Show
  ProjForm.WindowState = NORMAL    'Set dimensions
```

```
    ProjForm.ScaleWidth = 3225
    ProjForm.ScaleHeight = 2235
    ProjForm.ScaleTop = 1785
    ProjForm.ScaleLeft = 1170
    'Match Window size to list box size
    'MsgHgt% = PrjMsg.Height
    'PrjMsg.Move ProjForm.ScaleLeft, ProjForm.ScaleHeight - (MsgHgt% * .97),
    ...ProjForm.ScaleWidth, MsgHgt%
    PrjPrompt.Caption = "Double click or F2 to select"
    ProjList.Move ProjForm.ScaleLeft, ProjForm.ScaleTop, ProjForm.ScaleWidth,
    ...ProjForm.ScaleHeight - PrjPrompt.Height
    'Move Prompts with Window
End Sub

Sub ProjList_DblClick ()
    'Find first tab
    pos% = InStr(1, ProjForm.ProjList.List(ProjForm.ProjList.ListIndex), Chr$(9))
    'Grab project number from list entry
    ProjNo = CInt(Mid$(ProjForm.ProjList.List(ProjForm.ProjList.ListIndex), 1, pos%))
    Bugs.Show        'Show bug list
End Sub

Sub ProjList_KeyDown (KeyCode As Integer, Shift As Integer)
    If KeyCode = KEY_F2 Then ProjList_DblClick: Exit Sub
    If KeyCode = KEY_ESCAPE Then Unload ProjForm: Exit Sub
    Keys KeyCode, ProjMode
End Sub

Sub Quit_Click ()
    Unload ProjForm                        'exit project list
    MainMenu.Caption = "No Open BugBase"   'Reset main caption
    MainMenu.WindowState = MAXIMIZED
    MainMenu.Logo.Visible = True
    LogoMove
    MainMenu.Reports.Enabled = False
End Sub
```

TOOLS.BAS

```
Sub AutoLaunch ()
    Const BadFile = 0, NoFile = 1
    On Error GoTo LaunchErr                      'Error processing
    MainMenu.Logo.Visible = False                'Retire copyright screen
    'Used in other parts of the program for path names
    SavedPath = Command                          'Save command path
    Do Until x%                                  'Go til good
```

```
      x% = AutoOpen(SavedPath)                'Try to open files
       If x% = NoFile Then Exit Sub           'When no file
    Loop
    Set td = db.TableDefs                     'Get table defs
    Set tb = db.OpenTable("Projects")         'Focus on projects
    Main.Caption = "BugBase"                  'Caption of MDI form
    'MainMenu.Caption = BugFile                'Caption of main menu
    ProjForm.Caption = BugFIle                'Caption of projects
    MainMenu.Show                             'Ensure Menu shows
    ProjForm.Show                             'Display projects
    tb.MoveFirst                              'Go to first item
    FillProjList                              'Display project list
    ProjForm.ProjList.ListIndex = 0           'Set cursor
    Exit Sub
LaunchErr:
    If Err = 3021 Then
      Fatal Err, Error$
      Exit Sub
    Else
      Fatal Err, Error$: End
    End If
End Sub


Function AutoOpen (SavedPath As String) As Integer
    On Error GoTo OpenErr
    If InStr(SavedPath, ".") = 0 Then              'Is an extension there?
      SavedPath = Trim$(UCase(SavedPath)) & ".MDB" 'Add the Access 1.1 ext
    End If
    ext% = InStr(UCase(SavedPath), ".MDB")         'Get length of path
    For n = 1 To ext%: lastslash% = InStr(n, SavedPath, "\"): Next n 'find \
    BugFIle = Mid$(SavedPath, lastslash% + 1, (ext% + 4) - lastslash%)'get name
    BugFilePath = Mid$(SavedPath, 1, lastslash%)   'Grab path only
    Set db = OpenDatabase(SavedPath)               'Reopen data base
    AutoOpen = 2                                   'Opened request file
    Exit Function                                  'Leave
OpenErr:
    If Err = 20477 Or Err = 3044 Then              ' invalid file name passed to dialog
      Prompt$ = Error$ & " Please enter a valid path and file name. "
      Prompt$ = Prompt$ & "Press CANCEL or leave blank to start normally."
      SavedPath = InputBox$(Prompt$, "Error: " & Str$(Err), SavedPath)
      If SavedPath = "" Then                       'When no file picked
        AutoOpen = 1                               'Tell AutoLaunch
        Exit Function                              'leave
      Else
        AutoOpen = 0                               'Open failed
```

```
        Exit Function
      End If
    ElseIf Err Then
      Fatal Err, Error$: End                          'Exit Program
    End If
End Function


Sub CallNew (Mode As Integer, Src As Integer)
      Select Case Mode
      Case Adding:
        EditMode = Adding
        If Src = 1 Then ' Project Edit
          NewProj.AddProjBtn(0).Caption = "&Save New"
          NewProj.Caption = "Add A New Project"    'Set form caption
        Else
          BugForm.AddBugBtn(0).Caption = "&Save New"
          BugForm.Caption = "Add A New Bug"    'Set form caption
        End If
      Case Deleting:
        EditMode = Deleting
        If Src = 1 Then ' Project Edit
          NewProj.AddProjBtn(0).Caption = "&Delete"
          NewProj.Caption = "Delete This Project?"'Set form caption
        Else
          BugForm.AddBugBtn(0).Caption = "&Delete"
          BugForm.Caption = "Delete This Bug?"    'Set form caption
        End If
      Case Editing:
        EditMode = Editing
        If Src = 1 Then ' Project Edit
          NewProj.AddProjBtn(0).Caption = "&Save"
          NewProj.Caption = "Edit This Project"    'Set form caption
        Else
          BugForm.AddBugBtn(0).Caption = "&Save"
          BugForm.Caption = "Edit This Bug"    'Set form caption
        End If
      End Select
      If Src = 1 Then
        NewProj.Visible = True
      Else
        BugForm.Visible = True
      End If
End Sub
```

```
Sub CreateBugBase (BugFIle As String) 'Create new database
        'Builds new database at path
        Set db = CreateDatabase(BugFIle, DB_LANG_GENERAL)
        'Warns user if anything failed
        If db Is Nothing Then MsgBox "Could Not Create BugBase"
End Sub


Sub CreateField (TableNo As Integer, FieldName As String, FieldType As Long, FieldLen
...As Integer)
  NewField(FieldNo).Name = FieldName        'Create new data field
  NewField(FieldNo).Type = FieldType        'Set variable type
  If FieldLen Then                          'Depending on field type
    NewField(FieldNo).Size = FieldLen       'Set length
  End If
  NewTable(TableNo).Fields.Append NewField(FieldNo)'Add field to tabledef
  FieldNo = FieldNo + 1                     'Increment field number
End Sub


Sub CreateIndex (TableNo As Integer, IndexName As String, IndexFields() As String)
        On Error GoTo Trap
        NewIndex(IndexNo).Name = IndexName          'New Index
        For n% = 1 To UBound(IndexFields)           'For items in array
          NewIndex(IndexNo).Fields = IndexFields(n%) 'Add field to index
        Next n%
        NewTable(TableNo).Indexes.Append NewIndex(IndexNo)      'Add Index to table
        IndexNo = IndexNo + 1
        Exit Sub
Trap:
      MsgBox Error$ & ": " & Str$(Err)
      Exit Sub
End Sub


Sub Fatal (ErrNo As Integer, ErrStr As String)
      MsgBox "Error: " & Str$(ErrNo) & " - " & ErrStr, MB_OK, "Process Error"
End Sub


Sub FileMgr (Index As Integer)
      MainMenu.Logo.Visible = False  'Retire copyright screen
      'Chooses type of dialog and sets characteristics
      On Error GoTo DlgErr
      If Index = 1 Then          'on Open
        MainMenu.DBFiles.DialogTitle = "Choose Project Bug File to Open"
      Else
        MainMenu.DBFiles.DialogTitle = "Choose Path for New File Name"
      End If
```

```
MainMenu.DBFiles.DefaultExt = "BUG"
If Dir$(SavedPath) <> "" Then
  MainMenu.DBFiles.InitDir = SavedPath
End If
MainMenu.DBFiles.Filter = "Access File (*.MDB)|*.MDB|All Files (*.*)|*.*|"
MainMenu.DBFiles.FilterIndex = 1
If Index = 1 Then
  MainMenu.DBFiles.Flags = OFN_FILEMUSTEXIST Or OFN_READONLY
Else
  MainMenu.DBFiles.Flags = OFN_CREATEPROMPT
End If
MainMenu.DBFiles.CancelError = True
MainMenu.DBFiles.Action = 1
If Err = False Then
  SavedPath = MainMenu.DBFiles.Filename
  BugFIle = MainMenu.DBFiles.Filetitle
  BugFilePath = Mid$(MainMenu.DBFiles.Filename, 1, InStr(MainMenu.DBFiles.Filename,
  ...BugFIle) - 2)


  If Index = 0 Then                                'When creating
    Dim IndexFields() As String                    'Array of indexes
    ReDim NewTable(2)                              'Set number of tables
    CreateBugBase (BugFIle)                        'Build data file
    ReDim NewField(2)                              'Set number of fields
    ReDim IndexFields(1)                           'Set no of index fields
    ReDim NewIndex(1)                              'Set no of indexes
    NewTable(1).Name = "Projects"                  'New Project Table
      FieldNo = 1: IndexNo = 1                      'Reset counters
      CreateField 1, "ProjNum", DB_INTEGER, 0      'Build new field
      CreateField 1, "ProjName", DB_TEXT, 25
      IndexFields(1) = "ProjNum"                    'Build new indexes
      CreateIndex 1, "BY_ProjNum", IndexFields()
      db.TableDefs.Append NewTable(1)               'Add table to defs
    NewTable(2).Name = "Bugs"                      'New bug table
      ReDim NewField(8)                            'Reset no. of fields
      ReDim IndexFields(2)                          'Reset no. of index fields
      ReDim NewIndex(1)                            'Reset no. of indexes
      FieldNo = 1: IndexNo = 1                      'Reset counters
      CreateField 2, "ProjNum", DB_INTEGER, 0      'Build new fields
      CreateField 2, "BugNum", DB_INTEGER, 0
      CreateField 2, "BugTitle", DB_TEXT, 25
      CreateField 2, "DateIn", DB_DATE, 0
      CreateField 2, "Status", DB_BOOLEAN, 0
      CreateField 2, "Type", DB_INTEGER, 0
      CreateField 2, "Priority", DB_INTEGER, 0
```

```
          CreateField 2, "Notes", DB_MEMO, 5000
          IndexFields(1) = "ProjNum"                    'Choose index fields
          IndexFields(2) = "BugNum"
          CreateIndex 2, "BY_ProjNum", IndexFields()   'Build new index
          db.TableDefs.Append NewTable(2)              'Add New Table
        db.Close                                       'Close database
      End If
      Set db = OpenDatabase(BugFIle)                   'Reopen data base
      Set td = db.TableDefs                            'Get table defs
      Set tb = db.OpenTable("Projects")                'Focus on projects

      MainMenu.Reports.Enabled = True
      Main.Caption = "BugBase"                         'Caption of MDI form
      'MainMenu.Caption = BugFIle                      'Caption of main menu
      ProjForm.Caption = BugFIle                       'Caption of projects
      ProjForm.Show                                    'Display projects
      tb.MoveFirst                                     'Go to first item
      FillProjList                                     'Display project list
      ProjForm.ProjList.ListIndex = 0
    Else
      MsgBox "Error Opening File Dialog"
    End If
    Exit Sub
DlgErr:
    If Err = 20477 Then                ' invalid file name passed to dialog
      MainMenu.DBFiles.Filename = ""
      Resume
    ElseIf Err Then
      MsgBox Error$ + ": " + Str$(Err)
    End If
    Exit Sub
End Sub



Sub FillBugList ()
      'Could use .RemoveItem .AddItem to change List
      On Error GoTo FillErr
      dsort.MoveFirst      'Go to top of list
      'Insert titles
      Bugs.BugList.AddItem "Bug No." & Chr$(9) & "Date In" & Chr$(9) & "Status" &
      ...Chr$(9) & "Type" & Chr$(9) & "Priority" & Chr$(9) & "Title"
      Bugs.BugList.AddItem "-----------" & Chr$(9) & "-----------" & Chr$(9) &
      ..."----------" & Chr$(9) & "----------" & Chr$(9) & "-----------" & Chr$(9) &
      ..."-------------------------"
      Do Until dsort.EOF = True          'Look til end of file
        'Status
```

```
        If dsort("Status") = -1 Then     'When stat is closed
          Stat$ = "Closed"               'Display the word
        Else
          Stat$ = ""                     'Status not closed
        End If
        'Type
        If dsort("Type") Then            'When stat is closed
          Typ$ = "Enhance"               'Display the word
        Else
          Typ$ = "Error"                 'Status not closed
        End If
        'Priority
        Select Case dsort("Priority")    'When stat is closed
          Case 0:
            Pri$ = "Low"                 'Display the word
          Case 1:
            Pri$ = "Medium"              'Display the word
          Case 2:
            Pri$ = "High"                'Display the word
        End Select
        'Display record information
        Bugs.BugList.AddItem "   " & dsort("BugNum") & Chr$(9) & dsort("DateIn") &
        ...Chr$(9) & Stat$ & Chr$(9) & Typ$ & Chr$(9) & Pri$ & Chr$(9) & dsort("BugTitle")
        dsort.MoveNext                   'Go to next record
      Loop
      Exit Sub
FillErr:
    MsgBox Error$ & ": " & Str$(Err)        'Warn user of error
    Exit Sub
End Sub

Sub FillBugRec ()
    BugForm.BugNumber = "Bug Number: " & dsort("BugNum") 'Set bug number
    BugForm.NewBugTitle.Text = dsort("BugTitle")        'Set bug title
    BugForm.DateIn.Text = dsort("DateIn")               'Set date display
    If dsort("Status") Then BugForm.Status.Value = 1    'Show Status
    BugForm.Type(dsort("Type")).Value = True            'Show Type
    BugForm.Priority(dsort("Priority")).Value = True    'Show Priority
    If dsort("Notes") <> "" Then                        'Ensure notes
      BugForm.Notes.Text = dsort("Notes")               'Show notes
    End If
End Sub

Sub FillProjList ()
        'Could use .RemoveItem .AddItem to change List
```

```
        tb.MoveFirst                        'Start at top of list
        Do Until tb.EOF = True              'Read til end of table
          'Insert item in list
          ProjForm.ProjList.AddItem tb("ProjNum") & Chr$(9) & tb("ProjName")
          tb.MoveNext                       'Go to next record
        Loop
End Sub

Sub FillProjRec ()
   NewProj.ProjNumber = "Project Number: " & tb("ProjNum") 'Display number
   NewProj.NewProjName.Text = tb("ProjName")               'Display title
End Sub

Sub FindRec ()
    tb.MoveFirst                            'Go to top of list
    'Grab project number of selected item
    np = CInt(Mid$(ProjForm.ProjList.List(ProjForm.ProjList.ListIndex), 1, 2))
    Do Until tb("ProjNum") = np             'Read through list til find
      tb.MoveNext                           'Go to next record
    Loop
End Sub

Sub FixBugList ()
   On Error GoTo Trapper:
   'Could use .RemoveItem and .AddItem instead
   Bugs.BugList.Clear                   'Empty the list
   FillBugList                          'Refill the list
   'When not first item or last item
   If Bugs.BugList.ListCount >= ListPos And Bugs.BugList.ListCount Then
     Bugs.BugList.ListIndex = ListPos   'Set to current position
   Else
     Bugs.BugList.ListIndex = Bugs.BugList.ListCount 'Set to last item
   End If
   Exit Sub                             'Leave
Trapper:
  MsgBox Error$ & ": " & Str$(Err)       'Warn user of error
  Exit Sub
End Sub

Sub FixList ()
   'Could use .RemoveItem and .AddItem instead
   ProjForm.ProjList.Clear                     'Empty the list
   FillProjList                                'Refill the list
   LsCnt% = ProjForm.ProjList.ListCount
   If LsCnt% = ListPos Then 'When last item
```

```
      ProjForm.ProjList.ListIndex = ListPos - 1
   ElseIf LsCnt% > ListPos Then 'When not first item
      ProjForm.ProjList.ListIndex = ListPos          'Set to current position
   Else
      ProjForm.ProjList.ListIndex = ProjForm.ProjList.ListCount 'set to last
   End If
End Sub

Sub Keys (KeyStroke As Integer, Src As Integer)
 Select Case KeyStroke
   Case KEY_INSERT:
      CallNew Adding, Src        'Mode, Project or Bug
   Case KEY_DELETE:
      CallNew Deleting, Src
   Case KEY_RETURN:
      CallNew Editing, Src
 End Select
End Sub

Sub LogoMove ()
   Fwc% = MainMenu.ScaleWidth / 2
   Fhc% = MainMenu.ScaleHeight / 2
   lft% = MainMenu.Logo.Width / 2
   hgt% = MainMenu.Logo.Height / 2
   MainMenu.Logo.Move Fwc% - lft%, Fhc% - hgt%, MainMenu.Logo.Width,
   ...MainMenu.Logo.Height   'ltwh
End Sub
Index
```

Index